AF361320

A CONTINENT OF COLLEAGUES

GERMAN AND EUROPEAN STUDIES

General Editor: James Retallack

A Continent of Colleagues

Backroom Politics and Interwar Democracy

JAMES McSPADDEN

UNIVERSITY OF TORONTO PRESS
Toronto Buffalo London

© University of Toronto Press 2025
Toronto Buffalo London
utppublishing.com
Printed in Canada

German and European Studies

ISBN 978-1-4875-6563-3 (cloth)   ISBN 978-1-4875-6565-7 (EPUB)
                                  ISBN 978-1-4875-6564-0 (UPDF)

Library and Archives Canada Cataloguing in Publication

Title: A continent of colleagues : backroom politics and interwar democracy /
    James McSpadden.
Names: McSpadden, James, author.
Series: German and European studies.
Description: Series statement: German and European studies | Includes bibliographical
    references and index.
Identifiers: Canadiana (print) 20250262118 | Canadiana (ebook) 20250262223 | ISBN
    9781487565633 (cloth) | ISBN 9781487565657 (EPUB) | ISBN 9781487565640 (PDF)
Subjects: LCSH: Politicians—Europe—History—20th century. | LCSH: Democracy—
    Europe—History—20th century. | LCSH: Europe—Politics and government—
    1918–1945. | LCSH: Europe—Foreign relations—1918–1945.
Classification: LCC D443 .M37 2026 | DDC 940.5—dc23

Cover design: John Beadle
Cover photo: bpk Bildagentur / Erich Salomon (1886–1944) / Art Resource, NY

We wish to acknowledge the land on which the University of Toronto Press
operates. This land is the traditional territory of the Wendat, the Anishnaabeg, the
Haudenosaunee, the Métis, and the Mississaugas of the Credit First Nation.

The German and European Studies series is funded by the DAAD with funds from the
German Federal Foreign Office.

Publication of this book was made possible, in part, by a subvention grant from the
Center for Austrian Studies at the University of Minnesota.

University of Toronto Press acknowledges the financial support of the Government of
Canada, the Canada Council for the Arts, and the Ontario Arts Council, an agency of
the Government of Ontario, for its publishing activities.

DAAD Deutscher Akademischer Austauschdienst
German Academic Exchange Service

Conseil des Arts
du Canada

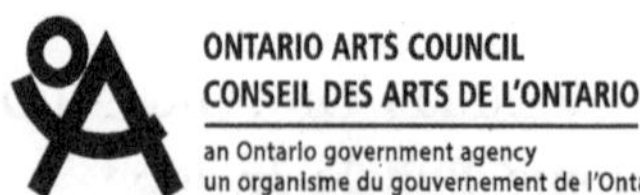

Funded by the   Financé par le
Government   gouvernement
of Canada   du Canada

Canadä

Contents

List of Illustrations

Acknowledgments

The task of acknowledging all those who have made my first book possible is daunting. Countless professors, friends, family members, colleagues, archivists, and others – not to mention vast institutional support across two continents – have helped this project grow from being just a glimmer in a graduate student's eye to a published monograph.

At its core, this book is the product of the time and energy that many teachers have invested in me. I am grateful to Ute Frevert for instilling an early fascination with German history. At Leiden University, Henk te Velde introduced me to histories of political culture and guided me through an initial exploration of the interwar Dutch past. A myriad of professors at Harvard, including David Blackbourn, Ann Blair, Mary Lewis, and Emma Rothschild, helped me hone the historian's craft. I am most indebted to my dissertation committee. Many thanks go to Derek Penslar for his insightful ideas about the project's narrative arc, to Daniel Ziblatt for helping me with concepts from political science, and to Alison Frank Johnson, whose steady support and encouragement throughout my graduate education and beyond have been deeply meaningful. As my *Doktorvater*, Charlie Maier pushed me to think comparatively in my scholarship and has fundamentally shaped how I think as a historian. I count myself lucky to have had this whole cast of professors whose dedication to teaching and mentoring is something I aspire to in my own career.

The book before you has more recently been shaped by the gifted Stephen Shapiro at the University of Toronto Press. Stephen is a brilliant editor with an eye for improving both arguments and prose style. He has walked me through the entire process of publishing a first book with care and kindness. In addition, this book's final version owes much to the insightful comments and helpful suggestions of the three manuscript reviewers. I am deeply grateful for the copious notes and constructive criticism of Erin Hochman and the two anonymous reviewers.

This book is also the product of years of generous institutional support. Most of the archival research was supported during my graduate education by Harvard's Center for European Studies, the Harvard History Department, a Pforzheimer Fellowship at the Harvard University Archives, the Weatherhead Center for International Affairs, and a German Academic Exchange Service (DAAD) Graduate Research Grant. Since 2018, my research has been graciously supported by the American Council on Germany, the American Historical Association, the Botstiber Institute for Austrian-American Studies, and the Hoover Institution Library and Archives. At the University of Nevada, Reno, the College of Liberal Arts, the Core Humanities Program, the History Department, the Office of the Vice President for Research & Innovation, and the Ozmen Institute for Global Studies have all supported my scholarly endeavors. I am particularly indebted to Thomas Weber not only for our yearslong friendship but also for introducing me to Ulrich Schlie who hosted me for a semester in Bonn on a DAAD grant, which afforded the time to finally complete my manuscript. The publication of this book has been generously supported with a First-Book Subvention from the Center for Austrian Studies at the University of Minnesota, as well as by funding from the Fred C. and Dennise Howard Endowment for European History and the Core Humanities Program at the University of Nevada, Reno.

I would be hard pressed to find one institution that has been more supportive of this project or of my career than the German Historical Institute (GHI) in Washington, DC. Since I first wrestled with German paleography on the GHI-sponsored Archival Summer Seminar in 2013, the GHI has been a steady supporter of my research through a short-term graduate student research fellowship, sponsoring my participation in the Transatlantic Doctoral Seminar, hosting me on a visiting postdoctoral fellowship in 2018–19, and enabling my more recent networking with Germanists across the region through the GHI's Pacific Office. The GHI brought me into contact with colleagues who have been cheerleaders and supporters, including Heike Friedman, Merle Ingenfeld, Simone Lässig, Simon Unger, and many others. The GHI also connected me to Richard Wetzell who is a scholar I deeply respect and who has become a trusted mentor and friend.

Teachers and institutions have made this book possible, but friends and colleagues have made the journey worthwhile. I first learned the importance of having an academic community of friends among graduate students at Harvard, where we commented on each other's chapters and chatted through ideas over drinks. Our community was enriched by Mou Banerjee, Andrew Bellisari, Marysia Blackwood, Brandon Bloch, Tomasz Blusiewicz, Charles Clavey, Elizabeth Cross, Barnaby Crowcroft,

Mattie Dungy, Josh Ehrlich, Carla Heelan, Erin Hutchinson, Tae-Yeoun Keum, Hannah Shephard, Michael Thornton, Michael Tworek, Stephen Walsh, among many others. I am especially lucky to count Heidi Tworek as a close friend. Early on, she took me under her wing navigating the ropes of academia, understanding the world of grant applications, honing my skill as a teacher, and so much more.

This project has also benefited from conversations at conferences and in archives with Ian Beacock, Adam Blackler, Erin Hochman, Teresa Walsh, and many others. The rock among my Germanist colleagues has been Robert Terrell. Since we first met in 2013, we have split hotel rooms at the GSA, hung out in Germany, run archival errands for each other, and decamped to Block Island for a writing retreat. I count myself extremely lucky for Robert's friendship.

More recently, a potentially lonely academic life has been enriched by the friendship of my colleagues at the University of Nevada, Reno. Several have gone above and beyond in helping me get this particular project over the finish line. Conversations in Lincoln Hall with Ned Schoolman prompted me to apply for key grants, Greta de Jong's delivery of summer vegetables from her garden provided sustenance during lonely months of writing, and invitations for coffee or meals from Linda Curcio, Renata Keller, Elizabeth Raymond, and Cameron Strang coaxed me out of the office. Jennifer Ng has gone above and beyond in listening to my anxious musings about work and writing, looking after the apartment when we were away, and being a wonderful friend. Finally, I am deeply grateful to both Suzanne Silverman and Dennis Dworkin. In addition to serving as department chair, conversations with Dennis about research have prompted me to rethink many of my own historical ideas.

The key transatlantic relationship that has supported me throughout the years I have worked on this project has been with Barbara and Willi Höfer. In the fall of 2008, Barbara and Willi hosted me for my first month as a Fulbrighter in Berlin. Since then I have returned – often annually – to Neue Kantstraße or Eichkamp. Whether stockpiling the books I had sent to their home address or saving a research trip by offering a place to stay when our Airbnb's water was found to be contaminated with legionella, Barbara and Willi have made this book possible. As my adopted German family, Barbara and Willi have experienced the ups and downs of my research, relationships, and life. They are the model of hospitality to which I aspire.

I would be remiss if I did not thank my family for all their support. My mom Kay and my brother Will have endured me being away for the holidays far too often. In the midst of working on this book, we lost my dad Randy McSpadden. Whenever I came back to my hometown in South

Carolina, Dad would pepper me with questions about my research. At the time, his questions often prompted my own anxious fretting about the job market or the publishing process. I miss those questions – and how they reflected how proud Dad was of me – now that he's gone. For encouraging my dreams and for his limitless love, this book is dedicated to Dad's memory.

I remember finding it cliché that so many authors thanked their spouses last and most profusely in their acknowledgments, but having wrestled with this book project for years, I understand why. I owe the most to my husband Joseph. We met on the cusp of me descending into the basement of the Center for European Studies to spend days secluded from the world frantically finishing my dissertation. Since then, Joseph has put up with me rethinking, re-researching, and rewriting this book. Sometimes this meant travelling with me to Europe for last-minute archival research (a burden he enjoyed). However, this has also necessitated Joseph being banished for two summers from northern Nevada so I could write like a madman. He has endured many nights with a cranky partner who spent too long a day in the office. Without Joseph's support, this book would not exist.

Reno, Nevada
December 18, 2024

List of Abbreviations

BVP	Bavarian People's Party [Germany] (Bayerische Volkspartei)
CHU	Protestant Christian Historical Union [The Netherlands] (Christelijk-Historische Unie)
CPIC	International Parliamentary Commercial Conference (Conférence parlementaire internationale du commerce)
CS	Christian Social Party [Austria] (Christlichsoziale Partei)
DDP	German Democratic Party (Deutsche Demokratische Partei)
DHK	Deutscher Herrenklub/German Gentlemen's Club
DHV	German National Association of Commercial Employees (Deutschnationaler Handlungsgehilfen-Verband)
DNVP	German National People's Party (Deutschnationale Volkspartei)
DVP	German People's Party (Deutsche Volkspartei)
GDVP	Greater German People's Party [Austria] (Großdeutsche Volkspartei, GDVP)
ILO	International Labour Organization
IPU	Inter-Parliamentary Union
NSB	Dutch Nationaal-Socialistische Beweging [The Netherlands] (National Socialist Movement)
NSDAP	National Socialist German Workers' Party (Nationalsozialistische Deutsche Arbeiterpartei)
SA	Nazi Stormtroopers [Germany] (Sturmabteilung)
SDAP	Austrian Social Democratic Workers' Party (Sozialdemokratische Arbeiterpartei or Sozialdemokratische Arbeiterpartei Deutschösterreichs)
SdP	Czechoslovak Sudeten German Party (Sudetendeutsche Partei)
SHF	Sudeten German Home Front [Czechoslovakia] (Sudetendeutsche Heimatfront)

SPD   Social Democratic Party of Germany (Sozialdemokratische
        Partei Deutschlands)
USPD   Unabhängige Sozialdemokratische Partei Deutschlands
        (German Independent Social Democratic Party)

Public Political Outsiders to Behind-the-Scenes Insiders

At the 1889 International Workers Congress in Paris, a charismatic Dutch revolutionary socialist strode up to the speaker's rostrum. Acclaimed by Frisian farmhands as a saviour who sported the beard of a Biblical prophet, Ferdinand Domela Nieuwenhuis was an ex-clergyman who had abandoned his pulpit to spread the gospel of socialism across the Netherlands. In 1888, Nieuwenhuis was the first socialist ever elected to the Dutch parliament, where he pointedly ripped up long-established norms. He scandalously voted against sending condolences to the king's widow, and his fellow legislators demonstrated their disdain for the firebrand by refusing to shake his hand. Nieuwenhuis's anti-parliamentary, left-wing radicalism horrified many in the *fin-de-siècle* Dutch bourgeois public.[1]

A year after his election to the Tweede Kamer, Nieuwenhuis traded the theatre of the Dutch parliament for a Parisian podium, where he had been invited to speak to the congress inaugurating the worldwide socialist Second International. Dubbed the "radical Dutchman" by his German detractors, Nieuwenhuis elected not to begin his speech with his pre-assigned topic – making the socialist case for the eight-hour workday – but to conjure up his old preaching skills to challenge his audience. Nieuwenhuis was livid that this left-wing assembly had been organized to ape a gentlemanly parliament. The congress' attendees heard dull, prepared speeches and merely rubber stamped pre-written resolutions. To the "radical Dutchman," this reeked of bourgeois parliamentarism, and Nieuwenhuis brought fire and brimstone down on his captive left-wing congregation for these sins.[2]

Glowering at the assembled crowd, the Dutchman declared that rather than talking about the eight-hour workday, he would take up the far more important question of parliaments and parliamentarism. "I personally expect nothing from parliamentarism, precisely because I am a member of a parliament and have witnessed all the playacting, and I ask all those here who are members of a parliament, starting with our chairman […] who is a member of the English parliament, whether they expect anything from parliamentarianism, yes or no." With the zeal of an angry prophet, Nieuwenhuis paused to look around, as if he were demanding an answer to his rhetorical question. "Parliaments are just talking shops, which is not only the fault of the individuals but of the system itself. We have seen it here. Our Congress is made up of an elite, no parliament in the world can compare with this assembly, and I ask you whether it has not made exactly the same mistakes? We have talked a lot, even excessively, and in the end we have to vote and make decisions, which have been prepared in advance, without the time and opportunity to discuss them seriously. The fault is therefore in the system." Nieuwenhuis saw no point in recreating a parliament that valued words over action. His revolutionary goal was to bring down the entire system to usher in a new utopia in which both parliaments and the bourgeoisie would cease to exist.[3]

Just shy of three decades later, Nieuwenhuis's revolutionary zeal had subsided among his left-wing Low Country posterity. Although Nieuwenhuis barely won one seat in the legislature in 1888, almost 22 per cent of the votes cast in the July 1918 Dutch election were for the socialists. Far more elected left-wing politicians – including the Netherlands' first female parliamentarian, Suze Groeneweg – were serving in The Hague. Nieuwenhuis had used every opportunity to challenge the foundations of government, but by 1918, Dutch socialist parliamentarians had long become accustomed to the ins-and-outs of parliamentary life. However, among bourgeois and conservative elements of Dutch society, there was still considerable fear of the left. The public's sense of foreboding intensified in 1918, when Dutch soldiers who had mobilized to defend the Netherlands' wartime neutrality revolted. The country's socialist leader, Pieter Jelles Troelstra, sensed the advent of a worldwide Marxist revolution and prophesied the imminent collapse of the government. Within a few days, Troelstra had retreated from his revolutionary prediction, and this riotous, red week went down in Dutch history as "Troelstra's blunder."[4]

Troelstra's 1918 revolutionary prognosis only confirmed to the majority of the Dutch body politic that the country's socialists were the unreformed heirs of Nieuwenhuis's virulent anti-parliamentary radicalism. In public, interwar Dutch socialists were deemed unacceptable for any sort of political co-operation. Unlike Nieuwenhuis's era, however, in private, socialist parliamentarians were conversing, corresponding, and mingling with their political rivals. After the would-be revolutionary Troelstra slurred a liberal parliamentary colleague as the "clown of the reaction" in a punchy 1919 speech, that same liberal sent the socialist leader a humorous telegram: "Best birthday wishes from the clown of the reaction."[5] In a private letter, Troelstra praised that liberal's "parliamentary qualities that I would wish on many of ours[:] your quick-wittedness, your sarcasm, and your striking way of both attacking and parrying."[6] Instead of being unwelcome in this behind-the-scenes interwar political world, Dutch socialists were writing confidentially to cabinet ministers and being formally appointed to international commissions. A left-wing critic might grouse that the socialists had been co-opted into the system, but this was a natural inclusion mechanism. Just as the radical liberals of 1848 had grown into the staid bourgeois politicians of the *belle époque*, the uncompromising working-class politicians of the *fin-de-siècle* were becoming a clubbable left wing. Within the private world of politics, Dutch socialists had become trusted insiders.[7]

In a larger sense, European political history between the world wars began with the political outsiders of the past entering halls of power, and it ended with a disastrous authoritarian high tide. As a revolutionary wave swept away old central and eastern European empires, there were renewed democratic hopes as reformers wrote new constitutions, introduced women's suffrage, abolished aristocratic privilege, and expanded civic rights. Political parties modernized to capitalize on mass movements, and they used new technologies and techniques to campaign. Despite creeping anti-globalism and the popular resentment that the postwar settlement brought to the former Central Powers, there was new internationalist energy, centred on the newly created League of Nations. There was an early flowering of democratic hope across Europe. Only later would authoritarian movements grow with paramilitary forces marching down streets and brawls breaking out in parliaments.[8]

This book takes as its focus interwar parliamentary politics, but it does not dwell on public speeches, press coverage, voting behaviour, or party manifestos. It documents the more private and informal world of sociability among elected politicians. From The Hague to Vienna and beyond, parliaments could and did serve as locations for creating an unexpected esprit de corps among rivals. Moreover, this book contends that personal relationships were essential to how European lawmakers wielded political power. In clubhouses, around committee tables, and at dinner parties, parliamentarians built robust cross-party networks that they used both for legislating and for personal favours. Moreover, this informal political and social milieu was not merely inhabited by mustachioed aristocrats or the gentlemanly liberals of the nineteenth century. Instead, these smoke-filled backrooms integrated political newcomers, including recently elected women and working-class politicians. Through secret conversations and backdoor lobbying, legislators who were sidelined in public could negotiate in private and influence decision-making.

In addition to illuminating the expansive world of interwar political sociability, this book demonstrates that many European parliamentarians came to understand their role as having a transnational component. Of course, these legislators came to power with a mandate to represent a national or local constituency. However, for many interwar parliamentarians, their political scope extended into the international arena. These legislators travelled on junkets, attended inter-parliamentary conferences, and served as under-the-radar diplomats. The 1920s were particularly marked by experimentation in using elected parliamentarians as formal diplomats abroad. National lawmakers – even those who opposed the sitting government – were appointed to the Assembly of the League of Nations and to other international bodies. This transnational world seeped into the social lives of parliamentarians as they hobnobbed with foreign journalists, ambassadors, and other travelling politicians who passed through European capitals. Serving in a national parliament could be an unexpected ticket onto the world stage, where parliamentarians joined a more international political elite.

Finally, backroom sociability and transnational parliamentary connections had a paradoxical relationship with interwar democracy. On the one hand, sociability and international ties could further inclusion. When more radical politicians encountered cross-party social networks, sometimes their revolutionary zeal was tempered as they entered into closer behind-the-scenes relationships with rivals. For instance, as newly elected legislators, women could exert political influence behind the scenes that was not possible in public. Similarly, when parliamentarians travelled abroad, they brought the penumbra of democratic legitimacy onto the international stage. This informal world of parliamentary politics could empower elected lawmakers vis-à-vis the executive. Rather than rubber stamping decrees from the cabinet, lawmakers conferred with trusted rivals behind the scenes. Rather than leaving diplomacy to patrician diplomats taking orders from a foreign minister, elected lawmakers tried their hand at diplomacy. Bolstering the influence of lawmakers and promoting collaboration across party lines was a plus for interwar democracy.

Moreover, in private, these social and international connections – even among political rivals – could help interwar democracies function. Socialists and conservatives who were publicly at each other's throats could privately agree on housing legislation, constitutional changes, or even military reforms. However, these behind-the-scenes connections also meant that decision-making and politicking were displaced from public view and moved into backrooms. Parliamentarians travelling to other countries to call in favours abroad was far from the lofty goals laid out by Woodrow Wilson in the Fourteen Points that promised "diplomacy shall proceed always frankly and in the public view."[9] By moving the work of compromise and negotiation behind the scenes, more legislators were included in governing and more concessions were possible among the political elite, but the public was excluded, which posed problems for the openness democracy requires.

Understanding Parliaments in History: From Outdated Methods to New Enthusiasm

The phrase "parliamentary history" conjures up images of old-fashioned armchair historians poring over the legislative manoeuverings of Otto von Bismarck in some futile attempt to rescue great-man history from the dustheap of antiquated methodologies. More avant-garde historians have long since moved to think of political power as contested in places like bread lines and street brawls, and these frontiers in Central European history have captivated scholars including Maureen Healy, Pamela Swett, and Belinda Davis.[10] Until recently, modern parliaments were largely abandoned by historians in the Anglosphere and left to political scientists and legal scholars.[11] Groundbreaking work has been done by others, including Giovanni Capoccia in *Defending Democracy: Reactions to Extremism in Interwar Europe*, which explores democratic resilience under threat by anti-system parties. Capoccia examined strategies of political leaders in Czechoslovakia, Belgium, and Finland to show that "skilled democrats" could and did blunt the rise of interwar extremism.[12] However, these competing disciplines are not always as sympathetic to historical nuance. Scholars beyond history can nonchalantly lump nineteenth-century Bohemian political culture together with the Czech parliamentary response to COVID-19. Historians rightly cast a skeptical eye on approaches that run roughshod over finer details – and a century of history – but until recently, there has not been a wealth of alternative historical work.[13]

Lately, a fresh scholarly wind has reinvigorated the historical study of both parliaments and politics during the nineteenth and twentieth centuries. Much of this new energy has emerged in continental Europe, where historians have creatively synthesized political and cultural histories, while also incorporating other interdisciplinary methods. The German scholars Thomas Mergel and Barbara Stollberg-Rilinger have advocated for methodologies including the "cultural history of politics" and the "cultural history of the political."[14] Large, well-funded European research projects have employed innovative approaches to political history, a political historical association has been founded, and a whole cadre of up-and-coming scholars are working on topics including monarchs and the press, parliamentary furnishings and revolutions, and national minorities and democratic representation – pushing the field of political history beyond any traditional primacy of an elite.[15]

This updated approach to political history is not merely the navel gazing of historians looking to find yet another lacuna to fill up with monographs. Instead, this new perspective can overhaul conventional scholarly explanations about the past. Thomas Mergel demonstrated this in his 2002 monograph *Parlamentarische Kultur in der Weimarer Republik* (Parliamentary Culture in the Weimar Republic). Mergel's book shook up the stagnant scholarship on the interwar German Reichstag. At the time, the key book in this subfield was still Karl Dietrich Bracher's 1955 *Die Auflösung der Weimarer Republik* (The Disintegration of the Weimar Republic). Bracher had concluded that "functional deficits" in the Reichstag, including an inability to compromise, contributed to the legislature's demise. Michael Koß, Philipp Austermann, and other more recent political scientists have returned to this breakdown of legislative norms and the lack of co-operation to explain the collapse of interwar German democracy. However, Thomas Mergel's work challenged narratives of a parliament paralyzed by functional deficits by asking how it functioned rather than how it failed. Unafraid to discover collegiality in a body tarred by its subsequent history, Mergel painted a picture of a parliament not frozen by division but instead governed by norms and in spaces that enabled fruitful political communication.[16]

Although this book returns the German Reichstag, it does not re-tread Mergel's pioneering steps. Mergel tended to emphasize symbolism and communication and once asked: "Is politics just communication or is it also power, its threat and use?" Mergel ultimately read power into political communication, but this was seen as too much of a scholarly fudge by academics in the Netherlands who took up Mergel's torch of reimagining political history.[17] Jouke Turpijn has highlighted a danger in dwelling too much on the communicative and cultural elements of politics: "By focusing too much on 'the soft side of politics,' the question of political power might slip out of the picture. Power is crucial to consider in writing political history. After all, politics is about who wins and who loses when power is divided, is used, or is absent. Whoever forgets this, forgets what politics was – and is."[18] Rather than reading power into political communication, this book examines power and influence as it was amassed and wielded through both political sociability and transnational connections.

This new European scholarly enthusiasm is a distant echo of older insurgent trends. In the 1920s, the British political historian Lewis Namier was putting the finishing touches on his seminal volume *The Structure of Politics at the Accession of George III*. Namier used collective biography to reconstruct the motives of members in the eighteenth-century British House of Commons. He was convinced that any analysis that remained at an institutional level was misleading, since Parliament was made up of individuals who pursued their own interests: "The student [of this history] has to get acquainted with the lives of thousands of individuals, with an entire ant-heap, see its files stretch out in various directions, understand how they are connected and correlated, watch the individual ants, and yet never forget the ant-heap." Namier's insight was that ant-heap-like institutions were the product of individual relationships, as well as of common action. His collective biographical method undermined the then-reigning Whiggish orthodoxy.[19]

Namier saw one of his tasks as untangling the web of past politicians' hidden motives. Today there is new interest in applying insights from early modern scholarship on patronage, corruption, and personal-political relationships to understand the ulterior motives of more modern politicians. The clear patron-client relationships that Namier noticed in the Georgian House of Commons had become muddled by the twentieth century, and modern politicians value intangibles like loyalty and trust in different ways than did their early modern predecessors. Nevertheless, the German historians Jens Ivo Engels and Volker Köhler have advocated using the broad term "micropolitics" to capture phenomena "that relate to personal connections in the context of political processes," which Namier had long ago identified in the British political past.[20]

In a 2018 monograph, Volker Köhler applied this micropolitical approach to rethink Weimar politics. Köhler developed three case studies that foregrounded the personal relationships of political actors in Red Saxony in the early 1920s, surrounding Konrad Adenauer as Cologne's mayor, and in the Junkers' pet project of aid packages for East Prussia. Rather than taking the spatial-communicative approach to politics favoured by Thomas Mergel, Köhler put personal relationships under the microscope to determine how "party patronage, friendships, and backroom dealings" shaped political outcomes. Köhler did not return to the outdated great man historical methods of the past, but he did do more to acknowledge the tangible effects of interpersonal ties. Building on Köhler's micropolitical angle, but moving beyond any single national context, this book centres politicians and their personal relationships in the service of documenting parliamentary sociability, transnational connections, and interwar decision-making.[21]

Interwar Parliamentary Politics Beyond the Nation-State

Yearning for more than narrow scholarly analyses, Fernand Braudel long ago hoped that "history can do more than study walled gardens."[22] Parliaments would seem to be perfectly bounded "walled gardens," rooted in one national context with a limited cast of characters but with a gold mine of source material. Reams of paper are produced in legislative work, parliamentary happenings are reported in the press, and legislatures publish nearly verbatim accounts of their debates. Parliamentary officials also tend to draft copious reports, correspondence, and the like, which is often still available to more archivally inclined scholars – unless a bomb fell on the parliament's offices in the Second World War and destroyed the majority of this material.[23]

Upon closer inspection, however, interwar parliaments were not the tightly circumscribed "walled gardens" one might expect. Instead, they were linked to networks that stretched across the world. Take, for example, the lower house of the Belgian parliament. Files in the official archives from the 1920s and 1930s are full of correspondence from legislative functionaries in Turkey, Austria, South Africa, Poland, Egypt, Hungary, Japan, and the Dutch East Indies. A steady stream of international visitors from Japan, South Africa, France, Luxembourg, and Germany appeared in Brussels as parliamentary guests.[24] When one moves to the personal papers of interwar lawmakers, there are even more records of politicians travelling across the Atlantic for inter-parliamentary conferences, conversing in Central European spa towns with lawmakers from neighbouring states, and supporting election campaigns in foreign countries. Interwar parliaments were not simply the ultimate manifestations of nationally bounded political culture; they were gateways to a wider transnational world of politics and sociability.

Robust international ties among interwar lawmakers clash with the usual "walled garden" approach to political history, since many historians working on modern European politics think and write wearing the blinders of one national history. On the one hand, this is understandable. National elections, political parties, and institutions like the presidency or parliament functioned within a country-specific context. Moreover, studying only one country's political past means that a scholar has fewer archives to visit, languages to master, or national nuances to learn. Because of these hurdles, scholarly attempts to compare international political phenomena like the introduction of women's suffrage have often been done through edited volumes. Contributors write on single case studies, an editor cobbles together synthetic themes in a pithy introduction, and readers are supposed to divine larger comparative conclusions by considering the volume in its entirety.[25] Europe's political historians have been slower to push beyond the bounds of the nation-state than scholars innovating in related fields who explore entangled, global, and imperial histories.[26]

Ultimately, this book takes a two-fold approach to consider interwar legislators beyond any single nation-state: first, it examines parliamentarians as transnational actors; second, it analyzes parliamentary cultures comparatively. In adding parliamentarians to the global cast of characters between the world wars, this book writes legislators into a burgeoning scholarship on interwar internationalism. For well over a decade, scholars have flocked to the international world of the 1920s and 1930s. From the Paris Peace Conference to the League of Nations, historians including Erez Manela, Susan Pedersen, and many others have explored the tension between self-determination and imperialism, often concluding that the League abetted colonialist projects.[27] Scholars like Caroline Fink and Natasha Wheatley have explored the League's minority rights system and interwar legal regimes. Patricia Clavin and Madeleine Dungy have worked to understand the League's restructuring of world trade.[28] This rosy picture of interwar internationalism has been more recently challenged by Jamie Martin and Quinn Slobodian who have used interwar thought and diplomacy as a springboard towards the global economic thinking that led to neoliberal structures that exist today. Tara Zahra's analysis of the rise of anti-globalism has tempered scholarly optimism about the internationalist past.[29] In this now well-studied interwar international world of economists, technocrats, colonialists, and even anti-globalists, parliamentarians have been missing, despite the fact that elected lawmakers served as formal diplomats at the League of Nations, as informal diplomats travelling across Europe, and in inter-parliamentary organizations throughout the 1920s and 1930s.[30]

Complementing the claim that interwar legislators were transnational actors, this book looks beyond nationally bounded parliamentary "walled gardens" by using comparative history. Classic comparative studies exploring the welfare state, analyzing the Sovietization of universities across the Eastern bloc, and understanding the return to economic and social normalcy after the First World War have all left their mark by "identify[ing] questions and problems that one might miss, neglect, or just not invent" when narrowly focused on one national example.[31] Among Europeanists who use comparative methods, there has been a divide between those who think of comparison as a rigorous social scientific method and those who use comparison for what Jürgen Kocka called "heuristic" effect. The former camp has included scholars like

Peter Baldwin for whom comparison is "fundamentally concerned with causation, particularly with explaining differences and convergences."[32] For other comparativists, juxtaposing historical examples can "clarify the profiles of single cases," which Kocka described as the "descriptive" power of comparison.[33] Drawing on Kocka's approach, this book uses comparison to disturb the assumptions that have developed in nationally blinkered political historiographies. For instance, if one were asked to create a comparative research project on the destruction of interwar democracy, scholars would undoubtedly turn to cases of Italian Fascists and German Nazis. These are implicitly accepted as paradigms for how autocracy supplanted democracy. However, in comparing German Nazi parliamentarians with anti-democratic legislators in Czechoslovakia and in the Netherlands, the German Nazis stand out as outliers, not as the archetypical case. Dutch and Czech historians have looked back on their countries' anti-parliamentary parties as a fascist fifth column that dutifully imported Hitler's radicalism, but meticulous comparison with German Nazis – which this book does – shows this is untrue and, thus, disrupts historical narratives developed in national contexts with untested assumptions about other European national histories.

While drawing on examples as far afield as Brazil, the United States, Japan, and Australia, this book foregrounds more extended national case studies from Germany, Austria, Czechoslovakia, and the Netherlands. As a supposed "republic without republicans," Germany is a natural focus for this project.[34] Austria and Czechoslovakia are connected to each other through Habsburg-era political ties and to Germany within Central Europe.[35] Removed from Central Europe's entangled political past and not having endured postwar revolutionary upheaval, the Netherlands might seem like an outlier. On the one hand, it can be comparatively productive to include a more distant case study in order to see commonalities that are not explained by a shared political history. Moreover, unlike France, the Netherlands expanded equal suffrage rights for women in the interwar period, which allows comparison of the experience of early Dutch female legislators. Finally, Dutch historians and up-and-coming graduate students have been particularly eager to apply new methods in political history to the Netherlands' past, which means that there is a robust secondary literature on Dutch parliamentary culture that does not exist to the same extent in Austria or Czechoslovakia.[36]

Rather than crafting a study of interwar parliamentary democracy that is only comparative or only transnational, this book mixes both approaches in order to peer beyond any single country and build larger claims about European political life. This approach takes up a possibility Jürgen Kocka saw in comparative history not only to analyze "parts or segments" but also to acknowledge them as "components of a larger whole." Kocka used the example of a comparative study of nineteenth-century Central European opera houses. Strictly speaking, a reader of this scholarship would learn the ins-and-outs of public support for the Viennese opera or the program of the Budapest opera; however, in a larger sense, a comparative approach lays bare "elements of a comprehensive culture of Central Europe" about which it also makes larger claims.[37] Ultimately, this hybrid approach blending transnational and comparative histories responds to an eloquent warning from Charles Maier in 1975: "Comparative history remains superficial if it merely plucks out elites in different societies[.] Flower arranging is not botany. A bouquet of historic parallels provides little knowledge about society unless we dissect and analyze the component parts."[38] This book tackles Europe's parliamentary elite, but it embeds these actors in both a transnational world and a national political context. This "bouquet" ultimately points to implications for interwar democracy, how it functioned, and how its collapse was experienced by lawmakers.

Sources and Chapters

At the heart of this book is the contention that political decision-making and outcomes were shaped by behind-the-scenes respect, co-operation, collaboration, skepticism and animosity among political rivals. For political scientists and political historians today, less energy is spent on the hard-to-qualify and hard-to-detect personal relationships of past politicians. Intellectual historians pore over political ideas, and political scientists tend to unpick the workings of cabinets or legislatures to understand governmental processes.[39] With the new frontier of digitized parliamentary records and newspapers, text mining is now possible for producing new conclusions about past rhetoric.[40] Newfangled digital techniques can open new pathways for research; however, big data can still miss evidence in analogue correspondence tucked away in former politicians' papers. Foreign collusion, gentlemen's agreements, and brokered legislative drafts are often only evident when one looks behind the scenes. Delving into this private domain of parliamentary politics can help us understand how power functioned and was contested in Europe between the world wars.

However, documenting past parliamentary sociability can be tricky. No bureaucrat was minuting chats in the hallway, and secret negotiations over drinks did not leave a paper trail. Contemporary newspapers did not trumpet opponents co-operating in parliamentary committees, and books hot off the interwar presses did not recount a British Member of

Parliament being secretly encouraged by the German government to ask favourable questions in the House of Commons.[41] However, diaries can provide evidence of who was spending time with whom, and guest lists for parties shed light on private socializing. Contemporary correspondence can bolster accounts in later recollections. Unpublished memoirs can be added into the mix in order to examine untapped sources. Of course, any political memoir must be read critically, since autobiographies are often couched in aggrandizement or apologia. The problem of bending the truth was particularly acute among interwar politicians. For example, any memoirs by a bourgeois German politician from the Weimar Republic that were written during the Nazi years were likely to emphasize how much the politician hated democracy and was a true-believing antisemite. However, if that politician survived the Second World War, there was a vested interest in omitting details like the fact that the writer mingled with Nazis. A massive grain of salt must accompany reading the later recollections of interwar politicians.

Given the minefield of drawing primarily on postwar memoirs, this book relies as much as possible on politicians' contemporary personal papers. Of course, the extent to which personal papers shed light on the informal social and political milieu is contingent on what any given person saved. Some politicians kept all their invitations to social events, while others did not. More importantly, intervening history determined whether politicians even have extant papers. Many European politicians lost all their records as a result of destruction during the Second World War. However, events before the war could also determine the extent of people's archives. For instance, Austria's interwar politicians retained particularly sparse personal collections. Many leading Austrian socialists were arrested en masse after the 1934 Austrian Civil War when left-wing paramilitaries rose up against the increasingly authoritarian state. Socialists destroyed their own records at that time so right-wing Austrian prosecutors did not have incriminating evidence to use against them or their friends. When Nazi Germany annexed Austria, traditional conservatives destroyed their papers so as not to offer proof to the Gestapo of their pro-Austrian and anti-Nazi sympathies. By 1938, almost all Austrian politicians who were prominent in the 1920s had good reason to have disposed of their papers. A critic might challenge the vignette-like nature of this archival evidence for past private connections. Is a calling card from a political rival with a hand-scrawled note asking for help enough to prove that opponents were best friends who plotted together behind the scenes? No, of course not. However, in tandem with a letter here, a journal entry there, and confirmation in later memoirs, this evidence helps builds the case against the scholarly assumption that interwar polarization was so crippling that robust political co-operation between the wars was impossible.

These sources are ultimately all mustered to document a world of interwar parliamentary sociability, to demonstrate transnational connections among legislators, and to show the complicated relationship of this backroom world of politics with interwar democracy. The chapters in this book move in a rough arc that begins in 1918 with postwar democratic change in domestic political cultures, continues through the vibrant international parliamentary world of the 1920s, and concludes with the challenges posed by anti-parliamentary and radicalizing parties on the right.

The first two chapters foreground national parliamentary cultures in the wake of the First World War, with a particular focus on the integrative power of parliamentary sociability. Chapter 1 uses case studies of female parliamentarians from Germany, Austria, and the Netherlands to demonstrate how these women encountered and exerted influence through the social world of politics. Whereas Dutch and Austrian female parliamentarians were active transnationally, the social world surrounding the German Reichstag was particularly expansive, which offered female lawmakers cross-party opportunities to shape decision-making domestically. Chapter 2 moves to Weimar Berlin to trace the shape, extent, and boundaries of the social-political milieu in the German capital, as well as to document how international this private world was. Although the social world in republican Berlin democratized by including women and working-class politicians, a conservative backlash prompted the creation of gentlemen's social clubs that were more reminiscent of the old regime.

The subsequent two chapters move beyond the collegiality of any single national parliamentary culture to lawmakers on the international stage. Chapter 3 shows how the rethinking of interwar diplomacy opened doors for parliamentarians as both formal and informal diplomats. Despite being overlooked by scholars, parliamentarians were transnational actors, campaigning in elections in foreign countries, calling in personal favours abroad, and lobbying foreign colleagues on certain issues. Chapter 4 foregrounds two competing inter-parliamentary organizations, the Inter-Parliamentary Union and the International Parliamentary Commercial Conference. Over the course of the interwar decades, both organizations abandoned their early advocacy for liberal democracy and acquiesced to the presence of faux fascist legislators and technocratic officials from authoritarian states. Inter-parliamentary advocacy for strong democratic safeguards had waned by the 1930s.

The final three chapters work in tandem as comparative examples of how sociability and transnational ties related to anti-parliamentary movements and radicalizing mainstream conservative parties. Chapter 5 focuses on Nazi parliamentarians in Germany's Weimar Republic to demonstrate their early concessions to parliamentary norms and limited forays into the Reichstag's social-political world. However, after massive electoral gains in 1930, the Nazi leadership reined in the parliamentary party to prevent cross-party ties. The spectre of regimented German Nazis has wrongly been assumed to be the model for how radical anti-parliamentary parties functioned everywhere; Chapter 6 demonstrates that this was not true. This chapter offers two case studies of far-right anti-parliamentary parties: the National Socialist Movement in the Netherlands and the Sudeten German Party in First Republic Czechoslovakia. Unlike the strictly disciplined Nazis, the Dutch and Czechoslovak right-wing legislators actually nurtured some cross-party social and political connections and participated within the democratic bounds of Dutch and Czechoslovak parliamentary cultures. Lastly, Chapter 7 employs examples of socialists and conservatives in Austria and Germany to show long-lasting, private working relationships among rivals. Ultimately, the death knell for the interwar period's robust world of political co-operation came from radicalizing and besieged conservative parties that purged moderates and prevented cross-party co-operation.

Uncovering a robust, friendly world of politics behind the scenes might seem heartening. In the present, when politics seems so noxiously divided, one might hope that in private political rivals are strategizing, collaborating, and befriending each other to prop up the system from within. However, no continent of colleagues – past or present – can replace a strong, public commitment to democracy. This was aptly illustrated in a radio conversation between Paul Löbe – a German socialist and long-serving president of the Reichstag – and the conservative German nationalist parliamentarian Axel Freiherr von Freytagh-Loringhoven. In the early 1930s, the German cabinet moved to rule by decree, and Löbe and Freytagh-Loringhoven took to the airwaves to share their thoughts with the German public. Framed as an interview, the two men were friendly and referred to each other as honourable colleagues. This was an aural remnant of the collegiality that one would have heard in the backrooms of the Weimar-era Reichstag. The socialist Löbe fretted that rule by decree was "a diminution of the civic rights of our fellow citizens." On the other hand, Freytagh-Loringhoven saw the fundamental problem as "the parliamentary system itself," which was chaotic and lacked strong leaders. The conversation was friendly, but the stakes were democracy or dictatorship. Not long after this recording, Freytagh-Loringhoven supported Adolf Hitler as chancellor, and Löbe ended up in a concentration camp.[42]

Chapter One

Entering the Smoke-Filled Backrooms: German, Austrian, and Dutch Women as Interwar Parliamentary Newcomers

The issue of the *New York Times Magazine* on June 14, 1925, contained two articles on women as European legislators. Splashed across the magazine's front page was a cartoon depicting a parade of well-heeled women – slightly reminiscent of the suffragettes – bursting into a room of bespectacled, top-hatted aristocrats. The accompanying article recounted the recent narrow defeat of British peeresses in their attempt to join the House of Lords. However, the author mocked the hereditary peers' flimsy attempts to "defend the House of Lords against the swish of silken petticoats," and predicted that aristocratic women would soon take up their place in "that last remaining citadel of unregenerate men." Women's social and political roles were changing at such breakneck pace in the 1920s, this article anticipated peeresses on the Lords' red benches in the very near future. In fact, lingering misogyny would keep women out of the House of Lords until 1958, and hereditary peeresses would be barred until 1962.[1]

The same 1925 *New York Times Magazine* issue that predicted imminent equality for privileged British peeresses featured an exposé on the parliamentary career of Katharina von Oheimb. Printed around a glamour shot of Oheimb, the page-long story "Katinka Pulls the Reichstag Strings" profiled the leading German politician who had recently lost her parliamentary seat. The feature trafficked in sexist tropes in describing Oheimb's "sibylline influence" on leading German ministers, and the article ignored many female colleagues to proclaim Oheimb "the first elegant lady to represent a constituency in Germany." According to this reporting, Oheimb was a conservative politician with "democratic tendencies" who, while in parliament, mobilized her personal relationships to powerful people to thwart the hyper-nationalism of the far right. Indeed, even out of office, Oheimb was said to have "lost nothing in power or influence, thanks to her charm, her brains, her money, her salon, and her friendships." Having garnered the attention of the foreign press, Oheimb had successfully used her four-year stint in the German Reichstag to cultivate her celebrity within the social world of interwar politics.[2]

Exploring the rarefied fight for peeress' equality on the one hand and Oheimb's political networking on the other, this 1925 issue of the *New York Times Magazine* captured the dramatic revolution in European women's political roles since the First World War. Both Germany and Great Britain had only a few years of experience with women as elected parliamentarians when these articles were published. Before the war, only a handful of European countries had pioneered the expansion of women's political rights. The 1907 parliamentary election in the Grand Duchy of Finland had marked the first time women in Europe voted for their national representatives, and 19 women won Finnish parliamentary seats, making history as the modern world's first elected female legislators. Norway and Denmark followed in expanding suffrage rights before the end of the war.[3]

By 1920, Europe's largely Scandinavian experiment with women's suffrage and parliamentary representation had pushed into Central and Eastern Europe. Many of the countries most impacted by the war were buffeted by political turmoil, and revolutionary governments attempted to curry favour with the populace by hastily extending suffrage to women. For example, after the czar's abdication, the non-Bolshevik Russian provisional government caved into calls for women's suffrage after a march in Petrograd in March 1917. Russian women won the right to vote in the free elections to the short-lived Russian Constituent Assembly.[4] Women's suffrage in national elections was then introduced between 1917 and 1920 in European countries including Albania, Austria, Czechoslovakia, Estonia, Germany, Hungary, Latvia, Luxembourg, the Netherlands, and Poland.[5] Not all states jumped to full suffrage from day one. Belgium and the United Kingdom tinkered with their suffrage systems to allow only some women to cast ballots. From 1921, Belgium permitted war widows to vote in national elections – essentially as stand-ins for their deceased spouses, most Belgian women waited until after the Second World War for the unrestricted franchise. The United Kingdom and Ireland permitted women over 30 who met property restrictions to vote and stand for election as MPs starting in 1918. It took a few more years – until 1928 – until British women were given voting rights on par with those of men.[6]

Although women's suffrage was on the march across the continent, for new legislators like Katharina von Oheimb, election to parliament was only the beginning of their political journeys. The road from parliamentary newcomer to a fully-fledged member of the wider political community was often a long one. The historians Jouke Turpijn, Erie Tanja, and Carla Hoetink have all explored the complex acculturation process for new parliamentarians in Dutch politics from 1848 to the 1990s, considering the historically contingent social barriers of class, education, and background.[7] During the interwar years, female newcomers had specific burdens, particularly in the world of parliamentary sociability. Although they were admitted to plenary chambers for debates and votes, political life also took place in the social milieu surrounding parliaments, and in these spaces there were often barriers based on gender. Political negotiations that happened over drinks in a private gentlemen's club would be impossible for women to attend. Schmoozing at a late-night gentlemen's dinner with the titans of industry was not on the calendar of these newly elected female politicians. Women had to find their own social and political spaces and explore opportunities for political action in parliamentary systems where they were among the most junior members.[8]

This chapter comparatively examines the experiences of four female legislators from three countries as they entered their national parliaments in the years after the First World War. Katharina von Oheimb from Germany, Anna Boschek and Gabriele Proft from Austria, and Frida Katz from the Netherlands were all elected as parliamentarians in the first few years of universal suffrage in their countries. Women's suffrage brought new female parliamentarians to high political office across large swathes of Northern and Central Europe, but scholars have tended to address both the expansion of voting rights and the work of these female legislators in national isolation. This chapter, on the other hand, takes a comparative approach to these women's experiences and political influence in all three national contexts.[9]

Political scientists and historians interested in party manifestos, voting blocs, or charismatic leaders often minimize or ignore the role and influence of these earliest European female politicians. This is surprising, since today's quantitatively minded scholars have repeatedly demonstrated the effectiveness of increasing the percentage of female parliamentarians on everything from reducing deforestation to promoting national economic growth.[10] In looking further back in time, a paucity of sources has instead prompted scholars to comb through public records to understand women's political influence.[11] The problem with this approach is that interwar female politicians often delivered far fewer public speeches on a narrower range of topics than their male counterparts. Interwar feminist discourse questioned whether to highlight a "gender-specific" politics that linked women with mothers, children, and conciliation, or whether to preach a more radical vision of equality. As the Austrian historian Gabriella Hauch has demonstrated, many early female legislators focused on these "gender-specific" issues that valorized "women's unique nature" but received less press or time on the parliamentary floor.[12] Moreover, female lawmakers often took up leadership roles in their political parties' women's organizations, which also received less attention than the male politicians headlining giant political rallies. Focusing on public records as sources can yield the incorrect conclusion that women played little role in legislative politics during this period. Therefore, this chapter will turn to diaries, correspondence, and memoirs that point to more private channels of influence for female parliamentarians.[13]

Delving into the smoke-filled rooms of Berlin, private letters written in The Hague, and closed committee rooms in Vienna, this chapter seeks out the world of private cross-party co-operation and parliamentary sociability experienced by these female legislators in order to highlight their political agency. In this behind-the-scenes world of interwar politics, all four women were transnational figures, although to varying extents. Despite ever giving only one speech in the Reichstag, Katharina von Oheimb amassed political influence within the vibrant, cross-party – and often international – social world in Weimar Berlin. Anna Boschek and Gabriele Proft's public and private parliamentary personas were far more combative in interwar Austria, but their party-political work propelled them onto the international stage. Finally, Frida Katz forged personal cross-party ties in The Hague, but her legal expertise was valued both domestically and internationally in a technocratic sense. These case studies illuminate differences in the three national parliamentary cultures these women encountered, particularly foregrounding the robust private world of politics in Weimar Berlin that had no equivalent in the Austria or the Netherlands.

The interwar years dawned as a new birth of democracy, promise, and hope across the continent. Over time, interwar democracy would be pitted against authoritarianism, but a key question in the immediate wake of the war was how expansive these interwar democracies would be. Were working-class men to be included? Were ethnic and linguistic minorities to be included? Were women to be included? Comparing Oheimb, Boschek, Proft, and Katz demonstrates that the first female parliamentarians were more than the outward expression of superficial interwar change, but they exerted their own political agency. These women navigated the clubs of interwar capitals, the working sessions of international conferences, and their own parliaments' closed committee rooms to influence political decision-making. That was a revolutionary – and more democratically inclusive – break with the nineteenth-century past.

Katharina von Oheimb: Celebrity, Charm, and Strategy in the Weimar-Era Reichstag

The German election of January 1919 was the very first in which German women could vote, and it produced a National Assembly that included 37 women among its 423 total legislators. Over time, four more women joined these ranks to replace outgoing members, which ultimately meant that almost 10 per cent of the German National Assembly was made up of female parliamentarians. These women represented parties across the political spectrum, ranging from the far-left independent socialists to the right-wing German National People's Party (Deutschnationale Volkspartei, DNVP). Although one-tenth of the parliamentary total might seem a trifling percentage of female politicians today, this was early high-water mark for women's representation and was not regularly surpassed by the West German Bundestag until the 1980s.[14]

When Germany's first democratically elected parliamentarians assembled in Weimar in February 1919, the socialist Marie Juchacz made headlines as the first woman to address a German parliament.[15] She had long travelled around the country speaking on behalf of the Social Democratic Party of Germany (Sozialdemokratische Partei Deutschlands, SPD), but on February 19, 1919, Juchacz was particularly conscious of her historical role. To grab everyone's attention, she began with the unconventional "Meine Herren und Damen! [Dear Gentlemen and Ladies!]" which prompted laughter that the parliamentary stenographers dutifully recorded. Although Juchacz praised Germany's socialist government for effecting the revolutionary change that guaranteed women the right to vote, she argued that German women owed her own party nothing for giving women what had always been due to them yet unjustly withheld. The minutes of the parliamentary session record the reactions of the audience to this speech, and it was met with enthusiasm from the socialists and no significant pushback until Juchacz attacked a leading conservative for his defense of war and the old regime. Right-wing politicians then interrupted her, and the commotion was so great that the presiding officer had to call the parliament to order. Juchacz's political rivals were content to sit silently as she marked the historic occasion of women's suffrage, but when she strayed into issues of war and peace, they tried to shout her down.[16]

In the earliest years of the Weimar Republic, leading feminists and women's organizations worked to encourage newly elected female parliamentarians to co-operate across party lines on so-called women's issues. The plan was to coordinate advocacy first among a cross-party group of female legislators and then to present results of women's deliberations to male parliamentary colleagues. The Federation of German Women's Associations (Bund Deutscher Frauenvereine) organized cross-party committees outside parliament for drafting laws. The association's committee worked on issues related to illegitimate children and included female legislators from the SPD to the DNVP, as well as additional technical experts. Essentially, this extra-parliamentary group became the de facto legislation-writing committee that presented ready-made draft laws to male politicians with the support of all the leading women across the parliament's political parties. In this way, Germany's first generation of female politicians co-operated in drafting laws for maternity protection, on regulating obscene film content, and related to youth welfare. In addition, these female politicians advocated for equal rights and opportunities for German women. Female legislators from various parties petitioned the government to open up the legal profession by allowing women to complete the same legal exams as men. A cross-party group of women also drafted a motion demanding the government replace the police vice squad's oversight of sex workers with social work and health counselling services. Of the myriad ways that German women worked on legislation, only formal petitions and motions would crop up in the published parliamentary records, which are often the only source base consulted by scholars. Looking beyond those materials into this private backroom world of politics is essential to understand the breath of women's interwar political activity.[17]

A persistent cross-party bloc of women in the German parliament can be seen in voting records, where female parliamentarians tended to vote together or politely absent themselves from votes where they would have had to take a stand against their party. For example, in a June 1919 vote to ban the death penalty – which ultimately failed – all the women present voted to ban capital punishment, including a Catholic Centre Party member who voted against her own party. During a different debate on the article of the Weimar Constitution regarding women's equality, German parliamentarians were presented with the draft text: "Men and women essentially [grundsätzlich] have the same civil rights and duties." The socialist Toni Pfülf then proposed striking the word "essentially," but another leading politician, Christine Teusch of the Centre Party, opposed this amendment on religious grounds. The debate between Pfülf and Teusch was decided by the whole assembly in favour of keeping "essentially," although when the vote was taken, many of the female parliamentarians simply were not present, so they would not have to vote against their conscience or against their party. Even as freshly minted parliamentarians, German female politicians built an informal cross-party community that flexed its legislative muscle in republican lawmaking.[18]

One early observer of this world of robust cross-party women's connections was Katharina von Oheimb. In 1919, she had come to the National Assembly in Weimar, not as an elected politician, but as an observer working on behalf of the women's committee of the right-liberal German People's Party (Deutsche Volkspartei, DVP). Cutting her teeth on German national politics for the first time, Oheimb met with the DVP parliamentary group, and she observed the National Assembly's proceedings. Katharina von Oheimb then won her own election in 1920 to the Weimar Republic's first regular Reichstag session. She served for the DVP for one parliamentary term from 1920 to 1924. In her new role as an elected parliamentarian, Oheimb cultivated a sense of celebrity that used her formal political role to bridge the social and political worlds in Berlin. After she left elected politics in 1924, she remained a key link between the political establishment and the social world of the German capital.[19]

When she sat in the Reichstag, she was known as Katharina von Oheimb, but she would later marry a DVP colleague and take the name Katharina von Kardorff-Oheimb. However, many interwar contemporaries knew this trailblazing woman simply as "Kathinka," which was the nickname used in the 1925 *New York Times Magazine* exposé. She married four times and divorced in a period when that was exceedingly rare. She ran factories, inherited a fortune, qualified as a hunter, set up training courses for middle-class women, pioneered political education for women, and was a regular newspaper columnist. From New York to Paris and London, reporters covered Oheimb's political activities; her glamorous photographs appeared in fashion magazines, and one contemporary song referenced her antics. She amassed a worldwide following, and after she departed elected politics, London's *Daily Express* called her the "uncrowned queen of Germany." The *Times of India* dubbed her "A Modern Madame de Staël" because of her social salon's central position in the political networks of Weimar Berlin. For her pioneering yet idiosyncratic biography, Katharina von Kardorff-Oheimb has earned herself a place in Germany's current feminist pantheon.[20]

Although Oheimb attended debates, voted, and signed on to motions presented in the Reichstag, during four years of parliamentary service, she only ever gave one plenary speech. In a debate about appointing women as jurors and judges, Oheimb spoke after the German justice minister, who came from her own conservative-leaning political party. In her speech, Oheimb agreed that women should be appointed to legal positions, but she pivoted to a party-political attack that ultimately ended in a racist dog-whistle. Speaking from the podium, Oheimb turned directly to her female colleagues in parliament: "Of course, ladies, I am not here to disrupt the esprit de corps among us." She then immediately did just that by throwing other women under the bus. Oheimb condemned the dogmatic tone of the schoolmarm-like campaigners for women's rights. She argued that "the role of women [in parliament] should be didactically influencing the men in parliament." Oheimb's less-than-feminist vision was that women were to educate and persuade men in private rather harangue in public. In wrapping up her intentionally divisive speech, Oheimb claimed that this whole debate about women jurors was less important than attacking Germany's enemies abroad. She polemically claimed that the biggest threat to the women of Germany was not legal inequality but Allied colonial soldiers of colour in the Rhineland befriending German women. This one and only speech Oheimb gave as a parliamentarian was incendiary, racist, and reactionary.[21]

However, focusing on Oheimb's one formal speech would give a wildly inaccurate perception of her political acumen. Oheimb's biographer Cornelia Baddack assessed this speech and a simultaneous increase in Oheimb's committee work as "the high point of all her participation in parliament."[22] Although this was true in terms of Oheimb's public parliamentary work, Oheimb was well aware that Germany's female politicians co-operated across party lines. In public, she had challenged her female colleagues in her lone speech, but, in private, she and other leading female lawmakers continued to parlay women's influence with specific men. The most stunning item in Oheimb's personal papers is a list of all the women serving in the Reichstag. On this list, these women have been rated for their intelligence, power, and influence. Oheimb likely collaborated with Marie-Elisabeth Lüders from the left-liberal German Democratic Party (Deutsche Demokratische Partei, DDP) on this ranking. A key explaining this document reads: "Those [women] marked 0 are complete blank slates, those with - irrelevant nobodies. Only those with + have obvious influence, of these the especially smart ones are marked !" This list identified influential and intelligent women in every political party. Lüders and Oheimb gave top marks to Paula Müller-Otfried from the conservative DNVP, Hedwig Dransfeld and Helene Weber of the Catholic Centre Party, Marie Juchacz, Mathilde Wurm, Antonie Pfülf, and Toni Sender from the SPD, and even Clara Zetkin of the Communists. In her lone public parliamentary speech, Oheimb trashed the left, but in private, she gave left-wing female politicians top marks.[23]

Oheimb's ranked list of female legislators included additional notes explaining the power of various women. Some of the bourgeois and Catholic women active in external women's groups were said to have those organizations' goals as "an agenda often separate from that of the party." These women could be worked with on projects that their women's organizations supported, even if their own political parties were lukewarm.

One Centre Party parliamentarian's influence was described as tending "more in a confessional than in a political direction," and a socialist was seen as having power over Paul Löbe, the president of the Reichstag. The bourgeois biases of this list's authors are revealed in a comment disparaging some the women in the working-class parties, while lifting up others: "In the SPD, only T. Pfülf and M. Wurm are from educated homes. The smartest of them was Klara Zetkin. She possessed a marvelously sharp mind, great reasoning, and brilliant ability as a speaker. [She was] earlier very radical but personally friendly." Respectable homes and class still mattered in the strategic thinking of this document's authors.[24]

This stunning document could serve as a blueprint for any woman trying to build a cross-party united front among her colleagues. This strategic political thinking reflected the social infrastructure that supported cross-party collaboration among female lawmakers in Germany. Cornelia Baddack rightly points out that Oheimb was less well connected to the organized women's movement and public "parliamentary women's work," but Baddack does not consider this particular archival source as evidence for the extent of Oheimb's strategic cross-party mobilization of female legislators.[25] This list prompts a re-evaluation of Oheimb's lone speech and public political persona. The minutes of the Reichstag record that conservative men loudly applauded Oheimb's one fiery parliamentary speech. Her vitriol for the Allies endeared her to her right-wing male colleagues. Indeed, Oheimb had claimed in the speech that "the role of women should be didactically influencing the men." Oheimb's strategy as a newcomer was to endear herself to her right-wing colleagues rhetorically, while behind the scenes influencing them to further goals that the women in the Reichstag wanted. If that required a speech or two throwing left-wing women under the bus to gain the ear of her right-wing male colleagues, Oheimb was not averse to doing just that.[26]

Katharina von Oheimb often made skilful use of her flirtatious sense of humour for the same strategic political ends. Oheimb wrote extensively in her memoirs about one incident that the official minutes of the Reichstag record as having taken place on November 22, 1921. The left-wing independent socialist leader Rudolf Breitscheid was taunting right-wing politicians in a speech. The socialist firebrand was recounting the period just after the German Revolution when large land-owning aristocrats were scrambling for assistance from the socialist-led revolutionary government. Breitscheid was then the Prussian interior minister, and he recalled that these nobles came hat in hand to him: "Humbly and wistfully, they showed up to beg for the position of a local official or for some other small concession." The back-and-forth between Breitscheid and his right-wing Reichstag colleagues led him naming Graf von Mirbach as one of these aristocratic beggars.[27]

The parliamentary minutes then record a shout of "lies" after which Breitscheid spoke directly to Katharina von Oheimb. Her own recollection was that she called Breitscheid a liar, after which "a roar of indignation burst from the left side of the chamber."[28] Oheimb remembered the parliament then fell to a dead silence. The formal minutes record Breitscheid addressing her allegation that he was being untruthful:

BREITCHEID: Deputy von Oheimb, where did you find the unfortunate courage to declare that the claim I am making is a lie?

(Deputy VON OHEIMB: Because he's my friend and because Graf Mirbach went to Ebert and not to you! – Great Commotion.)[29]

Katharina von Oheimb's use of the German word "friend" could imply a more intimate connection between her and the aristocratic Mirbach, something that was seen as funny for the then twice-divorced Oheimb. Her own memoirs recount the story as if the "friend" joke was the punch line. However, the formal minutes record that Breitscheid artlessly continued his remarks: "In no way do I want to deal with your friendly relationships." He then dismissed the whole matter with the sexist coda that "this is the thinking of housewives." Oheimb recalled that at the next meeting of the Reichstag, on her desk she "found an orchid and a note with unfamiliar handwriting: 'I want to be your friend.'" Both Breitscheid and the anonymous flower friend focused on Oheimb's humorous innuendo about her romantic past.[30]

However, Oheimb deployed far more political skill with this public political intervention. After she declared that Graf von Mirbach was her friend, she admitted that he went grovelling to the socialists for aid, but she claimed he went to German President Friedrich Ebert rather than to Breitscheid. She actually confirmed Breitscheid's larger allegation about the nobility asking for government handouts, while undermining Breitscheid's authority by suggesting he inserted himself into a scene where he was not present. If Oheimb's goal was "didactically influencing the men in parliament," she strategically ingratiated herself to conservatives with the humour that punctured Breitscheid's bubble. At the same time however, she also appealed to more moderate socialists allied with Ebert by admitting than the aristocrats had sought aid from the government.[31]

Even more important than Oheimb's deft political acumen in charming both sides in the Reichstag, she was a skilled operator in Berlin's behind-the-scenes political culture. She held her own in the smoke-filled rooms of posh social clubs, in the homes of aristocrats, and in private ministerial offices.[32] Women were not always welcome in these spaces, so some leading female politicians moved informal political meetings to spaces they could more effectively control. Marie-Elisabeth Lüders invited colleagues from other political parties to small meetings at her home on Berlin's Uhlandstraße.[33] Oheimb took a different approach. In keeping with her bold statements and edgy jokes on the Reichstag floor, she confidently barged into male-dominated social environments with grit and determination. She was the only woman invited to Walther Rathenau's political dinners. After she spent a whole day turning down her boring political colleagues' invitations to drop by for a formal tea, she "went in the evening to the Reichsklub [...] We played the card game Skat, I won 3 Marks 80." Clubs, card games, betting, and politics – Oheimb tossed her period's gendered stereotypes and expectations aside, thriving in this male-dominated social world.[34]

Katharina von Oheimb and her fellow female parliamentarians were not the first women in Berlin to build social and political networks surrounding the Reichstag. The wives of German politicians had long run social salons, advised their husbands, and were fixtures at formal events in the Wilhelmine capital. Indeed, during the interwar years, politicians' spouses still participated in this informal world in ways that were similar to their prewar predecessors.[35] Ultimately, a link developed between the pre-existing networks of German political wives and these newly elected female politicians. For example, a 1923 appeal entitled "The German People Are Starving" called for donations to support those who were in need during the economic chaos of hyperinflation. This charitable drive had the support of the wives of the German president, chancellor, and a German nationalist leader. However, liberal and Catholic women sitting in the Reichstag also endorsed this campaign. Oheimb hosted a reception to support this charitable appeal. There was, thus, a mingling of the older networks of the wives of powerful men and the new network of women who were elected to public office in their own right.[36]

The link between the social world surrounding the Reichstag and the workings of the parliament are humorously illustrated by one account from Oheimb's memoirs, compiled from interviews she gave later in life. Her memoirs are not always a perfect source for dates and factual details, with Oheimb misremembering things like her Reichstag committee assignment. Nevertheless, the social atmosphere of parties and private gatherings that Oheimb describes in her memoirs are largely corroborated by postwar autobiographies, as well as contemporary correspondence, dinner invitations, diary entries, and, in this particular case, the *New York Times Magazine* feature.[37] Oheimb recalled hosting a small dinner in a luxury hotel on Unter den Linden, just on the other side of the Brandenburg Gate from the Reichstag building. Luminaries from Berlin society, as well as one of her Reichstag colleagues, had joined her for a meal. "Just in the middle of the nicest conversation around the table there was a summons from the Reichstag: 'Return immediately for voting in the Reichstag! Tax bill, exceptionally important! Every vote counts! You must vote the party line!'" Despite misgivings about leaving her guests behind and her indifference to the tax law being debated, Oheimb rushed to the Reichstag with her colleague, but not before using a butter knife on the table to pry the tiara of pearls and diamonds from her hair and entrusting it to a friend at the dinner.

When Oheimb arrived at the Reichstag, she realized that in addition to the fashionable evening dress revealing her bare arms, she was wearing only a fur cape, which would be a faux pas to wear into the plenary chamber. She imagined the humiliation that would be heaped upon her, especially by the proletarian press, mocking her as a rich reactionary lavishly displaying wealth, so she frantically sought out another solution. "I was on especially good terms with the people working the Reichstag's cloakrooms; they were always polite, regardless of the party of which they were members [...] I loudly begged: 'Give me a man's coat – doesn't matter if it's from the right or left – I just need to cover up!'" After hurriedly throwing the coat of a short socialist over her arms, she ran into the Reichstag chamber, ready to vote. "The Reichstag was abuzz [...] The right-wing women who walked by all looked me up and down, almost contemptuous at my misfortune." To Oheimb's chagrin, she learned that she had rushed back too quickly. Many of her other parliamentary colleagues had not shown up yet and the debate was nowhere near over; voting would not take place until much later in the evening.

Distressed by the scorn of her fellow parliamentarians, Oheimb rushed to be alone in the women's bathroom. However, she was not by herself there for too long: "The doors opened and closed, and I heard women's voices – in the end I was standing among all my left-wing female colleagues!" Braced for an onslaught of criticism and undoubtedly thankful that she had left her pearl-and-diamond tiara behind, Oheimb waited for their reaction. She was surprised: "Everyone was kind and gentle and wanted to see my dress in the right light. They kept repeating: 'This dress is so pretty!' and 'It's so dumb that they summoned you.' Since I was so distraught, they touched my bare arms, and I regained my composure, thankful for their respect for my appearance and their compassion for my distress." This unexpectedly friendly reaction reflected a cross-party camaraderie among Germany's female politicians. The leading socialist Luise Zietz was there in the Reichstag bathroom and had a bit of feminist advice: "Don't work yourself up so much; men aren't even worth it."[38] Indeed, Luise Zietz had been the left-wing foil for Oheimb's scorn and racist jibes in her lone plenary speech, but in this private space, they connected on friendly terms.[39]

As a lawmaker, Katharina von Oheimb also navigated a budding intimate relationship with her fellow DVP parliamentarian Siegfried von Kardorff. This worried Oheimb's colleague Marie-Elisabeth Lüders, who sent handwritten notes from her sickbed to warn Oheimb about this relationship. Lüders employed zero-sum language of "winning" or "losing the game" to refer to women's political and social success in relation to men: "As long as you noticeably favour [Kardorff] socially & personally, you will not win the game. And he is counting on that." Lüders was concerned with the damage the chatter about their relationship could do. If rumours got out of hand, "all the opposing or jealous gossips – both men and women – would have won the game." Lüders counselled Oheimb to distance herself from Kardorff in order to gain political standing: "Only after this speculation is no longer accurate, others will see the situation & and only then will you have won."

Lüders understood that politically active women needed to be hyper-aware of social settings and personal relationships, so as not to lose the political "game." In fact, Lüders was writing from personal experience. As an unmarried woman, she had a child with a former justice minister and colleague in her own political party. Lüders wrote to Oheimb of how she struggled in the relationship until her partner "had completely lost a considerable portion of his social and political standing [and was] vulnerable." The picture of the social life around the Reichstag that Lüders painted was of a dangerous political minefield for women. A close friendship, intimate rendezvous, or slanderous gossip could ruin a woman's career. However, this letter was also evidence that Lüders and Oheimb strategically thought about this social-political world in terms of winning, losing, and gaining influence.[40]

Ranked lists of colleagues and strategizing about personal relationships with Lüders notwithstanding, Katharina von Oheimb's political influence as a newcomer in the Reichstag can still be hard to measure. On the one hand, she obviously had little staying power within her own DVP party because she was booted from office by her local constituency after only one term.[41] As a member of the slightly more left-leaning, socially oriented wing in the DVP who voted against her own party a few too many times, Oheimb alienated both the leadership and her own local party.[42] Even Cornelia Baddack discounted the idea that Oheimb had developed any central position within "the parliamentary game." Baddack argued that the Reichstag itself had more symbolic value for

Oheimb rather than being the "actual setting for her political activities." Baddack's strict segregation between the Reichstag and Oheimb's social networks unintentionally minimizes Oheimb's approach that mixed the personal and the political. Only valuing parliamentary politics that yields monumental legislative successes is a limited way of thinking about political power. Oheimb excelled in amassing a private parliamentary network that advanced her desired political ends.[43]

A pointed attack on Oheimb by Paul Moldenhauer, who was a more right-wing DVP colleague, is evidence enough of Oheimb's political influence. After a cabinet crisis toppled Gustav Stresemann as chancellor, the German President Friedrich Ebert asked Siegfried von Kardorff, then Oheimb's secret lover, to try to form a government. Moldenhauer mocked the idea that anyone would have supported Kardorff as chancellor: "For Ebert's decision there is just one possible explanation: Frau von Oheimb, who can strongly influence Ebert, pushed him to this action and Ebert ultimately gave in [...] At least he gave into the desire of an ambitious and loving woman, and Kardorff became *homo regius* for twenty-four hours." Kardorff failed at putting together a cabinet, and Moldenhauer depicted Oheimb as a crafty woman out for her own glory in aiding her paramour. The gendered tropes in Moldenhauer's tale are glaringly evident. A more convincing reading of these events sees in Oheimb's consultations with Ebert proof that they both trusted and benefitted from working with each another. A female member in the Reichstag had the ear and the respect of the German president in advising him on who to appoint as the head of government. That was undoubtedly real political power.[44]

Oheimb's own recollections about Friedrich Ebert strengthen the argument that she used her connections for her own political ends, including gaining Kardorff his chance at high political office. Oheimb had grown close to Ebert in part because her land bordered the hunting grounds formerly set aside for the emperor that were now used the president. Essentially, the two were neighbours, and Oheimb was often a guest at his hunting lodge.[45] Oheimb felt comfortable in inviting Ebert to her own home in Goslar, and her well-known connections to Ebert even prompted a friend to implore the Oheimb to convince the president to attend a film premiere as a marketing stunt.[46] Oheimb's close relationship with Ebert was not as naive as Moldenhauer had argued. In fact, Oheimb firmly believed that Ebert valued order over revolutionary chaos. She praised the socialist for putting the trade unions' "organized millions against the Spartacists' and soldiers councils' wild hordes." In the socialist Ebert, Oheimb found a strategic political ally from another party, and she built a behind-the-scenes social and political relationship with him that lasted until his death in 1925.[47]

Figure 1.1. Katharina von Kardorff-Oheimb (left) in conversation with other women at a social function in interwar Berlin.

Source: From bpk Bildagentur / Photographer: Erich Salomon, Art Resource, NY.

As a coda to Oheimb's four-year stint in the Reichstag, her skill as a networker did not fade when she left her elected role in 1924. Out of office, she saw herself as "a free politician, without a party whip or obligation to vote a certain way," and she was able to further develop her networks.[48] As in the case of Friedrich Ebert, Oheimb often fostered close relationships with the socialists, and these connections deepened after she left office. She frequently exchanged letters and postcards with Paul Löbe.[49] Oheimb was also particularly close to Hermann Müller, a long-time leader within the SPD who twice served as chancellor.[50] Oheimb touchingly wrote to Müller at his departure from the chancellery: "I only want to express my deep disappointment that developments drove you off Wilhelmstraße. When I learned even more details, I thought about the saying: 'May God protect me from my friends (especially friends in the same political party); I can protect myself from my enemies.'" At the end of the letter, Oheimb invited Müller to visit her in the near future.[51]

Oheimb was not only a friend of the German socialists. The breadth of her social connections appeared most plainly at the announcement of her engagement to her colleague Siegfried von Kardorff. Congratulations poured in from friends, colleagues, and Berlin's diplomatic corps. She even heard from the Conservative British parliamentarian Philip Dawson: "I beg to write and express to you my sincere congratulations and good wishes on your engagement to Dr. Kardorff. I always remember the very pleasant time I spent at your house in Berlin and the very interesting people you were good enough to invite to meet me."[52] Colleagues, particularly women, from the DVP, the DNVP, and the Bavarian People's Party wrote in to congratulate the new couple. Most surprising was a note from Wilhelm Kube, who was then serving for a far-right party in the Reichstag and would later join the Nazi Party. Oheimb's social and political world – both inside and out of parliament – ranged from the radical right wing through to the moderate socialists.[53]

Oheimb had long been known for combining her Reichstag seat with her position as a *salonnière* in the German capital. Oheimb's political salon became such a fixture in the German capital that it featured in popular culture and contemporary non-fiction. In blending the social and the political, Oheimb worked to cultivate a particularly international guest list. "Foreigners are always welcome in her house, for she likes new viewpoints and cannot stand the chronic disparagement of things French." In her lone Reichstag speech, Oheimb had attacked the Allies in jingoistic terms, but in private she was supportive of German reproachment with its wartime enemies. Presciently anticipating Robert Schumann and post-Second World War European integration, in the 1920s, Oheimb argued that "a Franco-German understanding is a necessity to Europe," and her internationally inclusive social-political guest list reflected this belief, as well as her own understanding of her transnational role as a politician and social networker.[54]

Katharina von Oheimb's influence in shaping political decision-making through Berlin's behind-the-scenes social world is evidenced by the contempt in which she was held by her enemies. Extremists on the radical right, led by the Nazi Joseph Goebbels, despised the political and social duo Siegfried von Kardorff and Katharina von Oheimb. Goebbels caustically referred to Oheimb's husband as "Kathinkus der Vierte," mockingly referencing the fact he was her fourth husband.[55] However, Oheimb was criticized by the left as well. The noted leftist satirist and social critic Kurt Tucholsky took aim at Oheimb and her social events in his poem "An Frau von Oheimb" (To Frau von Oheimb) including the caustic lines: "A homey parlour is not really a salon. / You know nothing about politics." Tucholsky couched his criticism as an attack on the world of politics behind closed doors where the forces of reaction amassed and no real reform took place:

> Die Republik gibt sich in deinen Räumen
> ein Stelldichein. O stell sie wieder weg!
> Schlafwandler sind sie, die regierend träumen …
> Und die Reformen sind wie Teegebäck.
>> Und blickte Salomo auf diese Scheitel,
>> er spräche: Hier ist alles eitel.
>> Auf hundert rechte Gäste kommt ein linker …
>> Kathinka–!

> The Republic comes together at your place.
> Oh, just banish it!
> They're sleepwalkers, dreaming of power …
> Reformist ideas are mere peanuts.
>> If King Solomon glanced down on this,
>> he would say: Here all is vanity.
>> A hundred right-wing guests and only one leftist …
>> Oh, Kathinka![56]

Kurt Tucholsky was wrong in claiming that Oheimb did not engage figures from the left, as her extensive connections across the political spectrum demonstrate. Goebbels and Tucholsky attacked Oheimb because they hated what she represented: a behind-the-scenes world of politics, deal-making, and co-operation in which a woman could wield political power. In her sole speech as a member of the German parliament, Oheimb had tipped her hand: "The role of women should consist in didactically influencing the men in parliament." In salons and backrooms, Oheimb worked to gain the ear of powerful men, educate them, and then direct them in the way she thought was best. In the end, any understanding of Oheimb's political acumen and influence would be incomplete, if one focused only on her public statements and formal votes. Oheimb, as well as many of her female colleagues in the Reichstag, mobilized and acted within a larger social world to advance political ends.[57]

Anna Boschek and Gabriele Proft: From Resentful Coalition Partners to Socialist Internationalists in First Republic Austria

The first interwar Austrian elections in February 1919 bought a cohort of eight women to the 170-person Constituent National Assembly. First

Republic Austria was born in the chaos of a crumbling Habsburg empire with uncertainties about the country's borders and future stability. Elections in the rump German Austrian state brought seven female socialists and one Catholic conservative Christian Social woman into the new parliament. Two of those socialists were Anna Boschek and Gabriele Proft who served as parliamentarians from the advent of the republic through the collapse of Austria's interwar democracy. Both women's experiences demonstrate an emphasis on party-political work and a lack of strong domestic cross-party connections in Austria. Political polarization at the rank-and-file level of parliamentary politics, as well as a largely two-party political system, promoted more division rather than cross-party collaboration within the interwar Austrian parliament. Nevertheless, both Boschek and Proft took on roles in the international arena that were linked to their own socialist activism.[58]

Anna Boschek and Gabriele Proft came to Austria's parliament in 1919 after years in the Habsburg-era socialist movement. Born in Vienna, Boschek grew up in a working-class family, herself leaving school after only five years of elementary education after which she worked stints in textile, metal, and harmonica factories. She quickly became active in socialist trade unions, and she was later the first woman elected to the executive committee of the Austrian half of the Habsburg Empire's socialist party, the Austrian Social Democratic Workers' Party (Sozialdemokratische Arbeiterpartei, after the First World War, Sozialdemokratische Arbeiterpartei Deutschösterreichs, both abbreviated SDAP). Boschek remained a towering figure within the moderate wing of the Austrian socialist movement throughout the interwar years. Gabriele Proft came from a German-speaking family in Troppau/Opava where her father was a master cobbler. Proft received some secondary education before working as a domestic servant and eventually moving from Czech Silesia to Vienna. From 1909, Proft held professional positions within the women's organization of the socialist party and became a party journalist. Proft was associated with the more left-leaning SDAP faction.[59]

After the February 1919 elections that propelled Boschek and Proft into parliament, the Austrian socialists took the lead in a coalition government between themselves and the conservative Christian Social Party (Christlichsoziale Partei, CS). After the First Republic's constitution was adopted and fresh elections were held in October 1920, that coalition ended with CS taking the helm without the SDAP, and the socialists would never again serve in a First Republic cabinet.[60] The political scientist Anton Pelinka has used the end of this early coalition as a turning point in Austrian political history between the "parliamentarism of consociational democracy" and a fully fledged majoritarian democracy with its consequent uptick in polarization.[61] The historian Erin Hochman has applied this idea of consociational consensus beyond 1920 to detect even more moments that bridged political divides during the First Republic.[62] However, Boschek and Proft did not experience the collaborative political world that both Pelinka and Hochman anticipated. Although the Austrian politicians were working and voting in a coalition, there was little love lost between the socialists and Christian Socials in the halls of parliament. Consociationalism can create co-operation among party elites, but Boschek and Proft were not among the highest ranks of the SDAP elite. They were parliamentary foot soldiers who voted with their CS rivals but had no qualms about attacking them rhetorically at the same time.[63]

When Boschek and Proft entered the Austrian parliament in 1919, they were immediately made legislative committee rapporteurs. Parliamentary procedures had been borrowed from the Habsburg era and included collaborative committee work. An assigned parliamentary rapporteur presented the committee's draft legislation and fielded questions from the parliament.[64] During the sessions of the Constituent Assembly, Anna Boschek served as rapporteur on two proposals. She was a committee rapporteur on a domestic servants' law and on a proposal to treat male and female civil servants equally. Boschek also delivered three other parliamentary speeches in 1919 – one on regulating women's nighttime work, one on helping the victims of the world war, and one introducing an eight-hour workday. Boschek later recalled that sometimes she struggled with the complex legal terminology bandied about in parliamentary work because of her lack of formal education, but she also worked to hold her own in debates.[65] Gabriele Proft served as a rapporteur on finance and budget proposals twice, and she also spoke separately on the household budget of Austrian women and on support payments to disabled veterans. In the early years of Austria's First Republic, Boschek, Proft, and their female peers in the Austrian parliament did far more of this public parliamentary work with speeches and interventions than Katharina von Oheimb or her female colleagues in Weimar Germany.[66]

Like their German counterparts, much of the parliamentary work of Austria's first female legislators involved advocating for topics related to mothers, children, and women. Hildegard Burjan, the lone conservative CS female parliamentarian, poured her time and energy into proposals creating a state-run intermediate girls' school and expanding home economics schools. Although the SDAP and CS were in a coalition government, Proft and Boschek nevertheless included frequent party-political digs in their speeches reporting on legislation related to these perceived "women's topics."[67] Sharp political rhetoric between socialists and Christian Socials even pockmarked the most successful example of Austrian women co-operating across party lines in the early years of the republic. The female socialists were joined by Hildegard Burjan in a committee to hammer out a new domestic servants' law. The committee collaboratively overcame constitutional objections and incorporated the feedback of both Catholic and socialist trade unions. The Austrian historian Gabriella Hauch has noted that co-operation among female legislators tended to produce support across the political spectrum; however, the public rhetoric did not often reflect this friendly collaborative ethos. When Burjan delivered her plenary speech on the draft law, she began with the historical significance of the moment: "Today is the first time that a law that was crafted by women has come up for discussion in the National Assembly." However, Burjan's nod to this historic moment quickly yielded to her pointed party-political critique of socialist newspaper reporting that set the expectations of domestic servants too high. Burjan could have lingered on the benefits of co-operation, but her quick pivot was to party-political differences.[68]

Although these public parliamentary interventions by women suggest an ingrained political suspicion of their domestic rivals, the private correspondence of Gabriele Proft and Anna Boschek pointed to a self-understanding within a larger socialist movement. Both Proft and Boschek had come of age in an expansive imperial SDAP. The Habsburg-era SDAP had tried to keep together moderates, radicals, and even different nationalities in one big-tent socialist family. This meant that when the Habsburg Empire collapsed, the German-speaking socialists had grown up in a party that had always included members from Bohemia, Moravia, Silesia, Bukovina, Trieste, and South Tyrol, which were no longer represented in Viennese politics.[69] Despite the new interwar national borders, Boschek and Proft maintained connections with their former colleagues who now happened to be in other countries. For instance, Ludwig Czech, the leader of the German Social Democrats in Czechoslovakia and a minister in the Czechoslovak cabinet of the late 1920s and 1930s, wrote to Proft in 1929 to mark her birthday. His friendly letter revealed that he had learned of her birthday from the *Arbeiter-Zeitung*, the Vienna-based newspaper of the Austrian Social Democratic party, which Czech still read daily. It might seem strange that the leader of a socialist party sitting in a different national government kept up with the birthday announcements in the neighbouring country's socialist press. However, this was natural for Ludwig Czech who, like Boschek and Proft, always saw himself as a member of the Central European German-speaking labour movement and Vienna as that movement's capital.[70]

Although Proft and Boschek had socialist friends all across Central Europe, there was a noticeable lack of cross-party relationships with Austrian politicians of other political persuasions. Friendly correspondence from a socialist women's union leader in Germany planning a get-together was not uncommon, but there is an utter dearth of archival records from Boschek or Proft about social events with Christian Social colleagues.[71] Instead, both Proft and Boschek focused primarily on party-specific work, even while serving as parliamentarians. Proft, Boschek, and their Austrian socialist colleagues dedicated themselves to political projects like the municipal socialism of Red Vienna, where both women also served in the Viennese city assembly.[72] Boschek and Proft were also particularly involved in the SDAP's women's organizations. When the SDAP's central women's committee elected nine members to the editorial committee overseeing the socialist women's publication *Die Frau*, all but three of the women were members of the Austrian parliament, and this included Boschek and Proft.[73] Both women, along with other male and female parliamentary colleagues, also took up teaching and leadership roles in the working-class women's school. Proft taught the series of classes on Austrian political economy, and Boschek co-taught the courses on working women in society, which included discussions ranging from the pre-capitalistic development of marriage to proletarian women's engagement for marriage reform. In Austria, party work dominated the female socialist parliamentarians' calendars.[74]

In addition to Boschek and Proft's regional socialist connections, both women travelled abroad on party-political trips. Gabriele Proft joined a 45-person travelling group sponsored by a Viennese socialist educational centre that went to the United States in the summer of 1930. The president of the Viennese Landtag and federal parliamentarian Robert Danneberg, who had previously been on lecture tours in the United States, led the group. In addition to visiting tourist sites in New York, Philadelphia, Washington, Chicago, Detroit, and Niagara Falls, Proft and her travel companions met with American trade union activists and officials at the US Labor Department. They were entertained by the mayor and city staff in Chicago where Danneberg hoped to find inspiration for improving Viennese parks and traffic patterns. Austrian consulates in the United States followed news of the trip closely, but with the exception of the Austrian consul general in Chicago, the socialist travellers declined to meet with Austrian diplomats who were seen as too close to the conservative government. The socialists' concern was not unfounded, since these same Austrian diplomats were criticizing Danneberg's revolutionary, anti-Austrian speeches in private dispatches back to Vienna. Ultimately, Proft's fact-finding trip was more party-political than inter-parliamentary, but she still connected being an international traveller with her political work in Austria.[75]

Anna Boschek had much more extensive international experience through her work with the International Labour Organization (ILO). Boschek had long served as a functionary within Austria's socialist trade unions, even founding and leading a women's section in the unions. Starting in 1919, she also had an international platform within the ILO as the permanent Austrian representative to the ILO's women's committee. Boschek had long been a frequent correspondent with leading socialist European trade unionists, and her biggest break on the international stage was when she was recommended by the Austrian socialist trade unions to be their representative to the International Labour Conference in 1931. ILO conferences brought together government officials, employees, and employers, and socialists had long dominated the ILO's leadership. Even the conservative Christian Social federal government in Austria acquiesced to Boschek's appointment and sent her formal accreditation to Geneva. The 1931 conference was attended by 141 delegates representing 46 states. Along with experts and assistants, 370 people were at the conference, of whom only 28 were women. Boschek was the first woman attending as a fully independent delegate representing her union, rather than serving as a substitute delegate or a designated expert.[76]

At the 1931 ILO conference, Anna Boschek advocated for a committee on women in the workplace, which the ILO then created and to which Boschek was appointed. Despite the crackdown on Austrian socialists and Boschek's own arrest by the authoritarian government after the Austrian Civil War of 1934, the authoritarian Austrian state could not remove Boschek from her ILO committee seat in Geneva, and her term was renewed in 1935. After being released from jail in 1935, Boschek remained internationally active through this ILO committee on women's work until Austria's merger with Nazi Germany in 1938, when she was required to resign. Ultimately, Boschek remained active as a transnational figure in the European left-wing world of labour politics long after Austrian authoritarians banned her party and evicted her from her parliamentary seat.[77]

In looking back at Boschek and Proft in First Republic Austrian parliamentary politics, their experiences were those of women closely tied to the SDAP, to its organizations, and to a wider Central European socialist network. Even their earliest speeches as parliamentary newcomers were full of political barbs for their erstwhile Christian Social governing partner. Both women took on transnational roles – Proft as a fact-finding traveller and Boschek with the ILO – that stemmed from their party-political parliamentary work. The extant archival collections suggest that neither Proft nor Boschek were members of any vibrant national cross-party social community in the same way that Oheimb was in Germany. On some level, collegiality was unnecessary for ordinary parliamentarians in First Republic Austria. After the SDAP left the government in 1920, cross-party co-operation was not needed to achieve majorities in parliament. Austria essentially had two large parties – the socialists and the conservative Christian Socials – and the much smaller pan-German nationalists and agrarians were distant third and fourth parties. Because the blocs were so large and coalitions did not need to be remade every election, there was little political gain from developing lasting cross-party connections among ordinary legislators. In the end, Proft and Boschek's power, influence, and drive stemmed from their positions within the SDAP and its trade unions. Serving as some of their country's first female parliamentarians was treated as yet another party-political task. In the end, cross-party co-operation in Austria was reserved for the men at the top of their political parties.[78]

Frida Katz: The Vocation of a Conciliatory Expert in the Dutch Tweede Kamer

"The ballot box cast Suze Groeneweg into parliament for the women. Our own Miss Rankin in the Dutch parliament has summoned up the compassion of her fellow women." A Catholic newspaper in Holland reached for a foreign analogy for the election of the first woman to the lower house of the Dutch parliament, the Tweede Kamer. Jeanette Rankin had won a seat in the United States House of Representatives for Montana in 1916, and this reference to Rankin catapulted the Netherlands into an international vanguard. However, the Catholic newspaper's journalist was also intentional in having the socialist Groeneweg magically "cast" by the ballot box rather than pushed forward by Dutch women, since the Netherlands' first female parliamentarian entered office without any women's votes. In 1918, Dutch women had only been permitted the halfway house of "passive suffrage," when they could stand for office but not actually vote themselves, a disparity which would not be rectified until 1919.[79]

Like many newly minted female parliamentarians of the interwar years, the 43-year-old grocer's daughter and educator Suze Groeneweg encountered the gaze of the press and the scorn of her colleagues immediately after arriving in The Hague.[80] News reporting on her first day in office focused on her clothing: "Suze Groeneweg was entirely appropriately dressed in a tastefully sober black outfit, and many parliamentarians of all political persuasions came to compliment her."[81] The reader was left in some doubt as to whether her colleagues were complimenting her attire or welcoming her to her new job. In fact, Groeneweg's arrival in The Hague had required renovations to create spaces in the parliamentary complex just for her. She was provided with her own break room and washroom that were accessed by a small hallway mockingly called the "Groenewegje" (little green path) by her male colleagues. This was a pun based on Groeneweg's last name, but her male colleagues undoubtedly appreciated the irony that "Groenewegje" also happened to be the name of a street in The Hague's red light district.[82]

Within weeks of Suze Groeneweg taking up her new parliamentary seat, multiple Dutch newspapers were condemning her for not giving speeches on women's issues. One suggested that her silence had proven that she had fallen victim to the "eternal feminine."[83] Despite the sexist pushback in the bourgeois press, Groeneweg delivered her first parliamentary speech on military matters on November 7, 1918. She emphasized her special concern for families, since husbands were often deployed far away from home due to the policy of armed neutrality. Groeneweg's speech was interrupted by her colleagues' derision, so much so that she directly addressed their disrespect by asking her fellow politicians to think about the message that laughing at her first speech would send to the wider world. At one point, Groeneweg even elicited supportive laughter when she challenged her colleagues who were peppering her remarks with questions: "Don't try to confuse me with interruptions [...] instead, you should actually do something for the women." The socialists and the audience in the public gallery cheered. Afterwards, one or two right-wing politicians even congratulated Groeneweg on her first parliamentary address.[84]

After the 1922 Dutch elections, Suze Groeneweg was joined by six female colleagues. One of these newcomers was Frida Katz of the conservative Protestant Christian Historical Union (Christelijk-Historische Unie, CHU). Katz was the only women in her party's 11-person parliamentary group.[85] She had first become politically active in the early 1900s working with organizations dedicated to promoting women's suffrage. She blazed her own career path, studying law and joining a legal practice in 1917. As a lawyer, she broke a glass ceiling in being appointed the country's first female clerk of court. During the early interwar years, Katz became more active in Christian women's organizations and won election in 1921 to represent the CHU on the Amsterdam city council. The following year, she was elected to the Tweede Kamer for the Protestant establishment party. As the only CHU woman and a leading lawyer, Katz was in a singular position to carve out a space for herself as a new political actor in The Hague.[86]

During Frida Katz's first two years in the Dutch parliament, she took to the podium five times in plenary debates. Like Boschek and Proft, Katz was very much a working parliamentarian who came to the Dutch legislature's podium far more frequently than Oheimb did in her four years in the German Reichstag. The majority of Katz's speeches were about women's issues or the justice system, with which she was familiar as a lawyer. These speeches did not contain the zealous rage of some of her female colleagues. Instead, Katz positioned herself as an advocate for gradual evolutionary change in policy. In her very first remarks in the Tweede Kamer, Katz spoke after a liberal female colleague's passionate speech demanding reform of Dutch marriage laws. The justice minister was present for the debate, and Katz attempted to appeal specifically to him. She distanced herself from her colleague's radical attitude and adopted an intentionally moderate tone that, nevertheless, aimed to nudge the Dutch cabinet towards change.[87]

Frida Katz's conciliatory approach exasperated her more progressive colleagues. Later in this debate about marriage laws, Katz outlined a compromise plan. In condescending fashion, a liberal parliamentarian interrupted her speech:

> MR. KETELAAR: If you start that way, you'll get nothing.
>
> MISS KATZ: In this, I completely disagree with you.
>
> MR. KETELAAR: Well, I've been here in parliament for 25 years, so I know this better than you do.
>
> MISS KATZ: You have been in parliament for a long time. I would simply point out that even if I only have a bit of experience here in parliament, in my law practice, I have had many cases where you have to try to reach a settlement. In those cases, you can get somewhere sooner whenever you assume the good intentions of the other side rather than obstinately standing your ground.[88]

Seeking out compromise became Katz's public persona in the parliament. Interestingly enough, she ended up on the same side in parliamentary votes as her more radical colleagues. However, her moderate tone and search for compromise permitted a flexibility in her ultimate voting behaviour that departed from her conservative CHU colleagues.[89]

Katz's political style was apparent from her first parliamentary speeches, but it was confirmed in her friendly, personal, and private connections with colleagues from other political parties. As testament to how non-polarizing she was, she befriended David Wijnkoop, a parliamentarian from the Dutch Communist Party. Wijnkoop was notorious in The Hague for being a loner. He did not attend dinners, go on junkets, or make small talk with colleagues. Instead, he used his parliamentary seat to further his radical revolutionary ideals.[90] However, Wijnkoop and Katz knew each other from serving on Amsterdam's city council, and they co-operated on some of Katz's own genealogical research. Although Katz was a confessional politician, Wijnkoop had known her father who had been an active socialist. Wijnkoop shared what he knew about her father's political activities, and he passed along suggestions for which socialist printers had published the elder Katz's speeches. Cordial letters helping a parliamentary opponent reconstruct a bit of family history were totally out of character for Wijnkoop, but the time he took to check his files for Katz demonstrated his sincerity. Katz made one friend in the Tweede Kamer who no one else could win over.[91]

Wijnkoop was not the only left-wing politician who sent Katz kind letters. The leader of the Dutch socialist party Willem Albarda wrote to Katz after a speech she gave in 1939. There had been a series of scandals involving Catholic priests that polarized the confessionally driven world of Dutch politics. In an earnest bit of confidential advice, Albarda encouraged Katz to continue speaking her mind: "In the Catholic press there were a few unfriendly and particularly inappropriate remarks […] I felt that I should tell you that I especially admired your speeches. They were both intelligent and courageous, and you deserve respect rather than condemnation for them."[92] Gestures like Albarda's comforting letter after Katz's speeches were not unheard of among political rivals in the Tweede Kamer, particularly among leaders of opposing parties. However, Katz was a more junior backbencher whose penchant for compromise meant that she was easily embedded in this private world of honest cross-party correspondence and personal connections.[93]

Moreover, Frida Katz was active as a Dutch parliamentarian on the international stage, attending a number of conferences of the Inter-Parliamentary Union (IPU). The IPU brought parliamentarians from around the world together to discuss the political issues of the day. Katz travelled to inter-parliamentary conferences in 1924 in Bern, 1927 in Paris, and 1928 in Berlin, and she carefully saved photographs, menus, invitations, and other ephemera from these events in scrapbooks. Katz had the habit of asking fellow participants she met or dined with to sign her dinner menus or event programs; these are now an excellent record of who she came in contact with on these trips abroad. At the 1927 Paris IPU conference she met the French foreign minister Aristide Briand, the Swedish IPU leader Theodor Adelswaerd, and the German president of the Reichstag Paul Löbe, and they all signed her program. She also accumulated the visiting cards and signatures of parliamentarians from Serbia, Poland, Britain, Czechoslovakia, and the United States.[94] Republican Senator Selden Spencer of Missouri even wrote down his home and Washington addresses for Katz to stay in touch. Being an elected Dutch parliamentarian propelled Katz onto this broader international stage.[95]

However, most of Frida Katz's foreign political trips focused on her professional area of expertise, which was the law. Katz attended meetings of the International Prison Conference several times, including in

London in 1925 and in Prague in 1930. The 1925 prison conference participants went on study trips to Bournemouth, Aberdeen, and Edinburgh, feted in every town they passed through. Because of this busy social schedule, Katz had the chance to meet a number of the other delegates, who were themselves not politicians but actively involved in the legal system as bureaucrats or judges. For instance, at a dinner in the Royal Bath Hotel in Bournemouth, Katz sat with an official in the German justice ministry who worked on criminal law, an American prison commissioner who had worked in Minnesota and Illinois, and a prosecutor and judge from Japan.[96] Unlike other participants, Katz was an active parliamentarian. The conference's organizers made a big deal about the presence of the Viscountess Astor, who was the first woman to take her seat in the British Parliament, but Lady Astor was more of a guest of honour than a participant in the conference. Frida Katz, however, was there to network with practitioners and build up a knowledge base she could take back to her work legislating in the Netherlands.[97]

Katz also attended a gathering of the International Association of Lawyers (Union Internationale des Avocats), an organization formed in the 1920s to bring together attorneys and representatives of national bar

Figure 1.2. Union Internationale des Avocats meeting in The Hague, July 1932. Katz is in the middle under the black X.

Source: From National Archief, Inv. 21, 2.21.190, C. Frida Katz Fam., NAH.

associations. Katz did not need to venture too far from her parliamentary workplace for the group's 1932 meeting held in the Peace Palace in The Hague. However, at the event she encountered the wider world of international jurists. Katz saved a photo of this event, which shows her as one of only a handful of women in judicial robes in a large crowd.[98] This gender imbalance was not only evident in the photograph's dearth of women but also in the fact that Frida Katz attended the technocratic gathering in the first place. Katz's male Dutch political colleagues jockeyed for spots at grand international gatherings hosted by organizations like the League of Nations.[99] Male politicians were seen as generalists who could learn anything and did not always have to prove their worth at subject-specific conferences or in specialized political portfolios. Dutch women like Katz were expected to excel in a specific field to advance any further. Since Katz's field was law, she served on parliamentary legal committees and was sent to legal conferences. This pigeonholing of Katz into her subject-specific area of expertise began even before she was elected to parliament. The CHU's executive had asked her to serve on party committees on Dutch law. This set the stage for her to speak on justice issues in parliament for the party.[100]

Katz reflected publicly on her role and the larger position of women in Dutch politics in a 1933 radio address on "The vocation of women in the Tweede Kamer." She spoke on a radio program geared towards Christian women and used religious language and imagery to make her points. She anticipated the conservative Christian objections that women should never serve in political office: "I always kept in mind that we are shown again and again in the Bible – the Old and New Testaments – that in difficult moments God called women to responsible positions in public life." Katz used the theological language of vocation to argue that some women were called by God to careers beyond the family, since "not all women marry, and these days women feel called to all kinds of duties in the world. Many professions are open to her, lots of social work calls for her dedication and her serving compassion."

In the radio address, Frida Katz's argument for why women should sit in parliament had two prongs, both grounded in traditional ideas about women's roles. First and foremost, "God created humans: man and woman. With their own talents and their own needs. [...] Her insight shall [...] thus sometimes be different than that of her male colleagues." Katz suggested that women have a unique perspective on issues that is valuable to include in parliamentary discussions. The second prong of Katz's argument was related to the first but was more forceful: a woman's "special insight is apparent in everything in which the woman is involved as a spouse and mother." Katz argued that women are better able to understand what it means to be a mother and a wife and should have influence over decisions made in these subject areas.[101]

Continuing her remarks, Katz considered how Dutch female parliamentarians should direct their energy in the Tweede Kamer. She went through the women in parliament to point out who focused on health, education, labour, or general social issues. Katz and one liberal colleague had the only non-stereotypical expertise on legal topics, but both were trained lawyers. However, Katz emphasized that even these female legal experts were still supposed to express their views and disagreements about legislation primarily in committees. She suggested that committees – a private forum for the technocratic shaping of legislation – were seen as the parliamentary domain most suited for women's activity.[102] Despite her modest radio proposal for women's work in backroom committees, legislatively Katz took bolder steps. She co-sponsored a tax law amendment in 1926 that would have given widows the same tax benefits as widowers. Moreover, Katz voted differently than her CHU colleagues in 1930 in favour of a motion to allow women to be appointed as mayors and municipal officials. That said, these public departures from the men in her party were uncommon, and her conciliatory approach directed her towards committee work, her expertise in the law, and a moderate tone to slowly bring the men along.[103]

Although Katz laid out a progressive perspective on women in politics within the context of her own Christian milieu, she still accepted the premise: "Of course, the woman's vocation shall remain primarily in the family, whether in her own family, in the family of her parents, or another family."[104] This belief was heartfelt; when Katz married in 1937, she planned on immediately resigning her seat in the Tweede Kamer. Only a last-minute intervention by her party's leader convinced her to continue. However, at least one colleague in the CHU opposed married women in politics on principle and prevented Katz from rejoining the postwar Dutch parliament. One might assume that this belief that marriage and children were a disqualification for women in political life was a religious issue, limited to the Dutch parliament's confessional parties, but that was not the case. Of the seven women who served as newcomers in the Tweede Kamer in 1922, three were married, and four were unmarried. Moreover, none of them ever had children. An unspoken rule for women in interwar Dutch politics was that marriage and children could not be combined with a political life.[105]

The earliest generation of Dutch female parliamentarians moved within a world bounded by the sexist norms of the era that pressured female politicians to speak up for mothers but also ushered mothers out of the world of elected politics. Frida Katz's approach to this interwar

Dutch political culture was to maintain close relationships with colleagues in other political parties and largely keep her head down to focus on her legal field of expertise, which included her travel to international legal conferences. Katz's approach aligns with a scholarly trend to see "transnational technocrats" as international actors in this period.[106] Ultimately, Katz used her parliamentary speeches to nudge male colleagues towards reform without beating them over the head with diatribes denouncing present conditions. Of course, Katz's background in a largely conservative Protestant confessional party helps to explain her political path. However, Katz's moderation and low-key approach cannot minimize the extent to which she built cross-party connections to shape Dutch legal policy by tinkering with legislation and proposals behind the scenes, including as a transnational actor meeting parliamentary colleagues and gathering information on her international junkets.

Interwar Women, Inclusive Democracies, and Wielding Power Behind the Scenes

After the First World War, monarchs fled, ministers were made responsible to parliaments, the electorate dramatically expanded, and – as this chapter has explored – women were elected as legislators in many Western and Central European countries. These revolutionary changes were a stark break with the political past. Despite the changing demographics among politicians, contemporary interwar intellectuals including Hans Kelsen and Carl Schmitt largely rejected the idea of any wholescale caesura in political institutions.[107] Indeed, as women entered parliaments in countries including Germany, Austria, and the Netherlands, they encountered an older world of political sociability and its gendered barriers. Nevertheless, within no time, Frida Katz was enlisting a Communist loner for genealogical research, and Katharina von Oheimb was beating the men at their own card games. This more inclusive world of private sociability is itself evidence for a interwar democratization process that could expand to include women.

Despite headwinds of sexism and bias, Frida Katz, Gabriele Proft, Anna Boschek, and Katharina von Oheimb all found spaces in their national parliamentary settings to advance issues that the gentlemanly politicians of the nineteenth century had overlooked. In Austria, female politicians from the SDAP and CS worked together on ground-breaking legislation on certain women's issues, but their political rhetoric still pointed to deep divisions. For rank-and-file parliamentarians, there was polarization in Austrian politics that inhibited the creation of a robust cross-party social world. Instead, Austria's socialist female politicians engaged in party-political work that was often outside parliament and on the international stage. On the other hand, the confessionally splintered political world of the Dutch parliament offered opportunities for Frida Katz's subject-specific specialization in the domestic arena, where she cultivated the image of a conciliatory political figure. As a transnational actor, Katz was an international traveller who understood her parliamentary role as extending to conferences abroad acting as a "transnational technocrat" gathering expertise on the law.

Most significantly, however, Katharina von Oheimb's interwar biography is an glimpse into the particularly robust nature of the cross-party social world in which German lawmakers could move. Beyond the earshot of parliamentary stenographers, cross-party groups of female legislators drafted laws and female parliamentary colleagues strategized how to influence ministers and fellow lawmakers. Oheimb cultivated a particularly robust network of friends and acquaintances through her political salon. Although she did not hesitate to include many foreigners as guests, Oheimb's international ties pale in comparison to Anna Boschek and Frida Katz. Ultimately, interwar democracies all grew to incorporate these newly elected women politicians but always in nationally specific ways.

Chapter Two

From Boozy Receptions to Private Clubs: The Social Landscape of Politics in Weimar Berlin

"Nüscht bei Kroll jewesen, nüscht in Berlin jewesen!" (If you haven't been to Kroll's, you haven't been to Berlin!) This bold claim in the local vernacular captured the importance of Kroll's gastronomic and entertainment mecca to the social life of the interwar German capital. Adjacent to Berlin's central Tiergarten park, Kroll's was just across the square from the German Reichstag. Part of the larger complex – Kroll's Opera House – would later be the venue for infamous moments of the Nazi era including the 1933 passage of the Enabling Act and Adolf Hitler's rabid 1939 speech prophesying the demise of European Jewry. In the earlier republican years, however, Kroll's had not yet been tarred by this grim fascist history, and it was a hub for Berlin's elite to mix and mingle.[1]

During the Weimar Republic, Kroll's was a one-stop shop for enjoying a beer in the garden, eating a fancy dinner, renting banquet halls, attending musical concerts, and even taking a medicinal mineral water cure. Kroll's management specifically targeted its marketing at overworked lawmakers just on the other side of the square: "Of course, we know that the job of a parliamentarian, the job of a lawmaker, is hugely taxing on a person's mental and physical faculties. During the parliamentary sessions, lawmakers spend the vast majority of their time in the parliament building itself. Committee meetings, plenary sessions, parliamentary party meetings, conferences, conversations, visits – one right after another. There is no quiet time to sit down and eat or a take a well-deserved break to relax." Of course, the implication was that there was always Kroll's – just a very short walk away for anyone in the Reichstag.[2] Kroll's was one of many locations on an ordinary German parliamentarian's mental map of political Berlin. Beyond Kroll's there was an entire world of clubs, foreign embassies, formal events, and informal dinners that represented the cross-party interwar sociability in which colleagues like Katharina von Oheimb thrived, as was demonstrated in Chapter 1.[3]

In his comprehensive study of the Weimar-era Reichstag, Thomas Mergel analyzed the interwar German Reichstag as a "social space" in a broad sense. Mergel's spatial tour de force first took readers through physical locations in the German parliament, ranging from the Reichstag's gymnasium, post office, and newspaper stand to the legally protected "Bannmeile" surrounding the building where demonstrations were forbidden. Mergel's expansive definition of "social space" encompassed parliamentary demographics including lawmakers' professional backgrounds, wartime service, and the like, as well as how these factors changed over time. Mergel's analysis stretched to parliamentary socializing, romantic dalliances among colleagues, and the shared committee work of political rivals. However, when Mergel uncovered cross-party social connections among political opponents, he tended to link them to demographics: "Shared previous experiences [...] were the expression of a similar horizon and social circles [as well as] a shared habitus. They shaped a specific perception of reality, common language, and set of political priorities." Mergel's assumption was that common interests and shared backgrounds explained why political rivals collaborated, but this is an assumption that can be hard to prove from contemporary evidence. Generally, unlikely friends do not leave a paper trail as to the reasons they forged behind-the-scenes relationships. It could be because they had overlapping beliefs on economic theory, for instance, or perhaps their offices were simply across the hall from each other. Rather than replicating Mergel and again plumbing the demographic depths of parliamentarians' backgrounds, this chapter turns to the spaces in which they moved across interwar Berlin.[4]

Gathering evidence from memoirs, published diaries, and select archival collections, Mergel gestured to several locations for cross-party social integration among Reichstag parliamentarians. This chapter takes up this baton from Mergel to explore the breadth of this interwar social world and the places where parliamentarians mingled in much greater detail. Mergel's study was more closely tied to the Reichstag and its immediate surroundings, but the social world of Weimar politicians stretched much further afield – from Kroll's to the horse racetrack at Hoppegarten and into clubhouses across Berlin. Moreover, this social world was incredibly international, which was absent in Mergel's description. Mergel saw an "integration dynamic" that functioned from the Social Democratic Party of Germany (Sozialdemokratische Partei Deutschlands, SPD) to the German National People's Party (Deutschnationale Volkspartei, DNVP).[5] Although this is true in broad strokes, the early social integration of newcomer working-class socialists and female politicians into parliamentary social spaces prompted a backlash. Exclusive German gentlemen's clubs that tended in a right-wing nationalist direction proliferated as conservative safe social spaces where a resentful old-regime elite could escape revolutionary change.

Over a century after the afternoon teas, evening balls, and political salons in Weimar Berlin, that era's distant social world can be exceedingly hard to pin down. Careful – yet still spotty – reconstruction is only possible by cobbling together one person's saved calling cards, another's detailed weekly calendar, and references to events mentioned in passing in private letters. Rather than adopting the comparative approach of Chapter 1, this chapter focuses on interwar Berlin for practical reasons. Thomas Mergel has already broken ground on this fertile area of study, but more important logistical considerations limit comparison. Evidence for a dinner party, afternoon tea, club lecture night, or guest list for a boozy reception is necessarily fleeting. Interwar Berlin is a stronger case study because there were so many more politicians who passed through Weimar Reichstag and had the chance to leave archival traces of this social world of politics. Although the Dutch Tweede Kamer had only 100 members and the Austrian parliament often had 165, German parliaments ranged in size from 421 to 647 members. There were far more German politicians and, therefore, more archival opportunities to find the traces of a century-old social world.[6]

One might also object that encounters among politicians, socialites, foreigners, and businesspeople at places like Kroll's, at a foreign embassy, or at a Berlin club were merely the window dressing of a lost sociability. Pinning down this social aspect of interwar Berlin's political culture could seem as futile as trying to "nail pudding to the wall" to invoke the political scientist Max Kaase.[7] However, interwar lawmakers would themselves disagree. The proof that these parliamentarians valued their contemporary political social connections is evident in the fact that a number carefully saved their many invitations to interwar social events. The personal papers of German politicians from the 1920s and early 1930s even include handwritten notes about whether an invitation was accepted or not and what reason was given for having to decline. Some elected parliamentarians diligently kept notebooks of who had invited them over for tea, drinks, or dinner. The presence of so many invitations in the personal papers of parliamentarians demonstrates the importance of this social world to Germans at the time and is not found to a similar extent in Austria or even in the Netherlands. In Weimar Berlin, this social world was part and parcel of networks of trust, co-operation, and reciprocity that these interwar politicians inhabited and valued.[8]

From Bismarckian Bierabende to the Outsiders and Insiders in Weimar Berlin

Germany's social world of politics between the world wars did not emerge *ex nihilo* out of the ether. Weimar Berlin's social-political milieu was rooted in a longer history, and this included the quintessential social event of interwar political life, which were dubbed *Bierabende*, literally "beer evenings." This almost untranslatable concept involved receptions where guests mingled over drinks and light hors d'oeuvres. However, Bierabende (singular: Bierabend) were not an interwar invention. In fact, Otto von Bismarck's imperial Reichstag had developed the practice of regular Bierabende where members of parliament would mingle with government officials in the Reichstag's foyer.[9] When the far-less-democratic and entirely male Wilhelmine parliament introduced these boozy gatherings, the more common German term for traditional social evening was a *Herrenabend*, literally a gentlemen's evening. Of course, this

Figure 2.1. Ernst Henseler and Bismarck in conversation with Reichstag deputies at a parliamentary soirée, 1894.

Source: From bpk Bildagentur / Stiftung Preussische Schlösser & Gärten Berlin-Brandenburg, Art Resource, NY.

word was exclusionary in terms of both gender and class. The competing term "Bierabend" had long been associated with working-class men getting together to spend their hard-earned wages at a local pub.[10] With shocking foresight, the Bismarckian Reichstag's regular Bierabende bucked the period's linguistic norms in adopting the less exclusive term for convivial evenings.[11]

Despite its somewhat more inclusive name, attending a Wilhelmine parliamentary Bierabend was seen by some as a political act. Socialists had long been outcasts in imperial German political society, hounded by anti-socialist legislation. There was actually a 1899 debate among socialist parliamentarians on whether socialists could attend a Reichstag Bierabend, which yielded lukewarm permission to attend but no endorsement of these events.[12] During the imperial years, German socialists had built up their own separate working-class political milieu, and among party activists this included giving each other endearing nicknames or even vacationing together.[13] Nostalgia for these older left-wing social ties bled into the interwar years in correspondence between left-wing notables like Adolf Geck and Clara Zetkin. These two old friends ended up in Weimar Germany's competing socialist and Communist parties. However, they remained close, fondly reflecting on their shared past. After the death of a comrade they had known well, Zetkin wrote to Geck: "Wilhelm's death increased my desire to spend a few weeks in your company. To exchange and relive memories, ask and answer questions of each other: Do you still think about that? How exactly was this or that? It would be an important bit of historical recollection that we could get through this way." With a nod to her far-left sympathies, Zetkin concluded her letter: "In steadfast thankful friendship, with a handshake, your old unreformed 'Radikalinski.'"[14]

This segregated socialist milieu reached into the halls of the Wilhelmine Reichstag. One younger imperial-era socialist legislator, Carl Severing, recalled infrequent cross-party contact among lawmakers, but the socialist parliamentary comrades spent considerable time in each other's company. Most rented rooms in the same Berlin neighbourhood. The older, veteran social democrats met for frequent drinks at the same working-class bar that they humorously dubbed "*Krüppelheim*" (the home for cripples). Severing fondly remembered informal socialist potlucks called "*Naturalienabende*," a German pun combining the idea of natural produce and payment in kind. Rather than having one socialist lawmaker treat everyone, each guest sent along specialty foods from his own home region to a Berlin comrade who organized an evening event. "This Berlin colleague then had the task of pulling together enjoyable courses from this higgledy-piggledy collection of foods – white asparagus from

Brandenburg [...] Westphalian ham and pumpernickel, wine from the Palatinate, Badenese tobacco products, and Hessian beer." Through a nostalgic haze, Severing favourably compared these socialist Naturalien-abende to the more inclusive Bierabende of Weimar Republic.[15]

As Berlin's new republican era dawned in 1919, the shape and extent of Germany's informal world of politics was up in the air. Compared to the imperial period, parliamentary demographics changed dramatically with the influx of women, more working-class representatives, and several populist rabble rousers. This moment was ripe for a revolution in the informal political milieu, but Weimar Berlin continued many of the social traditions of the Wilhelmine era. Compared to the imperial past, however, these interwar events were thrown open to a broader crowd that often had an international guest list. Indeed, socialists like Carl Severing no longer had to debate whether to attend a Bierabend or stick to a socialist Naturalienabend; socialists often made up the plurality of guests at interwar events.

Reminiscent of Bismarck's era, the pinnacle of Reichstag-specific socializing was the big-tent parliamentary Bierabend hosted by leading government ministers. In fact, high-ranking German officials were expected to invite parliamentarians as part of their official duties, and some resented it. One minister would have rather slept than stayed awake hobnobbing with colleagues late into the night. He recalled that the parliamentary guests would have stayed even longer at these official Bierabende if the beer taps had not been closed at 1 a.m.: "The guests stayed together into the early morning hours carousing, hooting, and singing – often no longer particularly sober."[16] Ministers who were less keen on these large Bierabende were undoubtedly grateful that during the Great Depression the government cancelled all these social events as unnecessary luxuries to donate the savings to disabled veterans. Indeed, the expense could be so high because the guest lists were so long. When the chancellor hosted a Bierabend for leading bureaucrats and politicians, 300 people attended. A Bierabend that focused more exclusively on parliamentarians could attract up to 150 lawmakers.[17]

Since the Weimar-era Reichstag usually had around 500 members and sometimes exceeded 600, just in terms of logistics, it was next to impossible to invite all the members to any one single social gathering. This was a ready opportunity for interwar Germans to draw bright-line boundaries in their social-political world; however, these events tended to be more inclusive than one might expect. Memoirists recalled antisemitic conservatives and Jewish socialists joking with each other over drinks. Prominent Communists like Clara Zetkin and even some Nazis like Franz Ritter von Epp attended. However, Bierabend invitations were not sent to the most radical politicians like the Nazi Joseph Goebbels because there was always the danger that a social invitation could be abused.[18] During an intense debate in the Prussian Landtag in 1922, a Communist state parliamentarian brought up the fact that the socialist president of the Landtag had invited him to an upcoming Bierabend: "[T]hen with the words – 'I will throw the invitation with contempt in his face' – he actually threw the crumpled-up invitation towards the president." The risk of this kind of political theatre in the Reichstag prevented invitations from going out to every politician, but the cross-party invitation lists extended from some Communists all the way to more clubbable Nazis.[19]

Two complete guest lists for large Bierabende hosted by the chancellor in 1920 and in 1925 survive. At the November 1920 Bierabend, alongside the government ministers and state secretaries, representatives of the German states, the national economic council, and the leadership of the Reichstag and Prussian Landtag were all invited. Important people from the press, industry, business, and banking attended. Only 30 members of the Reichstag came, six each from the SPD, Catholic Centre Party, German Democratic Party (Deutsche Demokratische Partei, DDP), German People's Party (Deutsche Volkspartei, DVP), and DNVP, and one from the Bavarian People's Party (Bayerische Volkspartei, BVP). This division meant that the SPD was slightly under-represented, but there was obviously a conscious effort to include most of the larger parties in the Reichstag, even though they were not in government at the time. However, parliamentarians from the more radical left-wing Unabhängige Sozialdemokratische Partei Deutschlands (German Independent Social Democratic Party, USPD) were completely excluded from the event. The USPD party congress had voted only weeks before to join the Soviet-aligned Comintern, which might have influenced the guest list.[20] Excluding radicals was often a feature of German social events and was repeated at another smaller Bierabend in the early 1920s, where the same six parties were represented, again excluding the USPD.[21]

On May 30, 1925, the German cabinet put together a much larger parliamentary Bierabend including representatives from a whole slew of Reich and Prussian agencies, representatives of cities, members of the art and cultural sector, and businessmen and bankers. Excluding the leadership of the Reichstag, 122 parliamentary guests attended, which was almost a fourth of the parliament's membership. This event was attended by members of the SPD, DNVP, Centre Party, DVP, DDP, BVP, Economic Party of the German Middle Classes (Wirtschaftspartei), and even the National Socialist Freedom Party. The social democrats were slightly underrepresented again, but bourgeois and Catholic parties were extremely overrepresented. No Communists were invited, but the right-wing extreme National Socialist Freedom Party did receive three invitations. Interestingly, however, even among these radical right-wing guests, two – Albrecht von Graefe and Ernst Graf zu Reventlow – were former members of the DNVP and aristocrats who were less directly associated with Adolf Hitler's radicalism.[22] The practice of allowing one or two token members of the more radical parties to attend semi-official social functions was repeated in the parliamentary Bierabende hosted by the president of the Reichstag. One or two Communists or Nazis were occasionally seen at these events, but they were always among the least radical members of their respective parties.[23]

Before 1914, socialists like Carl Severing were less likely to attend the formal parliamentary Bierabende in favour of their own exclusive Naturalienabende or other socialist get-togethers. Of course, party-specific socializing was by no means dead during the 1920s, and interwar German parties had regular bars and restaurants to which they would routinely adjourn after meetings.[24] However, the socialist parliamentary extreme of the Wilhelmine era had become the mainstream of the interwar period. The long-serving Weimar-era President of the Reichstag Paul Löbe was himself a socialist and was a frequent host of these big parliamentary Bierabende. The clubbable middle ground of the Weimar Republic was much broader than in the imperial era. Only the most radical Communist and Nazis remained social outsiders at these republican social events.[25]

The Busy Social Life of a Member of the German Reichstag

The interwar mailboxes of most run-of-the-mill German parliamentarians were filled with invitations to various social events across Berlin and sometimes those held even further afield. The kind and number of engagements parliamentarians would be asked to attend was often determined by how long they had served in national politics – which influenced how many people they knew in the capital – and whether they held leading positions in the Reichstag, in the government, or in their own political parties. The more power or influence politicians had, the more hosts wanted to invite them to exclusive events.

Just by virtue being members of the Reichstag, German parliamentarians would receive official invitations to events organized by ministries, government agencies, or the parliament itself.[26] Berlin's formal social-political calendar boasted recurring speeches, lectures, and special parliamentary sessions held on holidays and anniversaries during the Weimar Republic, and any politician would be welcome on these occasions.[27] Beyond the Reichstag's own events, ministers often held

receptions as part of their official duties and invited all parliamentarians –
or at least a representative sample – to attend. These types of events
would include ministers hosting a student charity reception at Kroll's or
a transport ministry dinner honouring pioneering aviators.[28] In October
1926, for example, the German interior minister sponsored two particularly well-attended events: one opening reception for an exhibition of
German art and another for a inaugurating a new memorial room for a
Prussian field marshal.[29]

One sober bit of social glue in interwar Berlin were funerals, but this
was not as true in the earliest years of the republic. The early 1920s
were marked by the assassinations of republican politicians including
Matthias Erzberger and Walther Rathenau whose memorial events
were politicized. For instance, when news of Foreign Minister Rathenau's assassination reached the floor of the Reichstag, chaos ensued.
Those on the left accused right-wing politicians of enabling the mur-
der. Tumultuous scenes and scuffles in the parliament, coupled with
Chancellor Joseph Wirth's declaration that "the enemy is on the right,"
set a more polarized tone for commemorating Rathenau's life. However, this politicized response to assassinations in the early 1920s gave
way to funerals that were more contemplative and collegial. Even by
1923, when the DVP parliamentarian Katharina von Oheimb delivered
a memorial speech for Walther Rathenau, she argued that "honouring
the dead is not a demand of the moment but a requirement of civilization itself." She then criticized her Reichstag colleagues for playing
party politics with Rathenau's memory who she instead honoured as a
great German.[30]

When President Friedrich Ebert died unexpectedly in 1925, parliamentarians from the across the Reichstag were invited to a series of cere-
monies including a memorial event in the Presidential Palace. Although
Ebert was a socialist and the embodiment of the German republic, this
event was far less politicized than those surrounding Rathenau's death.
Some parliamentarians even travelled on the special overnight train to
Heidelberg for the graveside memorial.[31] Parliamentarians also travelled
as a group to the 1926 funeral of the Catholic Centre party politician
Constantin Fehrenbach whose career had included serving as both the
last president of the imperial Reichstag and a president of the republican National Assembly in 1919. He was also chancellor for about a year
before serving in the Reichstag until his death.[32] When Fehrenbach died,
a special train of 50 parliamentarians and high-ranking bureaucrats was
dispatched from Berlin to Freiburg for the funeral. Although 32 of these
passengers were Fehrenbach's Catholic Centre Party colleagues, the travelling parliamentarians also represented the wider political spectrum.

Cooped up in train together for hours, political rivals chatted with each other.[33]

In addition to more formal events, an everyday parliamentarian during the Weimar years was inundated with invitations for various receptions, dinners, and countless Bierabende sponsored by private groups. In the mid-1920s, a German parliamentarian could choose to go to a "discussion evening" at the Hotel Continental sponsored by the Westphalian Agrarian League, to a Bierabend with stand-up comedians from the German theatre association, or to a film screening about spas in the Rhenish resort town of Bad Kreuznach.[34] Visits to the German Jockey and Horse Breeder conference, an anniversary celebration of the German Pursers' League, meetings of the German Colonial Association, or a social gathering of the Agricultural League were also possibilities.[35] If a parliamentarian wanted to take up more educational offerings, there were invites for exhibition openings on the work of various pedagogical institutes or new housing co-operatives.[36] There were even lectures on civil air defense, on Chinese political economy, and on European unity.[37]

Among the welter of these private social opportunities in the German capital, some events would have stood out to Weimar-era parliamentarians because they were endorsed by their Reichstag colleagues. The long-serving and well-liked conservative Gottfried Treviranus sponsored a birthday celebration for a liberal journalist, and invitations were sent out in Treviranus's name.[38] When representatives of rural Prussian localities met in Berlin for an annual congress, most parliamentarians were invited to the conference itself. However, some politicians also received personalized invitations from the DNVP lawmaker Günter Gereke to an exclusive Bierabend in the luxurious Hotel Adlon to mingle with the congress' delegates.[39] Similarly, the DVP parliamentarian Heinrich Schnee sponsored a special meal in the Reichstag restaurant marking the ten-year anniversary celebration of the Working Committee of German Associations (Arbeitsausschuss Deutscher Verbände), and Schnee sent out personalized invitations.[40] When the Association for European Rapprochement put together an event in the Reichstag building in 1926, the organizers likewise ensured there were five current and former parliamentarians (from parties ranging from the right-liberal to the socialist side of the spectrum) on the agenda in order to encourage more politicians to attend.[41]

Moreover, interwar German parliamentarians also grew close to colleagues from other political parties through socializing and collaborating in the course of their regular parliamentary work. Beyond bumping into each other in the corridors of the Reichstag, committees were especially good places to grow close as colleagues. In interwar Germany, legislative committees were not open to the public, so committee rooms themselves were semi-private in order for politicians and representatives of the government to work together in an isolated setting. Political scientists have paid particular attention to committees as productive areas for policy work, in part, because decisions by committees can be positive sum, when they are reached collaboratively.[42] When a Centre Party Reichstag member died suddenly in 1923, two parliamentarians from two different parties sent condolences to his widow that referenced their common committee work. One colleague wrote about working together for many hours on the Reichstag's social committee trying to improve people's lives, and another praised the late politician as a good friend on the tax committee. Committees could – and did – serve as locations for productive cross-party relationships beyond the glare of the interwar press.[43]

Parliamentary committees could even bring stranger political bedfellows together. For example, the Communist Reichstag member Karl Becker collaborated with his moderate socialist colleagues on the economic policy committee. Becker had worked as a blacksmith in the Silesian mining industry, and he was particularly close to three socialist parliamentarians who came from similar working-class backgrounds. Becker saw eye-to-eye with them, and they worked collaboratively on mining issues in the committee despite the fact that in public during plenary debates, their parties were at each other's throats.[44] On the other end of the political spectrum, there was co-operation between right-wing radicals in the committee investigating the grain market.[45] In this case, the conservative parties wanted to embarrass the government with revelations about corruption in the import and export of rye between Poland and Germany. The left-liberal DDP chairman of the investigative committee remembered that the more politically aligned right-liberal DVP committee secretary completely ignored him, but the right-wing German nationalist DNVP and the Nazi committee members co-operated in their joint efforts to ridicule the government.[46]

Beyond the social events or committee work that were accessible to most members of the Reichstag, the highest-flying backbenchers in the German parliament could move into a world of more exclusive dinners. For example, the state secretary in the chancellery, Hermann Pünder, frequently invited special guests to his home in Berlin's Lichterfelde district for meals. Pünder usually hosted members of the cabinet and high-ranking civil servants; however, ordinary members of the Reichstag, like the Catholic politician Christine Teusch, occasionally made it onto his guest list.[47] By 1930, up-and-coming backbench politicians formalized their own standing lunch date for middle-aged bourgeois politicians from different political parties. Even when parliamentarians spent their work days engrossed in the nitty-gritty of polarizing politics, there were ample opportunities for backbench politicians of various political persuasions to grow close in both formal and informal social worlds surrounding the Reichstag.[48]

When politicians had risen above the rank of backbenchers and into party leadership or even started serving as ministers, they received far more invitations to more elite social occasions. These prestigious official events included receptions for ambassadors and delegates at the Reich Chancellery, as well as occasions like a Bierabend marking the founding of a new national council on youth physical fitness or a special tour of renovated rooms in the Chancellery before a cabinet meeting.[49] The mayor of Cologne, Konrad Adenauer, also planned a small "Rhenish Evening" in Berlin in 1926 to bring together a group of about twelve men, primarily ministers and leading Catholic politicians. This was to be a "Gentlemen's Evening" and the invitation explicitly said "no women" were allowed. Only the *crème de la crème* of Berlin's political world were slated to attend.[50]

Leading German politicians also organized curated social experiences for guests who were to be wooed for political purposes. When an American journalist who was also the son-in-law of the New York banker Thomas Lamont came to Berlin, the president of the Reichsbank, Hjalmar Schacht, put together a breakfast with key players in German political, economic, and intellectual life to show off Berlin in its best light to this American VIP.[51] Sometimes these elite invitations crossed political divides. The former socialist Chancellor of Germany Hermann Müller, who was particularly reviled among conservatives for having signed the Versailles Treaty, received several invitations to private events with political opponents on the German right. Jakob Riesser of the right liberal DVP and his wife invited the socialist leader to a friendly evening together.[52] Most surprisingly, however, the socialist Müller was invited to a white-tie formal dinner at the Schöneberg City Hall sponsored by the conservative DNVP parliamentary group. The DNVP were avowed right-wing opponents of the socialists, so Müller politely declined the invitation. When one had risen high enough politically, being political opponents in interwar Berlin did not preclude invitations for joining someone else's table.[53]

For high-profile parliamentarians, charitable and foundation work could bring them together across party lines. Private associations often sought out elite politicians to join their organizations to lend them credibility. For example, the Walter Rathenau Gesellschaft included national and Prussian politicians, as well as bureaucrats who hailed from the centrist Weimar coalition of parties – the SPD, DDP, and Catholic Centre Party.[54] The German League of Nations Association boasted a similar cast of political characters, bringing together centrist politicians with representatives of business and academia in the association's executive.[55] These private organizations – and the social events and governing committee meetings they sponsored – meant that even when the constellation of the governing parties changed in the national government, politicians still bumped into each other. This was particularly true for the socialists, who spent a long time out of Germany's national cabinets.[56]

To take one specific example, legislators were particularly well represented in the German Pro Palestine Committee (Deutsches Komitee Pro Palästina), which was designed to promote Jewish migration to Palestine through both fundraising and lobbying. The organization was founded in 1919 and reorganized in 1926. At both junctures, the Zionist organizers sought out elite non-Jewish German members, particularly from the ranks of politicians serving in the Reichstag. In 1919, these members were as diametrically opposed to each other as the socialist Philipp Scheidemann, who proclaimed the republic and ushered the monarchy off the stage, and the German aristocratic nationalist Kuno Graf von Westarp. After a reorganization in 1926, the association's politician members came from the SPD, DDP, Centre Party, DVP, DNVP, and the centre-right Wirtschaftspartei.[57] Alongside individuals like Rabbi Leo Baeck and Albert Einstein, leading parliamentarians from the SPD to the DNVP all served in the executive leadership.[58] In the end, the German Pro Palestine Committee had one of the most diverse political memberships of the period.[59]

Having a high-ranking German politician at a public event in Berlin would raise the profile of the event itself and could, in turn, be used in future marketing to encourage more people to attend. For instance, when the world's first gay rights organization, the Scientific-Humanitarian Committee, marked its thirtieth anniversary in 1927, a public gathering was planned on "The Homosexual Question" that would culminate in a public petition to reform laws that targeted gay men.[60] The Scientific-Humanitarian Committee leaders wrote directly to movers and shakers in Berlin to encourage them to attend and speak at the event.[61] The lead organizer and famous sexologist Magnus Hirschfeld wrote to politicians, some of whom were puzzled by this invitation to address the crowd. Paul Löbe politely turned down the opportunity to speak, but he agreed to attend as an ordinary participant to honour Hirschfeld's work.[62] The former colonial minister and DDP parliamentarian Bernhard Dernburg wrote that he was happy to sign petitions against anti-gay laws, which he described as "harsh" and "unfair," but he drew a line at speaking publicly "in my capacity as a representative of a larger electorate that has strongly divided opinions."[63] Organizers of events like this Scientific-Humanitarian Committee celebration sought out political speakers because of the penumbra of their official blessing that would gin up support and greater attendance. In Hirschfeld's case, however, he need not have worried. Over 1,000 participants showed up in favour of gay rights, even without a famous politician's name on the marketing materials.[64]

The International Aspects of Weimar Berlin's Social Calendar

Weimar Berlin's interwar social milieu was also markedly international. German politicians' personal papers are replete with the calligraphed, gold-bordered invitations for a private dinner with an ambassador, a consul, or other diplomatic official stationed in the capital. The Soviet ambassador and his wife were particularly keen on inviting guests to their home or table, although many of these invitations were also declined.[65] Invitations from the Italian military attaché, the Austrian consul, the Dutch consul, the British ambassador, and the Polish consul are all scattered throughout German politicians' papers.[66] When the DDP parliamentarian and editor-in-chief of the *Vossische Zeitung*, Georg Bernhard, invited over 60 people to a holiday chamber music concert, his guest list included Greek, Belgian, Lithuanian, and Czechoslovak diplomats, in addition to socialist and liberal lawmakers and their spouses.[67] One of Bernhard's larger social events in April 1928 had over a hundred invited guests including sitting German politicians, ranging from the chancellor to lawmakers representing parties from the conservative DNVP through the SPD. All of these politicians mingled with a crowd that included everyone from an Italian opera singer to officials from the United States, Italy, and Japan. Foreign diplomats were nearly omnipresent in Berlin's social life.[68]

Moreover, when a foreign head of state or prime minister passed through Berlin, the German government rolled out the red carpet with various social receptions, often with extensive guest lists. When the king and queen of Afghanistan arrived, the cabinet invited parliamentarians, including those of the opposition, to the dinner honouring the royals.[69] In 1930, the Hungarian Prime Minister Count István Bethlen and his wife came to Berlin for a meticulously planned trip. After a series of reciprocal visits by German and Hungarian officials, a VIP tour of the Pergamon Museum was followed by an evening reception presided over by the wife of the German foreign minister. Subsequently, Countess Bethlen and women in the party departed for an evening at the theatre, leaving the men for a gentlemen's dinner. The socialist opposition was especially well represented at this men-only dinner. No Communist parliamentarian – one of the larger parties in the Reichstag at the time – was invited. Only one Nazi parliamentarian was on the guest list, but he declined his invitation. There were, thus, still boundaries in this lofty international social world in interwar Berlin.[70]

In addition to formal diplomatic visits, foreign visitors often passed through the German capital. Sometimes hundreds of international guests came for an organized event like the International Parliamentary Commercial Conference of 1929. These big international congresses were integrated into Berlin's calendar with social gatherings planned around them. For example, the Japanese ambassador invited numerous German parliamentarians to tea honouring the Japanese delegation to the International Parliamentary Commercial Conference in 1929.[71] Berlin's Chamber of Industry and Commerce marked the inter-parliamentary conference by inviting foreign delegates to mingle with local notables at a dinner held at the Zoological Garden's marbled grand hall.[72] Also in 1929, a leading French politician of the interwar years, the once-and-future Prime Minister Édouard Herriot came to Berlin on a speaking tour where he extolled the virtues of European integration at an event at the Hotel Kaiserhof in front of a broad swath of Berlin's social world.[73]

The wider international world also crept into interwar Berlin's social life through the presence of countless foreign journalists in the city. The city's Foreign Press Association hosted many events that German politicians were eager to attend. Much like an ambassador, the foreign press association's president Max Blokzijl wrote to leading German ministers and politicians asking them to join him and his wife for dinner at the Hotel Adlon.[74] The association also put together parliamentary Bierabende and lunches that were well attended by politicians, officials, and other key figures from the cultural and academic worlds. Foreign journalists mingled with the movers and shakers of German politics, following up on leads for news stories.[75] The high point of the Foreign Press Association's social calendar was its annual Foreign Press Ball that brought out a large crowd for dinner, dancing, and drinks in the luxurious Hotel Adlon.[76] The association kept extensive records of its guest lists to the balls in the late 1920s and 1930s; each year cabinet ministers, leading bureaucrats, and key parliamentarians attended. The papal nuncio was a frequent guest of honour. Communist and Nazi politicians declined to attend the ball during the republic; however, members of the German press were always invited, and these invitations went to journalists from Communist and Nazi party newspapers. Although Nazi journalists did

Figures 2.2. Two interwar posters advertising the annual ball of Berlin's Foreign Press Association from the period of the Weimar Republic.

Source: From Archiv des Vereins der Ausländischen Presse e.V.

not attend, the Communist *Rote Fahne* publication sent a representative in 1932.[77]

There was even a noticeable international element at the most parliamentary of social events in interwar Berlin. As president of the Reichstag, Paul Löbe hosted Bierabende that he referred to as "parliamentary evenings" in his later memoirs. These were Bierabende primarily for parliamentarians that included friendly mingling with political colleagues and luminaries from Germany's scientific and artistic community. These events could become quite chummy, and parliamentary rivals could grow close. Löbe remembered one Bierabend held during the National Assembly in Weimar with journalists from Russia, Finland, Sweden, the Netherlands, Italy, and the United States to which more radical socialists were also invited. Löbe and two of his socialist rivals squeezed together on one small sofa talking about topics including the merits of different candidates for upcoming elections.[78]

This robust mix journalists, politicians, and eminent foreigners was repeated during Berlin's "parliamentary evenings" where the Apostolic Nuncio Eugenio Pacelli frequently received special attention. Pacelli – known later as Pope Pius XII – was greeted with gestures of respect from the Catholic parliamentarians, but "he then joined in engaging conversation with Christians, Jews, and non-believers" until right before midnight when he needed to get home to sleep before Mass the next day. During one of these evenings, the conversation turned to the nuncio's German language skills. When one Reichstag member privately suggested that Pacelli's German was not that good, Chancellor Hermann Müller decided to put it to the test by recounting a joke from Upper Silesia in a thick local dialect. After the punch line, "[w]hen Pacelli joined in the hearty laughter, Müller won [the bet]. The nuncio really did understand German." Parliamentarians and ministers mingling and joking alongside diplomats, foreign journalists, and even a future pope until late in the night reflected just how international Berlin's interwar social world was.[79]

A German Clubland: Gentlemen's Clubs and Sociability in Interwar Berlin

Both before and during the Wilhelmine period, Berlin developed popular gentlemen's clubs as elite oases – often modelled on similar patrician social clubs in London. Many of these clubs survived into the interwar years, and they shaped the social and political milieu that developed in republican Berlin. Club members would often lounge around a clubhouse and work in club libraries, as well as eat their meals, attend speeches and presentations, and meet friends in these spaces. For anyone looking to lobby elected politicians, clubs were a perfect place to do so, since parliamentarians could mingle with bigwigs from business and industry. Moreover, clubs were helpfully removed from the prying eyes of the public. Elite clubs remained an anchor on Berlin's social scene despite dramatic regime change. However, there was also a boom in the founding of new clubs after 1918, particularly those with explicit right-wing goals, and there was fierce competition among German nationalist clubs for members within this political niche. Even for more centrist or centre-left politicians in the early years of the German republic, club life structured much of Berlin's social world.[80]

For a moderate bourgeois or conservative man who sat in the Reichstag and was based in Berlin, there were a plethora of clubs to join and club events to attend. Two of the oldest clubs that were active in the 1920s were the Ressource zur Unterhaltung, which traced its history back to 1784, and the Club von Berlin, which dated to 1864. The Ressource zur Unterhaltung had a building on Oranienburger Straße, and its events in the 1920s included a political discussion with a conservative politician, along with a club Christmas party to which women were also invited. After centuries at the forefront of Berlin club life, the Ressource zur

Unterhaltung ran into financial trouble during the Great Depression and sold its building in 1930.[81] By contrast, the Club von Berlin shaped interwar social life, and it still exists today. Politicians including Walther Rathenau, Gustav Stresemann, and Karl Helfferich were all members, and the erstwhile Chancellor Hans Luther dropped by during the Weimar years. The tasty lunch offerings and the seclusion of the clubhouse were known as appealing to business and political contacts making their way through Berlin. In 1932, the Club von Berlin served as the location for meetings and dinners between members of Franz von Papen's conservative cabinet and important industrialists and bankers.[82]

Moving beyond the centuries-old clubhouses of central Berlin that drew membership particularly from the world of business, some of Berlin's clubs brought together men – and sometimes even women – who shared common interests. The Lawn-Tennis-Turnier Club brought together tennis players, sometimes to play and other times for social events like their 1929 Christmas Ball in the Hotel Esplanade.[83] Founded in 1867, the Union-Klub was made up of men interested in horse breeding and horse races. Otto von Bismarck had been a member, frequently joining club members for the train ride to the racecourse at Hoppegarten outside Berlin.[84] During the 1920s and early 1930s, the members of the Union-Klub spent quite a lot of time in their particular clubhouse. Both erstwhile Chancellor Franz von Papen and DVP lawmaker Siegfried von Kardorff were members who frequently used the club's stationery for their own political letters.[85] Like other clubs in the city, the Union-Klub hosted an annual banquet open to invited members of the wider community, and another erstwhile chancellor, Kurt von Schleicher, would often attend.[86] Women in Berlin's high society also organized their own club, the Damenclub 1930, and put together political and informative events for the group's members. This women's club hosted a lecture series on history, finance, and politics with parliamentarians as featured speakers.[87]

Two Berlin clubs were explicitly tied to political parties. The right-liberal DVP was associated with the Reichsklub, and the left-liberal DDP was associated with the Demokratische Klub. The Reichsklub der Deutschen Volkspartei, to give the organization its full name, included a number of DVP parliamentarians among its members, but the vast majority of club members were supporters of the party in the greater Berlin area. The club hosted public presentations on topics like economic competitiveness and rapprochement with France.[88] The Reichsklub's events were not limited to party members. When a DVP parliamentarian spoke on Otto von Bismarck in 1925 at the Reichsklub, he purposely invited a politician from the conservative Wirtschaftspartei and two rival DNVP politicians.[89]

These more party-political clubhouses could also serve as a home away from home for parliamentarians who did not live in Berlin. When the Demokratischer Klub moved locations, it sent out a notice to the DDP members in the Reichstag encouraging them to use the clubhouse more often. In addition to a revamped series of talks and events and a restaurant, this letter noted: "The spaces for reading, library materials, and games have been expanded, and particular attention has been paid to furnishing them comfortably. A number of individual rooms serve as space to rest or change clothes." These two clubs could easily be the dining rooms and entertaining spaces for DDP and DVP politicians who did not normally live in Berlin. However, as predominantly single-party environments, they could also be ideological echo chambers. The Reichsklub and Demokratischer Klub both ultimately ran into financial problems as these two liberal parties waned in political importance and in membership during the later Weimar years.[90]

A larger number of social clubs tended in a general conservative or nationalist direction without an explicit party affiliation. Notably, the number of these more right-wing clubs grew dramatically in the early 1920s. Some of these clubs were more informal get-togethers that had an intellectual bent. For instance, the Mittwochsgesellschaft worked to bring academic topics to the broad audience of its members. It hosted Wednesday lectures on everything from honey bees and succulents to eugenics and constitutional reform. Only the more political topics veered in a more right-wing direction. Invitations to Mittwochsgesellschaft events are scattered throughout leading politicians' papers.[91]

An even larger nationalist intellectual crowd came out for a group created by the former general and DVP parliamentarian Hans von Seeckt, the independent former foreign minister Walter Simons, and the diplomat Wilhelm Solf. This club was never officially registered as an association but was referred to as the SeSiSo-Club by contemporaries, using the last names of its conveners. This informal group hosted a lecture and discussion series, usually with meetings taking place in the Hotel Kaiserhof, occasionally with one to two hundred people present. SeSiSo-Club presentation topics included an analysis of problems within the British Empire by a German journalist who had been a correspondent in London, the current status of the Polish Corridor from an East Prussian official, and various approaches to economic questions by leading civil servants and former ministers. The SeSiSo-Club also hosted smaller lunches with expert presentations and discussions on contemporary bureaucracy and parliamentarism, agriculture in Europe, and on colonial policy. The SeSiSo-Club included so many participants who were serving with the government that its presentation on agriculture in East

Prussia had to be rescheduled because a mandatory government event conflicted with the talk.[92] Solf's biographer devoted only one page to the club, ultimately dismissing its members as "the intellectual elite in German political life, but definitely not the most active or important." However, the SeSiSo-Club provided yet another space for right-wing politicians to mingle and was one of many clubs that appeared on numerous politicians' calendars.[93]

A formal club in Berlin that tended in an even more conservative direction was the Deutscher Herrenklub (DHK). The DHK was founded in 1924, bringing together conservative men from politics, business, administration, and the military. The club described its own goals in a contemporary publication: "The people joined together in this association see their special task as arousing and maintaining an understanding and involvement in pragmatic political issues among men and future politicians, who are bound together by ethnicity and national responsibility, regardless of party politics or narrow economic interests."[94] Despite the overt ethno-nationalism of their mission statement, the annual DHK banquet was another high point in Berlin's annual social calendar, and each year featured a different speaker. In 1927, the former Catholic Centre Party Minister Andreas Hermes spoke on agricultural issues, and in 1929, the long-serving German diplomat Albrecht Graf von Bernstorff was the keynote speaker.[95] Until a sharper right-wing turn in the 1930s, DHK talked up its annual banquets as the moment when representatives of "national ministries, the diplomatic corps, and the leaders of society" all came out for the club.[96] Historians have largely focused on the DHK in relationship to Chancellor Papen's right-wing "Cabinet of Barons," which had strong ties with the club. More recently, Larry Eugene Jones has written of the club as the "preserve of political reactionaries," although the club existed within a much wider conservative club landscape and grew more reactionary over time. Between 1930 and 1932, many of the centrist bourgeois members of the DHK left the club, leaving aristocrats in the majority.[97] This rump patrician club was linked with Papen's un-democratic and un-representative cabinet, so it was an easy target for both Nazi and socialist journalists to ridicule as part of the system they hated.[98]

Turning the clock back to the less reactionary days of the 1920s, day-to-day membership in the DHK revolved around dropping by the club-house for lunch, where more than one hundred people were usually present. For lunch, members often divided themselves up by occupation so that, for instance, bankers sat at one table and parliamentarians were at another.[99] In addition, Friday evenings there was an officially non-partisan political program. These DHK events were similar to those hosted by the SeSiSo-Club, but there were more talks on specific economic issues like manoeuverings on the Berlin Stock Exchange, the financial crisis in London, and the role of the German government in economic affairs. The trade attaché from the United States embassy also came to speak on the American perspective on the German economic situation. Sometimes there were events of more general interest, like a banquet welcoming a German traveler back from Tibet. However, the political topics that were discussed had a markedly conservative tilt. For instance, a presentation on the psychology of Russian youth was designed to discredit Bolshevism, which had been a stated goal of the club since the beginning. The former Reichsbank President Hjalmar Schacht provocatively sprinkled right-wing talking points into his talk on the Young Plan, and even the Nazi party member Walther Funk spoke in an early one-off speech on National Socialist economics.[100]

A final right-wing nationalist club in Berlin was the Nationaler Klub founded in 1919 with even more specific anti-Bolshevik and nationalist goals. From its founding, the Nationaler Klub claimed to be "built on a non-partisan national foundation." Nevertheless, the club became so tied to the DNVP that the leader of the DVP, Gustav Stresemann, joked that it should be called the "Deutschnationaler Klub," a pun that incorporated the DNVP's party name into the club's name.[101] Although the Nationaler Klub came to be associated with a more extremist DNVP party line, in the early 1920s, it took a progressive stance in actually inviting a female parliamentarian from the DVP, Katharina von Oheimb, to join its ranks.[102] Even in the early 1930s, the Nationaler Klub's president still expressed hope to reconcile various right-wing movements: "Our goal is to bring the groups together that were almost at blows with each other during the election but – because of their national German mindset – still must have common unifying goals."[103] However, the Nationaler Klub pointed to a more radical right-wing inclination in offering Adolf Hitler a platform for his debut speeches in the early 1920s. Joseph Goebbels and radical Nazis returned to the club in the early 1930s, hoping to steer the club towards Hitler's brand of right-wing extremism. Although these attempts failed until after the Nazi seizure of power, the Nationaler Klub was one of the few that gave the Nazi speakers a regular podium to speak to Germany's traditional conservative elite before Hitler was named chancellor.[104]

Most German clubs had public membership lists, but some interwar associations valued their privacy. This included a subset of Deutscher Herrenklub members who thought that an already exclusive gentlemen's club was not enough, so they formed a private club within the club called the Civil-Casino in April 1931. This group was to be no more than a hundred men who were also members of the DHK. The Civil-Casino's goal was to "be the somewhat conspiratorial place to exchange ideas among the functional elite in economic and political life."[105] This club-within-a-club was a smaller group, but invitations to their exclusive events still appear in politicians' personal papers. For instance, 26 invitations went out for a private Civil-Casino event held in the Hotel Kaiserhof with conservative and bourgeois politicians mingling with a small group of bankers and businessmen, as well as with Horace Rumbold, the British ambassador in Berlin.[106]

Another secretive association that brought together powerful political and economic actors was the Friedrich List Gesellschaft. Ostensibly, the List Gesellschaft was an organization founded by academics to publish and propagate the works of the nineteenth-century German economist Friedrich List; however, the association soon aspired to be more influential, including by bringing together politicians and academics. The scholars who led the List Gesellschaft tried to exert influence in the business world by bringing together economic theorists and practitioners. Attendees at List Gesellschaft events included bankers and businessmen, professors and scholars, central bankers and civil servants, and, of course, ministers and parliamentarians.[107] The minutes and lists of participants at private talks in Berlin or Bad Pyrmont were always marked confidential. However, one participant stands out: the erstwhile socialist finance minister and Marxist theorist Rudolf Hilferding.[108] Hilferding, who was the SPD's financial and monetary expert, actually took a conservative position on credit expansion, and agreed with many of the right-wing List Gesellschaft participants in terms of economic practicalities. Through private events hosted by this group, Germany's more conservative economic theorists and wealthy businessmen gained the ear of a leading socialist, who, in turn, hobnobbed with the financial elite.[109]

Whether public or more secret in their approach, all the clubs thus far were unlikely places to find members of the moderate left, which is why Rudolf Hilferding stands out so much in the List Gesellschaft. Almost all of these groups had a pronounced nationalist or conservative aristocratic bent. However, Berlin also had a few social clubs that did not fit squarely into this right-wing camp. The Gesellschaft der Freunde, for example, was originally a Jewish learned and charitable association. The organization had its own clubhouse that hosted large non-sectarian social events including the large congress of Prussian rural towns in November 1926. However, based on extant invitations in personal papers, most moderate or left-wing members of the Reichstag were not frequenting the Gesellschaft der Freunde's events as often as their right-wing peers visited conservative clubs.[110]

The one moderate big-tent social club in interwar Berlin was the Deutsche Gesellschaft 1914. This club had been founded in 1915 by leading German journalists, politicians, and cultural actors with 900 original members.[111] The group's name did not refer to its date of founding but was chosen to invoke the image of wartime unity.[112] This ideal of national cohesion was not mere lip service; from the founding of Deutsche Gesellschaft 1914, the club included socialists, who even served on the organization's executive boards. Wartime members ranged from the former chief the German General Staff Helmuth von Moltke to the Catholic parliamentarian Matthias Erzberger and the moderate socialist Albert Südekum. Many conservatives were skeptical of the club's bourgeois liberal leadership and left-wing members; interestingly, however, one historian has read incorporating reformist socialists into the club as a successful attempt "to bring moderate social democratic elements into the existing monarchical system."[113] This big-tent ethos persisted after the German Revolution of 1918, when the club staked out a position in the middle of German society, accepting the new republic and its leading officials.[114]

The clubhouse of the Deutsche Gesellschaft 1914 was frequently used by political groups, itinerant speakers, and for various meetings throughout the 1920s and early 1930s, making it a key location of Berlin's social-political world, much like Kroll's. In the early years of the republic, the SPD's own parliamentary "fortnightly convivial gatherings" were held in the clubhouse.[115] In 1932, the Gesellschaft hosted a political meeting of the leaders of the centre-right political parties trying to coordinate their election efforts to avoid a victory by either the most radical right or the radical left.[116] That same year – 1932 – when skepticism about democracy seemed to be on the rise, the pro-republican Walther Rathenau Gesellschaft hosted a social event at the Deutsche Gesellschaft 1914. These clubhouse events tended to draw from the middle of society, from the moderate socialists through the progressive conservatives, although socialists seemed to frequent the Deutsche Gesellschaft less and less as the years wore on.[117]

Like other clubs in Berlin, the Deutsche Gesellschaft 1914 also hosted its own program of presentations and discussions for its membership, and these were intentionally supposed to have a broader appeal than other clubs. Whereas economic topics dominated the speaker series in more conservative clubs, the Deutsche Gesellschaft's programs included academic lectures on science, archaeology, and history, as well as the reflections of practitioners from politics and economics, trip reports of adventurers to far-flung locales, and many presentations that included the cutting-edge technology of projected images. At the Deutsche Gesellschaft, a German delegate to the League of Nations spoke on international politics, an archivist from the German national archives addressed the role of annexationist thought in the First World War, and the famous political theorist and lawyer Carl Schmitt discussed a landmark legal case in Leipzig. The club was also the venue for a former Prussian minister to speak on Bali, where a naturalist lectured on "Noble and Odd Creatures from the Animal Kingdom," and the place for a French Jewish author to speak in French on poetry and modernity. There was even a tour of the State Porcelain Factory in Berlin, and the club organized group trips abroad to the United States and Canada, as well as to Egypt into the mid-1920s.[118] All of these membership-only programs were supplemented by a variety of musical concerts and parties to which the wives of members were invited. Many ordinary German parliamentarians of the 1920s would have come into contact with the Deutsche Gesellschaft, whether as a socialist using their facilities for gatherings, as a club member listening to lectures by academics, or as an invited guest for a concert.[119]

In looking back at these Berlin clubs, German participants in this club world were emulating the older culture of gentlemen's clubs in London. British clubs had a long history; they had developed out of the aristocratic coffee and gaming establishments of the seventeenth century but flourished in the nineteenth century. With over nine-tenths of British MPs as members of clubs in the mid-1800s, London's club landscape was so integrated into the world of politics around the House of Commons that this era has been called one of "club government."[120] One cannot quite assert that Germany was governed in the same way, but in the waning years of the Weimar Republic, Franz von Papen's cabinet of the barons was mocked as governing from the exclusive, right-wing clubhouses of Berlin. In 1932, the socialists critiqued this social world of politics in an election poster targeting the "Herrenklub government." Later, even the Nazis proclaimed that "Fat cats and the Herrenklub [were] with the Jews." Whether in humorous or antisemitic terms, German club government was mocked from both left and right.[121]

Interwar Germans were particularly interested in emulating the exclusive London clubs of the late nineteenth century that catered to aristocratic or high-ranking men in Victorian society. These clubs had luxurious clubhouses, decadent meals, and homosocial environments.[122] Not only were the Germans looking to the British, but so were other continental Europeans. The interwar Dutch publication *Club Kroniek* was a monthly newsletter on social clubs in the Netherlands and Dutch colonies. In addition to sections with tips on playing chess or billiards, there was the regular column on club life in Britain that included exposés on British clubs, descriptions of women's clubs in London, and essays on British club concepts like "clubbability." London's clubs were considered the gold standard for social clubs in both the Netherlands and Germany.[123] However, German and Dutch clubmen were several decades late in copying these British examples. London's gentlemen's clubs and the exclusive "clubland" of the city's St. James's district had waned in importance dramatically by 1914. Even before the First World War, London's up-and-coming gentlemen sought out mixed-gender spaces and ate in restaurants in the hopes of being seen, rather than remaining hidden away in homosocial clubhouses; London's club life was dealt an even sharper blow by the world war.[124]

Around the same time London's clubs lost their social importance, Berlin's right-wing politicians turned en masse to the security of club life. By the late nineteenth century, London had changed demographically, culturally, and spatially, and this was the moment when British clubmen left public spaces for private and luxurious clubhouses to isolate themselves from these changes.[125] In 1918 and 1919, German conservatives and the old aristocracy felt similarly unmoored in a society undergoing revolutionary change. Germany's imperial past, with its privileges for the traditional elite, had become a republic dominated by proletarian politicians. The interwar proliferation of more conservative German clubs reflected the anxieties of the old-regime elite. The exclusive parties and balls of Weimar Berlin were now populated by working-class parliamentarians. As the ordinary folk entered those lofty social spaces, the right-wing elite moved to more exclusive clubs.

Over the course of the 1920s and 1930s, the link between gentlemen's clubs and Berlin's political life became so self-evident to contemporaries that when the Nazis took power in 1933, eager socialites rushed to found yet another club. The new Reichsklub vom 30. Januar 1933 was established in the sleek, modern Columbushaus, right on Potsdamer Platz. The club's name echoed the Deutsche Gesellschaft 1914, but it wholeheartedly rejected the legacy of that broad-church club that had previously harboured socialist party meetings. The new Nazi club was to provide community for Berlin's leading gentlemen inspired by the "National Socialist Revolution of January 30, 1933." Prospective members had to certify that they were of Aryan descent and were not freemasons. Right-wing German politicians who had previously been content with the city's conservative club landscape rushed to join this new Nazified club. Even the political leader of the DVP was sent a membership application. The founding of the Reichsklub vom 30. Januar 1933 was a final gasp of Berlin's republican-era social milieu that expressly mixed parliamentary politics and gentlemanly social spaces. Berlin's club life lost its link to politics under the Nazi dictatorship, and long-standing clubs focused on their ostensible non-political roots by fostering tennis, supporting horse-racing, or providing elite spaces without the party-political programming or diverse membership of the Weimar years.[126]

A "Parliamentarized" Weimar-Era Social Elite?

The image of Germany's interwar political elite being so polarized and forced into party-political silos that they did not socialize with each other is off the mark. Parliamentarians, especially in the political middle, collaborated with their rivals through committee work, mingled at lavish social events at Kroll's, and dropped by a fancy club for concerts and conversation. The prominent DDP politician Erich Koch-Weser once wrote to his fiancée to assuage her concerns about his relationship with the leading socialist Toni Sender: "We are very good friends but that's not at all political."[127] Scholars like Thomas Mergel would tend to agree that there might have been lots of interwar socializing, but it was unlikely to have much to do with real politics. However, the sheer amount of evidence for social gatherings suggests that even if private chats or club-room meals were not quid pro quo arrangements among Weimar parliamentarians, they were a key aspect of a healthy and robust interwar parliamentary life. Interwar politics and sociability were intertwined.

There were also boundaries demarcating this social world. Women were excluded from most of Berlin's club life, for example. Elected female parliamentarians could even be banished from official events on the basis of gender. When the prime minister of Hungary visited Berlin and the men lingered for an evening of political chatter over cigars, Germany's female politicians were ushered away with Hungarian prime minister's spouse and other politicians' wives.[128] Moreover, the conservative bent of the private clubs meant that more left-wing politicians were not welcome. Now that the hoi polloi had entered the Reichstag itself, the conservative politicians ran in droves to Berlin's social clubs with memberships that were more reflective of the *ancien régime* rather than the new republic.

Extant guest lists from more official social events demonstrate the acceptable political spectrum at private or party-political events in republican Berlin ranged from the social democratic SPD to the DNVP. How acceptable the Communist left wing or the radical conservative right-wing was at a given time depended on the event's host or on the government in power. Moreover, the demographics within this private social world changed over time. Socialists were more frequent guests at bourgeois and cross-party events during the early years of the republic. With a diverse right-wing club landscape, there were far more interwar social spaces open to conservative and bourgeois politicians than to left-wing socialists or right-wing populists. Communists and Nazis were always few and far between in this informal social world. Joseph Goebbels once heaped criticism on his colleagues in the Nazi parliamentary party who mingled with political rivals as "parliamentarized" and contemptable "reactionaries." As radicals like Goebbels gained a firmer hold on Berlin's politics with more seats in the parliament held by anti-democratic figures who wholly rejected this world of sociability, the percentage of the Reichstag that was clubbable and could move in these mixed, cross-party social circles declined precipitously. The experiment at the beginning of the interwar years was to open the door to this social world of politics widely, but that experiment had faltered by the eve of the Nazi seizure of power as radical politicians opted out of this interwar world of sociability.[129]

However, the ghost of interwar parliamentary sociability lingered into the Third Reich after the parliament became a Nazified shadow of its republican self. The Reichsklub vom 30. Januar 1933 had been organized as a fascist echo of the gentlemen's clubs of the republic. After 1933, the Reichstag only had Nazi members who were merely a glorified audience for Adolf Hitler's declamations. The anti-Nazi German exile newspaper *Pariser Tageszeitung* ridiculed a Reichstag meeting scheduled in February 1938 as a Nazi attempt to "play parliament." The Reichstag session was a stage for Nazi propaganda; indeed, Hitler's parliamentary pronouncements would be broadcast from loudspeakers and on the radio, and all sporting events were cancelled for that Sunday afternoon, encouraging Germans to listen. However, even the Nazis had gotten the memo that parliaments – even fake parliaments like this Nazified Reichstag – should include a private social world, so a "Bierabend of comrades" was scheduled in Berlin's old Royal Palace on the night before this 1938 fascist parliamentary session. The Nazis had long ago killed off parliamentary democracy, but they resurrected the parliamentary Bierabend. On some level, even during the Third Reich, the Reichstag as an institution was still indelibly linked to a social world of politics.[130]

Chapter Three

From the League of Nations to Electioneering Abroad: Transnational Parliamentary Connections Between the World Wars

Filed away in Prague Castle's Czech presidential archives is a folder entitled "International parliamentary commercial delegations" containing an eclectic mix of materials from the 1920s and 1930s. Sandwiched between a bureaucratic note in Czech and a letter to a local Australian state politician is a nondescript envelope from the Japanese legation. The fancy cream-coloured heavy paper inside unfolds into a document about one metre long that records a speech in Japanese delivered to the president of Czechoslovakia in 1923. The Japanese parliamentarian Viscount Nishiōji Yoshimitsu had travelled to Europe for an international commercial conference in Prague. The aristocrat was a member of the Japanese parliament's upper chamber and was accompanied by other politicians from his country. Nishiōji's speech was itself a wide-ranging mix of the formulaic and the personal. It began with condolences marking the recent death of President Tomáš Garrigue Masaryk's wife but then quickly jumped to praise of First Republic Czechoslovakia's fiscal reforms. Viscount Nishiōji emphasized economic ties that linked Czechoslovakia with the rest of Europe, with America, and with the East, in the hopes of increasing trade between East Asia and Central Europe.[1]

Starting in the early 1920s, foreign politicians, particularly elected parliamentarians, came to Prague and met with the Czechoslovak president. A Belgian socialist chatted with President Masaryk in the library of the presidential palace in 1920. A Cuban parliamentarian set up high-level meetings on Cuban-Czechoslovak economic issues. The president of the Latvian chamber of deputies presented President Masaryk with a gift during a meeting in the mid-1920s. Sometimes individual ministers from other countries met with the president; Dutch and Norwegian ministers were hosted at Prague Castle, and French ministers were invited further afield to the presidential summer residence at Topoľčianky in central Slovakia. The presidential chancellery rolled out the red carpet in 1930, when six British members of Parliament from the governing Labour party travelled together on a junket to Czechoslovakia. Tours and travel were arranged for these MPs throughout Moravia and Slovakia with a formal meal with Masaryk at the Topoľčianky stately home. Masaryk's daughter, Czechoslovak parliamentarians, and leading Czech intellectuals all travelled with these Labour MPs, indicating how much the Czechoslovak government wanted to use the trip to win friends in London.[2]

These parliamentary visits and presidential audiences were not seen by contemporaries as meaningless formalities or an unimportant side show for a politician en route to a Bohemian spa town.[3] Instead, they were part of a larger political calculus on the part of both the visitors and the Czechoslovak government. On the one hand, when a Japanese socialist was travelling through Europe and requested a meeting with the Czechoslovak president, the foreign ministry reported that Japanese socialists had little influence, so a presidential audience was declined. On the other hand, despite the danger of angering the British government, the Czechoslovak foreign ministry pressed the president to meet with the Indian anticolonial dissident Subhas Chandra Bose. The economic perception that Czechoslovak exports might replace German exports to India and the diplomatic reality that Bose was headed from Prague to Berlin to meet with Nazi officials combined to prompt President Edvard Beneš to agree to the meeting. Audiences were seen as a soft diplomatic tool used to boost Czechoslovakia's standing in the word.[4]

Although these international political connections ran through Prague, they had limits, and this was thrown into sharp relief during the 1938 Munich crisis. After Austria was annexed by Nazi Germany in March 1938, the world's attention turned to Czechoslovakia with its restive German-speaking minority and threats of military mobilization in Central Europe.[5] From May 1938, the Czechoslovak presidential chancellery went into overdrive reaching out to European legislators, particularly from Britain and France. At least 12 audiences were granted to foreign politicians between May and September 1938, far exceeding the total annual number of recorded visits in any previous year. The francophile President Beneš hosted French parliamentarians of all political stripes – ranging from social democrats to moderate conservatives. During the escalating diplomatic crisis in mid-June 1938, 15 French conservative parliamentarians travelled together on a fact-finding mission to Prague to meet with President Beneš. Interestingly, the politically inclusive approach for French guests in Prague was in stark contrast the Czechoslovak presidency's long history of meeting only with left-wing UK parliamentarians. Until the desperate geopolitical scramble of August 1938, all seven presidential audiences with British lawmakers had been granted to Labour politicians. The Conservative MP Sir Thomas Moore showed up at Prague Castle only after the foreign ministry pressed President Beneš to meet with him in August 1938.[6]

This last-minute Czechoslovak attempt to shore up its foreign alliances through presidential and parliamentary diplomacy could not save the First Republic. This does not mean that these visits accomplished nothing; indeed, many of Edvard Beneš's guests returned to London or Paris as avowed supporters of Czechoslovakia. For instance, the Labour leader in the House of Lords, Lord Snell, had met with President Beneš in June 1938. In early October 1938, after Conservative Prime Minister Neville Chamberlain had endorsed appeasing Nazi Germany, Lord Snell delivered a passionate speech opposing the government's position: "I feel that the real heroes on this occasion do not reside in London, or Berlin, or in Paris, but in Prague." Lord Snell praised the Czechoslovak government and came to Beneš's defense challenging that "perfectly odious campaign of slander against his name." On the one hand, this was a diplomatic coup for the Czechoslovak government to have such kind words spoken about it in the British Parliament as a result of a presidential audience. On the other hand, it was not enough to avert geopolitical catastrophe. Even if this world of parliamentary diplomacy came up short against the international machinations of a war-mongering Nazi Germany, many interwar parliamentarians understood their role as including a transnational element, whether they were formally appointed delegates to the League of Nations or travelled as informal mediaries on the global stage.[7]

From the late 1990s, scholars have grappled with the historical contours of internationalism during the nineteenth and early twentieth centuries. On the one hand, there had long been calls for global equality from the working-class socialist movement that explicitly positioned itself as international. On the other hand, there were organizations managing shipping along the Rhine and promoting Esperanto that the historian Akira Iriye has written into a scholarly narrative of more amorphous nineteenth-century liberal internationalism. Glenda Sluga and Patricia Clavin have pointed to a diversity of internationalisms, although after the Brexit referendum and 2016 US election, scholars have raced to explore more right-wing past internationalisms. David Motadel has written of the issues-driven, practical "reactionary cosmopolitanism" of the right, and Tara Zahra has pointed to an interwar anti-globalism that was rooted in deep-seated economic concerns and should be seen as an oppositional counterpart to the optimistic internationalism surrounding the League of Nations.[8]

Whether socialist, liberal, or reactionary, scholars have combed the archives to pinpoint a variety of people as interwar internationalists.

Often overlooking seasoned diplomats and leading politicians, historians have instead spotlighted engineers, jurists, academics, trade unionists, journalists, businessmen, and colonialists.[9] Of course, not all interwar internationalists were warm and fuzzy progressive liberals, and considerable scholarship has tied imperialist sentiment to internationalism. Peter Weber's work on the German journalist and foreign policy guru Ernst Jäckh paints a picture of a liberally minded imperialist who later acquiesced to the new republican order in Germany to become a "nationalist internationalist." Jäckh transformed into a "civil diplomat," unencumbered by the constraints of a formal government position, but with an air of officialdom because of his connections to the German Foreign Office. Like other internationalists towards whom historians have gravitated, Jäckh was essentially a leader in civil society with cultivated expertise that was used on the international stage.[10]

Unlike Ernst Jäckh or League of Nations technocrats, parliamentarians have not been included among the interwar internationalists who have piqued scholars' interests. With the archival evidence of parliamentarians' transnational ties piling high, this chapter writes elected lawmakers' transnational activities into this larger scholarship on interwar internationalism. Moreover, parliamentarians were at the vanguard of new diplomatic experimentation that attempted to democratize foreign policy by wresting it from the executive and vesting it in the legislature. This chapter explores the breadth of these transnational ties, beginning with parliamentarians serving formally as delegates to the annual Assembly of the League of Nations. Subsequently, the chapter turns to parliamentarians travelling as more ad hoc representatives of their home countries when they toured the world, bringing with them a penumbra of officialdom as quasi-diplomats. Since parliamentarians were elected on behalf of a national or subnational constituency, these transnational ties are unexpected. Europe's interwar continent of colleagues was forged not only in the smoke-filled backrooms of national capitals but also on travel across Europe and during trips to international conferences.

The Rise and Fall of Parliamentarian-Delegates at the Assembly of League of Nations

Every September during the 1920s and 1930s, delegations from around the world converged on Geneva to attend the annual session of the Assembly of the League of Nations. One German delegate recalled how the gathering transformed the Swiss city; crowds of people speaking a multitude of languages wandered the streets, cars of diplomats raced around town, the worldwide press crowded into the salons of the city, and motorboats constantly plied the waters of Lake Geneva between the Assembly hall and the luxurious hotels where delegations took up residence.[11] One British delegate's memories were not quite as pleasant; he remembered "the gossip of the cosmopolitan politicians, the huge dreary dinner-parties given by different nations in turn [and] the depressing cocktail parties and receptions."[12] Whether one had fond memories of Geneva or not, the League Assembly's annual gathering was a high point on the public diplomatic calendar, where the historian Susan Pederson has somewhat cynically argued "the statesmen of the world, well-oiled by drink […] had to perform civility and espouse internationalism."[13]

The annual sessions of the League's Assembly might have focused the attention of the world's diplomats on Geneva, but the Assembly itself had an ambiguously defined role in the League's Covenant. Although the treaty laid down the Assembly's powers in Article 3, before any other part of the organization, the article was brief in specifying only that the Assembly would be made up of representatives of each member-state, that each state could have up to three official delegates but cast only one vote, and that the Assembly could "deal at its meetings with any matter within the sphere of action of the League or affecting the peace of the world."[14] Because of the vague framing for the Assembly in the Covenant, everyone could project their own hopes on this new body. In this spirit, Woodrow Wilson laid out a global role for the Assembly in a 1919 speech in San Francisco:

> [T]he real underlying conception of the Assembly of the League of Nations is that it is the forum of opinion, not of action. It is the debating body; it is the body where the thought of the little nation along with the thought of the big nation is brought to bear upon those matters which affect the peace of the world, is brought to bear upon those matters which affect the good understanding between nations upon which the peace of the world depends; where this stifled voice of humanity is at last to be heard, where nations that have borne the unspeakable suffering of the ages that must have seemed to them like aeons will find voice and expression, where the moral judgment of mankind can sway the opinion of the world.

President Wilson envisioned an institution much like the bourgeois legislatures of the nineteenth century where debate and discussion would sway the public, and he envisioned this "forum of opinion" galvanizing public opinion across the world.[15]

As this amorphously defined Assembly came into being, the entire world of international diplomacy was in flux. The era began with the Paris Peace Conference that remade geopolitics and conjured up a

"Wilsonian Moment" in which the language of self-determination was picked up by peoples around the world.[16] At the same time, the political scientist Mai'a K. Davis Cross has shown a change in the day-to-day world of interwar diplomacy that turned against old-regime professional diplomats – often upper-class independent envoys empowered to negotiate on behalf of their countries. Europe's "old diplomacy" – the secretive, behind-the-scenes negotiations of often-aristocratic plenipotentiaries – was discredited as having failed to prevent a cataclysmic war. There was the rise of a "new diplomacy" that was open, public, and shaped by political leaders through summits attended by democratic politicians rather than professional diplomats. The Paris Peace Conference represented this new diplomatic era, which later came to be embodied in the hopes vested in the nascent League of Nations.[17] Sean Wempe has argued that the League was the nexus "where international public opinion engaged with diplomacy and political action" and "influence politics" brought together disparate actors, including ardent colonialists, who wanted to shape policy in Geneva.[18] An interwar contemporary dubbed this more open international world "diplomacy by conference." Top-level politicians were in Geneva, as were the lobbyists and advocates jockeying for influence. Elected parliamentarians were also present, although they have so far been overlooked by scholars.[19]

Although the Assembly of the League of Nations was far smaller and much whiter than the United Nations General Assembly today, it still brought together an expansive cast of characters. Among the heads of government, foreign ministers, and countless ambassadors who peopled the conference rooms in Geneva during the Assembly, elected national parliamentarians milled around as Assembly delegates. Writing in an international relations journal, the historian Norbert Götz has applied the idea of "parliamentary diplomacy" to the phenomenon of elected lawmakers representing Scandinavian countries at the League of Nations Assembly. Even more surprising than having national lawmakers at an international assembly was that a number of these legislators came from opposition parties, so domestic political opponents served together in the same delegation. However, in 1920s, there were increased calls for parliamentary oversight of foreign policy, and there can be no better oversight than parliamentarians – even from the opposition – sitting at the negotiation table alongside ministers representing the executive. Götz described this phenomenon among Scandinavian delegations to Geneva, but "parliamentary diplomacy" at the League was far more widespread.[20]

Throughout the 1920s and 1930s, the makeup of delegations dispatched to the League of Nations changed. There were roughly three types of delegations: those led by ambassadors, those dominated by government ministers, and those that incorporated parliamentarians. Ambassadorial delegations represented an older and more traditional form of diplomacy spearheaded by professional diplomats and foreign service officials. Ministerial delegations put representatives of the national executive at the forefront of participation in the League, and delegations that included parliamentarians represented a belief that legislators had a role alongside the government in the conduct of foreign policy. These were not rigid categories; ministerial delegations often included ambassadors, and parliamentary delegations were often led by a foreign minister. However, these categories are useful in tracking change over time in who attended the Assembly.

Of the 41 national delegations dispatched to the First Assembly in November 1920, slightly less than a majority – the delegations of 20 countries in total – consisted of special envoys, ambassadors, or other officials based in Europe. For instance, both Liberia and Nicaragua sent the chargés d'affaires from their diplomatic missions in Paris to represent their countries at the Assembly in Geneva. Bolivia empowered a Bolivian industrialist who resided in Paris to represent its interests. Since the Assembly broke into various committees that met simultaneously, additional delegates guaranteed national representation in the individual committees. This is why Cuba ordered three envoys to leave their diplomatic postings in Paris, Berlin, and Rome to head to Geneva for the duration of the Assembly.[21]

In addition to ambassadorial delegations, nine countries sent ministerial delegations – often led by the foreign minister – to the First Assembly. These delegations were usually closely associated with the government in power in their home country. For instance, Czechoslovakia's delegation included the foreign minister, as well as the Czechoslovak ambassadors to Switzerland and France, and Greece's delegation included the foreign minister alongside the Greek ambassadors to Switzerland and the UK. The delegations of Spain and the Netherlands included a larger entourage including law professors and leading civil servants from the foreign ministry, but the foreign ministers were still the focus of these delegations. In fact, some of the heavy-hitter perennial delegates at the Assembly who amassed more influence in the League that their countries were usually accorded were long-serving European foreign ministers including Belgium's Paul Hymans and Czechoslovakia's Edvard Beneš.[22]

Thus, 29 of the delegations to the first League Assembly were composed similarly to how delegations to the United Nations or international conferences look today; they were made up primarily of foreign ministers, ambassadors, and special envoys. However, 12 Assembly delegations included current or former parliamentarians. For instance, Brazil's delegation was made up of an official from the foreign ministry, an ambassador, and a federal deputy who was serving in the lower house of parliament. This Brazilian parliamentarian already had experience from the Paris Peace Conference, so he was not completely new to this world of international diplomacy. Other delegations were made up entirely of sitting parliamentarians, including Italy's, which consisted of the president of the Senate and the speaker of the Chamber of Deputies. Chairing the meetings of one chamber of a bicameral legislature is not usually seen as a prerequisite for diplomacy, but the Italian government automatically appointed the country's parliamentary leaders as its delegates to the League Assembly.[23]

In a parliamentary system, a sitting government is challenged by an opposition, so a strong indicator of a belief in robust parliamentary involvement and oversight in diplomacy was a national government appointing members of its own parliamentary opposition to represent the country abroad. Among the parliamentary delegations to the First Assembly, four included politicians from political parties that were not represented in the national government. The French delegation included two former prime ministers who were then serving in the French parliament, but whose parties did not back the government in Paris. The 1920 Danish and Swedish delegations had been expressly created to include as wide a political spectrum as possible. The Danish delegation boasted parliamentarians from two left-wing parties that were not represented in the sitting conservative Danish cabinet. The Swedish delegation included two once-and-future prime ministers – one socialist and one conservative – as well as a liberal and an aristocrat, all of whom travelled to Geneva while a caretaker government without party-political backing governed in Stockholm.[24]

During the course of the early 1920s, there was a trend towards more and more Assembly delegations including parliamentarians. This was in keeping with early British and American proposals during the Paris Peace Conference that anticipated national legislators serving in the Assembly. In 1920, twelve delegations – or almost 28 per cent of the total League membership – sent delegations that included parliamentarians to the League's Assembly. By the 1925 Assembly, 23 countries, or over 43 per cent of the total League membership sent delegations that included legislators, and often these particular parliamentary delegates kept returning. For example, Cuba began sending a parliamentarian with the Second Assembly when Cosme de la Torriente was appointed to the delegation by virtue of his position as the chair of the Foreign Relations committee in the Cuban Senate. He was reappointed and was elected president of the League's Fourth Assembly in 1923. Unlike the First Assembly, by the 1925 Assembly, parliamentarians or former parliamentarians came from much further afield with legislators travelling all the way from Cuba, Venezuela, and Uruguay to Geneva.[25]

Although there was a marked increase in the number of parliamentary delegations sent to the League Assembly between 1920 and 1925, not all countries were eager to dispatch opposition parliamentarians. Diplomacy was – and still is – generally the responsibility of the executive, and parliaments had foreign affairs committees that struggled with the cabinet for influence. In the Netherlands, for example, the Dutch socialists and their allied trade unionists called for acknowledgment of "parliament's right to participate in decision-making about the composition of League of Nations delegations." Since the conferences of League of Nations were seen as diplomatically low stakes, the Dutch cabinet was willing to concede some ground here, appointing socialist senators to delegations dispatched to Geneva. All this took place before the Dutch socialists ever joined a national cabinet. Serving at the League of Nations as an opposition parliamentarian was seen by legislators as a way to exert more parliamentary influence on foreign policy. However, inclusion of opposition legislators felt only like a minor concession on the part of a government in power.[26]

Nevertheless, the enthusiasm for dispatching parliamentary delegations to the Assembly waned in the late 1920s and early 1930s. There was first a loss of interest in sending members of the parliamentary opposition to the League Assembly. Britain quickly abandoned the practice after sending a Labour MP representing a Conservative-Liberal ministry to the First Assembly in 1920. Although a conservative Australian cabinet dispatched a cross-party delegation that included a conservative cabinet member along with the Labor leader of the opposition in 1924, there was already pushback from some Australian Labor parliamentarians in 1924, and a similar effort for a cross-party delegation failed in 1926.[27]

Pretty soon the entire practice of sending parliamentary delegates – even representing the governing parties – lost steam. Sometimes there were country-specific concerns. In the case of the United Kingdom, British lawyers discovered that the House of Commons Disqualification Act of 1782 meant that defraying the travel costs of parliamentarians who were not ministers would automatically evict them from Parliament. Creative British bureaucrats were able to "pay actual out-of-pocket expenses in the form of hotel bills," but having to pony up the cash for other expenses made travel by backbenchers less attractive. Despite the idiosyncrasies of a centuries-old British law, the decrease in parliamentary delegates was a widespread phenomenon. In 1932, only 12 of 58 members of the

League dispatched parliamentary delegates who were not simultaneously ministers, and this number included Italy, whose delegates were parliamentarians in a Fascist state. Moreover, far fewer of these parliamentary delegations in 1932 included politicians who represented the opposition. The massive 15-person French delegation included 12 parliamentarians, but they all supported the governing coalition. In 1932, only the Norwegian and Danish delegations still included opposition politicians.[28]

France was one of the last bastions supporting parliamentary representation at the League of Nations. When French Prime Minister André Tardieu decided not to appoint a political delegation to Assembly one year, he was roundly criticized for having "decidedly broken with all traditions" and for displaying "an offhand attitude with regard to the rights of the parliamentary minority to be represented" at the League. However, this widespread pushback was limited to France. Indeed, a French lawyer's 1938 doctoral dissertation on national representation at the League still contended that the "trend favoring the democratization of foreign policy" was ongoing.[29] Despite the hopes of this idealistic Frenchman, by 1938, the League's flirtation with parliamentary delegations was dying. In fact, parliamentary delegations had only a sputtering and limited legacy after the Second World War. The shadow of these early interwar parliamentarian-delegates, however, can be found in holdover traditions like diplomatic delegations from the United States to the United Nations. To this very day, American representatives to the annual sessions of the UN General Assembly include one Republican and one Democratic lawmaker. However, this bipartisan façade does not change the fact that America's executive branch makes the ultimate diplomatic decisions. The question of executive or legislative control of foreign policy had not yet been settled in this interwar era of diplomatic experimentation that brought elected lawmakers to the League as delegates.[30]

Interwar Parliamentarians as Informal Political Travellers on the World's Stage

Although elected parliamentarians served in formal positions at the League of Nations, most of the roles that national legislators played on the international stage were more informal. Sometimes parliamentarians went off on official political junkets or fact-finding missions to other countries. Other times, parliamentarians were used for party-political exchanges, literally campaigning in elections abroad. Reconstructing this lost political world requires piecing together many separate references in personal archives and recollections of politicians from across

Europe. Although these vignettes do not comprehensively reflect this international political past, the volume of references and variety of roles elected politicians held on the interwar international stage proves that there was a contemporary expectation that lawmakers be active beyond their own national capital. Being a national parliamentarian had a transnational element that has been overlooked by scholars.

Part of the increased presence of parliamentarians on the interwar stage was due to a boost in the international mobility of ordinary politicians. The world champions at lengthy travel abroad were Japanese parliamentarians who often strung together a whole series of international visits and foreign conferences. Geography made trips from Japan to Europe or to the Americas particularly onerous, so groups of Japanese politicians would travel on extended junkets abroad. After an annual international or inter-parliamentary meeting in one country in Europe, interwar Japanese parliamentarians would often continue on to other countries to meet colleagues and visit foreign parliaments. Sometimes this took the form of private audiences; this was the case when the British foreign secretary informally met a member of the Japanese House of Peers who was in London for an industrial conference in 1926. However, other times, entire delegations travelled together around Europe, as happened after the 1932 International Labour Conference in Geneva when the Japanese labour delegation, which included a number of parliamentarians, travelled to Brussels and was welcomed into the Belgian parliament. Japanese parliamentary delegations also travelled extensively beyond Europe with visits in the 1920s to Australia and to the United States.[31]

Regular bilateral visits by parliamentarians or legislative officials were common, as is evident in the records of the unassuming interwar Belgian parliament. In addition to the Japanese labour delegation, a 1922 study visit by the clerk of the South African Senate included lengthy discussions about parliamentary procedures. This South African official passed through Brussels to gather information on Belgian rules for dealing with discrepancies in bills passed by each chamber of a bicameral parliament. Insights from Belgium were later used by a South African joint committee to amend that parliament's standing orders. A frequent set of parliamentary visitors to interwar Brussels came from France and Luxembourg. A 1935 visit of the members of the French-Belgian joint parliamentary group was received first at the Royal Palace in Brussels and then greeted by the leadership of both chambers of the Belgian parliament. This same association returned to Brussels in 1937, along with their Luxembourgish colleagues for a day of laying wreaths, receptions, and champagne toasts, as well as a tour of Brussels' famous Grand Place. During the interwar decades, Brussels hosted guests from South Africa, Japan, France, and Luxembourg several times. This international inter-parliamentary world reached even to the legislature of a small European state.[32]

Turning from a small interwar country to a large and supposedly isolationist one, inter-parliamentary ties even extended to the United States. Despite America's absence from the new diplomatic world centred around the League of Nations, during the late 1920s and early 1930s, one particular American was a focal point in these broad international parliamentary networks – Senator William Borah of Idaho. When Borah was the chair of the US Senate Foreign Relations Committee from 1924 to 1933, his private Senate office was a required stop for foreign dignitaries passing through Washington, DC.[33] One of Borah's political biographers has downplayed the senator's international effectiveness: "Endlessly professing his yearning for international co-operation, he opposed every serious effort to bring it about."[34] However, this assessment focused too much on Borah's public fights against the League and against a world court. Borah was still a transnational link on the global diplomatic stage as a correspondent with political leaders around the world.[35]

There were also regional associations that brought parliamentarians together from further afield. The Empire Parliamentary Association assembled parliamentarians from across the British Empire for regular conferences. In 1924, South Africa hosted parliamentary delegations from Britain, Canada, Newfoundland, New Zealand, and Australia. The juxtaposition of diplomacy and sociability was evident in combining fact-finding junkets and train travel across southern Africa. Witty headlines in the Australian press like "Parliamentary Tourists" and "A Parliamentary Picnic: Jaunt to South Africa" underhandedly criticized politicians' trans-imperial travel as an unnecessary perk of the legislative job. As more British colonies attained self-governing status, parliamentarians from more locations attended. When Canada hosted the Empire Parliamentary Association's conference in 1928, MPs attended from the UK, Australia, New Zealand, South Africa, the Irish Free State, Newfoundland, India, Malta, and Southern Rhodesia. These lawmakers spent three months travelling throughout Canada, stopping for conferences in Ottawa, Toronto, Edmonton, and Victoria, while discussing issues with both federal and provincial Canadian legislators as they moved across the country. Although it would be too bold to claim that the Empire Parliamentary Association and its ilk radically reshaped interwar parliamentary politics, three-month trips abroad shaped the calendars of lawmakers and, most importantly, put local legislators in touch with worldwide colleagues.[36]

The Transnational Party-Political Ties
of Interwar Lawmakers

International party-political ties were historically associated with social-ists who had channelled the famous slogan "Workers of the world, unite!" into international organizations from the middle of the nineteenth century. By the interwar years, two competing international associa-tions hoisted this left-wing red banner aloft on the global stage: a more moderate Labour and Socialist International and the Moscow-based Communist Comintern. The historian of nationalism Stefan Berger has read the moderate socialists of the Labour and Socialist International as abandoning real global commitments for mere internationalist "lip service," but this discounts the socialists' transnational links. There were deep connections among individual socialist legislators, and these con-nections could be called on across national borders for party-political purposes.[37]

Leading socialists travelled around Europe on their vacations, to con-ferences, and in the course of their parliamentary business. When local party groups learned that foreign socialists were in town, they often tried to convince the foreign guests to drop by, and these invitations are sprin-kled throughout the personal papers of interwar socialist legislators. For example, when the German Communist-turned-socialist Paul Levi trav-elled to Czechoslovakia, he was asked by the German-speaking socialist student group to address them. When the Austrian socialist Karl Renner attended the 1926 meeting of the International Co-operative Alliance in Hamburg, he planned a return trip via Berlin so he could speak at three different local socialist events in the German capital. Renner's fel-low Austrian socialist Julius Deutsch travelled to Oslo for an international socialist sporting event, and the Norwegian party members arranged additional speaking engagements for him in the country. Often, these international party-political events were tacked onto non-party-political travel. For instance, to complement a non-socialist speech at a republi-can association in Latvia in 1929, Paul Löbe arranged political visits to socialist groups in Tallinn and Riga. To the average European socialist supporter who attended regular party events, these travelling socialist parliamentarians would have left the impression that the socialist move-ment was deeply international. To the socialist political elite, these trips helped create networks that stretched across the continent.[38]

These socialist ties were particularly close across German-speaking Central Europe, especially among the countries of the former Habsburg Empire. German-speaking socialists of Czechoslovakia and Austria sent official party delegates to the other party's congresses. The social democratic parliamentarians in Prague sent their parliamentary activity reports to Vienna and tried to keep their party programs aligned. In fact, this cross-border local co-operation could even incorporate Czech- and Slovak-speaking socialists alongside German-speaking ones. For example, after the Labour and Socialist International encouraged national parties to focus on disarmament in October and November 1930, the Austrian socialists coordinated with Czechoslovak socialists – German, Czech, and Slovak speakers – to hold joint rallies in the border towns of Gmünd/ Cmunt in Austria and Bratislava/Preßburg in Czechoslovakia. In this way, close regional relationships in Central Europe were nurtured during the interwar years, so that new borders after the First World War were not impermeable in the political minds of European socialists.[39]

There was even more extensive European socialist co-operation during election campaigns. In the run-up to the 1927 Austrian Nationalrat elections, the Viennese socialist party planned a massive socialist sports competition that would transition into an election rally with 30,000 to 40,000 participants. The leading German socialist and ex-chancellor Hermann Müller travelled to Vienna for a keynote speech at the sports event and then remained in the country for additional rallies that were prominently advertised on the front page of Vienna's *Arbeiter-Zeitung*. Socialists from Germany, Austria, and the German-speaking parts of Czechoslovakia were all in high demand during election season, travelling around as if they were part of the same political community.[40] Members of the local branch of the Sozialdemokratische Partei Deutschlands (Social Democratic Party of Germany, SPD) in Schleswig-Holstein appealed to the Austrian Julius Deutsch so often, they humorously began a letter in 1930: "You'll definitely be surprised to hear from us out of the blue; you probably are thinking: 'Yeah, I bet the folks up in Kiel have just one more thing to ask.'"[41] During the 1928 Reichstag elections, the Austrian socialist Karl Renner spent 20 days in Germany travelling and campaigning across the country – from Aachen and Cologne to Selb and Munich. During the 1930 elections, Renner was back for two weeks of campaigning in southern Germany.[42] During the 1925 parliamentary elections in Czechoslovakia, the Austrian SDAP – a political party in a neighbouring country – helped arrange travel for both Austrian and three émigré Hungarian socialists who wandered around Czechoslovakia as itinerant election speakers. No election was too small for seeking this kind of external support; the SPD in Saxony reached out to Vienna for Saxon legislative elections, and the German socialist member of the Reichstag Maria Reese travelled to Lower Austria for local elections there in 1929.[43]

Socialist electioneering in Germany even got a boost from outside the German-speaking world when the British Labour Party sent help during the German Reichstag elections of July 1932. "Red" Ellen Wilkinson, an MP who would later become known throughout the United Kingdom for her role with the 1936 Jarrow Crusade of unemployed men marching to London, travelled to the continent to campaign with her German comrades. Wilkinson brought with her a letter of support from the British union movement and the Labour Party: "We have watched with deep concern the menacing advance of your enemies, who are the enemies of us all. [...] It is you, our German comrades, who will bear the brunt of that attack. You are fighting not only the battle of the German workers, but our battle – the battle of Socialism the world over." Wilkinson's visit demonstrated that the German national election was understood in international terms by socialists abroad, even beyond the German-speaking world.[44]

However, there was not only a warm and fuzzy international world of moderate socialists campaigning in each other's elections; there was also backroom international friction. In 1928, the German SPD had won a plurality in the national election, which the socialists had fought with the slogan "Meals for Kids instead of Battlecruisers!" When the socialist Hermann Müller then became chancellor, the SPD had to bow to wishes of its new coalition partners and permit the construction of a new armoured battleship. The news of the SPD's about-face and subsequent German naval expansion was used as a cudgel to attack socialists elsewhere in Europe. The leader of the Dutch socialists wrote a lengthy letter to Chancellor Müller in which he described Dutch Communist tactics: "When we held a number of demonstrations for disarmament [...] the streets were all decorated with giant drawings of battleships!" Similarly, the French socialists wrote to Müller pointing out that when they campaigned to remove French soldiers from the Rhineland, their French political opponents pointed to the new German battlecruiser as evidence of a dangerous uptick in Teutonic militarism. Ultimately, this episode revealed the tension between socialist goals in government and socialist goals on the campaign trail. As chancellor, Müller could not only think of the good of his party or of the socialist movement across Europe. He implored his foreign socialist colleagues to think pragmatically: "You must understand that at the very least the majority of the German people – and we live in a country ruled by parliament – would not support just firing these marines or instead using them to peel potatoes." The sailors had to be employed, the ship had to be built, and the SPD had to govern. These transnational political networks, even among socialists, were limited by the realities of governing.[45]

Socialists were not the only politicians involved in party-political European co-operation or electioneering across national borders.

Bourgeois, Catholic, and even conservative nationalist parties dabbled in this international political realm. For instance, from the 1920s, there were international organizations created for various strands of liberal and conservative parties. In 1925, an International of Christian Democratic Parties (International des Partis Démocratiques d'Inspiration Chrétienne) was set up with a secretariat in Paris to bring together European politicians who held to a Christian – often a Roman Catholic – tendency in their politics. European politicians who were active in the Catholic Church had transnational connections with co-religionists. For instance, the German Catholic Centre Party parliamentarian Friedrich Dessauer had strong ties to France where he participated in French Catholic gatherings and made a point of meeting French politicians. In 1932, Dessauer used these connections to French Catholic politicians to relay messages that were designed to promote a thaw in Franco-German relations. Dessauer had a similarly rich set of Catholic connections that passed through the Vatican, which meant that when trips sent him to international conferences in Rome, he mingled with Catholic ministers from other countries and relayed messages and connections back to his German compatriots.[46]

In addition to the transnational ties of Catholic politicians, in 1924, an International Alliance of Democratic and Radical Parties (Entente internationale des partis radicaux et des partis démocratiques similaires) was founded in Geneva as the brainchild of the centre-left French Radical party. Over time, this Alliance expanded to include liberal parties from 16 European countries, ranging from Spain to Turkey. Its annual conferences took place in locations like Boulogne-sur-Mer, Copenhagen, Karlsruhe, Paris, and London. The meetings' agendas paired a topic related to parliamentary government, such as election reform or party structure, with other burning political issues of the day. Rather than coming to a uniform policy standpoint, the various parliamentarians were provided with an opportunity to speak from their liberal viewpoint to a like-minded European audience. As with all of these international events, the Alliance's conferences promoted behind-the-scenes conversations among participants. For instance, in 1931, a left-liberal member of the Reichstag reported his experiences at the annual Alliance conference in Athens to the German Foreign Office. He dutifully relayed confidential information as well as rumours he heard from French centrist colleagues about changes to French foreign policy.[47]

Even German nationalist parliamentarians created a formal right-wing, pan-German international network. The Working Group of German Parliamentarians (Arbeitsgemeinschaft deutscher Parlamentarier) was founded in Linz, Austria, in November 1921. Members included both the right-liberal German People's Party (Deutsche Volkspartei, DVP) and more conservative German National People's Party (Deutschnationale Volkspartei, DNVP) from Germany, the Greater German People's Party (Großdeutsche Volkspartei, GDVP) from Austria, and German minority parties from Czechoslovakia, Danzig/Gdańsk, Romania, South Tyrol, Yugoslavia, and Poland. This group met for off-the-record conferences. At its very first meeting, the group worked to align party policies to be as similar as possible to favour German minority rights. Annual gatherings included discussions on general political topics, including economic issues, food distribution, and the "reform of parliamentarism." This international working group aimed to counter the more republican support of German minority groups abroad by yoking these minority politicians to more conservative Austrian and German political parties.[48]

From at least 1919, German and Austrian right-wing German nationalist parties also developed international political ties between parliamentarians in both countries. The pan-German GDVP has traditionally been seen as within the third camp of Austrian politics, which was outside the two larger competing blocs of the Austrian socialists and conservative Christian Socials. Internationally, the GDVP partnered with two heavyweight parties on the German right, the DNVP and DVP. In 1919, the GDVP arranged a summer speaking tour to Vienna of a DNVP parliamentarian who planned pro-Anschluss, right-wing speeches geared towards the liberal middle class in Austria. Like the German-speaking socialists exchanging speakers for their party congresses, the GDVP also dispatched annual delegations to the party conferences of the DNVP and, slightly less frequently, to DVP meetings in Germany. This internationalism of interwar parliamentarians was not merely a left-wing project, but a commitment of nationalist and conservatives across Central Europe, who embodied the "reactionary cosmopolitanism" that David Motadel identified in this period.[49]

The Political and Personal Benefits of Continental Parliamentary Connections

Interwar parliamentarians experienced the transnational sociability of this continent of colleagues everywhere from cocktail receptions during the League of Nations Assembly to hotel restaurants in Czechoslovak spa towns.[50] These international parliamentary connections could sometimes be fleeting, but on other occasions, they developed into lasting friendships. In an era where some scholars have imagined countries turning inward and being internationally isolated, parliamentarians were crisscrossing borders to campaign for politicians abroad; they thought of themselves in political communities that stretched beyond any one domestic context.[51] Most importantly, parliamentarians could and did cash in on these European connections for personal and political gain. Here a myriad of examples – from legislators ensuring treaties were ratified to helping ex-lawmakers get out of prison – can be mustered to prove that these transnational ties resulted in concrete actions. Although this may seem like a parade of vignettes, these are radical in that they link the transnational element of interwar parliamentary culture to political decision-making in specific ways.

International parliamentary travel, inter-personal connections, and concrete benefits all came together in an undated letter from the German liberal Walter Schücking to the centre-left French parliamentarian and minister Édouard Herriot. Schücking's letter to Herriot referenced a friendly conversation the two men had at an international inter-parliamentary reception and then moved on to Herriot's work on Franco-German reconciliation: "Along with your compatriots in Paris, at the time all people of goodwill in the entire world cheered 'Vive Herriot!' They still cheer that today." After such cloying and effusive praise, Schücking turned to something he needed. A German school director from Frankfurt who was a close friend of Schücking's was in Paris and could not get permission to observe classes in French schools. Knowing that Herriot was inclined towards rapprochement with Germany, Schücking vouched for this travelling German as a republican and a pacifist. This pairing of a fond memory and flattery with a personal request suggests how this international social network could work. Letters of introduction were crucial, and doors were opened based on who went to bat for you. These kinds of personal favours were common in a national context among political colleagues, and they existed on the international stage too, as can be seen with Schücking and Herriot.[52]

Walther Schücking has been a compelling figure for historians to analyze as an internationalist of the 1920s and 1930s. Schücking was a professor of international law, later a judge on the Permanent Court of International Justice, and a frequent nominee for the Nobel Peace Prize. Schücking has been identified as a "transnational technocrat" for his role in expert networks in the world of international law. Isabella Löhr has argued that Schücking's networks point to the larger "law community" of which Schücking was a transnational member. This is, of course, true, but Schücking was also a long-serving German Democratic Party (Deutsche Demokratische Partei) parliamentarian in the Reichstag. He wore many hats, but his interaction with Herriot was based on an inter-parliamentary rendezvous, which was a connection rooted in Schücking's Reichstag service. In the myriad of international networks in which transnational actors like Schücking moved, serving as a law-maker could open even more international doors. A memorial edition of the German internationalist periodical *Die Friedens-Warte* dedicated to Schücking's life included contributions on Schücking's legal career, but it also included articles on Schücking as a parliamentarian penned by a political rival and on Schücking's inter-parliamentary work written by a Norwegian colleague. Schücking's parliamentary and inter-parliamentary activities were seen as key parts of his legacy at his death but have been forgotten by scholars today who emphasize only Schücking's legal background.[53]

Sometimes these border-crossing requests from foreign parliamentarians could become far more convoluted than requesting a letter of introduction. For instance, in the summer of 1927, Valentino Pittoni, a former Habsburg-era socialist parliamentarian from Trieste, who had moved to Vienna after the First World War, was concerned for a family member. Pittoni's son had remained in Italy and had adopted the false name Vittorio Tosoni to protect himself from retribution for the anti-Italian and anti-Fascist politics of his father. Tosoni worked for a German-owned Siemens factory in Milan and had come to Berlin for further training before his planned return to Italy. There was growing concern that Tosoni would be arrested by the Italian Fascists because of his father's political activities. The Austrian socialist parliamentarian Wilhelm Ellenbogen reached out directly to Hermann Müller, the German SPD leader and former German chancellor, to see if he could intervene with the Siemens company to find a permanent space for Tosoni outside Italy.[54]

By letter from Vienna, Hermann Müller was entrusted with the life-or-death situation of the Italian son of a socialist anti-Fascist. Strictly speaking, this was a personal rather than political concern, but Müller quickly stepped up to see what he could do. Müller's Viennese socialist friends did not divulge Tosoni's Berlin address, so the former chancellor had to play detective to track down Tosoni. With his strong socialist union bona fides, Müller reached out to the trade union steward for the Siemens factories to find Tosoni. The deputized steward took a while to locate the errant Italian, but when he was located, the Italian was said to be "very anxious" about his future. The steward advocated for Tosoni to the management, but the responsible factory director was travelling and could not intervene before the planned transfer of Vittorio Tosoni back to Fascist Italy.

Hermann Müller then racked his brains for whom he knew working for the Siemens company who could protect the Italian Tosoni. Müller ultimately went straight for the head of the whole company, writing directly to Carl Friedrich von Siemens himself. Müller realized how odd it was that he, the leader of the German socialists, was appealing to a pre-eminent capitalist – "In turning to you today with an issue that is only peripheral to politics, I do so with great personal reluctance" – but Müller was desperate. Müller had served with Siemens in the Reichstag, and Siemens had invited Müller to dinner in the past. Müller was banking on this personal connection to save Tosoni.[55] Later correspondence indicates that Müller's pleas were successful. Wilhelm Ellenbogen, the Austrian socialist who asked for this intervention, planned to travel to Müller's electoral constituency to deliver "a spirited oration on 'Richard Wagner and the Proletariat' to the voters as thanks for your gallantry." In the end, international relationships between Austria, Italy, and Germany, as well as Müller's personal relationship with a former Reichstag colleague, ensured a positive outcome that kept an endangered Italian out of Mussolini's clutches.[56]

Just as Müller's international intervention took place against the backdrop of potential persecution, personal-political international connections among lawmakers were often called on to help those who were imprisoned in other countries. For example, a German-speaking Czechoslovak parliamentarian was allowed to visit the socialist former legislator Gabriele Proft when she was a political prisoner in Austria.[57] In Germany, when the wife and 21-month-old child of the former German socialist member of the Reichstag Gerhart Seger were imprisoned by the Nazi regime in 1934, a British Labour peer pressed the German government on the issue when he visited Berlin. Eventually, a female Tory MP stepped in to negotiate the release and secure safe passage for Seger's wife and child to Great Britain.[58] When the Austrian socialist leader Karl Renner was jailed in Austria, the US Senator Smith W. Brookhart wrote supportively to him: "[I]t is hard for an American to realize that any government would be autocratic and foolish enough to put you in jail. I want to extend to you the hope that you will soon be released and your broad and humane ideas will again triumph in your country." Brookhart's letter of support – which he knew would be read by the Austrian prison censor – came along with letters from Renner's high-ranking socialist colleagues and ministers from Belgium and Czechoslovakia. This correspondence indicated to the Austrian officials that Renner's case had not been forgotten abroad.[59]

However, not all international parliamentary favours were about saving friends or family from persecution or improving conditions of imprisonment. Many of these exchanges involved shaping political outcomes, and this was true especially among socialists who called in favours among comrades abroad. In 1932, the German-speaking socialist Ludwig Czech was the Czechoslovak minister of social affairs when he wrote to an Austrian socialist politician asking for help in speeding up approval of a bilateral social security treaty. Czech encouraged his Austrian socialist comrade to intervene with Viennese officials and trade unionists. Minister Czech also emphasized the importance of discretion: "I also must request that in your discussions you do not refer to me or to our correspondence, since any communication between your and our social welfare ministries – even related to social administration questions – should be passed through the foreign ministry."[60] Czech was using his personal socialist connections to Austria for the Czechoslovak state's political gain. This was a common behind-the-scenes practice; Belgium's socialist leader Émile Vandervelde did the same thing. Vandervelde wrote twice to socialists in Sweden asking for specific political favours, including ratifying two treaties on the harmonization of international maritime law.[61]

In 1930, socialist members of the Reichstag were deputized for particularly circuitous international communication when German national interests were at stake. Negotiations that could have led to a restructuring of German reparation payments were on the table in the French Chamber of Deputies. The German ambassador in Paris had reached out to André Tardieu, the conservative French prime minister, and Tardieu revealed he was likely to lose the parliamentary vote without support from the socialists and the centre-left French Radicals. The German Foreign Office wanted to reach out to the leaders of these parties directly to lobby them, but the German officials determined that "contact with both or either of them by [the German ambassador] would be problematic. However, some other parliamentary or personal connection could be used." The German foreign minister then asked Chancellor Hermann Müller to find socialist members of the Reichstag who might have better luck informally reaching out to French parliamentarians. Müller rejected the idea of sending German politicians directly to Paris in case that turned into a public relations fiasco, but the leader of the SPD in the Reichstag privately contacted two French socialists who approached the leader of the French Radicals with confidential information from the German government. German socialist parliamentarians, thus, built on long-standing international ties to lobby French socialists on behalf of a foreign government.[62]

In a particularly complex use of political friendships, the Belgian socialist leader Émile Vandervelde reached out to the leader of the French socialists, Léon Blum, with concerns about a rally that was to take place in Basècles, a Belgian town close to the French border. Vandervelde served in the Belgian cabinet at the time, so he was in the position of being both a government official and socialist leader when writing to

Blum.[63] The Belgian communists were planning a "Grand International Protest against War and Fascism" with speakers from both France and Belgium coming to the Walloon town.[64] The socialist minister of justice in Belgium had learned that hundreds of French Communists were planning to attend and potentially disrupt this event. Belgium's justice minister deputized Vandervelde to contact Blum and learn about the French Communists' plans. Vandervelde asked Blum to reach out to his Communist parliamentary colleagues to see if they could be dissuaded from attending the rally in Wallonia. This request eventually involved two Belgian socialist ministers asking the leader of the French socialists in the parliamentary opposition in France to contact a specific French Communist parliamentarian about a future demonstration in Belgium.[65] Ultimately, the event went ahead with the French Communist speaker but without the disruption that had been anticipated by the Belgian government.[66]

To the public, all this behind-the-scenes international co-operation and lobbying among politicians could look like untoward international collusion. Political opponents could use the mere allegation of an international conspiracy as rhetorical ammunition against their rivals. This happened in November 1933 when the conservative press in Austria used a speech in the Dutch parliament to attack Austrian social democrats. By the fall of 1933, Austria had slumped into Austro-Fascist authoritarianism with the parliament permanently shut down.[67] In the Netherlands, the Dutch socialist leader attempted to stall approval of a League of Nations loan to Austria with passionate speeches that condemned Austria as a dictatorship "on the threshold of civil war."[68] The conservative Viennese press accused the Austrian socialists of colluding with the Dutch social democrats for this anti-Austrian rhetorical campaign.[69] One right-wing Viennese newspaper's headline read: "New Austromarxist High Treason Scandal." The Austrian press alleged that Austrian socialists were providing secret documents to the Dutch: "In no other country in the world would it be possible for party leaders who blatantly conspire with foreigners against the interests and economy of their country to be tolerated as party leaders or even to remain free out of prison."[70] When the Dutch socialist leader learned of this right-wing journalistic smear, he wrote to the top Austrian diplomat in the Netherlands, citing the page numbers from the minutes of the Austrian parliament in the Tweede Kamer's library as proof that there was no untoward international collusion: "I declare with absolute certainty that my Austrian friends did not offer or give me any information from confidential discussions in any way whatsoever and that I would not have even wished for this kind of material."[71] Although the scandal died down in the Austrian press, this kerfuffle demonstrated how allegations of helping friends abroad could be twisted into a whiff of treasonous collusion.[72]

Collusion during elections by agents of another country would seem to be especially noxious, but private consultations about elections in other states were actually part of this interwar transnational world. As a professor pioneering the medical uses of X-rays and a German Catholic Centre party member of the Reichstag, Friedrich Dessauer straddled both an academic world in Frankfurt and the political world in Berlin. In January 1932, while at the university in Frankfurt, Dessauer was introduced by a colleague to César Chabrun. Chabrun was a French law professor and centrist parliamentarian visiting Frankfurt on an academic trip. Chabrun and Dessauer spoke at length about politics, including about the possibilities of French and German reproachment through the prescient idea of a "customs union." This 1932 private meeting at the university in Frankfurt focused primarily on German reparations. Chabrun proposed a secret meeting of Catholic Centre Party politicians and leading French politicians in Frankfurt, Paris, or Luxembourg to work towards private agreement to smoothe the path towards ending reparations.[73]

During the subsequent two-round German presidential election that the incumbent Paul von Hindenburg won against Adolf Hitler in 1932, Friedrich Dessauer continued to be the private conduit to French parliamentarians like Chabrun. The spring of 1932 included a series of important German and French elections ranging from the German presidential election to state elections in Bavaria, Württemberg, Hamburg, Anhalt, and Prussia – not to mention the French parliamentary election in early May. Elections could be a moment of jingoistic rhetoric, but both German and French politicians wanted to avoid speeches or statements during these elections that would tie the hands of the politicians afterwards when they were looking for possibilities for diplomatic rapprochement, particular in suspending German reparation payments.[74]

In secret, Dessauer coordinated with French politicians including Édouard Herriot to vet campaign language on reparations and Franco-German relations that would be circulated in both countries to guide election propaganda. Dessauer ultimately sent the approved language to leading German socialists as well as French Radicals[75]:

Whenever touching on the question of reparations and other topics that relate to foreign policy during the election, it must be said in no uncertain terms that we have learned that reparation payments are completely impossible and that resuming them, even at a later date, would delay – if not prevent – straightening out this economic crisis. In all this, any expression should be avoided that could be construed to make it seem that Germany wants to wantonly rip up the treaties it has signed. Germany desires to comply with signed treaties. However, insofar as agreements have been made that are impossible to execute in this postwar situation, the treaties must be revised.[76]

On the one hand, this statement would seem natural to guide the talking points of political candidates; however, in this particular case, it was circulated among both the socialists and Catholic Centre party in Germany, as well as among French politicians, including Herriot, who was soon destined to be the prime minister of France. The future leader of another country literally had a hand in drafting talking points for a neighbouring country's election.[77]

German and French voters were presented with talking points that were crafted in a foreign capital. Rather than being forged in an open and honest domestic political debate, a rarefied trusting international environment among parliamentary intermediaries yielded the approved language that was presented to voters. Although this might feel undemocratic, it worked. These secret negotiations tamped down rhetoric enough to enable international agreement on suspending German reparations payments at the Lausanne Conference in June and July 1932. However, by early June 1932, Heinrich Brüning, the German chancellor who had tacitly agreed to collaborate with the French behind the scenes via his parliamentary colleague Dessauer, had been replaced by the more authoritarian Franz von Papen as chancellor. Toned-down French and German election rhetoric meant that Germany sorted out its reparations problem, but the slide towards the Germany's democratic abyss only sped up with Papen's installation.[78]

Ramsay MacDonald's Expansive International Socialist and Parliamentary Networks

By the end of his life, Ramsay MacDonald's own political party thought of him as a villain, despite the fact he had made history as the first Labour prime minister of the United Kingdom. Born in the north of Scotland, MacDonald was the illegitimate son of a farm labourer and domestic servant. He dabbled in Liberal and then in more radical politics as a young man, eventually helping to found the British Labour Party. He won a seat in the House of Commons in 1909 and rose through the ranks of Labour's leadership to become the leader of the parliamentary party in 1911. MacDonald's own pacifism and opposition to the First World War brought about his fall from grace and the loss of his parliamentary seat in 1918.

Undaunted, MacDonald returned to the Commons in 1922 rising again to become leader of the opposition. In 1924, he formed a minority Labour government, becoming the first prime minister from the working-class party. Although MacDonald's first ministry only lasted nine months, he returned as prime minister in 1929. However, because of tension within his Labour Cabinet in 1931 about reducing public benefits during the Great Depression, MacDonald ditched the majority of the Labour party to form a new coalition government supported by the Conservatives, Liberals, and a rump Labour faction. MacDonald soon called a general election that his new National Government handily won by decimating the Labour party, which expelled MacDonald. A bitter and ailing MacDonald remained the prime ministerial figurehead of a Conservative-dominated National government until 1935.[79]

Between 1918 and 1922, Ramsay MacDonald was out of Parliament and had more time on his hands that he used to travel around on behalf of international socialist causes. In 1920, for instance, MacDonald partnered with a French socialist for a trip through Switzerland and Italy to talk up a new moderate socialist international organization. Sometimes MacDonald even ventured further afield as during his 1920 trip to the newly (and only briefly) independent Georgia as a member of an international socialist study commission. Another especially adventurous trip was to Egypt in 1922 during a wave of anti-British sentiment, followed by a side venture to Palestine to meet Jewish social democrats. More often than not, however, MacDonald's travel was to more official socialist conferences and to large international socialist events. When the Danish Social Democrats were celebrating the 50th anniversary of their party's founding in 1921, MacDonald and other leading European socialists were all on the invitation list. This three-day gathering in Copenhagen included several sessions at Christiansborg Palace, a reception at the city hall, a procession with speeches, and an international socialist conference.[80]

One might object that MacDonald's years sojourning around the world as an apostle of socialism slowed when he regained a seat in the House of Commons, so he should not be considered someone who forged his international connections while officially a parliamentarian. However, MacDonald continued to travel to international socialist conferences and maintain connections with his comrades abroad after he rejoined the House of Commons, and these socialist ties persisted into his two stints as prime minister. Sometimes MacDonald's foreign friends even called on him in the UK. When two socialist ministers from Belgium came to London to confer with Conservative British ministers, MacDonald, who was not in government at the time, set up a private walk through an exhibition of Flemish art to chat with these friends while they were in town.[81]

After his first period as prime minister in 1924, MacDonald's European network expanded to include more non-socialist politicians. During visits to Prague, MacDonald was always invited to lengthy meetings and receptions with the Czechoslovak president and foreign minister, neither of whom were socialists.[82] MacDonald's trips to Paris also attracted the interest of a wider swath of the political spectrum. In 1925, a dinner was given in MacDonald's honour by the then president of the French Chamber of Deputies Édouard Herriot. Herriot, who was a member of the centre-left Radical Party, invited leading French socialists and Radicals to the event.[83] In 1928, MacDonald returned to Paris to give a speech on "The Labour Party, its activities at home, and its international policy." This event was attended by the presidents of both chambers of the French parliament, as well as a broad range of leftist and moderate politicians. MacDonald was so popular on this visit to Paris that Léon Blum, then the leader of the French socialists, had a hard time getting onto MacDonald's busy schedule.[84]

Throughout MacDonald's European travels in the 1920s, few places attracted him as much as Berlin. MacDonald had been a frequent guest of the German socialists even before the First World War, and he frequently made a point to visit Berlin before or after a trip anywhere else on the continent. Although there were more direct routes from London to Copenhagen, MacDonald planned his trip to the 1921 Danish socialist party anniversary festivities via Berlin. The year before, MacDonald travelled to a conference in Geneva via Berlin where he watched a debate in the Reichstag.[85] On a 1920 visit to the city, MacDonald even had time to give an interview to a *Vorwärts* socialist newspaper editor in support of democratic socialism, in which he claimed that "[s]ocialism without democracy is an impossibility. The revolution could usher in dictatorship, but the dictatorship of the proletariat is ultimately no better than the dictatorship of the aristocracy." MacDonald made the front page.[86]

MacDonald's experiences confirm that Berlin had become a cosmopolitan centre of moderate socialism during the 1920s. He often coordinated his visits to Berlin to overlap with Belgian or other foreign socialist colleagues, who spent evenings together with socialist members of the Reichstag. MacDonald trusted his Berlin networks enough to send along personal letters of introduction for his Labour party comrades who were passing through the German city. MacDonald became so busy during his visits to Berlin that during a short 1928 trip when he intended to meet numerous friends in the Reichstag, the socialist German chancellor Hermann Müller had to personally encourage MacDonald to meet the

Figure 3.1. Ramsay MacDonald in conversation with luminaries from academia and politics in interwar Berlin, August 1931.

Source: From bpk Bildagentur / Photographer: Erich Salomon, Art Resource, NY.

British ambassador who was very anxious for an appointment and was afraid MacDonald would otherwise be occupied.[87]

Ramsay MacDonald's international political life was far more than an MP's pastime during parliamentary recesses or the simple window dressing of interwar sociability. MacDonald believed that nurturing these international connections would not only advance the cause of socialism but also help like-minded politicians govern. These hopes seemed to be realized when MacDonald's good friend Hermann Müller was serving as the German chancellor when MacDonald became British prime minister for the second time in 1929. Müller sent MacDonald a private letter congratulating him, to which MacDonald earnestly replied: "As you know, one of my greatest desires is to help to leave peace behind me as the contribution which this generation makes to civilization. This, I am convinced, can be done only by the co-operation of all [...] As was yours, this is of course a personal & not a governmental letter, but I too rejoice that at this moment we should both hold the positions we do. We can help best in that way." More than sappy language, MacDonald was convinced that this personal network was something he could call on during his tenure leading the British government.[88]

Similarly, MacDonald's German friends also felt that their personal relationship to the British prime minister should have concrete results, but they were later tragically disappointed. MacDonald's abandonment of his foreign comrades for pragmatic political reasons was poignantly illustrated in a letter from October 1933 to MacDonald sent by the German SPD former parliamentarian Otto Wels who had been exiled from Nazi Germany. MacDonald had recently reacted publicly to an unsuccessful attempt on the life of the authoritarian Austrian chancellor Engelbert Dollfuß, and Wels viciously attacked MacDonald:

> Why do you not express your shock about the thousands of murders, the unspeakable torment and the expulsions, the hunger and the hardship suffered by millions of people in Germany, who saw in MacDonald, their former party comrade, a high-spirted, warm-hearted person [...] Does the attack on the life of the world, on socialism and democracy, the Magna Carta of your own people, not matter to you at all?

Wels was "conscious of our many years of work for a common cause," and he obviously felt betrayed by the British prime minister, whose own aide pointed out in writing that "the inhumanity of the concentration camps has been a proven horror for over 6 months, and that you have made no public allusion to it." MacDonald's staff believed that Wels' letter might be enough to move the prime minister to bring up the issue at the next Cabinet meeting. Although Germany was a topic at that next British Cabinet meeting, it was discussed only in terms of new proposals for disarmament. MacDonald did not bring up the mistreatment of his socialist friends.[89]

Interwar Diplomatic Experimentation and the Transnational Agency of Legislators

After the guns of the First World War fell silent, the internationalisms developed during the nineteenth and early twentieth centuries seemed to be riding high. Imbued with new energy from the Paris Peace Conference and the nascent League of Nations system, a hodgepodge cast of characters in the form of engineers, colonialists, bankers, and other technocrats were inspired by this invigorated internationalist spirit. This realignment within global diplomacy was paired with a rethinking of national parliamentary control of foreign affairs. After all, Central Europe's toppled old regimes had often empowered the executive – whether kaiser or chancellor – over the legislature, and those regimes had tragically propelled the continent into a cataclysmic war. This led to experimenting with including representatives of the people, namely elected parliamentarians, in the world of foreign diplomacy as a check on the executive. Even opposition lawmakers were dispatched to the Assembly of the League of Nations in a grand diplomatic experiment to add national lawmakers to the transnational actors of the era.

Beyond the League of Nations, parliamentarians criss-crossed Europe forging under-the-radar connections on their fact-finding junkets and international election campaign trips. On the one hand, this chapter's many vignettes of travelling parliamentarians – whether they came from Belgium, from Japan, or beyond – might seem like a superficial historical curiosity. However, corresponding examples depict how these international connections could then be called on to ensure a treaty was ratified, election manifestos were coordinated, or political prisoners were released from jail. A scholar cannot go to the archives of international political collusion to find all these accounts; they are rare and only fleetingly preserved. However, the sheer number of examples demonstrates that many interwar parliamentarians understood their roles as having a transnational component that extended far beyond their own country. Most importantly, when used for political favours, these international parliamentary connections shaped national political decision-making. "Parliamentary diplomacy" could sometimes merge with pork-barrel politics and international electioneering. This transnational space for parliamentarians ultimately provided some behind-the-scenes agency on the international stage for legislators that was beyond the reach of the national executive.[90]

Ultimately, Ramsay MacDonald encapsulates both the interwar promise and the limits of these international networks. MacDonald had been seeped in socialist internationalism, and he travelled across Europe connecting with and supporting left-wing colleagues. After serving as Britain's first Labour prime minister in 1924, MacDonald's European networks became even more politically inclusive. When MacDonald returned to 10 Downing Street in 1929, he reached out to more foreign leaders, including Hermann Müller in Germany who he trusted because of a long-standing transnational friendship.[91] MacDonald's socialist comrades abroad later felt that these international connections would ensure that MacDonald spoke against the rising tide of authoritarianism in Adolf Hitler's Germany and Dollfuß's Austria. MacDonald's silence reflected the limits of these networks. International parliamentary connections paid off with information exchange, through advocacy by foreign colleagues, in coordinating election messaging, and even for personal gain. Neither historians nor political scientists should overlook parliamentarians on the global stage. However, these interwar transnational ties did not guarantee that a continent of parliamentary colleagues stood up for democratic values against the rising tide of authoritarianism.

Chapter Four

The Inter-Parliamentary Union, International Parliamentary Commercial Conference, and Interwar Parliamentary Democracy

"Yet another International?" Full of biting skepticism, this rhetorical question opened a 1935 Nazi news report on an inter-parliamentary conference. Politicians from around the world had met in Brussels for the annual meeting of the Inter-Parliamentary Union to discuss ways of promoting worldwide co-operation among elected lawmakers. Reporting in the Third Reich panned this entire endeavour, pointing out that parliaments were themselves as antiquated and out of date as the French Revolution. The most vitriol was heaped on these representatives' international aspirations: "At the end of the age of 'Internationals' yet another creature of internationalism takes the stage. Added to the existing manifestations of supranational forces like the Second (Socialist) International, the Third (Communist) International, the International of Freemasonry, among others, now a Parliamentary International wants to join the show." Condemning elected parliaments to the dustbin of history, this Nazi report predicted that no internationalist aspirations among elected parliamentarians could prevent democractic legislators' slide into total irrelevance.[1]

This fiery fascist critique of parliamentary internationalism appeared decades after elected politicians began building their own global inter-parliamentary movements. The Inter-Parliamentary Union (IPU) and the International Parliamentary Commercial Conference (Conférence parlementaire internationale du commerce, CPIC) were on the inter-parliamentary vanguard with missions to bring parliamentarians together across national borders in the period between the world wars. Although both organizations began focused on Europe, they worked on outreach to become more global during the interwar years. These two associations competed with each other for the attention of the world's elected politicians and to become a primary vehicle for their transnational aspirations.

The 1920s and 1930s were bookended by global conflict, and earlier generations of diplomatic historians wanted to draw a path of
increasing isolation, autarky, and nationalism between the two world
wars in order to explain causation and continuity. More recently, however, historians have refocused energy on the flourishing of international hopes, along with new global experimentation in economics
and diplomacy, particularly in the context of the League of Nations.[2]
In this uptick of scholarly interest in nineteenth- and early twentieth-
century internationalisms, the Inter-Parliamentary Union has largely
been overlooked, and the International Parliamentary Commercial
Conference has not entered historical consciousness at all. Although
the CPIC did not survive the Second World War, the IPU still exists
with a well-stocked archive in Geneva. The IPU and its various national
parliamentary groups have sponsored chronicles of the organization's
own history that take a more encyclopaedic approach.[3] A comprehensive academic survey of the IPU's history through 1914 was published
in German in the late 1980s, a dense legal-political analysis by a former IPU employee came out in 2005, and brief articles tackling the
long arc of the IPU's history have considered ideas like "parliamentary
diplomacy." Many of these IPU-sponsored and older scholarly histories place in the organization in the context of peace studies and of
disarmament.[4]

The most compelling recent scholarly treatment of the IPU has
been a *Journal of Global History* article by Martin Albers. Albers
explored how the Inter-Parliamentary Union pivoted from its pacifist goals of the late nineteenth century to aspirations of being a
world parliament aligned with the League of Nations in the 1920s.
Albers ultimately argued the IPU transitioned from a "liberal club of
proponents of international arbitration to a self-styled international
legislature in the making," which reflected "a transnational body
politic" and a "global civil society." Although there were rumblings
of transforming the IPU into a world legislature in the 1920s, Albers
slightly overstated the case in pushing global legislative desires to the
fore of the IPU's interwar history. Albers's interpretation focused too
much on the organization's annual conferences and the grandiose
language of the IPU's non-binding resolutions rather than on the
more typical experiences of IPU members. Ultimately, both the IPU
and CPIC fostered the transnational ambitions of parliamentarians,
often through social engagements both in a lawmaker's home country and during conferences abroad. Albers foregrounded the IPU's
transition away from a nineteenth-century "liberal club" to wannabe
global legislature, but there were lingering club-like elements of

inter-parliamentary sociability in both the IPU and CPIC throughout the interwar era.[5]

Albers is right to link the IPU to the "crisis of representative democracy between the wars," but this analysis can go further. In Albers's article, this crisis is linked to one specific IPU debate at the 1928 annual conference in Berlin during which delegates discussed tinkering with electoral systems.[6] However, the phrase "crisis of parliamentarism" had become a catch-all term for the ills of modern political life even before the First World War; it took on varied and often contradictory emphases in different national contexts. Academics like Carl Schmitt infamously invoked the "crisis of parliamentary democracy" in the 1920s, and as this discourse crescendoed, even parliamentarians at the IPU realized there was a problem.[7] The IPU began to produce copious expert reports for possible changes to democratic procedures. These reports amounted to technical fixes and included in-depth studies of first-past-the-post or proportional electoral systems. No reform was too small in this frantic hunt for a solution to the democratic malaise; one analysis even focused on permitting absentee voting rather than requiring everyone to go in person to a polling location on a given day. Adding absentee ballots to fix a worldwide "crisis of the parliamentary regime" seems like a bit of a stretch.[8] The 1928 IPU debate on which Albers focused was only really about technical fixes. However, the IPU itself was forced to take an even bigger stance on democracy in how it positioned itself vis-à-vis authoritarian states. Would the IPU permit parliamentarians without a democratic mandate to join the organization?

With the rising tide of skepticism about democracy – coupled with cannibalizing competition between the two associations – both the IPU and CPIC came to define their own "parliamentary international" in distinct ways. The IPU tried to grow into a big-tent organization, and the CPIC attempted to specialize in technical issues. Both organizations were presented with a fundamental question about how an inter-parliamentary body should relate to democracy. Should an inter-parliamentary group be a cheerleader on the global stage for democracy? Should it act like a trade union or advocacy organization for duly elected parliamentarians that challenged authoritarian regimes and stood up for the rights of legislatures? Should it merely be a global club for the parliamentary elite? Both the IPU and CPIC navigated these decisions. Tragically, they both ended up sacrificing their earlier commitment to democracy in order to cater to interwar parliamentarians who were becoming creatures of authoritarian regimes.

The Inter-Parliamentary Union and Its 1928 Berlin Conference

In August 1928, the German Reichstag's debating chamber hosted a more diverse crowd than usual. This strange cast of characters included a once-and-future socialist prime minister of Denmark, a Coptic Egyptian legislator, the pre-eminent philosopher of Italian Fascism, the first female clerk of court in the Netherlands, a Japanese prince, and the US Democratic vice-presidential candidate and senator from Arkansas, among hundreds of other international guests. These national legislators were attending the 25th conference of the Inter-Parliamentary Union, which brought 475 parliamentarians from 38 countries to interwar Berlin to mingle with each another, to debate the pressing political issues of the day, and to broaden their sense of an worldwide parliamentary community.[9]

These delegates were taking part in a long tradition of international gatherings hosted by the Inter-Parliamentary Union, dating back to its very first conference in 1889. That inaugural inter-parliamentary meeting was the brainchild of the British Member of Parliament William Randal Cremer and the French deputy Frédéric Passy. Before 1889, both men had been active in movements for international peace that focused on promoting arbitration as the way to solve world problems. At its founding, the IPU was dedicated to promoting peaceful co-existence and international arbitration by enlisting the world's parliamentarians as apostles in this pacifist cause. Before becoming a devotee of international arbitration, the Englishman Randal Cremer cut his teeth in this transnational arena as the secretary of the International Workingmen's Association, more commonly known as the First International, which Cremer left when the organization turned in a more radical direction under the influence of Karl Marx. When Cremer entered the British House of Commons in 1885 as a Liberal MP, he coupled his background working with international groups with his interest in peaceful arbitration. Cremer partnered with Frédéric Passy, a French economist, peace campaigner, and proponent of free trade to call an initial meeting of nine British and 25 French parliamentarians. Subsequently, the Inter-Parliamentary Union was formally inaugurated at an 1889 conference attended by 96 parliamentarians from France, Great Britain, Belgium, Denmark, Spain, the United States, Hungary, Italy, and Liberia. The following year, Germany, Austria, Greece, Norway, and Sweden sent parliamentarians to the second annual conference, quickly bringing representatives from across Europe together into one organization dedicated to peace through arbitration.[10]

In the optimistic years of the *belle époque,* this circle of parliamentarians steadily grew larger as even more European countries dispatched delegations to the IPU's annual conferences. These conferences were generally held in European capitals, with the exception of the 1904 meeting in St. Louis, which coincided with the World's Fair. Even before the First World War began, the IPU gradually expanded beyond the United States and European countries to incorporate Canada, the Ottoman Empire, Japan, and Australia. In these early years, the Inter-Parliamentary Union did not stray too far from its original mandate and backed calls for the Hague Peace conferences and supported the creation of the Permanent Court of Arbitration. As late as 1917, British MPs described the IPU's goals as "entirely restricted to the promotion of International concord by the advancement of International Arbitration, the establishment of a properly constituted International Tribunal and Code, and the guaranteed sanction of all International Treaties and obligations by the formation of a League of Nations." The British politicians did not want the IPU to go off message advocating dangerous ideas like worldwide democracy or decolonization.[11]

Nevertheless, even during the earliest years of the twentieth century, the IPU sometimes stumbled into tricky political thickets, especially when upheaval touched on the organization itself. For instance, in 1906, the First Russian Duma dispatched a delegation to the IPU's London conference, only to arrive in the British capital to the news that the czar had dissolved the Duma after a little more than two months. At the IPU conference, the British Prime Minister Henry Campbell-Bannerman heartily greeted the new Russian delegates, now ex-parliamentarians, in a public rebuke of the czar's heavy-handed, autocratic tactics against the Russian legislature. The 1906 Duma incident foreshadowed a larger interwar battle for the soul of the IPU and the extent to which it should advocate for parliamentary democracy. Was the IPU supposed to be an organization dedicated to liberal parliamentarism that condemned executive incursions into parliamentary sovereignty? Or, on the other hand, should the IPU welcome any member of parliament regardless of the legitimacy of the regime they represented?[12]

This longer organizational history was likely not the first thing on the minds of the world's parliamentarians milling around the Reichstag for the IPU's annual conference in August 1928. During that five-day conference, parliamentarians wrestled with issues including migration, a declaration of the rights and duties of states, and the future development of parliamentarism. Of course, the Berlin conference was not all work and no play; the evenings were full of receptions, dinners, and other private engagements. The German government sponsored an evening banquet at Berlin's Zoological Garden where guests listened to music from Wagner, Grieg, and Liszt, as well as a few speeches, while dining on pear pudding and sipping Rhenish sparkling wine. The next day there was yet another formal dinner, again accompanied by Liszt and Wagner, but this time sponsored by Berlin's local government and held in the city hall. Tea at the Chancellery, a boozy evening reception, and a special performance of Beethoven's *Fidelio* at the state opera house were also on the agenda. A healthy dose of informal social gatherings was seen by the organizers as the antidote for all the stress of parliamentary diplomacy.[13]

Although this was the 1928 conference of the entire Inter-Parliamentary Union, the local organizers were primarily members of the Reichstag. They earned the German cabinet's enthusiastic backing with promises of "around 500 to 1,000 prominent parliamentarians" travelling to Berlin.[14] Although the country's leading ministers were excited about the event, the conservative German president, Paul von Hindenburg, did not share their zeal. The president had already planned his Bavarian summer getaway and would be unable to welcome the members of the conference in person. The organizers panicked at this news, since "a greeting by the official republican or monarchical head of state belongs to the tradition of inter-parliamentary conferences." The former field marshal's absence would be taken as an expression of his lack of confidence in parliamentary democracy. The socialist Chancellor Hermann Müller was asked to step in and welcome the conference guests in such a way that he would "so strongly emphasize the regret [...] on behalf of the Reich President about his inability to attend so that it is utterly impossible to arrive at any sort of unwelcome misinterpretation about the Reich President's absence." Considering Hindenburg's well-known conservative skepticism of interwar democracies, the organizers' concerns were not without merit, although Hindenburg's absence did not end up overshadowing the conference.[15]

Both the German parliamentarians spearheading the conference and the German cabinet saw this large international event as a way to put the new Weimar Republic on display for the world. It was an opportunity to woo leading lawmakers in other countries. The German Foreign Office compiled a confidential list of VIP attendees based on information from embassies abroad and regional experts. This list of prominent participants was extensively annotated to include information such as which Italian delegate was known to be sympathetic to German claims about ending reparations, which Latvian representative was friendly to German interests, and which American representatives should be thanked for their support in returning German property seized during the First

World War. The importance of this soft diplomatic campaign to the German Foreign Office was obvious in the fact that although this was a confidential list of foreign parliamentarians, it was distributed so widely it crops up today in numerous archival collections. All the functionaries of the Weimar Republic were supposed to know which prominent foreigners should be cultivated to further German diplomacy.[16]

Although the 1928 IPU conference was seen as a foreign policy boon for Germany, it also presented headaches for diplomats when questions of the democratic legitimacy of delegations were raised. A perennial issue after Benito Mussolini's rise to power in Italy was whether parliamentarians from Fascist Italy deserved seats at IPU events. When this issue resurfaced on the eve of the 1928 Berlin conference, an angry letter from exiled Italian anti-Fascist former parliamentarians protesting the Italian delegation's makeup was quietly swept under the rug.[17] The IPU also confronted political developments in the Balkans. Only months before the conference in Berlin in June 1928, a Serbian parliamentarian shot five Croatian colleagues on the floor of the Parliament of the Kingdom of Serbs, Croats, and Slovenes in Belgrade. Three of the victims eventually died, and the Croatian politicians boycotted the national parliament in the wake of these assassinations. This meant that the 1928 parliamentary delegation from the kingdom excluded all Croatians. The Croatian Peasant Party challenged the legitimacy of the parliamentarians dispatched from Belgrade, demanding that the IPU both take a public position against the assassinations and require delegations be more representative of all political groupings in national assemblies. Rather than even expressing sympathy for the murdered Croatian parliamentarians, the IPU organizing committee dismissed these concerns with a milquetoast note. The IPU's leadership steered away from these larger questions about democracy in Italy and whether parliamentary delegations should reflect democratic legislatures or be free of political violence. Wilfully ignoring these issues in the preparation for the Berlin conference revealed the organizers' preference for a logistically smooth event without any bad publicity garnered from taking stances on controversial topics.[18]

However, one question of democratic legitimacy that the IPU conference organizers were not able to ignore related to the Egyptian parliamentary delegation. In August 1928, the king of Egypt suspended the parliament and limited civil rights throughout the country. However, the Egyptian parliamentary delegates had already left the country before the legislature's dissolution. Already on the IPU's list of participants, these Egyptian ex-legislators took up their conference seats in Berlin, ready to use the international spotlight to challenge the autocratic

Figure 4.1. Participants at the 1928 Inter-Parliamentary Union Conference in Berlin.

Source: From National Archief, Inv. 21, 2.21.190, C. Frida Katz Fam., NAH.

royal government in their home country. These former parliamentarians raised the issue of Egyptian democracy whenever possible in Berlin, including at one of the conference's closing banquets. They also proposed an amendment on the floor condemning the events in Egypt and taking a stance in favour of liberal democracies. Leading German parliamentarians, including Paul Löbe as the president of the Reichstag and host of the conference, offered public support for the Egyptian amendment. The legislators supporting Egyptian democracy staked out the position that the IPU must be a voice for the rights of parliaments around the world.[19]

The Egyptian government had anticipated this negative publicity in Berlin, so it started a private diplomatic campaign to squash news about these manoeuverings at the IPU. The Egyptian foreign minister summoned a German diplomat in Cairo for an urgent meeting asking for help to thwart the plans of the Egyptian ex-parliamentarians. Ultimately, both the French and German diplomats offered behind-the-scenes assistance to the Egyptian government. The French prevented the news agency Havas from broadcasting about the IPU conference to Egypt, and the German government curtailed reports on German state-controlled radio about the Egyptian ex-parliamentarians' agitation. The German Foreign Office also lobbied for strategic amendments to the conference's final resolutions to water down statements against the anti-parliamentary regime in Cairo. Ultimately, bureaucrats working for the republican governments of Germany and France collaborated with the autocratic government in Egypt to thwart democratic legislators' attempts to use the IPU as a vehicle to advocate as strongly and publicly as possible for democracy on the international stage.[20]

An International Organization of Diverse National Groups

International conferences like the 1928 meeting in Berlin were the obvious high point of the Inter-Parliamentary Union's annual calendar. The limited scholarly attention that has been paid to the IPU focuses on these marquee events and the aspiration to transform these gatherings into sessions of a global parliament. Martin Albers has claimed that "many IPU members aimed to become part of an international parliament, recognized in international law."[21] However, most interwar parliamentarians who were active in the IPU were not actually sailing off to foreign locales to participate in any wannabe international legislature. Instead, they first interacted with the IPU through their own parliament's national group. These groups were the self-governing local chapters of the IPU that collected dues, elected their own leadership, put together their own events, and then selected a subset of their membership to attend the annual conferences. However, these groups were not merely carbon copies of each other. For instance, many national groups had formal administrative and budgetary support from their government, but others relied on parliamentarians to shoulder the day-to-day running of the group's activities. Interwar lawmakers interested in inter-parliamentary cooperation had to step into this transnational world first through their national group.[22]

In terms of national membership numbers, there was significant variety among the IPU groups. Although in 1924, Japan's national group had a staggering 463 members, in 1936, the Austrian group had 86 members, and the Dutch East Indies group only had 39 members.[23] In a clever gimmick to increase the number of members in the United States, the American IPU group's president solicited new members from the House of Representatives and the Senate by sending everyone a membership card in advance of them actually signing up for one. He hoped to top the previous Congress' total of 250 members.[24] Many countries' groups prided themselves on the high total percentages of parliamentarians who had joined. For instance, the Czechoslovak group boasted that between 1923 and 1925 its total number of members was almost 300, fluctuating between 76 per cent and 82 per cent of the total number of members in the lower house of parliament along with 82 per cent to 90 per cent of the senators.[25]

A premium was placed on creating IPU national groups that were politically diverse. The interwar German group included members ranging politically from the moderate socialists through the right-wing German nationalists, whether or not the parties were in government at the time.[26] The 1936 membership roster of British IPU members shows that MPs from the three largest political parties were represented in the group's leadership. Moreover, when the number of Labour members of the British IPU Group slipped, the IPU's secretary general in Geneva personally wrote to a Labour member of the group to encourage him recruit more of his party comrades for the organization.[27] Although these national groups were often quite large and politically mixed, most of the delegations to the IPU's international conferences were only between five and 10 members strong, and this broader diversity was sometimes lost in the annual deputations for the conferences. Clearly, not all of these lawmakers who joined a local IPU group saw themselves as members of any international parliament, and, in the end, the vast majority did not attend the IPU's international conferences but instead experienced the wider association only through activities within their own national group.[28]

However, the IPU's national groups were not merely feeder organizations for international conferences; many were active in their own right. According to the IPU's governing documents, the groups were to serve as on-the-ground campaigners for national action to implement resolutions adopted by the international conferences.[29] The German IPU group was particularly diligent in this regard. In 1928, the German group sent the resolutions of a recent IPU conference both to other members of the Reichstag and to government officials, who distributed them to the relevant ministries. The ministries, in turn, sent specialists to meet with German IPU delegates to discuss the resolutions in more detail.[30] The extent of the German commitment to advocating for the IPU is evident in a letter dated April 4, 1933, from the socialist Paul Löbe to the German Foreign Office. Even after the Nazis had seized power, Löbe still lobbied for the IPU's concerns: "I would like to bring to your attention that a few days ago we were asked to advocate for the ratification by the

German government of the Convention for Limiting the Manufacture and Regulating the Distribution of Narcotic Drugs. Since the possibility of doing this in the Reichstag is not on the horizon, please allow me to enclose the relevant request of our Secretary General for your attention." Whether or not the German government acted in response to Löbe's letter is unclear, but the new Third Reich did ratify the treaty a few days later, on April 10, 1933.[31]

More than merely advocating for the IPU's resolutions at a local level, many of the national groups hosted events to educate their membership about international politics. The German IPU group convened its own committees to study issues like a European customs union and hosted these meetings in the Reichstag itself, blurring the line between official parliamentary business and a private IPU affair. Although only the largest and most active IPU national groups created such study committees, almost all groups put together banquets when IPU officials came to town. Passing through Berlin after a trip to visit the Scandinavian national groups, the organization's Secretary General Christian Lange was honoured at a swanky Berlin social club, where he gave a presentation on the "Inter-Parliamentary Union and the League of Nations."[32] The British group was visited twice by the secretary general in one year, with one of the visits accompanied by a lunch in the House of Commons for the British members of the IPU.[33] The Dutch group also welcomed the secretary general with a meeting for all the group's members in the parliament itself, followed by drinks at the private club Sociëteit De Witte.[34]

Of course, there were varying levels of enthusiasm and participation at the national level within IPU groups. In 1936, the Netherlands Indies group reported that it had held no meetings that year.[35] An Irish senator explained his local group's lack of activity: "I found it very difficult to get anybody to interest themselves in international politics and in the Inter-Parliamentary Union and our Group has undoubtedly been very somnolent for the past few years."[36] Chaotic national politics could even sidetrack the most active IPU groups. Because of an upcoming election in 1930 in Germany, the usual procedure of a formal group meeting to select delegates to the international conference was dispensed with in favour of an ad hoc meeting on the sidelines right after a Reichstag plenary session. In 1932, the leadership of the German group could not even find time to elect its own president.[37] Likewise, the Irish group responded ambivalently to the 1935 invitation to attend the IPU's annual conference because "July is generally a very busy month from the parliamentary point of view [...] I much doubt if anybody will be ready to promise to go until we see how the session is likely to develop, as there are a number of important Bills coming forward which will mean much discussion." Obviously desperate to have as many states as possible represented at the international conference, the IPU secretariat responded: "If at the time of the Conference there are important measures still before your Parliament, would it not be possible to form a delegation consisting of representatives of different parties, who would cancel each other out at the time of voting?"[38]

These national IPU groups were sometimes enlisted in the service of larger diplomatic goals. For instance, the French and Swiss IPU groups sent representatives to a special meeting in September 1930 in Lausanne. They discussed international issues, particularly a hold on a bilateral arbitration treaty between France and Switzerland in the French senate. The Lausanne group was small – five Swiss delegates and five French delegates – but the conversation was seen as productive enough for the IPU to encourage similar meetings in other contexts. Secretary-General Christian Lange tried to set up meetings between the German and French national groups in the early 1930s – when more public diplomacy between the two countries seemed politically fraught. Writing to a French senator who had attended the earlier meeting in Lausanne, Lange wrote of his faith in this form of private parliamentary diplomacy: "I still am of the opinion that contact between French and German parliamentarians, if it were quite private and without public knowledge, could be useful before the opening of the Disarmament Conference." Lange even tried to bring together the French, German, and Polish groups in keeping with his commitment to behind-the-scenes parliamentary co-operation, but the Nazi seizure of power in 1933 dashed Lange's hopes for a mini-diplomatic summit.[39]

One might be left with an overly rosy picture of collegial national gatherings of interwar parliamentarians dedicated to worldwide peace, made up of members from across the political spectrum, sometimes even conversing with colleagues in a neighbouring country to lessen global tension. There were also deep clashes within national groups, but few contests were as lasting as an acrimonious split in the Belgian group. After the IPU got back on its feet after the First World War, the Belgian group took a hard line against co-operation with any parliamentarians from the losing Central Powers. The Belgian group was horrified at the prospect of attending a conference "where they might run the risk of sitting with members of parliaments having endorsed the aggressions, depredations and other crimes perpetrated in Belgium by German barbarism." The Belgian IPU group instead proposed abandoning the previous Union and reconstituting it to "[e]xclude immediately [...] the Germans, the Austrians, the Hungarians, the Bulgarians, and the Turks" and welcome the new parliamentary democracies in Central Europe that had "chivalrously supported the cause of the Allies."[40]

The Belgian attempt to win over the British and other IPU national groups to this project of reinventing the Union as a club for politicians from victorious powers faltered, so the Belgian national group settled on a policy of boycotting the annual IPU conferences. At first, the French national group joined them in this protest, but in 1922, the French ended their boycott and sent parliamentarians to the annual IPU conference in Vienna. At this news, the Belgian group splintered between socialists who wanted to participate again in the IPU conferences and the remaining political parties, which insisted on principled opposition to any global organization that included the Germans. In protest, the socialists resigned en masse from Belgium's formal IPU national group and dispatched their own delegates to Vienna. The IPU was only too willing to accept these breakaway socialist delegates, and the Belgian socialists continued sending their own representatives to the annual conferences in later years. The obstinate Belgian boycott by diehard liberal and conservative politicians continued throughout the 1920s, although over time a few Flemish nationalists and defecting Christian democrats participated in the IPU's annual conferences via the breakaway socialist-dominated IPU group. Not until 1929 and 1930 did the entire Belgian group finally resume normal participation in the IPU's international events.[41]

In the end, the brand of parliamentary internationalism the Inter-Parliamentary Union embodied was one of local groups participating in a larger international organization. An individual parliamentarian would have associated the IPU with these national groups, which were the bread and butter of the organization. Only a select handful of these national members were even dispatched to the annual conferences. Moreover, within the IPU, not all national groups were created the same – some, like the American and Czechoslovak groups, tried to be as expansive as possible and prided themselves on having members from all political parties. The Austrian group, on the other hand, generally brought together only members from the large conservative Christian Social party with two minor parties. The rival Austrian social democrats were often excluded altogether. The IPU wanted to build a grassroots community of internationally minded parliamentarians that came together in national groups to advocate domestically on global issues. This IPU system of global conferences and national advocacy could have been enlisted in the service of propping up parliamentary democracy between the world wars. However, there was nothing inherently democratic about this structure, and by the end of the interwar years, the IPU had skewed towards being more like a social club for parliamentarians on the domestic scene with occasional opportunities for an all-expenses-paid junket somewhere in the world.[42]

The International Parliamentary Commercial Conference and Its 1927 Rio de Janeiro Conference

Tucked away in the Harvard University Archives in the papers of a former German chancellor is a curious photo of five men standing on the deck of an ocean liner. Only the man on the far right is smiling as he holds a cigar; the other four appear somewhat confused about where to look for the photograph. These men were the German delegates to the 1927 meeting of the International Parliamentary Commercial Conference in Rio de Janeiro. They include Heinrich Brüning of the Catholic Centre Party, who attempted to steer the German ship of state through the Great Depression as chancellor from 1930 to 1932; Rudolf Hilferding, a leading socialist theorist and former German finance minister; Oscar Meyer, the perennial delegate to these inter-parliamentary commercial conferences from the left-liberal German Democratic Party (Deutsche Demokratische Partei, DDP); the right-liberal German People's Party (Deutsche Volkspartei, DVP) parliamentarian and former economics minister, Hans von Raumer; and the German National People's Party (Deutschnationale Volkspartei, DNVP) legislator and later victim of the Nazis, Paul Lejeune-Jung. These men were the leading representatives of their parties on the Reichstag's trade committee and had been chosen to represent the Reichstag at the Rio de Janeiro conference. They came from competing political parties that were often at each other's throats in the interwar German public sphere, so it is jarring to see them all standing together as one team in this photograph.[43]

In August 1927, these five politicians and their spouses travelled first to Bremerhaven to embark on the ship *Sierra Morena* for their long trip across the Atlantic. To attract European politicians to South America for the conference, the Brazilian government offset their travel costs, and the German consul later estimated that the Brazilian government spent the equivalent of five million marks on the event. After a long sea voyage, the German delegates and their spouses arrived in Rio de Janeiro on August 25, 1927, where they were greeted on board the *Sierra Morena* by a Brazilian senator, the conference's secretary-general, and German consular staff who helped ferry them to the luxurious Copacabana Palace Hotel, where the Italian and English delegations were also staying.[44]

Similar to the conferences of the Inter-Parliamentary Union, a full social calendar awaited these men and their wives in Brazil. The critical Argentinian newspaper *La Prensa* mocked the conference's meagre

Figure 4.2. German delegation to CPIC Conference in Rio de Janeiro, 1927.

Source: From the Papers of Heinrich Brüning, Uncatalogued Accession, Photo of
Delegation to Inter-parliamentary Conference (1927) among Photos, Acs. 13632, Box 5,
HUA. Courtesy of the Harvard University Archives.

substantive agenda and its focus on "banquets, dances, excursions, and
strolls" rather than substance. In fact, the German delegation attended
quite a number of these social events before the conference officially
began – meeting or dining with the vice president of Brazil, the apostolic
nuncio, and over 60 leading members of Brazilian society. The five German delegates also travelled with their Austrian colleagues to São Paulo
on a three-day trip where they had a private audience with the Brazilian
foreign minister. The German delegation's extended stay prompted the
German-speaking community in Rio de Janeiro to organize a number of
gatherings including a special festival in their honour.[45]

From Brazil's diplomatic perspective, this trip was successful, since it
piqued the interest of these Reichstag members in South American issues.
On their return to Berlin, these politicians advocated upgrading German
diplomatic representation in South American states to full embassies and
for supporting German schools and teachers in the region. However, the
critic writing in *La Prensa* mocked mere soft diplomacy where the "main
concern has been to graciously host the conference participants, so that
they retain pleasant memories of their stay."[46] Interestingly enough, this

prediction of lasting recollections of the conference came true, since this particular meeting of the International Parliamentary Commercial Conference left such an impression on the German participants that well into the 1950s and 1960s, Heinrich Brüning still fondly wrote to his former travel companion Hans von Raumer about the trip: "During my illness I often thought about you, as well as your wife, who I specially admired. The memories of our trip to the economic conference in Rio became especially vivid to me."[47]

The memoirs and personal correspondence of the German delegates show that this trip to Brazil left such an impression because it brought them closer to each other. Although a group including a Marxist theorist and a conservative German nationalist was not a likely candidate to grow particularly close, the three months these lawmakers were cooped up together on steamships and in conference rooms did the trick. The DDP parliamentarian Oscar Meyer remembered one experience when on board the *Sierra Morena* en route to Brazil when the delegation saw the German national holiday pass unacknowledged on the ship: "On the new German national holiday we were on the high seas. Nothing marked the national day of remembrance. Two days later the ship was resplendent with flag decorations that we did not at first recognize; the captain's celebratory speech at dinner informed us that it was the national holiday of Uruguay!" This experience apparently made the German parliamentarians think of themselves as Germans first, rather than as socialists, Catholics, or German nationalists. Surrounded by blue and white flags, they realized they had more in common with each other than with the celebrating Uruguayan passengers. In particular, Meyer treasured the close relationships that developed among the German delegates, which meant "we set aside our party blinders and realized that we all really liked each other."[48]

These friendly personal relationships among German political rivals were apparent in a session of communal postcard writing. These parliamentarians and their spouses had the group photograph on board the ocean liner turned into a postcard they sent to absent friends and family. Hilferding's wife dispatched a note to her daughter that was signed not only by her stepfather, signing as "Uncle Rudi," but also by all the other delegates and their spouses. Oscar Meyer also wrote an exceedingly brief postcard to a relative: "Final greetings from the ship!" Before Meyer signed the card, he passed it around to collect the signatures of Hilferding, Brüning, Lejeune-Jung, and Raumer. Five political rivals signing friendly letters to far-flung relatives back in Germany was a personal gesture that showed the delegates had grown exceptionally close.[49]

The International Parliamentary Commercial Conference did not spring up *ex nihilo* in the interwar years. The organization's annual gatherings began right before the First World War, and it was inspired by the commercial committee in the British House of Commons, which shepherded trade-related legislation through the parliamentary process. At that time, Belgian parliamentarians wanted to create an international conference to bring together stakeholders in parliamentary discussions about trade and to replicate the approach of the Commons' commercial committee on an international level.[50] The formal statutes of the CPIC adopted right before the outbreak of war in 1914 defined the goal of the association: "The International Parliamentary Commercial Conference aims to bring together, through harmonious action, commercial committees where trade legislation is drafted in the primary parliaments, in order to continue together to harmonize legislation on commercial matters, and thus guarantee more efficient protection of interests abroad for the participating nations, due to the similarity in commercial law."[51]

Unlike the Inter-Parliamentary Union whose work ground to a halt during the war, the CPIC's second international conference took place in the Palais du Luxembourg in April 1916 in wartime Paris. Austria, Hungary, and Germany, which had participated in the CPIC before the outbreak of war, were obviously not invited in 1916. The conference refashioned itself as the Entente's international commercial gathering. In 1917 the conference was held in Rome, and the 1918 conference was held in London. The participating countries at these wartime meetings were only from Allied states; the Netherlands, which had attended in 1914 but was neutral during the war, did not dispatch delegations during the war, and states like Greece were only represented after they joined the war on the Allies' side.[52]

This Entente-only parliamentary bloc continued at the postwar 1919 CPIC conference, but the organization later grew more ecumenical in accepting delegations from around the world. By 1925, 37 national groups, of which 30 had been officially endorsed by a national parliament, attended. By the mid-1920s, the CPIC was even supported by a permanent secretariat in Brussels. The leadership of the CPIC pushed for faster growth, dispatching numerous letters to parliaments and governments encouraging attendance. In both the Australian and Austrian archives, there are many letters from the CPIC urging the countries to dispatch delegations; these were sent by the secretariat over and over again despite having been turned down previously. By 1928, the CPIC settled for incorporating an Australian state legislator into the British delegation, although it was undeterred in trying to add a national Australian delegation.[53]

Although Germany had been the major foe of the CPIC's members in the First World War, by the time of the 1927 conference in Brazil, German delegates held key roles on the meeting's agenda. In fact, Germany's delegate, Rudolf Hilferding, had been chosen to deliver a public address right after the formal welcome of the Brazilian foreign minister and thus had the rare honour of having his speech translated into Portuguese for the local press. Hilferding continued in this leading role by presenting a resolution he had prepared on cartels and trusts that was adopted by the whole conference. Hans von Raumer was also catapulted into the CPIC's leadership when he took over the chairmanship of the Coal Commission because the original chair was absent; there Raumer and Heinrich Brüning together helped usher a German compromise proposal towards adoption. Despite the conference's location in Brazil, a number of South American delegates later reported that European concerns – cartels and coal, for instance – had dominated the meeting's agenda.[54]

Politicians from around the world continued to attend these interwar meetings to discuss issues that were often more specialized than those handled at the IPU's conferences. The CPIC's topics of discussion included bankruptcy laws, shipping, circulation of capital, the world economic crisis, improving transport facilities, internal navigation, international broadcasting, agricultural credits, and price fixing.[55] The conference itself was run differently than the IPU, with work divided between, on the one hand, individual members who drafted and circulated resolutions before the conference began and, on the other hand, the committees that reviewed draft resolutions, debated them, adopted amendments, and finalized the definitive text that would be forwarded to the plenary session. Constructive debate and high-level discussion were relegated to committees where members were often experts on their topics. Different national delegations focused their efforts on different committees; for example, at the 1928 CPIC conference in Paris, British delegates attended the committee meetings on economic disarmament and on "Transport and Liberty of Transit" but completely skipped the meetings on "Long Term Treaties assuring equitable treatment" and "Legislative Measures to help international Commerce."[56]

Although CPIC committee work was a chance to muddle through finer policy details, the plenary discussion suffered: "The text [of a resolution] is presented to the conference by a rapporteur who is usually the originator of the project. The rapporteur briefly comments on the resolution, then a second speaker takes the floor to thank [the first speaker], then the resolution is put to a vote and unanimously adopted." A critic of the CPIC put it bluntly: "It is obvious that the plenary sessions are not interesting, which is made worse because the speakers just deliver a stream of compliments which are often exaggerated." In addition, unlike the League of Nations or the IPU, the CPIC was almost completely in French, which meant that time and resources did not have to be budgeted for translation but also dissuaded parliamentarians without a good grasp of French from wandering off script. Despite the more focused topics, emphasis on committee work, and dull speeches, the CPIC conferences remained well attended throughout the interwar period.[57]

Identity Crises and Competition Between Interwar Inter-Parliamentary Organizations

Although the annual conferences of the Inter-Parliamentary Union and the International Parliamentary Commercial Conference continued unabated during the interwar years, both associations sought out new directions for the future development of their internationalist goals. As Martin Albers has explored, in the early years after the First World War, the IPU specifically considered becoming an ancillary organ of the League of Nations. The IPU offered to give the League greater parliamentary support in return for funding. A League official reached out directly to the IPU's secretary general to offer assistance in the form of hosting IPU conferences in premises run by the League, providing interpreters, and sorting out accounting issues. This offer fell short of the IPU leadership's hopes in 1920, when the IPU's secretariat was particularly concerned with finding out how the League's Council might be able to endorse the IPU in such a way as to encourage renewed subsidies from national governments to solve the IPU's budget woes.[58]

Later in 1920, the secretary-general of the League of Nations actually considered the idea of creating or partnering with an inter-parliamentary organization in a more formal capacity. An internal League memo suggested that since the IPU was just now rebuilding its connections between parliamentarians and parliaments in the wake of the war, the League could closely work alongside the organization to remake the IPU as an affiliated institution through which the League could disseminate information and gain more democratic legitimacy. However, the League's leadership eventually stopped this partnership program in its tracks: "The League should not [...] officially separate Parliaments from Governments. What is of importance is that it should keep in contact with the various countries, or say nations as a whole, that is to say with their various elements [...] We must keep in touch with Governments, Parliaments, private associations, public opinion, and so on." Since the League backed off of a formal partnership, the IPU's annual conferences ultimately duplicated much of the work of the League's committees and commissions.[59]

Rebuffed by the League of Nations, the Inter-Parliamentary Union returned to its bread and butter – parliaments and parliamentarians. During the First World War, Christian Lange had written to the United States' IPU group with plans to expand the IPU's presence in Central and South America. Lange's US congressional contact could speak some Spanish, and this American politician offered to improve his language skills before serving as a roaming emissary for the IPU in Latin America. However, this congressman left politics soon after the World War I, and the IPU put the South American expansion on ice. After prospects of a partnership with the League fell through, the IPU returned to these worldwide expansion plans and dispatched representatives to meet parliamentarians across South America. These visits prompted the creation of Bolivian and Chilean national IPU groups. One Chilean legislator specifically commended the IPU for focusing on this growth in a period of bankruptcy and crisis of parliamentarism, pointedly contrasting the enthusiasm of the IPU for parliaments with larger trends within public opinion that were skeptical of democracy.[60]

During the 1920s the IPU's expanded membership included Brazil, Chile, Costa Rica, Cuba, the Dominican Republic, Egypt, the Dutch East Indies, Mexico, Panama, Peru, the Philippines, and Venezuela. The pace of new members joining slowed in the early 1930s, but even then Uruguay, Iran, Ecuador, Colombia, and Argentina joined the organization's ranks. The IPU's leadership had elected to redouble its efforts to transform itself into the biggest tent organization possible, bringing many new parliamentarians into the fold. This decision to grow was, in many ways, the IPU's response to an interwar identity crisis. Having left its *fin-de-siècle* focus on international arbitration behind and abandoning attempts to refashion itself as an organ of the League of Nations, the IPU opted to gain legitimacy as the biggest club for parliamentarians in the world. However, its choice to incorporate as many parliaments and political parties as possible led to conflicts over the question of whether the IPU still had democratic principles at heart.[61]

Like the Inter-Parliamentary Union, the International Parliamentary Commercial Conference also set out to remake itself during the interwar period. Unlike the IPU, however, the CPIC had remained active during the war and began the period as the Allies' international commercial congress. There was a similar push to add the CPIC to the League system, but this was through attempts in the early 1920s by the Belgian government to turn the Brussels-based International Institute of Commerce into the League's commercial statistics organization. The Belgian institute hosted the CPIC's permanent secretariat, so it would have been rolled into the League as well. Like the failed attempts at fusing the IPU and the League, this plan also came to naught. However, the idea of transforming the CPIC into parliamentary association supervising international statisticians reflected the far more specialized and technocratic nature of the CPIC, as opposed to the internationalist goals of the IPU focused on parliamentarians and their concerns broadly, more than any one topic.[62]

Although "parliamentary" was in the name of the International Parliamentary Commercial Conference, even in the early days of the organization, there was wiggle room in how rigidly this was interpreted. States could be represented at annual conferences by either parliamentarians or ambassadors specializing in trade policy. Allowing professional diplomats to sit alongside parliamentarians meant that as the interwar period progressed, the CPIC gradually moved further away from its founders' goal of being like an international parliamentary trade committee to being yet another diplomatic forum for discussion between official government representatives. Over time, the professional diplomats at the CPIC's events started to outnumber elected parliamentarians, who tended to come more from pro-free trade bourgeois liberal parties. An IPU observer at a CPIC conference felt that the parliamentary and representative quality was diminished because so many ambassadors were present. The CPIC's refashioned organization, which had technocratic dreams from its earliest days, entered its interwar heyday as a specialized club that was also a big tent. However, unlike the IPU, which encouraged as many parliamentarians as possible to sign up, the CPIC expanded to new countries by allowing ambassadors rather than parliamentarians to attend.[63]

Because of the growing prominence of both the IPU and CPIC, a rivalry between the two began. The IPU's executive circulated a memo to all its national groups taking a firm stand against the proliferation of these inter-parliamentary associations. It urged national groups to refrain from participating in organizations that duplicated the work of the IPU. This memo directly targeted the CPIC:

An "International Parliamentary Commercial Conference" was founded in 1913; its central office is in Brussels and it includes a certain number of non-parliamentary members. Annual conferences are called which now no longer, as was at first the case, limit themselves to commercial questions; last year, at Rio de Janeiro, questions of emigration and immigration were discussed.

According to the IPU, this shift in the CPIC's focus meant that there would be too much overlap between the two organizations, and the CPIC was now getting in the way of its hoped-for IPU-dominated inter-parliamentary world.[64]

The rivalry between these two organizations swung between outright competition and mild détente. After the anti-CPIC 1928 memo to all the IPU national groups, the CPIC's Secretary-General Eugène Baie invited an official IPU delegate to the CPIC's 1930 conference in Prague. This seemingly friendly gesture was instead used by the IPU to gather intelligence on the CPIC. The IPU leadership's sense of urgency was heightened with reports from national groups on the CPIC's manoeuverings. The clerk of the Dutch Tweede Kamer reported to the IPU leadership that there was a movement to create a separate national group for the CPIC in the Netherlands, which threatened to split the already small group of politicians interested in inter-parliamentary affairs. Another confidante of the IPU's secretariat in the Belgian Senate secretly sent the IPU leadership a letter saying that the CPIC expected 500,000 francs from the French parliament as a subsidy. Behind-the-scenes Belgian partisans of the IPU then used this information to try to get strings attached to Belgian funding for the CPIC so that the government would only disburse funds if the two inter-parliamentary organizations agreed to merge. As the older and larger organization, the IPU hoped to take on a dominant role in any fused inter-parliamentary organization.[65]

Other than these backroom informants dispatching memos to IPU headquarters in Geneva, how did most interwar parliamentarians experience the tension between these two inter-parliamentary clubs? At the national level, for the most part, these two organizations seemed redundant. After having hosted the IPU conference in Berlin in 1928 and then having the CPIC conference come to Berlin the following year, the German IPU group advocated that the two organizations merge. The Japanese delegation travelling to Europe for the 1928 IPU conference in Berlin aimed to have the same delegation in Europe to attend the CPIC that year.[66] Because some parliamentarians actually attended both conferences, lawmakers have gotten mixed up in their memoirs – writing about an Inter-Parliamentary Union conference in Rio de Janeiro, rather than the actual CPIC conference that took place there. Since many politicians could not even keep these organizations straight, the conflict raging behind the scenes between IPU and CPIC functionaries did not seem to perturb individual politicians who were members of one or both organizations. From the perspective of a run-of-the-mill politician's interest in inter-parliamentary co-operation, these international conferences were a chance to travel and mingle with foreign colleagues, while discussing the issues of the day.[67]

Advocating for Parliamentary Democracy or Representing Technocratic Interests?

During the interwar years, the Inter-Parliamentary Union and the International Parliamentary Commercial Conference wove together the transnational work of national lawmakers with the sociability of politicians travelling to locales ranging from Brazil to Prague. Both organizations grappled with evolving in the politically pitched decades between the wars. The IPU became a big-tent organization that welcomed as many parliaments and parliamentarians to its conferences as possible. The CPIC grew as well, but by permitting more specialist diplomats to represent countries in lieu of politicians. Ultimately, both organizations moved away from full-throated advocacy for parliamentary democracy, which had been a feature of the inter-parliamentary movement in the immediate aftermath of the First World War.[68]

At the 1928 conference in Berlin, the IPU was confronted with the extent to which the organization should support democracy in the aftermath of political violence and the Egypt royal coup. However, the IPU perennially confronted these issues whenever former Italian parliamentarians who had been forced into exile from Mussolini's Italy petitioned the IPU to stand up for democracy: "We cannot imagine that you tolerate powerful dictatorship and despotism [...] Your institution is, by itself, a living protest against any corruption of democracy or the parliamentary system." When this letter was read to the IPU council in 1927, the vast majority of the assembled parliamentarians wanted to sweep these concerns under the rug. However, Paul Löbe pointedly asked: "Is it not required that the Union now decide if it intends to act as a representative for a parliamentary system or simply as a representative of all the parliaments?" Löbe's answer was that the IPU should stand firm for parliamentary democracy, but only one socialist senator from Belgium supported Löbe's stance. The French socialists and bourgeois liberal politicians on the IPU's council sought a compromise to mollify the Italian Fascists rather than to support the true Italian democrats who were in exile.[69]

Paul Löbe's lonely stand in 1927 for an inter-parliamentary movement that was more than a club for legislators highlighted tension in the Inter-Parliamentary Union that would only increase as more and more countries abandoned democratic principles. Coincidentally, Löbe later found himself in a position similar to the exiled Italian parliamentarians. Löbe had become an undesirable former socialist parliamentarian in the Third

Reich, and his status as an early opponent of the Nazi regime meant that he was unable to find work. Unemployed and having no savings, he turned to friends abroad in 1935. Löbe reached out to the IPU via Walther Schücking, a former German liberal parliamentarian and then a judge on the Permanent Court of Justice in The Hague, who enlisted the IPU's secretary general to appeal to a select set of national groups for financial support for Löbe.[70] The IPU confidentially collected the handsome sum of 1,384 Swiss francs from a set of donors including the Irish national group, a private donation from a Welsh Liberal MP, a collection taken up from British MPs and members of the House of Lords, a large lump sum from the Danish group, and the largest donation from Löbe's friends in Geneva, particularly from members of the IPU secretariat.[71]

However, after receiving the money, Paul Löbe wrote to say how thankful he was for this support from the IPU. The secretary-general was horrified: "I was shocked [...] that he mentioned the Inter-Parliamentary Union itself. I would be grateful if you ask the bank to not mention the Inter-Parliamentary Union in this matter because the Union is neither officially nor semi-officially involved in this matter. Collecting donations has been organized by a few members of the Union in a personal capacity, which is very different."[72] In keeping with this idea that only individual parliamentarians could take a stand in favour of parliamentary democracy, at the 1937 IPU conference, 87 of the 376 participants petitioned the Nazi government for clemency on behalf of a condemned former communist parliamentarian. Their plea fell on deaf ears, and the former lawmaker was beheaded. Like the Löbe case, support for parliamentary democracy or for democratically elected ex-parliamentarians came to be seen a private matter, no longer the concern of the IPU as a whole.[73]

Strangely enough, the anti-democratic Nazi government provides a useful final take on the brands of parliamentary internationalism put forward by both the IPU and the CPIC. As the winds of fascist change blew over Germany in early 1933, the German Foreign Office put together a long report to the new Nazi leadership arguing that Germany should cut funding from the IPU and not attend future conferences. After a public spat about the legitimacy of the Italian delegation during the 1932 conference, Italy had responded by temporarily withdrawing from the IPU, and Japan had threatened to leave as well.[74] The German diplomats felt Germany should do the same. Moreover, if National Socialist members of the Reichstag were to attend the 1933 IPU meeting in Madrid, the Belgians would boycott the conference and fireworks would undoubtedly ensue. For the Nazis, the IPU was an uncontrollable parliamentary organization. In reality, the IPU had moderated in its stance towards illiberal parliaments, but the Nazi regime hated the idea of the IPU and the free debate at its conferences.[75]

On the other hand, the Nazis had far fewer qualms about participating in the International Parliamentary Commercial Conference. In 1935, the state secretary in the Nazi foreign ministry argued in a lengthy memo that "right now the Reichstag should not go through with cancelling its membership in the International Parliamentary Commercial Conference." By this time, Germany had left the League of Nations, the Disarmament Conference, the IPU, and other international organizations, but the state secretary argued that a decision to leave the CPIC would isolate Germany even more in the international arena. The German Reichstag had ceased to function as a real parliament by the mid-1930s, but to the CPIC that did not matter. Germany would get a seat at the table with a professional Nazi diplomat sent in lieu of actual legislators. Remaining active in the CPIC allowed Germany a back door into the international arena that it had earlier left in such a huff by withdrawing from the League.[76]

The proof that the Nazis were willing to accept the CPIC and its technocratic brand of parliamentary internationalism comes from the minutes of the Reichstag session on March 23, 1933. That day is infamous for the passage of the Enabling Act. Nazi stormtroopers had surrounded the Reichstag's provisional chambers at Kroll's Opera House, across the street from the burned-out parliament building. The social democrats who were not already in jail or in hiding had braved a gauntlet of stormtroopers to take their places for one final defense of German democracy. However, the Enabling Act was not actually the last act of that infamous Reichstag session. Among the procedural measures that Reichstag President Hermann Göring brought up right before he adjourned the meeting, one empowered him to consult with the various parliamentary parties to select the delegates to the CPIC's conference in Rome later that year. In the Reichstag's minutes, tucked in between the excitement and bravos of the National Socialists, the parliament voted Göring that power, and German attendance at the 1933 CPIC meeting was assured – the same day Germany's republic was legislatively undone.[77]

Ultimately, interwar European parliamentarians were active as transnational agents through formal appointments to the League of Nations Assembly, on party-political campaign missions, and as informal agents calling in favours from foreign colleagues. In both the IPU and CPIC, the international ambitions of parliamentarians took on more organized and more global dimensions. However, there is nothing fundamentally democratic in all of these transnational ties among parliamentarians. The CPIC abandoned its early plans of acting like a border-crossing legislative commercial committee by embracing specialized diplomats over democratically elected lawmakers. The IPU never disavowed its parliamentary roots, but its hopes for growing into the biggest tent for parliamentarians meant it ultimately became more a social and debating club for legislators, whether or not they had any democratic mandate. The ideal of a parliamentary international presented by both these organizations changed during the period between the world wars. By the late 1930s, advocating for strong parliamentary democracies had vanished from the agendas of both the IPU and CPIC.

Chapter Five

"Wolves Among Lambs": Nazis in the German Reichstag

In 1931, an 84-page booklet called *Der Reichstag 1930* (The Reichstag 1930) appeared on bookshelves. It had been written by a newly elected German lawmaker who hailed from the second-largest parliamentary party. The author was a leading campaigner in the September 1930 election, and his party's press published this primer on how the parliament functioned. In *Der Reichstag 1930*, the writer presented answers to common questions about German politics, ranging from who could vote in national elections to which mathematical formula translated the votes cast into parliamentary seats. The booklet moved provision-by-provision through the Reichstag's rules of procedure and reproduced comprehensive charts of vote totals by constituency and membership lists for all the parliamentary committees. As a technical primer, *Der Reichstag 1930* might have easily fallen into historical obscurity except for the fact that the author was the newly minted German legislator Heinrich Himmler, whose infamy stems from later orchestrating Nazi terror and genocide. Himmler's earlier reference work on the republican Reichstag largely presented material without party-political commentary. *Der Reichstag 1930* was essentially a Nazi-endorsed guide to Weimar-era civics and its hated democratic parliament.[1]

Although Himmler's booklet generally presented parliamentary information factually, there were exceptions. The framing of the book – beginning with the subtitle *Das sterbende System und der Nationalsozialismus* (The Dying System and National Socialism) – foregrounded a hatred for parliamentary democracy. Brief asides mocked specific socialist parliamentarians for their lack of working-class roots, and Himmler assembled data on all the corporate and supervisory board positions held by lawmakers, concluding that legislators held a total of 106 board positions, but the National Socialist German Workers' Party (Nationalsozialistische Deutsche Arbeiterpartei, NSDAP) had no board members in its ranks.

The text's most obvious national socialist bugbear was an analysis of how many parliamentarians were "racial Jews." Charts, lists, and percentages were meant to indict almost all other parties as being nefariously influenced by Jewish members. Although this overtly antisemitic analysis was contained to a handful of pages, this part of the book attracted the most attention after publication because Himmler falsely accused the liberal politician and later president of West Germany Theodor Heuß of being Jewish. Under pressure, Himmler retracted this claim.[2]

As a primer on parliamentary politics with hastily added Nazi antisemitic and anti-capitalist framing, *Der Reichstag 1930* was not an outlier on the bookshelf of a committed Nazi in the waning years of the Weimar Republic. The Nazi parliamentary leader Wilhelm Frick also published two lengthy compendia of the NSDAP's parliamentary activities. Frick would later serve as the Nazi interior minister and be executed at Nuremberg for his crimes, but in the early 1930s, he spent time amassing material to prove how productive his avowedly anti-parliamentary Nazi legislators were. Frick's books would have made dreadfully boring reading; they included lists of all the resolutions, questions, and votes put forward by Nazi lawmakers, without an index, table of contents, or commentary.[3] Nevertheless, a Nazi review of one of Frick's compilations insisted that this text was crucial for professional party speakers, activists, and even enemies to know what the NSDAP parliamentary party was doing: "In the future, there will hardly be any actively involved national socialist who does not have a copy of this book for reference."[4]

The NSDAP even sponsored the National Socialist Parliamentary Service (Nationalsozialistischer Parlamentsdienst) that reported the standpoints and activities of Nazis in parliament like a wire service. These political news items could then be reprinted by local Nazi publishers. Weekly reports included NSDAP parliamentary positions on topics such as whether Germany needed colonies (according to the service: yes, but not overseas) and how to help German artists and musicians (only hire Jews and foreigners for cultural jobs if there are no qualified German Aryans available). The service even reprinted NSDAP legislative proposals from regional parliaments. In early 1932, for instance, two Badenese Landtag proposals were reproduced in full. One would have banned importing Alsatian lettuce to protect local German farmers, and the other would have banned slaughtering animals without anesthesia, which was an antisemitic attempt to forbid kosher butchering.[5] Historians have tended to coalesce around the position summed up by the historian Volker Ullrich that Nazi parliamentarians' "only aim was to bring the Reichstag to a standstill by subverting negotiations, filing frivolous motions and submitting nonsensical queries."[6] However, publishing compendia of frivolous motions or telegraphing out the complete text of Badenese draft laws suggest that Nazi parliamentarians thought they were doing something more meaningful; otherwise why would they devote so much ink to their parliamentary work?

One could easily read this proliferation of Nazi party publications on NSDAP parliamentary activities as part of the party's strategy to gain power legally. After the failed Beer Hall Putsch of 1923, Adolf Hitler adopted the policy of gaining power through constitutional means rather than by a violent coup. Ian Kershaw has referred to this strategy as a more "parliamentary tactic," and Benjamin Hett quoted Hitler embracing this idea with the trepidation of someone who despised democratic institutions: "We shall have to hold our noses and enter the Reichstag against the Catholic and Marxist deputies."[7] However, Hett read Hitler's legal strategy as a charade, since it allegedly produced parliamentarians who "conduct[ed] themselves with the coarse brutality of the Stormtroopers."[8] Richard Evans similarly highlighted the NSDAP lawmakers' "incessant points of order, chanting, shouting, interrupting and demonstrating total contempt for the legislature."[9] When Nazi parliamentarians crop up in these longer, synthetic histories, scholars have tended to dwell on 1932 brown-shirted boorishness rather than examine the daily grind of NSDAP parliamentary life over the eight-and-a-half years Nazis were in the republican Reichstag. That parliamentary drudgery was spotlighted in these contemporary NSDAP publications by men like Himmler and Frick.[10]

Although Nazi parliamentarians feature briefly in grand historical narratives on the coming of the Third Reich, historians minimize these legislators' agency.[11] Swimming against this scholarly tide, Martin Döring comprehensively examined the Nazis in the Reichstag in a doctoral dissertation published in 2001 as *"Parlamentarischer Arm der Bewegung": Die Nationalsozialisten im Reichstag der Weimarer Republik* ("Parliamentary Arm of the Movement": National Socialists in the Weimar Republic's Reichstag). Döring set out to investigate the "paradox of having to exist as avowed opponents of parliamentarism within this parliamentary system" through in-depth, chronologically nuanced analyses of Nazi lawmakers and their Reichstag activities.[12] Döring's encyclopaedic work drew on the parliamentary minutes, archival collections of Nazis and other right-wing German politicians, and contemporary publications and memoirs. Although Döring's monograph has appeared prominently in footnotes of later scholars, many overlook Döring's sensitivity to change over time and his ultimate conclusion that "between 1924 and 1932 [Nazis in parliament] were not merely Hitler's tool."[13]

Building on Döring's foundation by centring interwar Nazi parliamentarians and taking seriously their own agency, this chapter focuses more specifically on Nazi legislators' relationship to the Reichstag's democratic norms both in public and in private. For example, Döring has read the creation of the NSDAP parliamentary press service as the natural professionalization of the party. This could be true, but a truly well-oiled propaganda apparatus for an anti-democratic party would not have printed so much on policy positions, motions, and resolutions. Instead, these many publications can be read as a concession to the Weimar Republic's norm that parliamentarians should be productive in working for their electorate and advancing their ideology. There was obviously a disconnect between these publications and the reality of Nazi legislators thwarting the will of the majority through obstruction, but printing so much on the productivity of NSDAP politicians in a hated republic was a concession of sorts to republican norms.[14]

Parliaments are always governed by written rules and unwritten conventions, and these parliamentary norms extended to the social world of politics where some radical politicians mingled with more moderate colleagues. Private sociability could provide a bridge from anti-democratic radicalism to implicit acceptance of parliamentary conventions. While serving in the Reichstag, Nazi legislators were confronted with the dilemma of how much to acquiesce to behind-the-scenes parliamentary norms and how much to unabashedly undermine the institution, even in private.[15] Before 1930 there were some limited attempts by NSDAP lawmakers to reach across party lines and into the Reichstag's world of sociability, but the landslide 1930 election helped transform the NSDAP legislators into a united anti-democratic cadre. This chapter explores that change over time in order to set up a larger comparison with the following chapter on radical right-wing parliamentarians in the Netherlands and Czechoslovakia. Nazi parliamentarians' eventual complete rejection of Weimar's democratic norms – both in public and private – was not replicated among all fascist parties abroad, as Chapter 6 will demonstrate.

Exploiting Parliamentary Privileges to Subvert the System

In the late 1920s, Hans Fabricius was a lawyer and Nazi party member working his way up the Prussian bureaucratic ladder. He was suspended from the German civil service as a high-ranking finance official in 1929 because of his Nazi politics. Although Fabricius would fight this suspension, losing his day job freed up time for him to redouble his commitment to the Nazi party by standing for and winning election to the Reichstag in 1930. After the Nazi seizure of power, Fabricius resumed his civil service career, moving between the Nazi interior ministry and the NSDAP party apparatus. Fabricius reached the acme of his career as a leading judge in the Third Reich's administrative court in 1944, just as the entire regime was going down in flames.[16]

During the Nazi years in power, Hans Fabricius tried his hand at writing, and in 1936, he published a short 59-page history of the National Socialist movement. Fabricius's pamphlet challenged unnamed "superficial and malicious critics of recent history" who believed Nazi political success had been the product of "general desperation and its manipulation through shrewd and demagogic propaganda."[17] In contrast with these accounts, Fabricius laid out his own version of the world-historical Nazi movement. He explored everything from Hitler's boyhood antisemitism to the movement's setbacks during the Weimar years. Fabricius's rendition of this Nazi past seemed fairly ordinary until he devoted several pages to Nazi parliamentarians during the Weimar Republic. Warm words for Nazi legislators were not the staple of the Third Reich's historical propaganda. Fabricius stood out for insisting that Nazi parliamentarians played a key role in the party's rise to power.[18]

Perhaps unsurprisingly for a man who highlighted the importance of Nazi parliamentarians, Hans Fabricius had not only been an NSDAP member of the republican Reichstag from 1930 but also was the party's chief parliamentary whip from 1932. Undoubtedly, Fabricius proudly wore the special swastika armband augmented with two gold stripes that was reserved for NSDAP parliamentarians. However, after the Weimar Republic was swept away, the NSDAP's copious publications about work in the Reichstag were quickly forgotten, and Nazi-era histories pivoted to emphasizing the world-historical importance and genius of men like Hitler or Goebbels's "relentless, stirring propaganda" rather than the drudgery of parliamentary work.[19] Until Martin Döring's monograph, most later historians also ignored the Nazis in the Reichstag, reasoning that the parliamentary service of an anti-democratic party was not worth analyzing.[20]

Although Fabricius trumpeted the importance of Nazi parliamentarians to the overall fascist movement, he also emphasized how radically anti-system Nazi legislators had to be. According to Fabricius, the guiding principle of any Nazi member of parliament was that he – and they were all men – "may never become a 'parliamentarian.' He was to remain a fighter and to understand his main purpose was still in arousing the people."[21] Since at least 1928, Adolf Hitler had called on Nazi parliamentarians to be "wolves among the lambs," subverting and devouring the system from within. Hitler's own phrase and related ideas of NSDAP lawmakers being like "snakes in the grass" or "wolves among sheep" were repeatedly echoed in parliamentarians' contemporary diaries, in late-1920s Nazi propaganda, and in Fabricius's later tract. Being wolf-like actors among the democratic parliamentary lambs was the contemporaneous self-understanding of Nazi legislators.[22]

Fabricius emphasized that serving as an anti-democratic parliamentarian offered both benefits and risks. He wrote that a Nazi parliamentarian must "with calculating expediency, exploit all advantages that parliamentarism offers for the movement but systematically avoid or steadfastly resist all the pitfalls of the parliamentary system."[23] From the perspective of the NSDAP leadership, the primary danger for Nazis serving in parliaments was that they might become complacent. Joseph Goebbels scornfully derided those Nazi politicians as "parliamentarized," who were happy to mingle with colleagues, to temper their incendiary language, or to draft constructive legislation rather than take cheap political shots.[24] To avoid this danger of "parliamentarization," Fabricius emphasized that Nazis were "to strictly isolate themselves from parliamentarians from other parties even in private situations, to consider the parliamentary stage solely as a place for propaganda, and to make it difficult for all the other parties whenever the possibility presents itself." Moreover, Nazi legislators were to physically avoid the Reichstag as much as possible, and "to linger in the parliamentary complex only when it seems to be absolutely necessary in a given situation." Fabricius saw sociability and its cross-party overtones as the danger that committed NSDAP politicians must avoid.[25]

Despite the temptations of parliamentary life, Fabricius highlighted three major benefits of national legislative service for the Nazis: "parliamentary salaries, the free train pass, and legal immunity."[26] These were all constitutionally mandated rights for parliamentarians in republican Germany. These privileges were designed to enable legislators to support themselves, to travel, and to speak freely. However, anti-parliamentary parties – both the NSDAP and the German Communists – used these rights to spread their anti-democratic message. In the Nazi newspaper *Der Angriff*, Joseph Goebbels sardonically celebrated his election to the German parliament in 1928. He wrote about his new role as a M.d.R. (Mitglied des Reichstags – Member of the Reichstag). In addition to M.d.R., Goebbels invented abbreviations for himself: "I.d.F." (Inhaber der Freifahrkarte – Bearer of a Free Train Pass) and "I.d.I." (Inhaber der Immunität – Bearer of Legal Immunity). Goebbels's satirical abbreviations represented the Nazi approach to exploiting their parliamentary rights, and Goebbels mocked "the stupidity of democracy[:] it will always be one of the best jokes about democracy that it offers its mortal enemies the exact weapons they need to destroy democracy."[27]

Of Fabricius's benefits for Nazis in the Reichstag, the first was "parliamentary salaries." Indeed, Reichstag pay was seen as a source of income by parties across the political spectrum. Most German political parties took a cut of their own legislators' salaries. This money was used to fund political staff and offset office costs, as well as to support the party and election campaigns. However, the Nazi party in the Reichstag broke with the tradition of taking a percentage of parliamentary pay to instead take 100 per cent of a legislator's salary. Nazi lawmakers were to act as "trustees of the Nazi party," destined to pass all the money on to the party for the party's use. Financially, the NSDAP parliamentarians were a funnel directing government money to the anti-parliamentary movement, and the party reimbursed some of their expenses in return.[28]

Fabricius's second benefit from Nazi seats in the Reichstag was the ability for politicians to access free train travel. Since 1873, German Reichstag members enjoyed at least some free transportation. Until 1906, salaries for Wilhelmine parliamentarians were constitutionally prohibited, so free train travel to and from the sessions of the Reichstag amounted to meagre in-kind compensation for legislators. Both salaries and free train travel throughout Germany for parliamentarians were enshrined in article 40 of the Weimar Constitution, in part, to enable new representatives from the working class to take up seats in parliament without having to struggle financially. However, more radical parties were able to exploit these rights. Fabricius claimed that all NSDAP members were expected to use this train travel for propaganda purposes, travelling across the country "on the republic's dime" spreading the Nazi gospel.[29] Although all incumbent lawmakers used their travel privileges for some political advantage, the radical anti-parliamentary parties saw free transportation as a big plus of serving in parliament. In fact, a German Communist recalled that radical left-wingers "were put on the electoral list, in order to be able to use the free train pass and thus be better able to carry out their work outside the parliament" campaigning for the party. Selecting potential parliamentarians not based on their qualities as future lawmakers but because of their skill as on-the-ground campaigners revealed a distain for the parliamentary process by radical parties on both the left and right.[30]

Fabricius's final benefit for NSDAP parliamentarians was legal immunity. Three articles of the Weimar Constitution regulated parliamentary immunity. Article 36 banned "judicial or official" reprisals for votes or statements made by Reichstag or Landtag parliamentarians in their capacity as lawmakers. This prohibition was absolute, and since the Reichstag's minutes could be freely distributed, this meant that elected Nazi parliamentarians would always be able to get their message out by delivering vitriolic speeches in parliament that could then be distributed across the country. The constitution's article 37 banned all prosecutions or investigations of members of the Reichstag or a Landtag without the consent of the parliaments themselves. Finally, article 38 allowed parliamentarians to bring others into their confidence without the obligation to testify and protected parliamentary premises from search and seizure.[31]

Politicians whose aggressive campaigning might run afoul of German libel or treason laws were happy to take advantage of these various layers of parliamentary immunity. For instance, the Communist trade unionist Hans Stetter gamed the immunity rules, both as a member of the Württemberg Landtag and of the Reichstag. Stetter was imprisoned in investigative custody in Stuttgart until early 1924, when the Communist party announced he was a candidate for the Reichstag. He was released for the election, and despite being elected, police investigations continued against him. "Since the Reichstag convened only at the end of May and my immunity as a Landtag member expired on May 15, I was arrested just after midnight on May 16." Stetter was only freed after his wife's doctor asked that he be allowed to care for her after a nervous breakdown. A trial against Stetter and his comrades continued in Leipzig, but before a verdict could be reached, he went into hiding in Berlin until the Reichstag met and his new term of parliamentary immunity began.[32]

The Nazi propagandist Joseph Goebbels also gamed the immunity system to avoid prosecution for libel as an editor of the Berlin Nazi newspaper *Der Angriff*. When Goebbels was first elected to the Reichstag in 1928 he wrote privately in his diary "So now I'm an M.d.R. [...] Immune, that's the main thing." Goebbels still had to face trial for earlier libel allegations, but his immunity prevented him from being as easily accosted in the future. Like the Communist Hans Stetter, parliamentary immunity was often on Goebbels' mind, and he worried that the dissolution of the Reichstag in 1930 would prompt the police to immediately arrest him. In 1931, the Reichstag moved to limit Goebbels's parliamentary immunity after he ignored several legal summonses.[33] However, in the public debate over lifting Goebbels's parliamentary immunity, anti-system parties like the NSDAP were able to position themselves hypocritically as the true defenders of the free speech of democratically elected parliamentarians: "If a democracy attempts to curtail the rights of national socialist parliamentarians, it would only deny its own raison d'être, which would diminish it in the eyes of its own proponents." Championing the destruction of democracy yet invoking democratic rights for protection was a common tactic among radical parties that ran roughshod over parliamentary norms and helped make the NSDAP parliamentarians "wolves among the lambs" in both their public and private Reichstag personas.[34]

Nazi Obstruction Both Inside and Outside the Reichstag

Rather than co-operating behind-the-scenes with political rivals in the German Reichstag as other parties sometimes did, a frequent Nazi political tactic was obstruction. In master narratives of the collapse of the Weimar Republic or the rise of the Third Reich, scholars have drawn attention to violent obstruction by Nazi parliamentarians, sometimes arguing that this tactic did not conform to Hitler's strategy of a constitutional path to power.[35] However, parliamentary obstruction is a much older tactic that political scientists and historians have traced from ancient Rome to the filibuster in the US Senate. The Dutch historian Henk te Velde has argued that the systematic parliamentary obstruction by Irish nationalists in the British House of Commons in the late nineteenth century was the advent of modern obstruction. Then Parliament was bogged down by opposition politicians who brought business to a halt by filibustering and using the rules to gum up the system. Since crippling parliamentary obstruction was similarly deployed by nationalists in the Habsburg-era Cisleithanian legislature, Te Velde identified larger worries around 1900 about a "crisis of the parliamentary system" that presaged interwar anxieties. Te Velde differentiated the *fin-de-siècle* parliamentary obstruction of nineteenth-century nationalists who believed in democracy but in a different place – for instance, in Dublin rather than in London – from the "anti-democratic obstruction of the interwar years." Strictly speaking, however, obstruction to disrupt parliamentary business can be a tactic. Whether it is anti-democratic is only evident based on severity and motive. Frivolous points of order might have pushed the parliamentary envelope, but as was true with German Nazi lawmakers, there was obstruction that amounted to a larger rejection of democratic norms.[36]

Systematic Nazi political obstruction began on the campaign trail, long before lawmakers entered the Reichstag. Nazi campaign rhetoric was incendiary and deployed pointed ad hominem attacks. For instance, in 1931, the NSDAP parliamentarian Gregor Strasser declared in a speech in Stuttgart: "When we are in charge we will throw [the socialist] Breitscheid and his comrades into the mud. A number will be hanged, the rest will be imprisoned." Strasser's personal death threats against his parliamentary colleagues were beyond the pale of normal republican speech.[37] Moreover, Nazi campaigners subverted age-old German election practices. Since the Wilhelmine era, Germans had developed the institution of the "discussion speaker" for campaign rallies. The idea was that to educate the public, a speaker from an opposing political party would give a shorter speech outlining his or her positions to which the candidate sponsoring the rally would respond. This was a mix of a modern election debate with a traditional political rally. The need for discussion speakers meant that politicians would often agree to go to opponents' events and then switch places for a subsequent rally. However, Nazis challenged the norms of this institution. One right-liberal German People's Party (Deutsche Volkspartei, DVP) parliamentarian recalled that he had been invited to headline a DVP rally in a medium-sized town with a Nazi discussion speaker who was to kick off the event with a short speech. However, the "National Socialist discussion speaker unabashedly demanded the same amount of speaking time that I would use as the leading candidate for the DVP in the constituency – an entire hour." The Nazi discussion speaker kept talking, and attempts by DVP leaders to intervene failed, since Nazi thugs had come to disrupt the meeting. The Nazi filibustered for almost 30 minutes.[38]

After subverting political traditions on the campaign trail, Nazi politicians then worked to challenge parliamentary conventions in the Reichstag's plenary chamber. Sometimes in violation of Prussian law, they appeared in brown stormtrooper uniforms for legislative sessions. They also turned their backs on speakers they did not like and boycotted the Reichstag for an extended period of time. The Nazis shared many of these tactics with their Communist enemies in the Reichstag. A left-liberal German parliamentarian wrote: "National Socialists and Communists sometimes sought out opportunities to shout each other down, although in other cases they worked together to throw up obstacles to challenge the parliamentary work of the chancellor and the parties supporting him." This legislator recalled a common Nazi-Communist front in thwarting the orderly processes of the parliament.[39]

The specific obstructionist tactics employed by NSDAP parliamentarians evolved over time, often based on the number of Nazis in the Reichstag. In the wake of the Beer Hall Putsch in 1923 that sent Hitler to jail, the National Socialist Freedom Movement (Nationalsozialistische Freiheitsbewegung) was formed as right-wing *völkisch* electoral alliance. It entered the Reichstag with 32 seats and 6.5 per cent of the vote after the May 1924 elections but then lost all but 14 seats in the subsequent December 1924 elections. Infighting among *völkisch* and Nazi politicians in the alliance hampered the work of this early parliamentary group. However, these radical politicians were not averse to delivering incendiary speeches or introducing legislation for propagandistic purposes.

In 1924, *völkisch* parliamentarians presented a draft law to exclude Jews from all public offices. In a January 1928 Reichstag speech, the Nazi Wilhelm Frick called for the destruction of the democratic parliamentary system, which he characterized as under the yoke of "inferior folks, the lower races, Jews, and moneybags." Other parliamentarians repeatedly shouted Frick down, and the Reichstag president called him to order for his language, but he was undeterred in exploiting the parliamentary bully pulpit.[40]

After the party skyrocketed to second place in the 1930 Reichstag elections, the Nazis brought their obstructionist and anti-parliamentary approach to parliamentary committees. As a larger party in the Reichstag, they were permitted both representatives on all committees and could appoint the chairs for several leading committees. Although the first wave of sugarcoated memoirs and sympathetic scholarship after 1945 insisted that the NSDAP had "worked properly" in day-to-day parliamentary life, in fact, Nazi committee chairmen tried to sabotage their own committees' work. In the budget committee, for instance, the Nazi vice chair refused to rein in one of his NSDAP comrades who slandered a socialist committee member as "a Marxist Jew who has no right to have a say in Germany."[41] In 1932, the Nazi Gregor Strasser used his role as chair of the one standing committee to ignore valid requests from members to convene the committee. Since Strasser refused to call the committee into session, the president of the Reichstag ordered another member to do so, but Strasser challenged this for "having egregiously violated parliamentary procedures and thus the constitution." Strasser borrowed from the tried-and-true radical playbook of calling out democrats for not playing by the democratic rules, while Strasser himself was subverting German democracy, even from his lowly station as a committee chair.[42]

One left-liberal German parliamentarian remembered that Nazis in the Reichstag "had no interest in any type of real co-operation." Since parliamentary committee work was about the finer points of legislating, the Nazis were particularly uninterested in these details.[43] Nazi politicians seemed keen on instead using committees to embarrass opponents and try out their talking points. The socialist parliamentarian Gerhart Seger recalled his experiences with his Nazi colleagues in the Reichstag's Foreign Affairs Committee. The Nazi party theorist and notorious anti-semite Alfred Rosenberg was a member of that committee, and Seger remembered challenging him there, once saying: "Facts are facts. You can evaluate them differently, you can place your own emphasis on a particular selection of facts, and you can draw your own conclusions from the facts. But to dispute the facts themselves is obviously nonsensical."

Rosenberg nonchalantly responded: "We National Socialists are not here to recognize facts but to alter them."[44]

In another episode during a committee debate on the Foreign Office's budget, Alfred Rosenberg condemned Germany's foreign service for employing too many foreigners at diplomatic postings abroad. When pressed to give an example, Rosenberg cited the German legation at Kaunas, the capital of interwar Lithuania. At the next committee meeting, the chancellor reported back that he had investigated the legation at Kaunas and determined that only the maid was a foreigner, underhandedly attacking Rosenberg in pointing out: "This woman was born in the same city as Mr. Rosenberg himself: Riga." Despite debunking the Nazi talking points in the committee, when the budget reached the floor of the Reichstag, "Rosenberg got up and made exactly the same speech with the same complaints – that German legations did not employ enough German nationals – as if nothing had happened in the committee." German parliamentary committees met in private, so Rosenberg had not yet presented his fake facts to the public. The socialist observer concluded: "You might just as well have talked to the wall as debate with the Nazis, and that of course made the work in the national legislature absolutely futile." Ultimately, the committee served as a dry run for Rosenberg's public plenary speech.[45]

The Nazis were also notoriously bad colleagues for their habit of revealing confidential information to the press and misusing material in their own party newspapers. In democratic parliaments, secret meetings and private negotiations were often necessary to reach political compromises. Attempts had been made since 1924 to bring *völkisch* and Nazi politicians into the confidence of their colleagues. For example, in July 1925, the new German president and former military field marshal Paul von Hindenburg reached out to the *völkisch* lawmaker and his former military colleague Erich Ludendorff to set up a private meeting. Ludendorff accepted the invitation but then publicized this event in the right-wing press. Hindenburg elected not to carry out the visit: "I would have happily visited you as a friend and comrade in arms, but an article in a *völkisch* newspaper has given this planned visit a political complexion and greatly excited everyone's passions. Considering this situation, what I would very much happily do as a friend and messmate, I sadly am unable to do as president. It is with the greatest regret that I must cancel our plans."[46]

However, Ludendorff's indiscretion was only the tip of the iceberg for radical right-wing politicians flaunting confidentiality. For example, when Hitler met Chancellor Brüning about a parliamentary extension of President Hindenburg's term of office, a report of the meeting was immediately published by the Nazis to discredit the government.[47] The Nazi leadership felt that this misuse of information was acceptable in the zero-sum game of politics. Even Hitler's conservative German National People's Party (Deutschnationale Volkspartei, DNVP) ally Alfred Hugenberg called Hitler out for not putting things down in writing because of the Nazi leader's morbid fear anything he wrote would be used against him: "Your principle of not answering letters – to prevent them from falling into the wrong hands or being misused – makes co-operation very hard." Hitler's phobia about producing a paper trail of political agreements reflected the anti-parliamentary Nazi belief that politics was not about collaboration but about discrediting enemies and winning at all costs.[48]

When Germans went to the polls for snap national elections in late July 1932, a staggering 13.7 million of them cast their votes for the Nazi Party. The NSDAP doubled its vote share from the 1930 elections, captured 37 per cent of the total vote, and won 230 of 605 seats in the Reichstag. This was almost a hundred seats more than the second-largest party, the Social Democratic Party of Germany (Sozialdemokratische Partei Deutschlands, SPD).[49] According to German parliamentary tradition, as the largest parliamentary party, the NSDAP was entitled to select the parliament's president. Hitler passed over candidates with previous experience in the Reichstag's leadership and instead tapped the famous fighter ace Hermann Göring to be the Nazi-nominated president of the Reichstag. Parties on the left recoiled at electing Göring to the legislature's highest office, especially since the Nazis had flaunted parliamentary tradition so often in the past. However, enough moderate lawmakers supported Göring, and he was elected. The role of the president of the Reichstag was to be an impartial presiding officer representing the interests of the entire body, but Göring's decision to take his presidential seat still dressed in his Nazi party uniform hinted that neutrality would not be the hallmark of his presidency.[50]

The dignity of the Reichstag was never on Reichstag President Göring's mind. The plump fighter ace brought Nazi political gamesmanship to his presidential duties. When a DVP politician was "repeatedly physically assaulted" by a Nazi colleague, Göring did not even acknowledge the DVP's complaint.[51] On September 12, 1932, two weeks after Göring's election as president, the Reichstag was set to debate a motion of no confidence in the cabinet of the conservative Catholic aristocrat Franz von Papen. Chancellor Papen led a presidentially backed government that ran roughshod over the parliament and ruled by decree. Papen had earned enemies on both the left and right, and the Communist party had submitted a motion of no confidence in the government. When the unpopular chancellor realized that his cabinet was set to lose the parliamentary vote, he rushed to the presidential palace to get a decree from the aging President Hindenburg to dissolve the parliament and call fresh elections.[52]

According to established parliamentary procedure, the president of the Reichstag should have called on the chancellor to address the parliament when he requested the floor, but when Papen arrived, ready to read the dissolution decree, Göring intentionally overlooked Papen's request to speak and instead called for a vote on the Communist motion of no confidence. The official parliamentary minutes do not record Papen's asking for the floor, but stenographers noted that when Göring called for the vote on the motion of no confidence there was "persistent great turmoil." Göring called for silence and moved into the vote despite "lots of constant movement in the hall." Papen cropped up in the Reichstag's minutes at this juncture: "Chancellor von Papen puts a document on the president's table and departs the hall with the cabinet ministers."[53]

Göring insisted on carrying out the vote, which Papen's government lost 512 to 42, the worst parliamentary defeat for a German government in history. As if to spite Papen, Göring then read the presidential decree dissolving the Reichstag. However, Göring declared the cabinet deposed since it "was just toppled by the parliament by an overwhelming majority," so he declared it was legally unable to dissolve the parliament.[54] Backroom dealing by more moderate parties eventually meant that the decree was recognized and the parties geared up for new elections, but Göring remained proud of his theatrical outmanoeuvering of Papen even into his imprisonment by the Allies during the Nuremberg Trials. On the one hand, Göring flaunted parliamentary practice by refusing to recognize Papen. On the other hand, he claimed to be the better democrat because he called for a vote and accepted the will of the parliamentary majority.[55]

Not all political obstruction is a rejection of parliament or democracy itself. Releasing a private conversation to the press or giving antisemitic speeches after being called to order by the president do not necessarily clear the bar of trying to destroy democracy. However, the pattern of rejecting the Reichstag's norms and using parliamentary privileges to get Nazis out of jail for libellous claims, to travel for free across the country, and to enrich the party to achieve Hitler's avowed goal of "achiev[ing] decisive majorities in all legislative bodies so that, if we're successful, we can remould the state in a form that corresponds to our ideas" does tend towards the "antidemocratic obstruction" that Henk te Velde noticed interwar era.[56]

From a Small Parliamentary Party to the Nazi Political Earthquake of 1930

From the Nazis' fractious early alliance with *völkisch* parliamentarians in 1924, there was always tension in corralling NSDAP parliamentarians into a party group that could function collectively in the common project of destroying the Reichstag's legitimacy. Indeed, early candidates were often selected for their ability to attract voters rather than form a disciplined team in office. This was the case with Franz Ritter von Epp who was elected to the Reichstag in 1928. Epp had made his career in the military, having fought in colonial wars, served in the First World War, and led a paramilitary Freikorps in the early days of the German republic. Epp's experience crushing the Bavarian Socialist Republic cemented his hatred of socialism. Epp had early connections with leading Nazis like Hitler and Stormtrooper (Sturmabteiling, SA) leader Ernst Röhm because of Epp's stint in Munich. However, Epp only joined the NSDAP right before the May 1928 elections. Having Epp on the ballot was a political coup for the Nazis.[57]

Intrigue and jockeying for power occurred among the handful of Nazis in the Reichstag when Franz Ritter von Epp was first elected in 1928. Among this smaller number of NSDAP parliamentarians, there was no love lost between certain party comrades. Joseph Goebbels wrote disparagingly of the avowed monarchist, long-time soldier, and fellow NSDAP lawmaker Epp calling him "still bourgeois" and warning that Nazis must "pay special attention to him." Epp's self-assuredness prompted him to challenge Nazi party unity in dramatic fashion when he abstained on a vote on a Communist resolution on financial policy. The other members of the NSDAP supported the motion, and Epp's solitary abstention prompted the party to develop disciplinary measures to ensure future Nazi legislators always followed the party line. Epp was chastised, but he did not fall from grace. These experiences of the late 1920s were used to build a united NSDAP parliamentary party in which stepping out of line was nearly impossible.[58]

Even for an anti-democratic party, the humdrum of Reichstag life shaped Nazi parliamentarians' time in Berlin. As with any parliamentary party, there were meetings to attend and staff to manage. Official leaders had to be appointed, and in Hitler's selection of Wilhelm Frick as the party's Reichstag leader, there was even a concession to parliamentary expectations. Frick was not a Goebbels-like firebrand but was a Bavarian civil servant who was seen as a technically minded "expert in the mastery of the tools of parliamentary procedure."[59] Although one might expect that an anti-parliamentary party did not devote much day-to-day energy to the Reichstag, some of the Nazi lawmakers forged friendships with each other during the time they spent in Berlin. Even during the Third Reich, an occasional birthday card to another Nazi who had served in the Weimar-era Reichstag would include a reference to becoming friends serving together for the NSDAP in the republican parliament.[60]

From 1930, it is virtually impossible to find the same vibrant networks of cross-party collaboration that existed in Berlin's private clubhouses or among Germany's female politicians among the Nazis. There was, however, the faintest whisper of cross-party ties among NSDAP parliamentarians and their fellow lawmakers between 1928 and 1930, paradoxically because the NSDAP was so poorly represented in the parliament. In the 1928 election, the Nazis captured only 2.6 per cent of the vote, which yielded 12 parliamentarians. This fell below the 15 members required to officially form a recognized parliamentary group, which would have given the party rights to bring motions forward, to have members in committees, and to speak for longer periods in plenary debates. The small number of Nazi parliamentarians meant the NSDAP members were treated almost as an afterthought in the Reichstag's processes, including in the seating chart. The assigned seats for the party were at the very back of the plenary hall. In fact, the parliamentary newcomers Göring and Goebbels had to make do with seats on an extra sofa in the far-right corner of the chamber.[61]

Because of the Nazis' weak presence in the 1928 Reichstag, they needed to reach out to colleagues in another party to do anything of substance legislatively. The Nazis found receptive colleagues in the lawmakers from the Christlich-Nationale Bauern- und Landvolkpartei (Christian-National Peasants' and Farmers' Party, Landvolk). The Landvolk had broken with the DNVP over agricultural issues, but their nine parliamentarians were also too few to reach official parliamentary group status. The Landvolk and the Nazis decided to co-operate to sponsor proposals in order to get these issues on the Reichstag's agenda. Attempts to fuse the two parliamentary groups were opposed on both sides, but they still co-operated pragmatically. Whether this was an alliance of expediency or true ideological affinity is still a matter of debate.[62]

The cross-party practical working relationship between the Landvolk and NSDAP was a political necessity, but it also brought these rival politicians together on a personal level. These connections later paid dividends in the 1931 project to unite right-wing forces in Germany into a national opposition. A rally was scheduled in Bad Harzburg, and the NSDAP Reichstag leader Wilhelm Frick worked to convince colleagues in other parliamentary parties to attend. Historians tend to focus on the alliance of the DNVP and NSDAP at this event, spotlighting Hitler and

Hugenberg's alliance, but Reichstag members from the Landvolk, the Economic Party of the German Middle Classes (Wirtschaftspartei), and the right-liberal DVP all travelled to Bad Harzburg. The relatively high number of Landvolk parliamentarians who attended appears to be an aftereffect of the Nazis' strategic alliance with them between 1928 and 1930.[63]

Fabricius and Goebbels fretted about the dangers of Reichstag sociability for the Nazi movement, and Goebbels once rhetorically asked: "Do any of you really believe that after marching into the Reichstag's plenary chamber we would share a friendly drink with [the socialist] Philipp Scheidemann?"[64] Goebbels expected the answer to be no, but in fact, there were several fleeting personal connections between Nazis and colleagues in other parties that appear in memoirs and archives. For instance, the DVP lawmaker Heinrich Schnee and Franz Ritter von Epp were connected because they knew each other from their previous careers. Schnee was a former imperial colonial governor who was president of the Working Committee of German Associations (Arbeitsausschuss Deutscher Verbände). Schnee knew Epp from their common service in the German colonies, as well as their public right-wing advocacy against the idea that Germans were responsible for the outbreak of the First World War.[65] In another attempted personal connection, the right-liberal DVP leader Eduard Dingeldey sent a condolence letter to Hermann Göring after the death of Göring's wife in 1931.[66] With this, Dingeldey tried to pull Göring into a collegial world around the Reichstag, but Göring's apparent lack of response reflected the Nazis' resistance to joining the informal culture of respectful, collegial correspondence. One of the most surprising examples of cross-party informal contact between the NSDAP and another party also involved Göring. An SPD lawmaker recalled that after the infamous Reichstag vote on the Enabling Act in 1933, Göring conferred with the socialists' leadership and warned them privately "to not yet leave the building, since the excited crowds of people outside might not treat [you] especially kindly." However, these cross-party relationships among Nazis and rivals were incredibly rare, and they most often occurred with veteran NSDAP parliamentarians who had served in the Reichstag before 1930.[67]

One striking feature of the NSDAP's more regimented parliamentary practice was an oath that all Nazi parliamentarians were eventually obligated to take. Wilhelm Frick put together a declaration that was edited over the years to eventually include five points. The first three points reflected the antisemitism and anti-capitalism of the NSDAP; the parliamentarians affirmed they had "no ties or connections to Jews," served in "no supervisory board positions in banks or other enterprises," and would not take up these positions in the future. The fourth and fifth points related to party unity and discipline. NSDAP parliamentarians promised they would "at all times consider the party's interests," recognize the NSDAP party program, and "subordinate themselves to Adolf Hitler and his commands." The final point made clear that the party thought of the parliamentary seats as the property of the party and that it required Nazi legislators who left the party to resign from the Reichstag rather than keep their seat and join another party.[68] This oath violated the spirit of the Weimar Constitution, which stated: "The delegates are representatives of the whole people. They are subject only to their own conscience and are not bound by any instructions." Contrary to the constitution, the NSDAP oath treated politicians as representatives of the party, bound by the party program and obedience.[69]

Although the Nazis overtook the SPD as the largest party in the parliament after the July 1932 election, that political earthquake was not as much a turning point for the history of the parliamentary NSDAP as the earlier elections of 1930. Even among historians who minimize Nazis in the Reichstag, the 1930 election is rightly seen as the watershed moment of change.[70] In September 1930, the NSDAP had gone from having parliamentarians sitting on the Reichstag's corner sofa as an afterthought to 107 parliamentarians. When the Nazi parliamentary party experienced such rapid growth, it had to teach newcomers the ropes of the Reichstag. The party worked to discipline its legislators from the beginning by drawing boundaries between them and colleagues from other parties. A long list of instructions to parliamentary newcomers reminded them how to behave, reflecting a more regimented approach than other parties took. The Nazi parliamentary leadership even divided its parliamentary party into four plenary seating blocs, each with an appointed bloc leader. These seating blocs were further subdivided into groups of 10, each with their own sub-leader. There was no equivalent in the other Reichstag parties and reflected the Nazi fixation on defined hierarchies and leaders.[71]

The NSDAP's insistence on order and obedience was also reflected in the correspondence of the party leadership to average NSDAP parliamentarians. A dress code – "brown shirt with armband (no coat)" – was spelled out explicitly for parliamentary and committee meetings, and notices that mandated attendance made clear "only serious illness when one is completely bedridden" would be excused.[72] This regimented NSDAP parliamentary life limited Nazi legislators' ability to mingle with colleagues from other parties or to indulge in Reichstag sociability. The NSDAP leadership explicitly wrote: "It is especially undesirable that members of the party who do not have some official business in the Reichstag sit or stand around pointlessly the halls when the parliament is in session." Instead parliamentarians were supposed to keep as far away from the parliament as possible, preferably travelling around Germany in the service of the party.[73]

Glimmers of individually minded resistance to this monolithically driven Nazi parliamentary system were exceedingly rare. For instance, in private correspondence with Wilhelm Frick as the leader of the NSDAP in the Reichstag, an NSDAP parliamentarian who came to office in the first election of 1932 protested attempts to force him out of the Reichstag after the November 1932 elections. Heinrich August Knickmann was a professional soldier and local bureaucrat who had risen to be a local leader among the local Nazi SA organization in northern Westphalia. The Nazi regional Gau level of party organization had put together the electoral list on the basis of which Knickmann was elected in July 1932. According to Knickmann, the Westphalian Gau rearranged the list for the subsequent November 1932 election at the last minute, contravening an earlier gentlemen's agreement. The Nazis then won five seats in the area, but since Knickmann had been moved from place 5 to 7, he had not been elected. Knickmann objected to this whole procedure in a lengthy letter to Frick and trotted out a series of arguments ranging from the impropriety of changing the rules to the importance of having Knickmann in the Reichstag "in the interests of the SA as the core of the movement." Knickmann recruited his SA superiors to support his last ditch appeal to remain in the Reichstag, but Knickmann's plea was unsuccessful. He only rejoined the Reichstag when a resignation opened up a seat in January 1933. This kind of intraparty tension was intentionally kept under wraps.[74]

Ultimately, the defining feature of the parliamentary NSDAP was that its leader Adolf Hitler was not himself a member of the Reichstag. As a former Austrian citizen who renounced that citizenship in 1925, Hitler was stateless and ineligible to serve in any German parliament until 1932. Hitler did not even live in Berlin, but whenever he came from Munich to the German capital, he led the meetings of the parliamentary party. For instance, in August 1932, the 230-man NSDAP parliamentary group assembled at the Kaiserhof Hotel to commit itself publicly to the Führer in a festive ceremony. Hitler's control of the parliamentary party had not always been absolute; after the 1924 elections when Hitler was in prison, he had to share power with the *völkisch* lawmakers. After 1928, however, the NSDAP was no longer tied to those allies, so Hitler consolidated his power over his legislators, making all determinations about the party leadership and candidates put forward for higher office. As the party grew in size and importance, the red carpet was rolled out for Hitler whenever he visited Berlin. In addition to his work chairing the parliamentary party, Hitler mingled with aristocratic guests in Hermann Göring's apartment. Hitler frequented Berlin so often that a middle box at the opera was reserved for him when he was in town.[75]

Because the NSDAP's structure had Hitler at the apex, cross-party negotiations always had to involve him. Other political parties' leaders were members of the Reichstag and conducted negotiations from their Berlin offices, but Hitler was not based in the German capital. Instead, the NSDAP parliamentary party often served as Hitler's Berlin secretariat and a conduit to get messages to and from him. For example, the NSDAP parliamentary staff went into overdrive supporting Hitler's presidential run in 1932, setting up meetings with other parliamentarians to shore up right-wing support for the Nazi presidential candidate.[76] Lawmakers from other parties sometimes even reached out to their Nazi colleagues as a way to contact Hitler. For instance, a vice president of the Reichstag from the Centre Party wrote to a leading NSDAP parliamentarian asking to set up a meeting between leading members of the Centre Party and the Nazi leader. Only as an afterthought, did he also arrange a meeting with Wilhelm Frick as the Nazis' parliamentary leader. This party structure dominated by Hitler meant that even if Nazi lawmakers had thrown themselves into the Reichstag's social world, any cross-party relationships never had the potential to transform into political partnerships in the way friendships among other parliamentarians could. After the 1930 election, NSDAP legislators had ceded more and more political agency to Hitler, and the parliamentary party redoubled its efforts to strictly regiment the interactions of its lawmakers to isolate them from colleagues.[77]

A Brown-Shirted, Regimented Anti-Parliamentary Cadre

In the small NSDAP of the late 1920s, Franz Ritter von Epp was able to go out on a limb and vote differently than his fellow Nazis and put out social feelers to colleagues in other parties. However, when Epp was first elected in 1928, he lamented: "I shall be a parliamentarian. At the moment it is doubtful whether I have the necessary qualities – I don't have these qualities, and I don't want them."[78] His colleagues in other parties disagreed, and he was considered clubbable enough to invite to social events in Berlin. On some level, the nineteenth-century liberal belief in parliaments was that individual members – captive to their consciences more than party discipline – would act for the good of the country. Epp began to do this before he was reeled back into the Nazi world by the massive influx of new parliamentarians in 1930. This disciplined NSDAP group was remade as an organized Nazi cadre bent on destroying the Reichstag despite serving in it. Any hopes of truly "parliamentarizing" the Nazis to moderate them died with the 1930 election.[79]

Paradoxically, there was room for greater individual agency in the smaller NSDAP parliamentary party of the 1920s, and Epp took advantage of this in abstaining when his colleagues did not. However, by the early 1930s, Adolf Hitler served as the ultimate arbiter of party and parliamentary disputes. This was particularly evident in a factional conflict between Gregor Strasser's populist take on Nazism and Hitler, and in this dispute the NSDAP parliamentary group played a role that ultimately demonstrated its powerlessness as an autonomous centre of authority. Gregor Strasser and his brother Otto had advanced a more anti-capitalist brand of National Socialism, and contemporaries saw an insurgent Strasserian wing in the NSDAP that could challenge Hitler's power. Historians have since debunked the myth of a truly viable Strasserian opposition; nevertheless, by 1932, Strasser had amassed significant power within the NSDAP as the Reich Organizational Leader. In this role, Strasser had particular influence in putting together the NSDAP candidate lists for the Reichstag elections. Although Wilhelm Frick, as the parliamentary leader, had formal control of these electoral lists, Strasser had the supervisory role in the candidate selection process. Nazi candidates ended up sending one brief declaration of interest to Frick and a longer, more detailed application to Strasser. Strasser's power in the party, particularly in approving candidates, led to him having party comrades indebted to him among the Nazi Reichstag members.[80]

The Hitler-Strasser crisis came to a head near the end of 1932. After the Nazis' electoral losses in the November elections, Strasser advocated entering a coalition with more traditional right-wing parties without insisting on the chancellorship, which was vehemently rejected by Hitler. When the new Chancellor Kurt von Schleicher secretly offered Strasser the vice chancellorship, Strasser privately mulled it over, which enraged Hitler. A series of meetings between Hitler and the NSDAP parliamentarians revealed that although Strasser lacked support among the run-of-the-mill party members, up to one-third of the NSDAP parliamentarians were sympathetic to Strasser. Nevertheless, when personally confronted by Hitler, none of them came to Strasser's defense. Gregor Strasser resigned all his offices in the party in early December 1932, and eventually he met a grisly end on the Night of the Long Knives in 1934. Sizeable support within the Nazi Reichstag party was not enough to defend Strasser from Hitler's wrath.[81] This episode points to the receding agency of NSDAP parliamentarians by 1932. However, it also shows that Strasser used his years in the Reichstag to build up close personal connections to his Nazi colleagues. Nevertheless, Strasser's work came to naught, since his colleagues' sympathies buckled under direct pressure from the Führer.[82]

When they entered the Reichstag in the mid-1920s, Nazi parliamentarians were not foreordained to serve as mindless automatons marching towards dictatorship. Of course, Nazi lawmakers did not robustly participate in the 1920s' cross-party parliamentary social world or understand their legislative role with any transnational element, as had become common among their German parliamentary peers. However, until the very early 1930s, there was creeping acceptance by Nazi lawmakers of some of the conventions surrounding the Reichstag. The glut of publications about NSDAP parliamentary activities was a tacit concession to the norm that parliamentarians should be legislatively active to further their political beliefs. Franz Ritter von Epp's decision to vote against the Nazi party line accepted the constitutional norm that legislators were "subject only to their own conscience and are not bound by any instructions."[83] Even Gregor Strasser's belief that he could use Nazi members of the Reichstag to build an independent power base implicitly adopted the democratic norm that lawmakers had their own agency. These extremely limited concessions to Weimar's parliamentary norms lost out, particularly after the Nazi landslide enabled the creation of a more strictly regimented Nazi cadre in the Reichstag. Paradoxically, the more NSDAP lawmakers there were, the easier it was to control the entire parliamentary party with Hitler at the apex. This enlarged Nazi parliamentary group disciplined its members to not integrate themselves into the Reichstag's social world, to use political obstruction wantonly, and to reject all of Weimar's democratic trappings.

Chapter Six

Gentlemanly National Socialists and Co-operating German Nationalists in the Dutch and Czechoslovak Parliaments of the 1930s

By March 1940, Europe was engulfed in the Second World War. Poland had been devoured by Nazi Germany and Soviet Russia. German U-boats were attacking Allied ships, and the world's attention was turned towards Finland's Winter War against the Soviet Union. In retrospect, this period would come to be called the Phony War before German blitzkrieg came to Western Europe. However, even contemporaries had an ominous sense of foreboding about the continent's future. In the Netherlands – which had maintained neutrality throughout the First World War and had declared its neutrality in this current conflict – the Dutch ministry of defense was scrambling to build new fortifications along the country's borders. Nazi Germany was obviously an aggressive power, and the Dutch were frantically shoring up their defenses. In the midst of this hasty military construction effort, Dutch parliamentarians in the Tweede Kamer requested that the country's military authorities arrange a formal visit for them tour these new defensive works in March 1940.[1]

The Dutch defense ministry pulled out all the stops for a two-day and two-night parliamentary tour of various military installations on March 28 and 29, 1940. Parliamentarians were shuttled between 's-Hertogenbosch and Arnhem with fancy meals scheduled alongside walks through freshly dug trenches, inspections of temporary military bridges, and conversations with officers along the border. Sixty-two of 100 Dutch parliamentarians signed up to go on this military junket. Among the politicians participating in the tour were two of the four parliamentarians from the Dutch Nationaal-Socialistische Beweging (National Socialist Movement, NSB). In fact, one of these national socialists was M.M. Rost van Tonningen – the most radical fascist member of the Dutch parliament and a close friend of Nazi Germany. He had never before gone on a parliamentary junket.[2] Rost van Tonningen was so obviously a Dutch national security threat that he was preventively detained by the authorities in early

Figure 6.1. Photo of the March 1940 parliamentary visit to the Dutch defenses along the German border.

Source: From Nationaal Archief, Inv. Nr. 3381, 2.02.22, Tweede Kamer der Staten-Generaal, 1815–1945, NAH.

May 1940. However, since this particular visit in March was arranged for all lawmakers, even the Dutch national socialist lawmakers were invited. Less than two months later, the army of Nazi Germany would invade the Netherlands over these very fortifications.[3]

The reason that Rost van Tonningen was allowed to travel with his parliamentary colleagues on this military junket was rooted in the broad informal social milieu surrounding the Dutch Tweede Kamer. The interwar networks of politicians in The Hague were politically expansive and were forged in a robust world of behind-the-scenes political sociability. There were chic receptions and fancy dinners for parliamentarians at top hotels in the city. A banquet hosted by the speaker of the Tweede Kamer in 1928 brought together 66 parliamentarians. That particular evening, a socialist, a traditional right-wing Protestant politician, and a liberal all sat together to dine on turbot filets and racks of lamb.[4] The standard practice in the Netherlands was to invite all 100 members of the Dutch

Tweede Kamer to any event outside parliament. In the 1930s, lawmakers received invitations to see a battle cruiser being built in Rotterdam, to visit the colonial institute in Amsterdam, to listen to a scholarly discussion on Suriname, to attend a national commercial fair, to travel to Rotterdam to visit a tunnel under construction, and to observe various military parades and naval fleet reviews. Sometimes interest from parliamentarians was limited; only two legislators – a socialist and a Catholic party member – planned to attend a talk in Amsterdam on fishing in the IJsselmeer. However, these events could also attract well over half the members of the Dutch parliament. Sixty-nine members travelled on a special train to show off a new diesel-electric railroad route.[5]

What do you do with avowed anti-parliamentary forces and common social events? As a general rule, parliamentary guest lists for social events or junkets in the Netherlands were not curated to keep out radicals. Communists, revolutionary socialists, and Dutch national socialists were forwarded invitations like any other member of parliament. One might imagine that anti-democratic parliamentarians opted out of this informal world of junkets and social functions entirely, as happened in Germany among the Nazis after the 1930 election. However, this strict rejection of parliamentary sociability by radical parties was not actually the case in the Netherlands. For instance, the Dutch Communist parliamentary leader Lou de Visser cropped up at many parliamentary social events. De Visser went on the electric train ride, and he belatedly requested tickets for reserved seating on the viewing platform at Princess Juliana's wedding in 1937. De Visser lived in The Hague, so perhaps he and his family wanted a better view of the royal couple. Nevertheless, the image of an avowed Communist clamouring for good seats at a royal wedding is astonishing. In larger parliaments, it was always necessary to exclude members from attending informal events on the basis of numbers. In Germany, there was just no way to invite 600 people to visit a newly opened tunnel. Logistics led to curating guest lists, which limited attendance to politicians from governing parties and the clubbable opposition. In the Netherlands, that convention never developed, and radical opposition members could and did attend these social events.[6]

How does a democratic parliament cope with anti-democratic forces in its midst? With creeping authoritarianism across Europe in the years between the wars, the problem of anti-parliamentary politicians was not only confronted in the German Reichstag with its regimented cadre of Nazi parliamentarians. Many of Europe's far-right parties were themselves inspired by Italian Fascists and the German Nazis and shared a similar disdain for parliamentary processes. However, individual national circumstances – ranging from the number of elected lawmakers to whether or not an anti-democratic party represented a national minority – shaped how these avowedly anti-parliamentary parties engaged in their own national legislatures. Political tactics were different in different countries, and comparing them points to distinctions that nationally blinkered historical perspectives miss.

In the flurry of scholarship from the 1990s and early 2000s on fascism, its origins, and typology, there was sometimes a flattening of smaller fascist parties in comparative studies. Stanley Payne and Robert O. Paxton both briefly addressed minor fascist movements, but far more academic attention has been paid to Fascist Italy and Nazi Germany. Parties like Belgium's Rexist movement, Ireland's Blueshirts, and the United Kingdom's British Union of Fascists have been given shorter shrift or even minimized as unsuccessful.[7] Moreover, since fascist parties beyond Germany often became the quisling agents of the Nazis during the Second World War, there was a natural tendency to see all these fascist parties as always aspiring towards the radicalism that was later unleashed by wartime German occupation.[8]

This chapter focuses on the Dutch NSB and Czechoslovak Sudeten German Party (Sudetendeutsche Partei, SdP) before the Second World War in order to provide a different picture of how two anti-parliamentary parties functioned within their national political contexts. Comparing these two parties' formal and informal approaches to parliamentary life and democratic norms shows they were not always mirror images of the German Nazis. No one can gainsay the fact that these two parties were opposed to interwar democracy and were enraptured with authoritarian reforms in Fascist Italy and Nazi Germany. However, parliamentarians could publicly espouse anti-parliamentary sentiments, while privately making concessions to democratic norms. This did not mean these radical parties were not dangerous, but it did tether them to interwar parliamentary democracies in unexpected ways.

Pulling back the curtain on these two anti-democratic parties' approaches to and experiences of interwar parliamentary life challenges larger narratives that group all anti-parliamentary parties together. In fact, in both the Netherlands and Czechoslovakia there was some acceptance of cross-party political connections, even by radical, anti-democratic legislators. The patrician leader of the Dutch NSB did not wholly reject the social norms that underpinned sociability in the Tweede Kamer, and the Sudeten German Party in Czechoslovakia nurtured working relationships with the Czechoslovak state in order to advocate for German minority interests. Only through comparison with the regimented radicalism of the Nazi parliamentarians in Germany do these two examples of unexpected accommodation with Dutch and Czechoslovak democracy stand out as distinct.

"Posting a Guard for the Dutch People!" The NSB Enters the Tweede Kamer

In 1937, four new members of the Dutch Tweede Kamer were elected as the first parliamentarians for the Dutch National Socialist Movement. In aesthetics, structure, and ideology the NSB resembled the many fascist knock-off political groups that emerged during the interwar years. The first four NSB parliamentarians, however, were a disparate group. Max graaf de Marchant et d'Ansembourg was an aristocratic, Roman Catholic Germanophile from southern Limburg who chaired the NSB parliamentary party. Meinoud Marinus Rost van Tonningen was a radicalized erstwhile League of Nations economics official. Jan Woudenberg was a former socialist trade unionist, and Gerhardus Dieters was a modest farmer from rural Drenthe.[9]

As the leader of the NSB parliamentary party, d'Ansembourg declared that these men were "parliamentarians against our wishes and without gratitude" who were only taking up seats in the Tweede Kamer "to announce the coming apocalypse" and "to speak as prosecutors of a system."[10] These bold, anti-parliamentary proclamations could have been lifted from the German Nazi Hans Fabricius's own writings on the tactics and goals of a parliamentarian in the National Socialist German Workers' Party (Nationalsozialistische Deutsche Arbeiterpartei, NSDAP). Fabricius had written that an anti-democratic Nazi legislator "was to remain a fighter and to understand his main purpose was still in arousing the people."[11] Indeed, Anton Mussert, the Dutch national socialist leader, also wrote of his hopes to rid the Netherlands of democratic traditions, as the Nazis had done in Germany: "We are only going to the Tweede Kamer to post a guard for the Dutch people! As soon as we seize power in the state, we will abolish parliamentarism [...] and all of its excesses!"[12]

When these NSB parliamentarians arrived in the Tweede Kamer in 1937, they engaged in provocative parliamentary behaviour that was reminiscent of NSDAP legislators in the German Reichstag. Fabricius had written that the NSDAP's parliamentary goal was "to make it difficult for all the other parties whenever the possibility presents itself."[13] In a similar vein, the new NSB parliamentarians decided to support a Dutch Communist proposal to institute a state pension for people older than 65. The Communists introduced this legislation every year, but since their own party never had five parliamentarians, the minimum to advance a proposal to a floor debate, the legislation always died without discussion. When the NSB joined the Tweede Kamer, they opportunistically supported the Communist proposal, setting it up for public debate. The NSB had no sympathies for the Communists or their ideas, but the NSB parliamentary leader relished the tension this caused in the Tweede Kamer in forcing moderate politicians to take a stand against old-age pensions. This kind of obstruction, however, was the pestering of skilled opposition parties and was not necessarily anti-democratic, even if the two parties collaborating to embarrass the government were the Communists and the NSB.[14]

The NSB's ability to promote conflict among the other parties through parliamentary manoeuvering was limited by the party's poor showing in the 1937 Dutch national elections. These were the first national parliamentary elections in which the NSB participated, and it won only 4.21 per cent of the vote, sending four lawmakers to the hundred-person Tweede Kamer. Of course, this was a higher percentage of the vote than the German NSDAP and its *völkisch* allies won in either the December 1924 or the 1928 German elections, but the Dutch NSB was deeply disappointed with the 1937 result. The NSB's leader, Anton Mussert, declined to take up his parliamentary seat despite being first on the NSB's electoral list. Like Adolf Hitler, Mussert committed himself to building his political movement from outside parliament.[15]

Although the NSB had not contested elections for the Tweede Kamer before 1937, it had burst onto the Dutch political stage in 1933, the year of the previous national election. In Dutch political history, 1933 was a year marked by numerous crises. In the run-up to the April 1933 election, there were wildcat strikes across the country, as well as demonstrations by both far left-wing parties and a populist farmers' movement. Perhaps most notably, in February 1933, there was a mutiny on board *De Zeven Provinciën*, a Dutch warship off the coast of the Dutch East Indies. The mixed Dutch and Indonesian crew seized control of the ship to protest pay cuts, and the Dutch authorities ended the mutiny with force, ordering an airplane to bomb the ship, killing 19 sailors. Many on the Dutch left were sympathetic to the striking sailors, while the more bourgeois and right-wing parties argued there was an systemic erosion of respect for authority in Dutch society. Of course, 1933 also marked the advent of the Third Reich in the country next door. In this national and international context, the NSB grew to be a formidable political force on the far-right side of the Dutch political spectrum. At the party's first national meeting in January 1933, there were only about a thousand party members, but by the end of the year, more than 20,000 had joined, and there was a waiting list for new members.[16]

Anton Mussert's Dutch brand of national socialism had copied the NSDAP's party program without the passages on racial science or the Führer principle. The NSB itself at first tended in a more Italian Fascist direction, allowed Jews to join the party, and tried to remain bourgeois enough to appeal to the middle of Dutch society. The NSB was originally seen as non-threatening by the existing political parties, but in 1934, political pressure from the socialists helped force the government's hand to prohibit civil servants from being members of the NSB. The NSB used this prohibition to attack the government as being undemocratic for clamping down on a legitimate political party. In the provincial elections of 1935, the NSB won a respectable 7.94 per cent of the vote, winning over 11 per cent in both Limburg and Drenthe where residents felt particularly distant from politics in The Hague. The NSB worked for a better result in the national Tweede Kamer elections of 1937, but by then, the party's political momentum had evaporated to only 4.21 per cent of the vote.[17]

Like the NSDAP in Germany, the NSB had to organize its legislators to function as a unified force in the halls of power. NSB parliamentarians had entered Dutch provincial legislatures after the 1935 elections. Dutch provincial parliaments indirectly selected the members of the Dutch upper house, the Eerste Kamer, so NSB legislators first appeared in The Hague in 1935. The NSB leadership approved guidelines regulating the behaviour of its provincial parliamentarians, and, on the surface, these rules seem similar to the regimented practices of the German NSDAP. First and foremost, the NSB legislative groups were "directed by the parliamentary group leader." There was clear chain of command with the parliamentary group leader subject to the national leader, and all of these leaders were "appointed and removed by the General Leader." Decision-making in the provincial NSB groups was also laid out clearly: "Differences of opinion would be dealt with in the parliamentary group, and afterwards decisions would be made by the group leader." Appeals of these decisions were possible to the national leader. This clear hierarchy with designated decision-makers differed from the early days of the NSDAP in the Reichstag when, for example, Franz Ritter von Epp was allowed to cast his vote differently than his colleagues.[18]

Once national NSB parliamentarians arrived in The Hague, the NSB purchased and outfitted a residential and office building, several minutes' walk north of the Binnenhof parliamentary complex. This Willem de Zwijgerhuis was set up with bedrooms for legislators to use during their stays in the city. NSB lawmakers were required to pay 2,500 guilders annually for the upkeep of these facilities in The Hague. This mandatory contribution shows that the NSB, like the NSDAP, saw the salaries of parliamentarians as a crucial source of party income. Although the NSB was headquartered in Utrecht, the Willem de Zwijgerhuis hosted several other NSB offices including the party departments for economics, housing, and agricultural issues. These offices took receipt of the parliamentary reference materials that were sent to NSB legislators. In practice, official Tweede Kamer documents often did not even reach the NSB parliamentarians but instead formed the research basis for party publications. NSB lawmakers could reach out to these party departments in The Hague for statistics to use in parliamentary speeches, but these departments were not seen as parliamentary support staff as much as a think tank for the NSB's general political work.[19]

In terms of the day-to-day work of the NSB's Tweede Kamer parliamentary party, there was a less regimented and structured dynamic behind the scenes. Between 1937 and 1940, there were only around five formal NSB parliamentary party meetings.[20] Rather than taking marching orders from the parliamentary leader or co-ordinating plans through regular meetings, the NSB parliamentary party divided subject areas up among its four parliamentarians. For instance, one member took engineering/ water management and another the Dutch East Indies.[21] The individual legislator assigned to a given subject area was given wide latitude in his domain and had little support and no guidance from the party. No NSB official ever stepped in to alter speeches. This meant that the position an NSB parliamentarian took on a given issue could be a surprise. One NSB parliamentarian recalled: "No one ever knew what anyone else would say. What's more, the party was only marginally interested in the work of the Tweede Kamer group."[22]

In 1932, 230 German Nazi parliamentarians filed into the Reichstag clad in stormtrooper uniforms, divided into seating blocs and subdivided smaller groups each with bloc leaders to maintain group discipline. In the run up to the 1937 Dutch elections, there were fears that the Dutch national socialists would win such a large percentage of the seats in the Tweede Kamer that they would be able to muster a similar show. However, when d'Ansembourg delivered the first NSB speech to the Tweede Kamer and declared that the NSB stood for freedom, a Protestant confessional parliamentarian theatrically coughed. The speaker of the Tweede Kamer recalled in his diary: "I beckoned to him and offered him a cough drop to soothe his throat. This worked, and the tense situation was diffused." Humour and disdain, rather than fear and theatrics, greeted the NSB in the Tweede Kamer. Ultimately, the NSB's parliamentary practice was far less co-ordinated than that of the German NSDAP, in part because of their measly electoral performance and subsequent small number of only four elected members.[23]

Fireworks and Fistfights: Rost van Tonningen's Radical Vision for the NSB

Meinoud Marinus Rost van Tonningen is today remembered as the quintessential *fout* (literally, "wrong"), which refers to a Dutch collaborator during the Second World War. Rost van Tonningen was one of the most ardent prewar fans of Nazi Germany, hoping to import Hitler's rabid antisemitism and introduce a hatred of political Catholicism to the less radical Dutch NSB. He earned infamy as a *fout* because he was an active agent of Nazi wishes during the war, first liquidating the Dutch socialist parties and then taking control of the Dutch national bank to finance the occupation. Captured after the liberation of the Netherlands, Rost van Tonningen died in the Scheveningen prison, likely having committed suicide. His widow, Florrie Heubel, also helped cement his grim legacy. She had joined the NSB's youth movement and studied in Nazi Germany, where she fell under the spell of Nazi racial science. Heubel never renounced the family's rabid Nazism, treasured a ring kissed by Hitler, was prosecuted for spreading fascist literature, publicly campaigned for her husband's rehabilitation, and encouraged the publication of Nazi apologist literature until her death in 2007. Heubel was the fitting widowed inheritor of the dark legacy of M.M. Rost van Tonningen.[24]

Rost van Tonningen was born on Java in the Dutch East Indies as the son of a Dutch noblewoman and a colonial military general. After studying law in Leiden, Rost worked in Vienna as an economic and financial expert for the League of Nations. Based in Austria, he imbibed the antisemitism and anti-Bolshevism of that country's politics. By the 1930s, however, he was most drawn to the radicalism of the Austrian Nazis. Instead of working with the dictatorial Austro-Fascist Chancellor Kurt Schuschnigg, Rost van Tonningen befriended Franz von Papen, then the ambassador of Nazi Germany in Vienna. When Rost van Tonningen returned the Netherlands in 1936, he turned his back on the work of the League of Nations and joined the NSB. Rost became the editor of the NSB newspaper *Het Nationale Dagblad,* where he used the platform to spread his more radical, antisemitic, pro-German version of national socialism.[25]

In the Tweede Kamer from 1937, Rost van Tonningen represented the most rabid faction of the NSB, and he constantly challenged parliamentary norms. His speeches were laced with offensive and unparliamentary language. The Tweede Kamer's speaker repeatedly exercised the speaker's prerogative to strike inappropriate passages in Rost van Tonningen's parliamentary contributions from the minutes. Thirty-four excerpts in

Rost's speeches were struck from the record, as opposed to only 25 by Rost's NSB colleague d'Ansembourg, who spoke for the party more frequently. Rost's most offensive remarks included personal antisemitic attacks on parliamentary colleagues. In a foreign policy debate that had been called by the Communist parliamentarian David Wijnkoop, whose father was Jewish, Rost van Tonningen spoke of a conspiracy involving a "racial comrade of Mr. Wijnkoop." Although this fiery and personalized language set Rost van Tonningen apart from his NSB colleagues, it was similar to the NSDAP's ad hominem attacks and pointed language in the German Reichstag.[26]

The apex of Rost van Tonningen's public parliamentary career was a series of incendiary speeches on the 1938 Oss affair that led to a fist fight in the Dutch parliament. Because of the high crime rate in the predominantly Catholic town of Oss in North Brabant, Dutch gendarmes had been sent in to assist the local police. There was tension between Catholic locals and predominantly Protestant gendarmes, and the situation exploded when the gendarmes uncovered a series of sex scandals, arresting a Jewish businessman on suspicion of "lewd acts with his female staff" and detaining two Catholic priests for sexual crimes with both men and women.[27] Rost van Tonningen was enthralled by this scandal's ability to bring together anti-Catholicism and antisemitism, and Rost even personally went to Oss to speak with residents to put together a dossier of alleged crimes in the city.[28]

Stewing on this scandal, Rost van Tonningen spoke on the Oss affair in the Tweede Kamer with as many fireworks as possible, and his flamboyant speeches prompted such raucous applause from the parliament's balconies that the speaker had to order the public out of the chamber. In one speech, Rost attacked two Catholic priests by name, and the parliament's speaker ordered Rost to quit giving his speech and leave the chamber. Rost tried to continue, but Catholic parliamentarians shouted him down. One even yelled that Rost was a "traitor." Although a parliamentary official directed Rost van Tonningen to the door, Rost and a Catholic lawmaker ended up exchanging blows.[29] Rost's NSB colleague Jan Woudenberg later recalled that he "was standing in the middle of the plenary chamber [and] quickly rushed to get between the two and to help Rost out if he needed it. This 'quick' rush was more of a 'frantic dash' during which he ran over [another lawmaker]." The parliamentary staff jumped on Woudenberg and ushered him to the door to break up the fight. In reflecting on Rost's approach to Oss, Woudenberg remembered: "He presented his allegations crudely. In a manner that was uncommon in the parliament." Coming to blows with a colleague was unheard of, but it demonstrated Rost's commitment to use the Tweede Kamer as a stage for propaganda.

Although Rost van Tonningen poured himself into his work on Oss, he had very little interest in parliamentary minutiae. In fact, Rost was not averse to shirking his duties altogether. Woudenberg remembered one day when he received "a big envelope with hard-to-read handwritten notes, many typed pages of work, and a series of appendices" from the parliamentary staff. Rost van Tonningen had sent the material along with a note saying that he was not able to be in the Tweede Kamer that day, so he asked Woudenberg to deliver his speech on the Dutch East Indies budget. Woudenberg was shocked to learn that he was next on the speakers' list, so before he could glance over Rost's speech or order his notes, he was called to speak: "It was a pitiful presentation. The pages were already or had gotten mixed up, and Woudenberg read in a monotone voice, page after page, full of numbers and statistics, jumping from tobacco to domestic governance and from rubber to warships." After hours of giving a meandering and dreadfully dull speech, Woudenberg realized he was speaking to an empty parliament and the minister – who was obliged to stay and listen – was ignoring him, so he just gave up and stopped speaking. Woudenberg's disaster of a speech was the product of Rost's disinterest in the day-to-day work of the Tweede Kamer that had no propagandistic value.

Rost van Tonningen was of the bourgeois class that was readily accepted socially in the Tweede Kamer, and he had experience mingling with dignitaries from around the world serving for the League of Nations. Nevertheless, Rost recoiled at connecting with his parliamentary colleagues; he was remembered as exuding contempt and speaking with no one. Rost van Tonningen's intelligence nevertheless caught the eye of one of his colleagues, the confessional Protestant politician Hendrik Tilanus. However, Tilanus's experiences also explain why Rost ultimately was on such bad terms with most of his colleagues: "The only [NSB parliamentarian] who I thought was smart was M.M. Rost van Tonningen. I liked him at first. [...] But for my part, I broke off all contact when he brought up something that I had told him in a private conversation in the discussion of the defense budget." Rost's misuse of Tilanus's private words for political gain was similar to Nazi parliamentary practices in Germany that disregarded secrecy for propagandistic purposes. Ultimately, Rost van Tonningen represented the wing of the NSB that was radical, only wanted to provoke, and was at home copying the NSDAP playbook for the Netherlands. Making friends or abiding by parliamentary rules was not part of his approach.[30]

Graaf de Marchant et d'Ansembourg and a Patrician Approach to Dismantling Dutch Democracy

Although the NSB parliamentary group's stated goal was to "present itself publicly as a unified front," Rost van Tonningen's political and personal approach to parliamentary life was not the only one put forward by NSB parliamentarians. There was also a more moderate and less radical attitude represented by the Limburg nobleman M.V.E.H.J.M. (Max) graaf de Marchant et d'Ansembourg. D'Ansembourg was more conciliatory behind the scenes and was respectful of the parliament's work despite his strong – and unwavering – opposition to democracy. Even in 1974, only a year before his death, d'Ansembourg still doubted any government based on majority rule: "Democracy has only one measure – numbers – and it cannot have any other benchmark! What a weak foundation! Since the French Revolution, numbers or the majority, have determined what happens in the world."[31]

D'Ansembourg's anti-democratic sentiment permeated his speeches in the Tweede Kamer in the late 1930s, but he did not ostentatiously challenge all norms of Dutch political life. D'Ansembourg's distance from Rost's radicalism was evident in his response to the fistfight that Rost provoked with Catholic lawmakers over the Oss affair. Rost and Woudenberg entered the fracas with fists flying, but d'Ansembourg prevented the fourth NSB parliamentarian from joining the fray: "Dieters, who reacted a little slowly, was stopped by d'Ansembourg, who ordered – or asked – him not to get involved." The patrician d'Ansembourg aimed to replace Dutch democracy with the strong institutions of a fascist, corporatist state, but he did not want to sully himself by brawling to achieve that goal. For Rost, on the other hand, no stunt or tactic that could discredit the democrats or boost support for the national socialists was out of bounds.[32]

Max graaf de Marchant et d'Ansembourg was the eighth of eleven children born to Iwan graaf de Marchant et d'Ansembourg and his wife, an Austrian countess. The family was a wealthy and powerful aristocratic clan that had historic links to the Dutch royal family and whose members had long served as mayors and provincial officials in Limburg. The elder d'Ansembourg helped found the Dutch Roman Catholic political party and had served in parliament. The younger d'Ansembourg was brought up in a home environment that was suffused with aristocratic traditions and pronounced Prussian influences. D'Ansembourg's first language was French, which was only the language he ever spoke to his father, and he attended German-language Jesuit schools, speaking German to his mother. During the First World War, d'Ansembourg enlisted in the

Kaiser's army, fighting for Germany, earning an Iron Cross first class, and was naturalized as a Prussian citizen in the process. After the First World War, d'Ansembourg returned to the Netherlands, first working in the banking sector in order to learn Dutch before beginning a career with the state mining service and then serving as the mayor of Amstenrade as a member of the Catholic party that his father founded.[33]

In 1933, d'Ansembourg broke with the expectations of his family and the Catholic political world of southern Limburg by joining the Dutch National Socialists. He had met the party's leader Anton Mussert that year and later insisted that he had only joined the NSB after being convinced that it was a moderate conservative movement. For the NSB, having d'Ansembourg as a member was a huge coup. Like Adolf Hitler convincing the aristocratic general Franz Ritter von Epp to join the NSDAP, d'Ansembourg added the prestige of having an actual nobleman and a sitting mayor sign up for the Dutch NSB movement. D'Ansembourg remained the mayor of Amstenrade until state officials were forbidden from being members of the party in 1934, and he had to stand down as mayor. D'Ansembourg even allowed the NSB to use the park surrounding his stately home in Amstenrade for its political rallies.[34]

However, after d'Ansembourg joined the NSB, he faced pushback from his immediate milieu, which pointed to the disciplining power of sociability. His former party colleagues in the big-tent Dutch Catholic party treated him like a traitor, and the policy of the Dutch Catholic bishops was to withhold communion from NSB members. Over time, d'Ansembourg had adjusted to this social stigma so much so that he was surprised when a Catholic student society in Tilburg invited him to an annual celebration in 1937. Although this type of invitation might have been expected for a normal local notable, d'Ansembourg was also a leading member of the NSB. He wrote for clarification about the invitation: "As one of the leaders in the N.S.B., I am treated as an apostate and banished from the community by practically everyone in public life representing the Catholic part of the country." D'Ansembourg inquired if this invitation was sent in error or if there were actually people in Tilburg who wanted him to be there. Immediately, a professor from the university wrote back that the secretary had made a mistake in sending d'Ansembourg an invitation; of course, he was not invited. Although the movers and shakers of Catholic society had ostracized d'Ansembourg, the voters sent him to the provincial legislature in Limburg, which in turn elected him to the Eerste Kamer in The Hague.[35]

In July 1935, 25 of the 50 members of the Eerste Kamer were elected by the provincial legislatures, and d'Ansembourg and an NSB colleague joined the Dutch senate as first members with legislative role in The

Hague. The Eerste Kamer played second fiddle to the Tweede Kamer in the Dutch constitutional system, but d'Ansembourg took over leadership of the NSB in the upper chamber. As a member of the Eerste Kamer, d'Ansembourg was dispatched as the NSB's official representative to the 1936 German NSDAP party congress in Nuremberg. In fact, both d'Ansembourg and his soon-to-be Tweede Kamer detractor Rost van Tonningen were in Germany for this Nazi rally, but they only ran into each other briefly in Nuremberg.[36] Later, d'Ansembourg and an NSB Eerste Kamer colleague were dispatched to the Dutch East Indies to gin up party-political support in 1938, but there was a general lack of transnational links among NSB politicians, with the exception of formal trips to Nazi Germany. This is perhaps surprising, since Rost van Tonningen had been a member of expatriate networks in Vienna as a League of Nations official, and d'Ansembourg was tied to aristocrats beyond the Netherlands by blood. NSB politicians' transnational links skewed towards Nazi Germany without the international junkets to Inter-Parliamentary Union conferences noticeable in the parliamentary careers of their colleagues.[37]

When Rost van Tonningen and d'Ansembourg entered the Tweede Kamer in 1937, both men delivered pointed anti-democratic speeches, extolled the virtues of an authoritarian state, and defended Nazi Germany. However, within the NSB parliamentary party there was often friction between Rost and d'Ansembourg. As the leader of the NSB parliamentary group, d'Ansembourg spoke at the annual government policy debate and on new parliamentary motions. One recurring topic was the question of new naturalizations, which had to be approved by an act of parliament. Rost van Tonningen repeatedly challenged the choice of allowing d'Ansembourg to give these kinds of speeches: "Not against the speeches themselves but against the fact that d'Ansembourg, with his French name, his German accent, and – as far as Rost was concerned – his less than sterling background." Rost instead thought "that Dieters or Woudenberg, who seem more like average Dutchmen, should be used for these speeches." Rost van Tonningen did not think highly of d'Ansembourg's parliamentary presence.[38]

When the NSB members first arrived in the Tweede Kamer, many of their fellow parliamentarians tried to ignore them. An NSB newspaper reported: "While the NSB parliamentarians sat quietly at their seats [...] the other members spread out into a swarming mass that moved spiritedly through the chamber with everyone shaking hands."[39] Although this decision not to greet colleagues could be seen as performative with the press watching from the balconies above, NSB parliamentarians were often given a cold shoulder behind the scenes. The NSB trade unionist

Woudenberg recalled trying to reach out to his colleagues, reaching out to shake hands in the cloakroom, "but his outstretched hand just floated there in the space between him and several other gentlemen who completely ignored him and started a conversation right over his head."[40] These interactions in the social world of Dutch politics helped denote insiders and outsiders, and it was clear that the NSB politicians were considered outsiders.

On the other hand, d'Ansembourg seemed to connect more effectively with his colleagues in private. Of course, d'Ansembourg had experience in politics, first as a mayor and then in the Eerste Kamer, so he knew the ropes of socializing. More importantly, however, he was a high-ranking aristocrat. Although Woudenberg could not get a handshake, of d'Ansembourg he recalled: "He was a real count, and there were not many – or any – others in the Tweede Kamer; there were probably some old-fashioned members who responded to that. In any case, he conversed with various members and was seen to shake hands with others every once in a while." Ultimately, d'Ansembourg's automatic high social standing as a patrician was something that brought people close to him in a way that did not happen with the working-class NSB legislators.[41]

D'Ansembourg publicly performed his role as a radical NSB parliamentarian, but he did not adopt the slash-and-burn tactics of his firebrand colleague Rost van Tonningen. First and foremost, d'Ansembourg tried to do the parliamentary work that was expected of him. Rost delved into the Oss affair with zeal because he saw the possibility of political points being scored, but Rost pawned off the debate on the colonial budget because it had little value for his work as a propagandist. On the other hand, d'Ansembourg remembered that the amount of work he was juggling in parliament prevented him from spending time in Amstenrade. "Life in the Tweede Kamer carried on as usual. I had a whole lot to do and often had to attend every possible meeting because my 'colleagues' in the parliamentary party were not always there."[42] Unlike his fellow NSB parliamentarians, d'Ansembourg also engaged in lengthy behind-the-scenes correspondence with the parliamentary staff and stenographers about the final versions of his speeches that were to be published with the official minutes, since language deemed too offensive or unparliamentary was prohibited. D'Ansembourg wanted to push the boundaries in the Tweede Kamer, but by participating in this dialogue with staff, he still engaged in behind-the-scenes parliamentary give and take and therefore accepted some of the democratic norms and legislative guardrails, something that Rost van Tonningen completely ignored.[43]

Moreover, d'Ansembourg entered into friendly conversations with his parliamentary colleagues. While serving in the Eerste Kamer, d'Ansembourg privately chatted with a Protestant confessional colleague about the upcoming 1937 election, exchanging friendly predictions about the final vote share. D'Ansembourg's colleague trusted that the NSB politician would not attempt to use the private conversation to score political points, something that Rost van Tonningen was known to do. D'Ansembourg kept up these collegial conversations when he was in the Tweede Kamer, critiquing a colleague's maiden speech in a chat with the speaker, for instance. D'Ansembourg even remembered conversations with Hendrik Colijn, a long-serving conservative Protestant prime minister. These conversations began when d'Ansembourg left office as mayor of Amstenrade and continued when he and Colijn continued to converse on political matters in the Tweede Kamer. Keeping the confidence and trust of rival politicians is not something the NSDAP did in Berlin, but that d'Ansembourg did in The Hague.[44]

In Edwin Klijn and Robin te Slaa's tome on the history of the Dutch NSB, drawing chiefly on official minutes and contemporary reporting led to the natural conclusion that NSB parliamentarians acted homogenously in seeing the parliament "as a platform to broadcast their propaganda."[45] However, there was nuance in the approaches of individual politicians, and ultimately, d'Ansembourg knew that being an NSB politician meant giving over-the-top speeches for propaganda purposes, but when the journalists left the room and the potential to produce election leaflets dried up, there was little purpose in being as radical. D'Ansembourg always "understood honour and propriety as the chief standards for the aristocratic life," and accordingly, he would have been hard pressed to misuse information from private conversations or to flaunt social conventions. D'Ansembourg felt that being a parliamentarian was a slightly distasteful, yet necessary, role. On the other hand, Rost van Tonningen seemed to take pleasure in the most radical speeches, attacking his colleagues, and mocking the rules of the democratic system he hated. In comparing the two men, Woudenberg wrote of d'Ansembourg: "He did not break off his ties with the 'distinguished' world but still moved in circles of aristocrats, diplomats, and large industrialists. In that world he would play the usual game of poker or bridge. Rost van Tonningen, on the other hand, essentially cut off all ties to his previous life and completely and only lived in the world of the NSB." As the parliamentary leader of the NSB, d'Ansembourg still accepted the social norms of high society and life in the Tweede Kamer. Via parliamentary sociability, d'Ansembourg was tethered to the Tweede Kamer's republican norms.[46]

Dutch society of the 1930s and the fractious Weimar Republic of the late 1920s had different political demographics. In the Netherlands, the years between the world wars have been seen to mark the apex of a social structure called pillarization (*verzuiling*) that limited the appeal of the NSB. In pillarized Dutch society, services, stores, social circles, political parties, and other institutions were seen to be segregated by religious or political ideology. The main social "pillars" in the Netherlands were Catholic, Protestant, and Social Democratic, and there was a potential fourth liberal pillar, as well as sub-pillars for the various Dutch Protestant denominations.[47] In 2011, Peter van Dam challenged the concept of unyielding pillars and strict social segregation as a totemic Dutch myth. Historians had come to uncritically invoke pillarization as a "unique Dutch phenomenon" that was a marked departure from the European mainstream. Van Dam contended that, in fact, most Western European countries developed exclusive communities and subcultures for certain demographic groups. In Germany, for instance, there were organized political parties, social organizations, and economic structures for Catholics and socialists, and this pattern was repeated with social groups elsewhere. Rather than bucking European trends, the slight Dutch difference – shared incidentally with Switzerland – was in having an organized, strong Protestant pillar.[48]

Regardless of the later myth about pillarization, Dutch interwar politics reflected the pillarization model insofar as Catholics, socialists, and others tended to vote for that group's political party. Moreover, in 1918, the electoral system in the Netherlands had transitioned from one of local districts to national elections based on proportional representation. This system meant that the Tweede Kamer was more representative, since smaller groups that were geographically dispersed could win parliamentary seats. This electoral system, coupled with strong political support within each pillar, produced an electoral stability that insurgent parties like the Communists or NSB had a hard time overcoming. In the case of the NSB, the Dutch cabinet, made up of parties that benefitted from the stable voting blocs provided by pillarization, also challenged the NSB with a ban on officials being members of the party in 1934. More importantly, the Dutch bishops banned practising Catholics from becoming members or voting for the NSB. The impact of this ban was especially evident in the Catholic province of Limburg where the NSB won 11.7 per cent of the vote in the provincial elections of 1935 but only 5.3 per cent in 1937.[49]

In 1940, d'Ansembourg exasperatedly bemoaned the strength of Dutch pillarization in alleging that the Dutch government cared less for the needs of the people as a whole than for the narrow interests of the "four pillars: a red pillar, a Catholic pillar, a liberal pillar, and a Protestant pillar."[50] Peter van Dam has conceded that pillarization can be helpful in explaining how the NSB was crowded out of Dutch electoral politics. In comparison with interwar Germany, the Dutch difference of an strong, politically organized Protestant milieu also explains why the NSB did not gain traction. Benjamin Hett pointed out that during the Weimar Republic the Nazi party co-opted the camp of Protestant middle-class voters, while the socialist and Catholic camps in Germany did not crumble entirely. On the other hand, the organized Protestant confessional parties in the Netherlands were stronger than in the Weimar Republic, and Dutch voters did not abandon them en masse for the NSB, as Hett argued happened in Germany.[51]

Although both the NSDAP and NSB were dedicated to anti-parliamentary goals, the parties took different approaches to parliamentary work. In Germany, Franz Ritter von Epp's attempts to blaze his own path by voting differently than the majority of the NSDAP and by mingling with colleagues from other parties were reined in after 1930. In the Netherlands, d'Ansembourg took a conciliatory stance in the Tweede Kamer in that he did not want to overthrow social hierarchies and norms along with the system of government. Rost van Tonningen, on the other hand, wanted to use the NSDAP blueprint to radicalize the NSB and remake Dutch society in the image of the Third Reich. This division within the NSB was not overcome until the German invasion of the Netherlands lifted Rost's radicalism over the moderation of d'Ansembourg.

The Activism-Negativism Binary and the Sudeten German Party in First Republic Czechoslovakia

One would assume that far right-wing, anti-democratic fascist-inspired parliamentarians in mid-sized interwar European countries like the Netherlands and Czechoslovakia would have modelled their parliamentary approaches on Hitler's Germany or Mussolini's Italy. As was true in the Dutch case, there was actually more diversity in the approach of anti-parliamentary politicians. Lock-step parliamentary regimentation was not a feature of the NSB in the Netherlands, where social mores were still respected by the moderate wing of the party. This same departure from the radical NSDAP playbook was also true in the case of Czechoslovakia's right-wing Sudeten German Party. Specifically, any SdP radicalism in behind-the-scenes parliamentary manoeuvering was limited by its status as national minority party in a fragmented Czechoslovak political landscape.

Emerging from the crumbling Austria-Hungary, First Republic Czechoslovakia was a multinational state with raucous national minorities. From the proclamation of the new country, however, the government was dominated by the Czech political elite. The Czechoslovak Revolutionary

National Assembly (Revoluční národní shromáždění), which was tasked with governing the country and drafting the constitution between 1918 and 1920, consisted of 272 members, all of whom were either Czech or Slovak. Of the 40 seats set aside for Slovaks, many were actually given to "Czech friends of the Slovaks" like the later president Edvard Beneš and the president's daughter Alice Masaryková. In fact, only around 65 per cent of the country's citizens were identified as "Czechoslovaks"; there were sizable German, Polish, Hungarian, and Ruthenian minorities. Moreover, there was a higher percentage of citizens in the new Czechoslovak state who identified as German rather than Slovak, although the Slovaks were generally combined into the larger Czechoslovak category. Despite early Czech political dominance, the country was itself quite nationally diverse.[52]

Turning to First Republic Czechoslovakia's largest minority, the country's German speakers universally rejected the new state at its founding in 1918. German speakers within the traditional borders of the Czech lands had campaigned to be a part of German Austria. However, Czechoslovak troops quickly occupied the German-majority regions, which culminated in massive protests on March 4, 1919. Ultimately, 55 German-speaking residents and two Czechoslovak soldiers were killed in the March 1919 clashes. Against this bloody background, when German-speaking politicians were first elected to the new Czechoslovak parliament in 1920, they were faced with the decision whether to co-operate with their Czech and Slovak colleagues or to maintain their principled opposition to the Czechoslovak state.[53]

At first, all German parties in Czechoslovakia banded together against the new state. However, within a few years, a division emerged between so-called activist German-speaking parties – those willing to work with the government in Prague – and "negativist" parties – those that refused to co-operate. Over the course of the 1920s, more German-speaking parties joined the activist camp. Franz Spina, a German-speaking professor of Slavic literature and a leading agrarian politician, developed the scholarly concept of a historical "symbiosis" between Germans and Czechs. This intellectual and historical acceptance of national diversity helped pave the way for a major turning point in 1926, when two German-speaking ministers – including Spina – joined a Czechoslovak cabinet. However, the binary between activism and negativism still undergirds much of the history of German minority politics in interwar Czechoslovakia, and the right-wing Sudeten German Party has often been read as a radical negativist reaction against creeping activism among German-speaking parties.[54]

Up through the 1929 Czechoslovak national elections, the largest German-speaking parties in the lower house of parliament were either the German social democrats or the more moderate agrarians. Although both of these parties had originally taken a negativist stance that rejected the Czechoslovak state in favour of joining German Austria, in the mid-1920s, both of these parties had joined the Czechoslovak cabinet as activists. On the other side of the activist-negativist dichotomy, the two largest far right-wing rabid negativist German-speaking parties in the country disbanded in 1933. Czechoslovakia's German National Socialist Workers' Party (Deutsche Nationalsozialistische Arbeiterpartei) and the German National Party (Deutsche Nationalpartei) had roots in the antisemitic pan-German movement in Austria-Hungary and supported both anti-Slavic and anti-clerical policies. When the Czechoslovak government moved to ban the two parties for their pro-Nazi radicalism, they disbanded in the fall of 1933. This opened up a vacuum on the conservative, negativist side of German-speaking politics.[55]

A new German-speaking party stepped into this right-wing gap. The Sudeten German Home Front (Sudetendeutsche Heimatfront, SHF) had been created by the German gymnastics leader Konrad Henlein. The SHF was ostensibly a big-tent conservative German political party. However, many of the former members of the two disbanded right-wing parties were looking for a political home just as Henlein's party was founded, and they quickly joined the SHF. This early influx of dyed-in-the-wool negativist party members would shape the party base within the SHF, which was later renamed the Sudeten German Party.[56] Tara Zahra was not alone in focusing on this overlap in grassroots membership to read the SHF/SdP as negativist from day one. The Czech historian Věra Olivová noted this radical SHF membership and argued the moderate party leadership preached loyalty to the state disingenuously. Activist German-speaking parties within the Czechoslovak government campaigned to ban the new SHF, but President Tomáš Garrigue Masaryk rejected any prohibition, in part, since it would clash with fundamental democratic principles.[57]

Indeed, many Czechoslovak contemporaries immediately adopted the view that the SHF/SdP represented exactly the same the negativist, anti-state, anti-democratic ideas of the disbanded German nationalist parties.[58] German-speaking socialists mocked the SHF in cartoons with Hitler pulling the strings of a puppet Konrad Henlein.[59] The Czechoslovak foreign ministry official Ján Papánek recalled that he held this view from the day he first met Konrad Henlein: "In a closed meeting of about fifteen people, several members of Parliament, several high officials and [me], he tried to convince us that he supported the basic policy of the country and that he wouldn't take any action against the country."[60] Papánek was skeptical, and Edvard Beneš also argued that the

Figure 6.2. Anti-Nazi and Anti-Henlein cartoon from the *Nordböhmischer Volksbote*, May 25, 1935. The cartoon reads: "The jumping jack toy and who is really pulling the strings." The small jumping jack figure is Henlein and is holding a "Message to Masaryk."

Source: *Nordböhmischer Volksbote* Newspaper, May 25, 1935.

SdP's work in stirring up virulent nationalism was "Henlein's fraudulent political agitation" that masked irredentist goals.[61] From the founding of the SHF/SdP, many Czechoslovak officials felt the party was merely "camouflaged Nazism."[62]

On some level, it might seem pointless to study SdP parliamentarians, since from the middle of the twentieth century, both Czechoslovak historians and German émigré scholars have forged the consensus that the SdP party apparatus was essentially a foreign "fifth column" that moved in lock step with the wishes of Nazi overlords in Berlin. Although this was true in the months immediately preceding the Munich Agreement, Věra Olivová, Radomír Luža, and Johann Wolfgang Brügel have all argued that the SdP was made up of Nazi stooges from the party's inception.[63] Drawing on this older work, the political scientist Giovanni Capoccia has claimed that the German Nazis "probably" prompted the founding of the Sudeten German party and shaped the party's work of "political camouflage" that prompted Henlein's movement to hide its radical fascist goals.[64]

Indeed, these scholars can seemingly point to smoking-gun evidence that the SdP – including its parliamentarians – were really Nazis in disguise. To bolster their case, they turn to a particularly revealing letter that Konrad Henlein sent Adolf Hitler in November 1937:

> The Sudeten German Party must camouflage its profession of National Socialism as an ideology of life and as a political principle. As a party in the democratic parliamentary system of Czechoslovakia, it [the SdP] must, outwardly, alike in writing and by word of mouth, in its manifestoes and in the press, in Parliament, in its own structure, and in the organization of the Sudeten German element, employ democratic terminology and democratic parliamentary methods. [...] at heart it [the SdP] desires nothing more ardently than the incorporation of Sudeten German territory, nay the whole Bohemian, Moravian, and Silesian area, within the Reich.[65]

It seems that Henlein literally admitted in this secret document that the SdP was a political movement hiding its true motives, serving as a fifth column for the Nazi state.

However, this open-and-shut case against the SdP is more complicated than it first appears. This often-cited quotation has been robbed of its context. Henlein's words appeared buried a lengthy letter to Hitler on the political situation in Czechoslovakia. Henlein was trying to make the case that "the broad masses of the Sudeten Germans themselves no longer believe in a compromise with the Czech people within the Czech State." However, in Henlein's enumerations of the indignities suffered by the Sudeten Germans, he only belatedly came to his profession of national socialism and his commitment to hiding the SdP's true motives.[66] This wandering letter must also be read in light of the explosive political context of the Rutha Affair in Czechoslovakia. Heinz Rutha, one of the leaders of the moderate wing of the SdP who helped set up a behind-the-scenes meeting between Czechoslovak officials and Henlein, was arrested in early October 1937 for violating the Czechoslovak ban on same-sex conduct. This investigation grew to include more and more men associated with the SdP's more moderate wing. Henlein had been an ally of Rutha, but in the dust up after this scandal, Henlein quickly made huge concessions to the radical national socialist wing of the party to secure his position as leader. Henlein's letter to Hitler emerged within this fraught domestic and internal party context. Any reading of a long-running cloak-and-dagger game by the SdP to subvert the Czechoslovak state from the party's founding earlier in the 1930s that hinges on a 1937 letter is overwrought.[67]

More recently, there has been some scholarly acknowledgment that the rigid activist-negativist dichotomy has not been the most effective way of understanding the SHF/SdP. The older historiographical tradition that saw good and evil in the First Republic past is embodied in Věra Olivová's decision to brand pro-state, activist German parties in Czechoslovakia "democratic," which necessarily means that the negativist parties were not.[68] Mark Cornwall has valiantly worked to challenge these older traditions by placing the SHF/SdP in a longer Habsburg-era and inter-war Bohemian context to argue that Henlein appealed to a bigger tent than rabid German nationalists. However, even Cornwall conceded "that the SHF was compromised at birth" because of its radical membership that that tainted its public perception.[69]

A myriad of scholars in the last two decades have echoed the idea that the SHF/SdP was not a reincarnation of the disbanded radical negativist parties and was not even irredentist before the elections of 1935. However, scholars all agree that the party turned negativist and radical, but they differ on when that happened. One Czech historian has argued that the SdP's impressive election victory in 1935 got the attention of Nazi Germany, and Nazi cash later transformed the party into Hitler's stooges.[70] Considering local politics in České Budějovice/Budweis, Jeremy King pinpointed the geopolitical changes of 1936 with the remilitarization of the Rhineland and German involvement in the Spanish Civil War that prompted the Nazis to open the financial taps for SdP activities across Bohemia as the final push towards negativism.[71] Examining the Saxon-Bohemian borderlands, Caitlin Murdock saw a grassroots transition to anti-state negativism within the SdP as cross-border propaganda and violence reached a fever pitch in 1937.[72] Rather than adopting the older scholarly view that the SdP's entire party organization was born opposed to the Czechoslovak state, here the SdP parliamentarians in Prague are shown to have practised activism reluctantly up until 1938 when the party's legislators became a Nazified fifth column marching towards the Reich.

Of course, contemporaries were not wrong that the SdP always included radical elements that were explicitly linked to the German NSDAP. Dossiers put together at the Nuremberg Trials showed that "the Sudeten German Party was supported by certain allocations from the [German Foreign Office] since 1935." This money allegedly flowed to the party through the German consulate in Prague, as well as via the SdP office in Berlin.[73] Members of the SdP also regularly communicated with officials in Nazi Germany to allow Sudeten Germans who demonstrated "*völkisch soundness*" to enter Germany to work under the radar in the agricultural sector. This plan aided unemployed Sudeten Germans, provided labourers in Germany, and was organized by the SdP. This patronage sponsored by the Nazi state was supposed to earn the party votes. The SdP also dispatched representatives to Berlin to advocate at the propaganda ministry for financial grants to support German-speaking theatre and festivals across Czechoslovakia. The party also implored the Nazi officials to send famous German actors and musicians to Prague for charity activities benefitting the German community in the country.[74]

All of this financial support from Nazi Germany for the SdP has been frequently referenced in Czech historiography from 1989 as evidence that the Nazis had transformed the party into a negativist fifth column aiming to dismantle Czechoslovakia. King and Murdock also acknowledged the extent of Nazi financial assistance in the borderlands and during elections. Modern Czech scholars have tended focus on the SdP members and politicians as disingenuous stooges because they were bribed by Nazi cash.[75] This cross-border political funding looks like foreign collusion, but when considered comparatively, election assistance from foreign countries across Europe was not unique. As demonstrated in Chapter 3, democratic politicians were embedded in campaigning networks that saw Austrians socialists dispatching and funding left-wing speakers in First Republic Czechoslovakia back in the 1920s. German and French politicians secretly drafted common campaign language in early 1930s.[76] Even before the dawn of the Third Reich, German Nazis had crossed into First Republic Czechoslovakia in solidarity political marches. Financial support for the SdP was notable, but comparison indicates that transnational election support – including cash and in-kind assistance – regularly flowed across interwar borders.[77]

Links between the SdP and Nazi state cannot be denied, but the allegations of total and complete "political camouflage" by the party run counter to evidence from the SdP's political and parliamentary activities. Even before the party had entered the Czechoslovak parliament, its leader Konrad Henlein had directed a lengthy dossier be created to be used in the event that the SdP was disbanded and the party leaders arrested. Henlein's secret dossier included speeches, press statements, and letters to be sent out if the Czechoslovak government acted against the party. Henlein had a signed letter ready to be dispatched to the League of Nations, circular letters for members of the party, and a pre-written speech that had blank spaces for the names of the Sudeten Germans who had been arrested. This was a sober text for an eventuality that never took place. In his draft speech, Henlein asked Czechoslovakia's German speakers to remain loyal to him as their leader. Furthermore, he declared that the party had been banned because of the slander that it was merely the movement of "disguised Nazi swastika bearers" and argued this was untrue.[78]

If one believes that the SdP was constantly using political camouflage, one could read this unused, secret party file on what to do if the party was banned as an elaborate ruse full of falsehoods to throw the Czechoslovak police off the trail of the SdP-Nazi connection.[79] However, that reading seems exceptionally tortured. Why would an imprisoned Henlein call on his supporters to remain loyal to him rather than Adolf Hitler? Why would these documents argue for a common Sudeten German future rather than a greater German future? This cache of speeches and letters is better understood as more evidence that "political camouflage" was not the main goal of Henlein's party in 1935. Instead, Henlein aspired to create one right-wing broad church that would represent all German speakers in Czechoslovakia. Only much later did the SdP transform into a group of Nazis-in-waiting, eager to dismember the Czechoslovak state. A thorough examination of the SdP parliamentary party yields evidence that the Sudeten German politicians were willing to work with First Republic Czechoslovakia as reluctant activists far longer than has been assumed.[80]

Reluctant Activists? The SdP Parliamentary Club at Work

The May 1935 national elections were a watershed moment in the political history of First Republic Czechoslovakia. A German-speaking party won the plurality of the vote and the highest number of seats of any single political party. Previously, Czech and Slovak parties had always captured the top spot. In 1935, the German vote in Czechoslovakia abandoned the German-speaking agrarians and social democrats, and it coalesced around Konrad Henlein's more radical conservative party. Ultimately, 44 Sudeten German Party members joined the 300-person lower house of parliament, the Czechoslovak Chamber of Deputies (Poslanecká sněmovna/Abgeordnetenhaus). Twenty-three SdP senators headed to the 150-member Senate (Senát/Senat). Following an older Austrian imperial tradition, all these senators and deputies formed one large parliamentary group that met together.[81]

From 1935, the Sudeten German Party's 67 parliamentarians worked in the predominantly Czech-speaking national capital, and they looked to carve out social spaces for themselves. They primarily moved through German-speaking cultural and political bubbles around town, especially surrounding the Deutsches Haus in Prague's Old Town. Just around the corner from the Deutsches Haus, the SdP had a spacious three-floor complex on Hybernská/Hibernergasse as its Prague office. This building hosted SdP party departments that were like "miniaturized ministries," each led by an SdP parliamentarian. The only major party offices found elsewhere in the country were Konrad Henlein's leadership office in Asch/Aš, and the party treasury in Eger/Cheb. The Deutsches Haus and SdP party office were safe, party-political spaces for these right-wing German nationalists in the Czechoslovak capital.[82]

In Prague, an SdP deputy or senator might also be found lingering in the parliamentary club rooms in the Rudolfinium where the parliament met. The parliamentary complex was designed to be a convenient workplace for lawmakers who travelled to the nation's capital from elsewhere. Importantly, unlike the NSDAP during the Weimar Republic, the SdP encouraged its parliamentarians to linger in the building. Party staff were available to help with SdP political work, and two non-partisan parliamentary officials were present to make reservations at the parliamentary restaurant, order a taxi, reserve a spot in the parliamentary spa and shower facilities, or have cigarettes delivered. SdP parliamentarians could also check their correspondence and official documents held in their assigned mailbox in the party's conference room, which is where the party hoped to corral many of its parliamentarians when they were in town. Even with competing languages and nationalities among the parliamentarians at the Rudolfinium, hanging around the spa and restaurant put SdP politicians in contact with their rivals.[83]

SdP parliamentarians often also met outside Prague. Sometimes these trips were to western Bohemia to assemble and receive instructions from the party leader Konrad Henlein, who lived in Asch/Aš. Like Hitler in Munich or Mussert in Utrecht, the party leader and parliamentary party were physically based in different places, but Henlein still appointed the SdP's parliamentary leadership and coordinated his parliamentarians. The SdP parliamentary group also sponsored training and events throughout Bohemia to help the party's parliamentarians come into contact with the German-speaking portions of the country. For instance, the parliamentary party hosted a legal workshop in Konstantinsbad/Konstantinovy Lázně in western Bohemia. Lawyers in the parliamentary party were obligated to attend, and other lawmakers who might speak on legal topics in parliament in the future were encouraged to go to the event. One finds little evidence of these types of parliamentary training sessions being held by either the NSB or NSDAP, whose party schools focused on propaganda more than the minutiae of public law and minority rights.[84]

The SdP also sent out a lengthy memo on procedures for its parliamentary group. Unlike the highly regimented NSDAP, SdP parliamentarians were not divided into rigid seating blocs for plenary meetings, and sharply worded meeting reminders did not demand attendance with militaristic discipline. In stark contrast to the incendiary and uniformed Nazis in Berlin, the SdP's guidelines made clear that parliamentarians were expected to observe a sense of decorum: "Going up to the ministers' seats during the session, shouting out and making noise is generally not recommended [...] Everyone is reminded that consideration should be paid to the dignity of the parliament when dressing for parliamentary sessions." However, like the NSDAP and NSB, SdP parliamentarians were required to divide their earnings with the party. Very much unlike the NSB whose four parliamentarians were on their own in The Hague, the SdP parliamentary party wanted to keep close tabs on its members and their parliamentary activities. Members were required to report to party staff by telephone whenever they were Prague, even when the parliament was not in session, and they were asked to submit monthly reports, as well as any speeches that were to be given in the plenary chamber.[85]

Even in the SdP parliamentary club's day-to-day correspondence with other parties and parliamentary officials, the SdP did not set out to thwart parliamentary or social norms. For example, the Czechoslovak parliament offered the opportunity for parliamentarians to buy into a common life insurance system. Parliamentarians could pay into a common pool at 50 Czechoslovak crowns (Kč) a month which was deducted directly from one's parliamentary pay. The fund would pay out Kč 25,000 to a parliamentarian's beneficiary on his or her death. This life insurance fund was administered by parliamentarians themselves. Rather than publicly rejecting this system as the trapping of a decadent democratic system or a program in a country that was doomed, the SdP recommended that its senators accept the insurance and allowed deputies to elect to take on the insurance if they wanted. Lawmakers participating in the parliamentary death benefit scheme meant that the SdP would take less from their salaries and meant co-operating financially with political rivals.[86]

The SdP also kept the lines of communication open with other parliamentary parties. When the British Labour Party leader Arthur Henderson visited Prague, he expressed a desire to meet with SdP parliamentarians. A Czech political party secretary contacted the SdP club office to arrange this meeting, indicating that there was no cordon sanitaire preventing behind-the-scenes contact. Moreover, the SdP had particularly strong connections with other national minority parties. In February 1938, several

SdP parliamentarians met in the northern Slovak town of Ružomberok/ Rosenberg with Monsignor Andrej Hlinka, a fellow lawmaker and leader of the Slovak nationalist Slovenská ľudová strana (Slovak People's Party). The SdP presented Hlinka with a plan to collaborate with several ethnic minority parties, and he agreed to appoint a Slovak party representative for this process. At this meeting, Hlinka "bluntly advocated the idea of an independent Slovak nation, which must demand autonomy for itself within the State." This idea of strong, autonomous national minorities was music to the ears of the SdP politicians, and they were willing to co-operate to advance this goal. Even as late as June 1938, the SdP reached out to other minority parties, like the Polskie Stronnictwo Ludowe (Polish People's Party), about joint legislation to create a nationality card for identification.[87]

The Czechoslovak political establishment was horrified to find out that the SdP was investing in party offices in Prague and that this complex would include places to eat and sleep for parliamentarians. Rumours of this parliamentary expansion plan were coupled with the news that SdP parliamentarians were travelling to meet Konrad Henlein to pledge their loyalty to him in a festive ceremony. For the moderate Czech-speaking political establishment, this conjured up images of near "military discipline" among the SdP parliamentarians that was reminiscent of the NSDAP in Germany.[88] However, when compared historically to Nazi parliamentarians in Germany around 1930, the SdP parliamentarians' attitude to legislative work was totally different. German Nazis had been instructed never to linger in parliament and always be out in the country winning converts for fascism. Of these NSDAP legislators, Joseph Goebbels had written the warning: "Whoever goes into parliament will die there! That is, if he goes into parliament to become a parliamentarian." Rather than being "parliamentarized," Nazis in the German Reichstag had to be "revolutionaries" who had no intention of "contributing matter-of-factly and positively." Despite fears within First Republic Czechoslovakia's political establishment, a revolutionary attitude to rip up all republican political norms was not evident among the SdP politicians when they first entered parliament.[89]

In the end, much of the SdP's constructive political work was done out of the limelight. This meant the Czechoslovak public did not know what to expect when the SdP parliamentary leader Karl Hermann Frank took to the floor in the Chamber of Deputies for the very first time in 1935. Frank's opening statement was a surprising olive branch to the Czechoslovak state. His speech rehashed the negativist position of the Sudeten Germans as being deprived of self-determination and "incorporated" against their will into the new Czechoslovak state. At the same time, however, Frank promised that the SdP would be "a constructive opposition [that] offers its hand for domestic peace."[90] Frank highlighted the role that the SdP could play in the parliament: "The Sudeten German Party hereby announces the legitimacy and the legality of its parliamentary work." Frank was not apologizing or dismissing the SdP's national goals, but he strove to distance it from the earlier German nationalist parties that were banned in 1933: "The Sudeten German Party is a national party but not along the lines of the nationalist chauvinism that unfortunately characterized older [parties] but is national in the spirit of a cultural, achievement-affirming, creative self-confidence that also respects other nationalities."[91]

The Czech press immediately rejected Frank's speech as insincerely mixing "rejection and participation, resistance and co-operation." As has been shown, many scholars have followed this early judgment about the SdP's parliamentary intentions, understanding the SdP politicians as masterful actors of in a performance of political camouflage. However, considerable evidence speaks against this argument. As yet another example countering these claims, in September 1935, the SdP sent its politicians on a retreat to Hirschberg-Thammühl/Doksy-Staré Splavy for three days of lectures and discussions that began with a talk entitled "The Czech Nation as Adversary and Partner in Tradition, Sentiment, Approach, and Goals." Envisioning Czechs as partners is not the kind of event that would be hosted by a party rabidly committed to tearing apart the country.[92]

None of this is to say that the SdP was averse to making waves in the Czechoslovak parliament, but its political stunts were more often designed to support the German minority or challenge the entrenched power of Czech elites rather than cast doubt on democracy as whole. For example, in October 1935, the SdP protested that other parties were ignoring SdP complaints about social welfare for German speakers. The SdP sent "loaves of poor-quality bread, that allegedly were sold in northern Bohemia" to fellow parliamentarians as a gimmick, and, only after additional parliamentary pressure, the Czechoslovak interior ministry promised to investigate this matter.[93] The SdP's tactic was designed to call attention to unemployment and the welfare of German speakers, implying that the governing coalition was biased against them. The stunt was needling and obnoxious, but it was reasonable for an opposition party, especially one representing a national minority. In addition to public relations gimmicks, the SdP parliamentarians also assembled memos of alleged discrimination against German speakers and lists of concrete reforms that were dispatched to Czechoslovak ministers. The goal in these behind-the-scenes parliamentary activities was to improve the lives of German speakers.[94]

Much of the SdP's day-to-day parliamentary work focused on interventions with the Czechoslovak government on behalf of the German minority. Article 22 of the Czechoslovak Constitution anticipated that parliamentarians would advocate for constituents: "They [Members of Parliament] shall not address to public authorities requests in the personal interests of individuals, unless they do so in their professional capacity."[95] The SdP's parliamentary headquarters had three rooms set aside as an intervention office, along with a waiting room for petitioners. *Die SdP im Parlament* (The SdP in the Parliament), the SdP's own published reflections on its parliamentary successes in 1935 and 1936, highlighted the party's interventions on behalf of German speakers with the Czechoslovak bureaucracy: "No one will want to deny that the majority of the work of many deputies and senators consists of making visits to various offices and authorities in Prague and outside Prague" on behalf of constituents. The workload of the SdP's intervention office eventually required a second office in Brno/Brünn. The SdP claimed it was so good at cutting through red-tape that it angered entrenched Czechoslovak parties, since the SdP's work helped the country's "administrative offices pick up their pace."[96]

The SdP kept extensive records of these interventions and publicized them for the party's German-speaking base. In 1935, the party handled 3,577 intervention cases and followed up with ministries and officials 4,773 times about these issues. Over 1,500 of these cases – the plurality – dealt with questions related to social welfare and employment, which was to be expected in a period of economic downturn. Almost 1,000 involved tax questions, help with business issues, and support on issues related to schools, which would seem to be within the mainstream of politicians' intervention with bureaucrats on behalf of constituents at any time or place. Only a handful of the cases could be read as related to the SdP's nationalist perspective. These included 64 questions on local self-government – an important, nationally charged issue for German-speaking parts of the country who resented federal, and therefore Czech-dominated control – and 268 cases on "bureaucratic encroachment or harassment," a pointed intervention category aimed directly at the Czechoslovak state. Nevertheless, these politically charged national issues only account for 9.28 per cent of the SdP's invention caseload in 1935.[97] Over time, however, certain SdP parliamentarians developed expertise in, for example, intervening successfully on behalf of the children of German-speaking parents who had inadvertently or allegedly through coercion been enrolled in Czech-speaking schools.[98]

One concrete case illustrates the regular work of the SdP parliamentary intervention office. In early 1938, the wife of the railroad employee

Ernst Horn approached the SdP office with concerns about her husband's employment. Horn was originally assigned to by the state railroad to work in Aussig/Ústí nad Labem, where the family lived. However, Horn was transferred to Zásmuky/Zasmuk in a Czech-speaking part of the country, arguably to improve his language skills. Horn had successfully passed the railroad's Czech language test, but his wife suspected that a denunciation prompted the transfer. Horn's wife struggled to pay down debts on their home near his original workplace, since her husband's salary now had to cover expenses in the family home, as well as an apartment in Zásmuky/Zasmuk. The SdP appealed first to an high-ranking civil servant in the Czechoslovak railroad ministry, and once the SdP politician heard that the ministry was hoping to transfer Horn back to his hometown, the whole file was sent directly to Railroad Minister Rudolf Bechyně to ensure the case was resolved quickly. All of this was done into the summer of 1938 – a politically fraught year in which the Sudetenland would eventually join Nazi Germany. Nevertheless, the SdP still co-operated behind the scenes with the Czechoslovak state on behalf of constituents. The SdP and its individual parliamentarians had to maintain working relationships with ministers and Czechoslovak bureaucrats in order to satisfactorily intervene on behalf of the country's German speakers. Putting the SdP's anti-parliamentary beliefs into action à la Rost van Tonningen to tear down the whole political system would have left the SdP's constituents in a vulnerable position vis-à-vis the Czechoslovak state.[99]

Sudeten German Party: From a Private Political Partner to a True Nazi Fifth Column

In the Czechoslovak election of 1935, Konrad Henlein played up his decision not to run for a parliamentary seat: "My comrades, I stand in front of you not campaigning for office. You all know that I will not take up a parliamentary seat or seek a position as minister. I am a normal man of the people, and I want to stay a normal man."[100] The real reason Henlein elected not to run in the elections was unclear; there was some speculation that his lack of Czech language ability might have been too much of a burden in Prague. However, even before the SdP won the 1935 elections, Henlein positioned himself as the SdP's chief negotiator both with other political parties and with the Czechoslovak government. At the founding of the SHF/SdP in 1933, Henlein flirted with idea of transforming the SHF into one big-tent Sudeten German party taking a more moderate activist approach. To this end, Henlein met with the more moderate parties and even a German-speaking Czechoslovak cabinet member about how to turn the SHF into a group that was not seen to be competing with the existing parties but brought all German speakers together.[101]

Henlein was not even averse to talking to the Czech political parties. In 1934, SHF officials reached out to the Czech Agrarians, who like the German Agrarians, were willing to tolerate Henlein's party. Henlein and his secretary even met with Přemysl Šámal of the Czechoslovak presidential chancellery, who reported that President Masaryk had read a draft of a conciliatory speech Henlein was to give in 1934 and that the president was impressed.[102] Although Henlein was supposed to be an up-and-coming unabashedly anti-Czechoslovak Nazi this entire time, consular reports of Nazi diplomats writing back to Berlin were horrified that Henlein had agreed on work with the Czechs at all: "Once again Henlein offered the Czechs his hand in reconciliation, once more he emphasized that the Germans in Czechoslovakia had no interest in redrawing the borders."[103] Even in late 1934, opposition to Henlein's course of détente with Czech parties and the state earned him anonymous letters within the SHF declaring that he had betrayed Germans in Czechoslovakia and demanding a much stronger anti-Czech course.[104]

Behind the scenes, the SdP also participated in a world of collegial correspondence with Czechoslovak ministries and institutions. On March 5, 1935, Konrad Henlein wrote to President Masaryk on behalf of the SHF wishing him a happy 85th birthday: "The Sudeten Germans honour in you the selfless pioneer of your nation and happily commit themselves to the ideals of democracy and humanity that you have proclaimed, as well as the consequent mutual respect and esteem among the nations living in this common country."[105] Henlein continued to send congratulatory letters to Masaryk's successor Edvard Beneš on his election as president in late 1935 and to mark his birthday in 1936. Even before winning their parliamentary seats, the SdP had sent copies the party's emergency program for unemployed people in the Sudetenland to various ministers in the Czechoslovak government. Secretaries in the defense and interior ministries sent Henlein formal letters in Czech thanking him for the pamphlet, and the agriculture ministry sent Henlein a letter in German signed by Minister Milan Hodža promising to read the pamphlet. As prime minister, Hodža would be the one member of the Czechoslovak government most interested in exploring ties with the SdP. Hodža gestured towards his openness for rapprochement in directly responding to Henlein's proposals in German – rather than in perfunctory Czech – in January 1935.[106]

After the SdP's 1935 election victory, there was a flurry of SdP telegrams to members of the Czechoslovak government, but the reaction to these messages revealed differences in the commitment of the party's various factions to engage with the state. On election night, the SdP leadership and supporters had gathered in Asch/Aš in the gymnastics hall. As the election results trickled in by radio, it was clear that the SdP had doubled their wildest expectations: "The more election results that came through, the more we were surprised that the election victory began to look like an earthquake."[107] This political earthquake was felt across Czechoslovakia, so to calm the waters, conciliatory telegrams were sent from the SdP leadership in Asch/Aš to President Masaryk, Prime Minister Jan Malypetr, and Interior Minister Jan Černý the day after the election. The telegrams were not the same, but they all tried to diffuse the tension. Henlein wrote to Masaryk to assure him that the SdP would work productively "on the basis of our country's constitution despite all misrepresentations about me and my associates by the party's opponents." In the telegrams to Malypetr and Černý, Henlein emphasized one of his past conciliatory speeches and pledged to exercise his democratic mandate within the confines of the law.[108]

However, these mollifying telegrams immediately became a discussion point within the SdP. Some in the party were angry that Henlein had tried to pacify the Czechoslovak elite when the party had just won a stunning victory. This internal SdP dispute revealed a divide between those who wanted to follow Henlein's conciliatory, mildly activist approach to the Czechoslovak authorities and those who wanted to ride the triumphant wave to Prague in order to make anti-democratic German nationalist demands. Behind the scenes, SdP politicians eventually began to express concerns that despite the party emphasizing its willingness to work constructively, both the government and the police were still too suspicious of the SdP. Confidential memos reveal that the Czechoslovak government doubted Henlein's loyalty and kept tabs on his travel into Germany with extensive customs checks at the border. However, for Henlein's part, the SdP reached out to the prime minister in advance of sensitive foreign travel to ensure he had tacit approval to leave the country to attend events like the Olympics in 1936 in Nazi Germany.[109]

For the SdP, transnational ties tended to go through Konrad Henlein rather than parliamentarians based in Prague. On occasion, party functionaries and politicians would meet with ambassadors in the Czechoslovak capital, but Henlein managed the SdP's foreign outreach to other countries directly, including through the opening of party offices in Paris and London. The SdP's top brass first reached out to Central European powers including Hungary, Austria, Italy, and Sweden, eventually settling on focusing their international attention on Great Britain. Henlein travelled at least four times to London where he met men including

Winston Churchill, the leading civil servant in the foreign ministry Robert Vansittart, and the Slavicist Robert Seton-Watson. Although Henlein did not snag appointments with sitting ministers, he did meet with Foreign Office staff who reported to their superiors: "Our view is that the Sudeten [Germans] are being, in a general way, badly treated." The SdP leadership hoped that the British would use their influence at the League of Nations on behalf of German speakers in Czechoslovakia.[110] Moreover, Henlein's appearances also garnered attention among the British chattering classes. In December 1935, he delivered remarks at Chatham House that pitched himself as a conciliatory figure who only wanted Sudeten Germans to "act[] as mediator between their German mother-nation and the Czech people." In the subsequent question-and-answer session, Henlein was pressed on whether his party had any secret relationship with Nazi Germany, which he strenuously denied, and which was not true, since money flowed into the SdP's coffers from German organizations. Indeed, the most important transnational ties between the SdP and any foreign country were with Nazi Germany, despite Henlein's attempts to deny this in London.[111]

Moving from the SdP's transnational ties to its domestic entanglements, the high point of the SdP exploring co-operation with the Czechoslovak state was a three-hour-long face-to-face meeting between Konrad Henlein and Milan Hodža at the prime minister's private apartment in Prague in September 1937. This meeting took time to organize through an intermediary, in part because of Prime Minister Hodža's insistence on treating Henlein like a private citizen, since he was not a legislator. Moreover, Henlein demanded that an invitation for a meeting come directly from Hodža to bolster Henlein's legitimacy as the leader of Sudeten Germans. Around the same time as the negotiations about setting up this meeting, the SdP parliamentary leader Karl Hermann Frank met with Hodža informing him that Henlein was planning on going to the annual Nazi Party Congress in Nuremberg to confirm that Hodža had nothing against Henlein's attendance. Although Hodža did not object to these travel plans, Henlein elected not to go to Nuremberg in part to smooth the waters to help to set up this top-level meeting. Henlein literally turned down a meeting with Germany's Hitler to ensure he had a face-to-face chat with Czechoslovakia's Hodža.[112]

On September 16, 1937, Hodža, Henlein, and their intermediary finally sat down for a private meeting. In Hodža's later memoirs, he recalled that the death of former President Masaryk was used as the pretext to get the two men together and overcome objections to a one-on-one meeting with an unelected politician. Henlein's minutes of the meeting also recorded that the conversation began with Henlein's condolences on Masaryk's death, but the conversation quickly transitioned into a discussion of the importance of nationality rights in Europe. Henlein then pivoted to a litany of complaints about the government's treatment of the SdP. Henlein pushed Hodža on issues about which any democrat would care. Henlein was frustrated that the existing parties had sidelined the SdP after its electoral victory in 1935. Henlein also wanted bills that the SdP had put forward in the parliament to become law. Henlein then argued that local elections should be held, and the SdP should be allowed to prove it could govern locally. Hodža had actually been pressured by foreign government to make concessions to the Sudeten Germans, and he hoped to avoid the further internationalization of these issues through this conversation. To conclude the meeting, Hodža expressed his hope that the SdP did not develop a "totalitarian perspective" and become an "offshoot of Hitlerism" but continued to respect democratic rule. Their conversation ended with the hopes of co-operating in the future. This lengthy cordial discussion with archrivals serving in the government is impossible to imagine in either the cases of the NSDAP or NSB.[113]

Scholars have read the meeting between Konrad Henlein and Milan Hodža as a failure, pointing out that there were no follow up conversations, and there was no permanent reconciliation of the Sudeten Germans to Czechoslovak state. Nevertheless, Prime Minister Hodža promised to look into issues that the German minority raised and to support SdP interventions on behalf of constituents. SdP politicians invoked that top-level promise in their later advocacy for German speakers. In his memoirs, Hodža linked his government's later concessions on the "just demands of the Germans" and his meeting with Henlein.[114]

Less than a month after this meeting between Hodža and Henlein, the German consul in Prague noted a "calm and conciliatory" speech by Prime Minister Hodža. The consul "request[ed] urgently that German press abstain from attacks on Hodza [*sic*], who is just now going to great ends to settle the conflict with Sudeten German Party." A few weeks later, Joseph Goebbels ordered the end of the anti-Czechoslovak press campaign in Nazi Germany. Rather than serving as proof that the SdP members were the rabble-rousing, anti-democratic instruments of the Nazi Party, this German consular correspondence in late 1937 suggested that the German Foreign Office was actually giving Hodža a chance at reconciliation with Henlein's SdP. Hope for a more activist and engaged future between the SdP and Czechoslovak government lived on for longer than one might have expected.[115]

Into early 1938, Henlein and his SdP parliamentarians understood their work as advocating on behalf of German-speaking constituents even in meeting with Czechoslovak political leaders. They harboured anti-parliamentary goals, and Henlein's megalomania helped cast him-self as the sole leader of German speakers in the country. Henlein's SdP had long played a low-key reluctant activist political game, but that changed in 1938. By the time another private meeting took place in mid-April 1938 between two SdP parliamentarians and Prime Minister Hodža, the two sides were talking past one another. In looking back to a point of no return for the SdP and the Czechoslovak state, the final turning point was undoubtedly the Anschluss of Austria on March 12, 1938. Austria joining a Greater Germany proved to the Sudeten Germans that changes in European borders were possible. This inspired grassroots hope of a union with the Third Reich.[116] In Edvard Beneš's own mem-oirs, Beneš similarly recognized that Anschluss was a political watershed, and he referenced the SdP parliamentarians praising the Anschluss "with joy," which hinted that the party's new ultimate goal for German-speak-ing regions across Czechoslovakia was union with Nazi Germany.[117]

Only days after the Anschluss, any hope for lasting SdP activism was dead. Henlein wrote a succinct letter to the German foreign minister that did not equivocate: "We shall render thanks to the Führer by redou-bling our efforts in the service of the policy of Greater Germany."[118] On March 28, 1938, Henlein and Frank visited Berlin and met with Hitler for almost three hours: "The Führer stated that he intended to settle the Sudeten German problem in the not-too-distant future." Hitler instructed Henlein to make "demands [...] which are unacceptable to the Czech government," but not yet push the Czechoslovak state to its limit.[119] Scholars have unfairly read this moment of Hitler issuing orders to the SdP in March 1938 back into the party's earlier political history. After March 1938, there is little doubt that the SdP had become a foreign legion for Nazi Germany in the heart of Czechoslovakia. By May 1938, a sense of inevitability in the Sudeten question being resolved in Ger-many's favour permeated German-speaking society in Czechoslovakia. The German consul reported back to Berlin: "The mass[es] are intoxi-cated by the overwhelming success in Austria; they will neither await nor accept any other form of political solution." The march towards Munich was inexorable.[120]

Nevertheless, routine behind-the-scenes conversations between Czechoslovakia's ministers and SdP parliamentarians continued with even more frequency into the summer of 1938. Czechoslovakia partially mobilized its army to defend itself against Germany. With the annexation of Austria in March 1938, Bohemia was literally surrounded by German territory. This new geopolitical situation added to tension and overshad-owed conversations between Hodža and Henlein. Whereas earlier con-versations pushed for specific reforms to aid German speakers, a late

August 1938 conversation between SdP parliamentarians and President Beneš turned on loftier intellectual topics. The SdP legislators debated with the country's president about the nature of democracy and accused the Czechs of being authoritarian. One SdP lawmaker boldly declared that Czechoslovakia "is today essentially a pseudo-authoritarian state and not a democracy." This kind of language did not exist in private top-notch political conversations before Nazi Germany's annexation of Austria. After Anschluss, the SdP both inside and outside parliament had become a real Nazi fifth column.[121]

The Diversity of Anti-Parliamentarian Parliamentarians

Interwar Europe's republics were toppled by the machinations of anti-democratic parties like the Nazis in Germany. Surprisingly, members of these anti-parliamentary parties sometimes looked back with longing on their stints in democratic legislatures. Just as the rabid Nazi President of the Reichstag Hermann Göring fondly remembered outmanoeuvering Chancellor Franz von Papen later in life, members of the Dutch National Socialist Movement were bitter about their lack of parliamentary success.[122] In 1941, Cornelis van Geelkerken, one of the founders of the NSB, reflected back on the movement's 10-year history. When he set pen to paper, the NSB had been co-opted and radicalized by the Nazi German occupiers of the Netherlands. As a former moderate in the movement, Geelkerken wistfully looked back on the NSB's earlier years, paying special attention to the handful of Dutch national socialist lawmakers who had served in The Hague. Like any self-respecting anti-parliamentary politician, Geelkerken attacked the "gentlemen democrats" in their useless "palaver parliament." Although the German occupation in the Second World War ultimately offered the NSB domestic political supremacy, Geelkerken harboured regrets that the NSB had not been able to come to power on its own: "The ultimate goal the [Dutch] national socialists were striving towards in entering the representative bodies, i.e., acquiring power in the state through democratic means, was not achieved."[123]

Ultimately, "acquiring power in the state through democratic means" was the goal of many interwar anti-parliamentary lawmakers, but there was tension in how this should be done. In the NSB, d'Ansembourg pushed the boundaries and the legislative guardrails, but he was still willing to interact with his parliamentary rivals, especially behind the scenes. Rost van Tonningen, on the other hand, wanted to burn everything down and intentionally broke all the unwritten social rules to ensure that people would not cozy up to him. D'Ansembourg was at one gentlemanly anti-democratic end of the spectrum, and Rost van Tonningen was at the other. However, rather than helping the NSB to speak to both moderates and radicals, the Dutch NSB's parliamentary party was simply rendered dysfunctional. There were disagreements over political tactics, and each of the NSB's parliamentarians could do or say whatever he wanted with little supervision. D'Ansembourg could mingle with his conservative confessional parties, and Rost van Tonningen could brawl with the Catholics on the floor of the Tweede Kamer.

In the Sudeten German Party in Czechoslovakia, there was similar political tension, but it was between the rabid party base, on the one hand, and the SdP's leadership and lawmakers directed by Konrad Henlein, on the other. The radical elements of the SdP kept pushing Henlein and the elected politicians to take a more negativist stance. Although many scholars have read Heinlein's SdP as a wolf in sheep's clothing from day one, the party's legislative activities prove the SdP was clearly far more committed to using their parliamentary seats to help German constituents and serve as an advocate for the German-speaking minority in the country. This prompted pushback from the party base for selling out. On some level, this tension within the SdP was a political strength. The party could seem like a nationalist big-tent unity party to connect with more moderate voters but, at the same time, retain the radicals which enabled the party to court the German NSDAP for financial support. As late as July 1938, the SdP parliamentary leader in Prague conceded that "within our worldview parliamentarism is of only limited value," but he still felt that elected politicians had been crucial to the overall Sudeten German movement and its achievements.[124]

The robust social and transnational worlds of interwar parliamentary life are largely absent among these radical right-wing parties in parliament. In Nazi Germany, Franz Ritter von Epp's connections to more moderate colleagues in the Reichstag stand out as exceptional, especially considering that from 1930, the NSDAP tried to prevent its parliamentarians from lingering in the Reichstag building at all. D'Ansembourg's aristocratic title bought him more social connections in the Netherlands, which reflected his relative moderation and clubbability. Sociability among SdP politicians in Prague was possible without the rigid guardrails, such as those imposed in Germany by the NSDAP. None of these parliamentarians, however, were travelling to the annual gatherings of the League of Nations Assembly or the International Parliamentary Commercial Conference. Transnational links tended to be party-political and to tie the NSB or SdP to Nazi Germany more than to third countries.

Through comparison with the parliamentary approaches of the NSB and SdP, Germany's NSDAP stands out as a far more regimented and single-minded party. Of course, before 1930, a handful of German Nazi politicians dabbled with political co-operation and pragmatism. However, any development within the NSDAP towards greater cross-party co-operation was completely halted as the numbers of Nazi parliamentarians skyrocketed in the 1930 German elections.[125] Afterwards, the NSDAP felt that it no longer needed support from other parties and pushed forward with a single-minded radicalizing agenda. The NSB and SdP were far less rigid in regulating their parliamentarians, in part because the four-person NSB in the Netherlands needed colleagues to effectively shake up the Tweede Kamer. The SdP needed to keep the lines of communication open with the Czechoslovak government to aid German-speaking constituents. Imagining that all of the fascist, Nazi-inspired political parties across Europe were copycat movements that mimicked Nazis in the Reichstag is incorrect. In the end, parliamentary democracy collapsed in both Czechoslovakia and the Netherlands, but it was not ultimately due to the machinations of those countries' own radical right-wing politicians. Czechoslovak democracy died because Hitler's Germany sponsored the dismemberment of the country at Munich, and Dutch democracy collapsed when Nazi Germany invaded.

Chapter Seven

From Cross-Cutting Interconnections to the Primacy of Parties in Interwar Austria and Weimar Germany

In the ordinary German town of Neustadt on an election night in the early 1920s, Herr Müller anxiously waited. Müller had lost two previous elections to the Reichstag, but he pulled out all the stops for his third campaign, ultimately delivering 63 political speeches in only 28 days. In the early morning hours after election day, Müller received an official telephone call that he had won a seat in the German parliament. Soon afterwards, the doorbell rang and late-night visitors – ranging from friendly neighbours to campaign assistants – dropped by with their well wishes. The very next day, a rushed telegram from his political party summoned Müller to Berlin for his first party meeting in the Reichstag. Two days later, a gold-embossed leather wallet arrived with a new parliamentary identification card and official first-class train travel ticket. Müller set off to the capital as a duly elected representative of the German people.[1]

Not far from the iconic Brandenburg Gate, Müller walked through Reichstag's members' entrance for the very first time. There he was greeted by staff who ushered him to the cloakroom where an employee noted the parliamentarian's presence by flipping the electronic switch "Müller-Hinterwalden." Müller now had his electoral district affixed to his last name, since there were too many Müllers serving in the Reichstag. The newly rechristened Müller-Hinterwalden found his way to his party's conference room for a first meeting on the post-election political situation. Afterwards, his party's lawmakers adjourned to their usual pub for drinks and informal campaigning for the parliamentary party's leadership offices. Over the following weeks, Müller-Hinterwalden searched for accommodation in Berlin, navigated the festive opening of legislative session, attended committee meetings, and developed a regular routine. Müller settled into a usual pattern of eating in the Reichstag's restaurant, dropping by the parliamentary library, working diligently in his appointed office, and observing his new colleagues.[2]

Müller-Hinterwalden quickly discovered that his activities in the Reichstag were regulated – to the greatest extent – by his own parliamentary party. His committee assignments were determined by the party, any opportunities to deliver plenary speeches were provided by the party, and socializing was most often with other members of his own political party in their regular pub after party-political meetings. Within this party milieu, Müller "felt similarly to when he became a soldier. Just as then, strangers were compelled by an external force into a community."[3] Müller's own political party was acting like a drill sergeant moulding new recruits into a disciplined collective. After all, parliamentary processes required generating majorities, so political parties had to stick together: "What is possible in parliaments only comes about with united parliamentary parties. The individual is nothing; the party that gives up its unity ultimately makes itself a laughingstock." Like a soldier, Müller ceded much of his political autonomy to the parliamentary group in order to advance a common cause.[4]

Since Müller-Hinterwalden observed this primacy of political party, he was dumfounded when he wandered around the Reichstag and observed run-of-the-mill parliamentarians from rival parties strategizing with each other. Müller set out to understand what was going on: "He took the handbook of the third session of the Reichstag, drew out a clean seating chart depicting the party divisions in the plenary chamber, and marked all the seats of agricultural parliamentarians on the chart." Müller-Hinterwalden used biographical information in the Reichstag's published handbook to show that rather than all being clumped in one political party, legislators with ties to agriculture were found in large numbers in the right-wing German National People's Party (Deutschnationale Volkspartei, DNVP), as well as the Catholic Centre Party and the regional Bavarian People's Party (Bayerische Volkspartei). However, there were even politicians with links to agriculture among socialists and communists, as well as among the far-right national socialists. Müller-Hinterwalden realized that he was looking at a chart mapping out a built-in agricultural lobby embedded in the Reichstag. "Whenever anything related to agricultural tariffs, questions of state economic regulation, taxation of agricultural enterprises, or transport policy for the countryside came up," these agriculturally minded legislators would band together to advocate on these issues within their own parties and across the parliament.[5]

Having uncovered a world of cross-party agricultural advocacy, Müller-Hinterwalden drew out new seating charts of parliamentarians active in the industrial sector, those who were small tradespeople, and politicians active in trade unions. Müller "gradually recognized that the whole Reichstag was not only vertically structured by parties but that horizontal interconnections cut straight through the parties. The effectiveness of these connections cannot be denied, even though they play out almost completely in secret." Müller-Hinterwalden called these cross-party ties "*Querverbindungen*" (cross-cutting interconnections) because they brought politicians with common interests – particularly economic interests – together. However, Müller imagined analogous interconnections linking parliamentarians of similar religious traditions, with the same career trajectories, from the same social class, or even just hailing from the same part of the country.

Müller came to realize that these behind-the-scenes interconnections functioned as a system of lobbying, coordination, and contact that competed with regimented parliamentary parties. He recalled a recent vote on civil servants' pay and pensions that unexpectedly went against the government. The cabinet's proposal abandoned even the pretense of equity by privileging men over women who were working for the state. All the female members of the Reichstag – whether or not they were in the ruling coalition – voted with the opposition to scuttle the legislation. In terms of the parliamentary math of the ruling coalition, the sexist proposal should have carried the day. However, Müller saw that women were also a parliamentary interconnection that could shape – or, in this case, derail – policy. With his marked-up seating charts, Müller-Hinterwalden had uncovered a hidden world of cross-party groupings that could challenge the power of political parties and forge an esprit de corps across the parliament.[6]

At least, Müller would have discovered all these things, if he had really existed. Müller-Hinterwalden was actually a fictional character in the 1926 book *Die Herrschaft der Fünfhundert* (The Rule of the 500). The author of this creative take on German legislative life was Walther Lambach, an actual member of the Reichstag, who served for the nationalist conservative DNVP. As an author, Lambach blended his real-life experiences, those of colleagues, actual election results, parliamentary documents, and seating charts to create Müller-Hinterwalden. This was a character who could credibly guide readers through the inner workings of the Reichstag. Through Müller's fictional eyes, Lambach pointed to a very real tension between the power of one's political party and the influence of cross-party interconnections. On the one hand, parliamentary parties would be more unified if they were ideologically pure and united behind a strong leader. On the other hand, common interests and political goals almost always spilled beyond the bounds of any one single party.[7]

As was demonstrated in Chapter 5, the most rabid anti-parliamentary parties, like the National Socialist German Workers' Party (Nationalsozialistische Deutsche Arbeiterpartei, NSDAP), stressed party unity at all

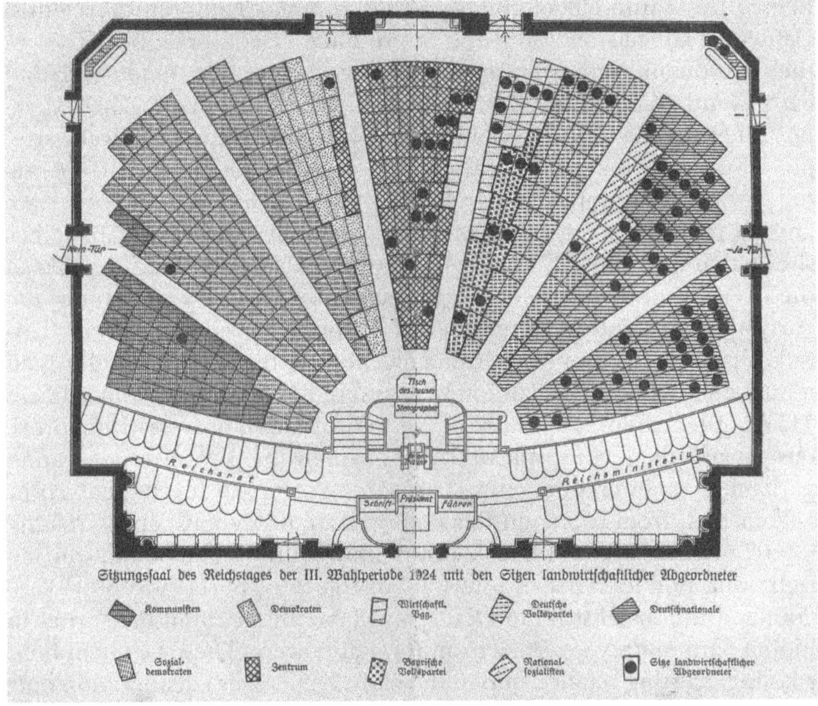

Figure 7.1. Chart depicting the seats of interwar parliamentarians connected to agriculture in the interwar German Reichstag from Walther Lambach's *Die Herrschaft der Fünfhundert*, 1926.

costs. Despite the vibrant social world and robust clubland in Berlin, the parliamentary NSDAP discouraged mingling with colleagues and worked to exploit any information shared in confidence by trusting rivals for political gain.[8] Nazi legislators had sworn "at all times to consider the party's interests," to "subordinate themselves to Adolf Hitler and his commands," and to return one's seat to the party leadership rather that join any other parliamentary grouping. As shown in Chapter 6, the NSDAP was not a rigid blueprint for far-right wing parties in the Netherlands or Czechoslovakia, but it represented the absolute embrace of party and total rejection of cross-cutting political interconnections.[9]

By themselves, interwar anti-parliamentary parties did not have the power to rip apart domestic cross-party parliamentary interconnections or the international esprit de corps that had developed over the course of the 1920s. Instead, radicalizing mainstream conservative parties helped this continent of colleagues to crumble. The political scientist Daniel Ziblatt has explored the importance of conservative parties in the creation and support of modern democracies of the nineteenth and early twentieth centuries. Comparing Britain and Germany, Ziblatt demonstrated the key role a "viable and robust conservative political party" played in integrating old-regime elites for a new democratic dispensation. A strong conservative party kept right-wing forces tied to the state and to democratic institutions more generally. However, Ziblatt has shown that in Weimar Germany there was a backlash within the ranks of the DNVP after its 1928 election defeat that prompted a takeover of the party by extremist forces that coalesced around Alfred Hugenberg. This radicalized DNVP then kept losing elections to the far right, with which it ultimately allied in a coalition that ushered Hitler's Nazis into office.[10] This chapter explores a feature of this radicalization process within previously mainstream conservative parties, namely the pivot from tolerating parliamentary interconnections to insistence on party loyalty at all costs.

Four men from two countries demonstrate how robust cross-crossing interconnections could break down under the strain of radicalizing right-wing politics. First in interwar Austria, the conservative Carl Vaugoin and the socialist Julius Deutsch collaborated behind the scenes in hiding paramilitary weapons from foreign powers. These two men built a lasting, trusting relationship in the early 1920s. This collaboration only faltered during a heated Austrian election campaign in 1930 when the mainstream conservative Christian Socials sensed increasing pressure from their erstwhile allies, the paramilitary-backed *Heimatblock* (Homeland Bloc), which openly rejected parliamentarism and the "multi-party state."[11] In Germany's Weimar Republic, the conservative legislators Walther Lambach and Siegfried von Kardorff both had been open to cross-party connections in the Reichstag of the 1920s. Over time, they were tarred as moderates and expelled from their radicalizing right-wing political parties in Germany. The breakdown in these personal-political relationships left a more polarized national political environment in their wake.

Political Rivals Hiding Illegal Weapons in First Republic Austria

Since the 1950s, scholars of interwar Austria have foregrounded political polarization through the existence of three competing sociopolitical "camps." These three groupings included the country's two largest political blocs – the conservative Catholic Christian Social Party (Christlichsoziale Partei, CS) and the Social Democratic Workers' Party of German

Austria (Sozialdemokratische Arbeiterpartei Deutschösterreichs, SDAP) – as well as a smaller pan-German nationalist camp. Political scientists and more politically minded historians have used this scholarly paradigm to help explain how Austria's parliamentary arithmetic functioned with stable blocs and little need for co-operation between the socialists and the conservatives to create governing majorities.[12] More recently, however, intellectual historians including Janek Wasserman have emphasized discursive similarities between the Christian Social and German national camps and collapsed them into one. Instead of a three-way tension, these scholars have argued for a marked left-right divide between the socialists versus a big-tent conservative grouping.[13]

Whether Austrian politics was divided between two or three camps, this division has narratively functioned to spur the polarization that drove Austria's First Republic towards its demise. Reacting against this teleology of impending doom, Erin Hochman has argued that focusing on unbridgeable cleavages between political camps still misleadingly foregrounds the collapse of democracy. Drawing on new trends in the historiography of the Weimar Republic, Hochman has reframed Austria's First Republic terms of its promise by demonstrating the potential for democratic mobilization and looking to the "myriad relationships among representatives from the rival *Lager* [camps]."[14] Hochman has expanded on the work of Evan Burr Bukey in *Hitler's Hometown: Linz, Austria, 1908–1945*. Through a regional case study of politics in Upper Austria, Bukey identified a "local political culture [that] was imbued with a sense of legitimacy, a commitment to democratic procedures, and a willingness of elites to engage in dialogue and co-operation." Bukey contrasted this co-operative local political culture in Linz with the Austrian federal system's "unstable order marred by little real consensus, intense societal cleavage, and a highly polarized system." Bukey argued for a regional consociational democracy in Upper Austria, but this was framed in contrast to the federal system.[15] However, Hochman applied Bukey's analysis to the national level. Whereas Bukey had assumed that Vienna was riven with unbridgeable ideological divides, Hochman posited a more collaborative and even more widespread consociational democracy in interwar Austria.[16]

On the one hand, as shown in Chapter 1, rank-and-file Austrian legislators like Gabriele Proft and Anna Boschek experienced a less collaborative and more politically charged environment in parliament. On the other hand, there are fleeting archival glimpses of meaningful cross-party personal contact among high-ranking Austrian political rivals. For instance, the Catholic priest and Christian Social Chancellor Ignaz Seipel, who has been seen as a key figure in the polarization of the First Republic, made a personal request – scrawled out on the back of a visiting card – of Robert Danneberg, who was a leading socialist politician. Seipel needed help negotiating with socialist municipal officials in Linz to find accommodation for a lieutenant colonel who was temporarily in the city. Seipel and Danneberg's brief personal favour reflected the fact that there was not a cordon sanitaire preventing cross-party encounters.[17] For the political establishment, Viennese society was even replete with "invitations to the so-called '*jours*,' or get-togethers for tea in the afternoon or evening" when politicians mingled with the Viennese artistic, musical, and social elite. This cross-party world of sociability that could bring opponents like Seipel and Danneberg together was reserved for the highest ranks of the political elite in interwar Austria. By definition, Hochman's hypothesized consociationalism would tie party elites together far more than ordinary party members – or even regular legislators – and that was, in fact, the case with these co-operative interactions among high-ranking political rivals.[18]

A personal chat about an apartment in Linz over tea might not be enough evidence of robust political interconnections, but there was long-term private political co-operation between socialist and Christian Social leaders on one of the most unlikely of topics: military-grade weapons. In the fall of 1918, interwar Austria emerged in fits and starts from the crumbling Habsburg empire, with its borders and future uncertain, and a population inundated with weapons from the First World War. As the revolutionary state's police powers faltered, paramilitary organizations picked up the slack. The provisional Austrian authorities tolerated distributing surplus guns to private groups in order to maintain some semblance of order. When the Treaty of Saint-Germain limited weapons manufacture and retention, Austria was awash with illicit firearms. The treaty's provisions were to be enforced by an inter-allied commission that sought out and would destroy weapons, parts of weapons, and other war materiel exceeding predetermined limits or not previously reported to the Allied governments. Behind the scenes, however, from the early 1920s, rival politicians from the SDAP and the CS worked together to conceal and manage secret weapons caches, particularly at the Viennese Arsenal. The two key figures in this backroom co-operation on firearms were Carl Vaugoin and Julius Deutsch.[19]

The Christian Social politician Carl Vaugoin was born into a liberal Viennese family in 1873. He first trained as a soldier but then worked in the financial administration of Lower Austria. He departed his family's centrist politics to join the conservative Christian Socials in the final years of the Habsburg monarchy. After wartime service in the army, Vaugoin began a political career in local Viennese politics. In 1920, he was elected to Austria's new republican Nationalrat and began a rapid rise to the cabinet. He first took over the army ministry in April 1921. With an interlude of only few months from 1921 into 1922, Vaugoin held the army ministerial brief for over a decade until 1933. Vaugoin later served briefly as vice chancellor and then as chancellor, while also taking up the political leadership of the federal CS party. Despite other top jobs, Vaugoin never gave up his military portfolio; he always combined his ministerial oversight of the Austrian military with other roles.[20]

The socialist bigwig Julius Deutsch was Vaugoin's counterpart in overseeing illegal firearms. Although Deutsch had been born into a poor family in Burgenland and originally apprenticed as a printer, the Habsburg-era socialist leadership supported Deutsch's education – first encouraging him to complete secondary school before sending him to the University of Zurich. In Switzerland, Deutsch completed his doctorate in 1908 with a prize-winning dissertation on child labour. This budding socialist academic was then drafted into the army of Austria-Hungary during the First World War. Because of his academic and political ties to trade unions, he was eventually assigned to the Habsburg army ministry to improve its relationships with the working class. Deutsch found himself at the army ministry when revolution tore apart the Habsburg empire, which meant that Deutsch was quickly promoted into top leadership of the Austrian ministry in November 1918. In March 1919, Deutsch was made army minister in his own right.[21]

At the army ministry, Julius Deutsch was instrumental in creating the first republican Austrian army. Deutsch dubbed this force the "Volkswehr" (people's militia), which was designed to defend democracy in close alignment with the working class. At the same time, the Volkswehr had to be a fighting force, since it was dispatched to Burgenland and Carinthia in order to secure the new Austrian republic's borders. Deutsch's legacy of a democratized army was steadily rolled back by his ministerial successors, especially Vaugoin. The Christian Social minister reshaped Deutsch's Volkswehr into the Austrian "Bundesheer" (federal army) that was to have fewer socialists in its ranks and be more loyal to the sitting government rather than to the parliament as a whole. However, Vaugoin's transformation process for the Bundesheer did not happen overnight, and the army's restructuring lasted through the end of the 1920s, in part because of legislative oversight of the army ministry that kept the socialists directly involved in army affairs long after they had left the governing coalition in 1920.[22]

In addition to the regular parliamentary committee that supervised the army ministry, there was a special standing parliamentary commission on army affairs. Three commissioners – one each from the three largest political parties – provided democratic accountability for the military even when parliament was not in session.[23] Although the socialists were in the opposition, Julius Deutsch was one of the parliamentary commissioners; he transformed this role into being a forceful advocate for the concerns of various socialist-leaning constituencies. When SDAP members serving in the army complained to Deutsch about members of the Bundesheer appearing in uniform at party-political events and about soldiers being compelled to attend events at military cemeteries dominated by right-wing paramilitaries, Deutsch's advocacy prompted ministerial reminders to commanders that these practices violated army policy.[24] As parliamentary commissioner, Deutsch negotiated agreements with Vaugoin to prevent the minister from firing all the socialist-leaning army personnel whenever budget cuts loomed. Deutsch also advocated for the recruitment of more socialist party members into the Bundesheer. Managing this left-wing recruitment drive from his official parliamentary commissioner office in the army ministry building, Deutsch's staff sent instructions to potential recruits on how to enlist.[25] On the cusp of Austria's lurch into dictatorship, this parliamentary commissioner system was ruled unconstitutional by the courts in 1932 and dismantled. However, as a parliamentary commissioner during the 1920s, Deutsch had frequent access to Carl Vaugoin which provided the opportunity for private negotiations about weapons stockpiles.[26]

Carl Vaugoin and Julius Deutsch did not only have opposing perspectives on how the army should function, but they also had different views on the armed paramilitary forces in the country. In the immediate post-war chaos when private actors were armed and wandering the streets, both left-wing and right-wing Austrian militias emerged. On the left, there were organized workers' militias. On the right, conservative militias and resident self-defense groups, often made up of veterans from the war, coalesced into the Heimwehr (Home Guard). The Heimwehr would ultimately grow into national organization of 200,000 men that dwarfed the Austrian army, which explains why Vaugoin frequently attempted to ally them with his federal army. As the militias on the right seemed to gain more strength and the blessing of the federal government, Julius Deutsch created the Republikanischer Schutzbund (Republican Protection League, Schutzbund) in 1923 to unite the working-class militias into a socialist-affiliated paramilitary group. Deutsch would remain a leader in the Schutzbund throughout the years of the First Republic. This meant that when Deutsch met with Vaugoin, the socialist wore many hats. He represented the SDAP by virtue of his seat in the Nationalrat and his party leadership position; however, he was also a special parliamentary commissioner overseeing the military. At the same time, he was the paramilitary leader of the left-wing Schutzbund.[27]

Vaugoin and Deutsch's secret, cross-party co-operation in hiding weapons would later be called the Arsenal Pact. The Viennese Arsenal had been built by the imperial Habsburg government after the 1848 revolutions and was a sprawling complex that included cadet academies, the military historical museum, laboratories, and storerooms. In 1918 and 1919, workers and soldiers who were trying to preserve order and defend the new Austrian state hid munitions in bricked-up cellars, halls, and the sewers throughout the Arsenal complex. Since the workers and Volkswehr soldiers who originally squirrelled away these arms were socialists, they knew where they were located. This meant that later the workers' militias, the SDAP, and later the Schutzbund felt some sense of ownership over these hidden weapons. Left-wing concern about these firearms grew after 1920 when the conservative federal government worked to exclude the socialists from more and more of the army. To allay these concerns, a private agreement was reached in 1922. This first Arsenal deal nominally allowed the SDAP to maintain some control over the weapons. A military officer – Alfred Marek – who was himself a socialist, was appointed to safeguard the munitions. The deal also stipulated that the weapons would remain in the Arsenal complex without the socialists and government both agreeing to any move elsewhere.[28]

In the mid-1920s, Carl Vaugoin and Julius Deutsch built on the trust created by the 1922 Arsenal pact in collaborating during a crisis with Fascist Italy. Italian jingoism had reached a fever pitch over the recently annexed, former Habsburg territory of South Tyrol. Benito Mussolini's government had imposed rigid Italianization policies in the predominantly German-speaking province, which had been rechristened Alto Adige. The Duce even suggested that an invasion of Austrian Tyrol might be in the cards in a letter to the editor of a regional newspaper: "Fascist Italy may, if necessary, carry its flag beyond the Brenner, but lower it, never!" With the dictator of a neighbouring state threatening to cross the newly fixed border on the Brenner Pass, provincial government of Austrian Tyrol frantically planned the defence of the region. This was such an existential crisis that the Austrian army reached out to all the local paramilitary organizations about mustering men to defend the territory should Italy invade. This included both the right-wing Heimwehr and the socialist Schutzbund.[29]

With a desperate need for men and materiel to repel an Italian invasion over the Alps, a series of conversations between the Republikanischer Schutzbund, army ministry officials, military officers, and even parliamentary committee members took place. Vaugoin and Deutsch were the key players. The Schutzbund and the government hammered out a deal on joint military co-operation in the event of an invasion. The socialists agreed to place up to one thousand men from the Schutzbund under the "supreme command" of the national army in Tyrol, and the federal government agreed to feed, equip, and help arm them. Arms were accordingly transferred to Tyrol for the socialist Schutzbund. The conservative government that was rolling back democratic controls in the army and cozying up to the right-wing militias was, nevertheless, willing to arm socialist paramilitaries to defend the Austrian state. The Schutzbund despised the right wing in Austria, but these socialists obviously hated Italian Fascist invaders even more. For Deutsch and Vaugoin, this agreement fostered additional trust that the two men could work together effectively and secretly on contentious military issues.[30]

Behind the scenes at the army ministry, there was a long-running concerted effort to cover up any information about weapons at the Viennese Arsenal. In 1925 when a confidential letter arrived at the army ministry that expressed concerns about supposed attempts to export the hidden Arsenal weapons, generals intercepted the letter and ensured it was not officially registered in ministry files, and Vaugoin approved this secrecy.[31] The fragility of the Arsenal weapons deal was pushed to the fore in March 1927 when a break-in in one of the weapons storerooms was reported in the press. Policemen and military officials discovered old rusty guns and publicly declared that they were seizing socialist weapons caches at the Arsenal. Mysteriously, the electricity to the Arsenal was then cut off – perhaps by socialist power plant workers – so the policemen and soldiers had to continue their work of confiscating firearms by lamplight. The local left-wing Schutzbund detachment mustered, surrounded the Arsenal complex, and called for a fight with the conservative government for taking these weapons. Julius Deutsch showed up in person to plead with his angry socialist comrades by claiming that this weapons cache was merely "old materiel, stocks, and barrels" and that nothing taken actually belonged to the Schutzbund. Grudgingly, the socialist paramilitaries dispersed, but this Arsenal weapons discovery was the talk of the town. The right-wing *Christlichsoziale Arbeiter-Zeitung* lambasted the socialists, while praising Minister Vaugoin and the police for seizing these firearms.[32]

About two weeks after this fraught moment on the streets outside the Arsenal, Julius Deutsch and Carl Vaugoin had a scheduled meeting about a draft law on army provisioning. Deutsch's notes recorded that the socialist mentioned the recent events at the Arsenal, but Vaugoin took the conversation in a curious direction:

v[AUGOIN]: At the death of my wife you sent me a few words that I found very touching. May I say something to you perfectly honestly, man to man?
d[EUTSCH]: Of course.
v[AUGOIN]: On your word of honour that this issue does not leave this room.
d[EUTSCH]: Agreed!

Vaugoin's reference to Deutsch's condolences is jarring after the socialist brought up a near-bloodbath by paramilitaries only weeks before. For Vaugoin, emphasizing a collegial gesture of sympathy was seemingly meant to highlight a personal connection that had grown during co-operation on the Arsenal pacts and the Tyrolean affair.

After mentioning Deutsch's condolences, Vaugoin shared his top-secret information about the Arsenal break-in with the socialist. The Christian Social revealed that Alfred Marek, the socialist army officer responsible for managing the weapons cache, had staged the whole incident. According to Vaugoin, Marek betrayed the SDAP and tried his hand as a double agent, providing the government soldiers with a map of all the Arsenal weapons caches. Vaugoin did not trust him: "The entire Marek family has been playing with us for a long time […] Marek has betrayed to us everything he knew from you. On the other hand, he has probably also told you everything he experienced from us. This man is the biggest scoundrel I know." Vaugoin said his hand was forced by the break-in, and the police had to be seen to do something. Although the CS minister now knew where all the weapons were, Vaugoin intentionally ordered that only worthless, rusted gun parts from one section of the Arsenal be seized in the hopes of maintaining the confidential agreement with Deutsch.

Both Vaugoin and Deutsch wanted to prevent Marek or others from going to the Allies to reveal the existence of all the other illegal weapons. Although Deutsch and Vaugoin were on opposite sides of domestic politics, they had made common cause to keep more weapons in Austria in violation of the Treaty of Saint-Germain. At the end of their March 1927 conversation, Deutsch suggested exploring "common control of all illegal weapons stores," with the Schutzbund and army co-operating. Moreover, Deutsch offered an olive branch to the entire Christian Social government led by the conservative Ignaz Seipel. "We [the socialist leadership] have already told Chancellor Seipel that we are for mutually sorting out the Arsenal Affair. We could best do that after the elections. Until then things need to be quiet." Deutsch and Vaugoin – members of two parties that were at each other's throats and were in the midst of campaigning for every last vote in the country – agreed not to bring up the Arsenal weapons for political gain during the 1927 elections. Illegal weapons stores could have been used as a brilliant vote-winning cudgel against opponents, but the whole issue was hushed up.[33]

After the April 1927 national elections, the SDAP and Minister Vaugoin came to a new agreement about the Arsenal weapons that was signed in mid-May 1927. The two parties decided to move all the weapons out of the Arsenal – sending two-thirds to army barracks and one-third to Neugebäude Palace in the Viennese district of Simmering. This sixteenth-century palace had fallen into disrepair and had recently come into the ownership of the municipality of Vienna. The city government – which was controlled by the socialists – agreed to rent out several rooms in the palace to the army ministry where these weapons would be stored. Both parties agreed to appoint one SDAP and one CS representative to administer the deal and each be given one key, both of which needed to be used to unlock the storerooms. Unlike the 1922 agreement, neither representative could be an active military officer, which sidelined Marek who had been proven untrustworthy. In fact, after this new Arsenal deal was negotiated, Marek's apartment was raided and 700 pistols, several rifles, and plenty of ammunition were discovered squirrelled away in the house and likely for sale to the highest bidder. Having removed Marek from the mix, Vaugoin and Deutsch agreed that no part of the new deal could be changed, and no weapons could be moved without the consent of the other party. The formal letter confirming this agreement was left vague, referring to the weapons as "the material assets stored in the Arsenal" so both parties had plausible deniability.[34]

This backroom wheeling and dealing might not be what one would expect in interwar Austria based on the decades of copious scholarship on the country's crippling political polarization. Historians of the First Republic have often read the authoritarian anti-parliamentary regime under Chancellor Engelbert Dollfuß and the subsequent 1934 Austrian Civil War back into the politics of the 1920s in crafting narratives about the origins of interwar Austrian political catastrophes. No one can gainsay that this was a polarized world, but reading Carl Vaugoin as a reactionary mastermind, who carefully built up an Austrian army loyal to the Chistian Socials by constantly lying to socialist politicians, would be tantamount to a historical conspiracy theory. Vaugoin agreed to arm socialists in Tyrol in 1926, and, as a grieving widower in 1927, he built trust with Julius Deutsch and made certain campaign issues off limits.[35] The lasting co-operation between Vaugoin and Deutsch supports Erin Hochman's contention that politicians from Austria's various camps were not "completely siloed," and this particular example points to co-operation among interwar elites that amounts to private, consociational democratic negotiation.[36]

In the 1920s, there might have been impassioned potshots and little cross-party mingling among rank-and-file socialists and conservatives in the Nationalrat, but the party elite still navigated cross-cutting interconnections and negotiated political deals. For instance, there had been grand compromises between the right and the left in agreeing on both the original 1920 national constitution and revisions nine years later. The same year the 1929 Austrian constitutional revisions increased the power of the executive over the legislature, all four political parties represented in the Nationalrat signed an agreement approving a draft law related to housing.[37] It may be easy to disregard these cross-party connections or read them as one-way attempts by clerical or authoritarian Austrian conservatives to manipulate their adversaries, but Julius Deutsch, for one, did not feel that he was being exploited. He and Vaugoin built a trusting political relationship over secret weapons to achieve the common goals of ensuring that order was maintained on the Viennese streets and that Austria was secure from foreign invasion.[38]

The Acrimonious Election of 1930 and a Permanent Political Falling Out

The Arsenal Pact endured even as the blood of protestors was spilled on Austrian streets. In the July Revolt of 1927, a popular protest led to a general strike in Vienna. Angry demonstrators broke into the Palace of Justice and set the building alight. The socialist mayor of Vienna pleaded with the crowd to disperse, but the police intervened with force, and ultimately 89 people were killed and hundreds were injured. These pitched battles in Austrian cities contrasted with the painstakingly developed working relationship between Julius Deutsch and Carl Vaugoin. The two men had earlier hammered out a deal to stash weapons that were themselves similar to those used by the authorities to gun down working-class protestors.[39]

Behind the scenes, the personal relationship between Deutsch and Vaugion became somewhat more strained. In a private meeting in late 1927, Vaugoin complained that Deutsch was being too critical of him in the socialist *Arbeiter-Zeitung* with underhanded insults such as accusing Vaugoin of being a coward.[40] A few months later, Vaugoin responded to a private letter from Deutsch with the laconic response that the minister would not give in to the socialist's attempt at "censoring his speeches before they are given."[41] Ultimately, the Arsenal deal itself frayed in

October 1928 when Vaugoin wanted to push forward with one clause of the agreement that would have enabled relocation of the stored weapons from Neugebäude Palace to a munitions factory in Simmering under the control of the Austrian army. In correspondence with the socialists, Vaugoin expressed a desire to move the weapons. Moreover, the Christian Social hinted this could be done unilaterally. Deutsch's frustrated response emphasized that he was reading Vaugoin's letter charitably as a request for the SDAP's opinion rather than the unilateral abrogation of the deal: "Would it not be better [...] if the two of us first discuss the situation? I think that we would be more likely to reach a solution this way." The agreement survived.[42]

Publicity is often deadly for backroom political deals, but the Arsenal agreement had weathered several storms in the press over the years. In fact, the 1927 revised Arsenal agreement was reported by the Viennese Communist newspaper *Die Rote Fahne* within a few months of being agreed. The small Austrian Communist party wanted to discredit the big-tent left-wing SDAP for making a deal with the right-wing government, so it reported at length on this incriminating collusion. No other publications followed up on the Communists' accurate reporting, but the news gained international attention in that the German consul followed up on the Communist lead and confirmed the deal's existence. The Arsenal agreement received even more press attention during a 1929 libel trial involving the alleged double agent and weapons smuggler Major Alfred Marek. The court proceedings brought the negotiations between the SDAP and Vaugoin to light. However, the socialist *Arbeiter-Zeitung* newspaper only obliquely reported on the deal.[43]

As with the age-old tension between cross-cutting interconnections and the primacy of party, electoral politics in Austria's 1930 federal election finally destroyed the Arsenal Deal. In 1929, Carl Vaugoin's party-political star was rising, and he was made vice chancellor, while retaining control over the army ministry. In a bid to shore up the party's right flank, Vaugoin profiled himself as the most anti-socialist minister possible. With this new reputation to secure, Vaugoin doubled down on anti-socialist and confrontational policies both in the army and in developing a new railroad strategy against the left-wing trade unions. By the end of September 1930, Vaugoin had been asked to form a government in his own right as chancellor, which he did by bringing in more radical right-wing Heimwehr militia leaders into the Austrian cabinet. The first act of his new government was to set a national election date for November 9, 1930. With no honeymoon as chancellor, Vaugoin had to pivot to campaign mode, speaking at 116 different events trying to secure victory.[44]

Seeking to bolster his anti-Marxist bona fides and cement his alliance with the radical right-wing militias, Chancellor Vaugoin arranged for a wave of weapons seizures on November 4, 1930, just five days before the national election. However, the plans for raiding these known caches of illegal firearms were drawn up several weeks in advance and distributed widely. There was plenty of time for news of the raids to leak out, and it did. Most of the illicit weapons belonged to the socialist Schutzbund, and with this advance notice, the left-wing militia ensured any valuable guns were hastily relocated. On November 4, when the police showed up where arms should have been stored, there were very few weapons present. However, this news that the police were scouring the country seeking illegal socialist guns would seem to be fortuitous political propaganda to reel in middle-class, anti-Marxist voters for the conservative bloc in the midst of an election.[45]

Carl Vaugoin's apparent plan was to stage weapons seizures to score electoral points, while not actually taking too many firearms. However, Vaugoin miscalculated and underestimated the SDAP's resolve. In the election campaign, both the SDAP and CS were trying to one up each other, and Chancellor Vaugoin publicly boasted of his government's seizure of illegal Schutzbund weapons.[46] The day before the election, on November 8, 1930, the socialist *Arbeiter-Zeitung* ran two explosive stories about Christian Social duplicity in seizing firearms. The newspaper's main story related to the Christian Socials' claim that they uncovered illegal weapons in Tyrol. The *Arbeiter-Zeitung* published letters pointing to long-standing co-operation between the Schutzbund and the national army in Tyrol dating back to 1925. This revelation made Chancellor Vaugoin seem like a hypocrite for taking credit for seizing these weapons: "Vaugoin has just had his military police in Tyrol confiscate weapons that his army allowed to be given to the Republikanischer Schutzbund in order to protect the state of Tyrol!"[47] The *Arbeiter-Zeitung* also ran a story about the Arsenal weapons in Vienna, including facsimiles of the documents that had sealed the agreement between the socialists and Christian Socials. Chancellor Vaugoin's anti-socialist election campaign actually undermined the trusting relationship that he had developed with the SDAP as army minister.[48]

Julius Deutsch had provided all of his notes on the years of co-operation with Vaugoin to the socialist *Arbeiter-Zeitung* newspaper for its two bombshell features. According to Deutsch, these explosive socialist newspaper stories were a response not only to Vaugoin's countrywide weapons seizures but also to his government informing the SDAP that it was unilaterally seizing guns from Neugebäude Palace and moving them to a federally owned army depot.[49] This contravened the Arsenal agreements of 1922 and 1927, so Deutsch retaliated by passing his records to socialist journalists. Vaugoin was livid, and with a day to go to the election, he attacked Deutsch with renewed intensity at his public rallies: "Dr. Deutsch's actions seem to me to border right on high treason [...] We are sick and tired of the high treason of our social democrats."[50] The same day Vaugoin also furiously wrote in private letter to Deutsch that these private agreements were to be "handled at the top levels," and that, for his part, "the agreement was not incorporated into the office files." Vaugoin made it clear that he would never trust Deutsch again: "I will not go in depth about the reasons for this secrecy here, since based on my previous experience, I must expect that you will turn this letter over to your party newspaper in your reckless pursuit of party-political goals." Chancellor Vaugoin declared all his agreements with Deutsch null and void.[51]

Carl Vaugoin and Julius Deutsch's co-operation on paramilitary issues survived for eight years until it finally buckled under the pressure of an intense election campaign. In 1930, Chancellor Vaugoin needed to score big electoral points against the socialists to shore up his right flank and to continue to partner with the anti-parliamentary Heimwehr politicians. Austria's Christian Socials publicized all the government's weapons seizures to boost Vaugoin's credibility as the most anti-socialist candidate. Confiscating weapons despite Vaugoin's deals with the SDAP seemed to be the politically expedient thing to do. Betrayed for electoral gain, Deutsch publicized all the secret agreements. Deutsch ended this long-standing political interconnection by writing to Vaugoin: "You will also be responsible if your violation of the agreement, which you did for self-serving party reasons for an electoral boost, leads to the loss of these weapons, which had been protected so carefully, for the state of Austria."[52]

This final acrimonious collapse in the collaboration between Vaugoin and Deutsch was disastrous on many levels. First and foremost, Vaugoin's gambit was not electorally productive for him. The CS party lost ground in the elections, and the SDAP overtook Vaugoin's party in the 1930 election to become the largest party in the Austrian parliament for the first time since 1919. Moreover, for Vaugoin's career, the stunt failed as well. He was now tarred as the Christian Social who lost an election, and he was ushered out of the chancellorship before the end of 1930. However, this breakdown of trust between two political rivals in the run up to the 1930 election was disastrous for the whole country; the 1930 election was actually the last free election in interwar Austria. The SDAP leadership had long tried to moderate the most radical impulses of its left-wing base, to talk them down from violence, and to work with the government, much as had happened during the Habsburg years.[53]

The collapse of the Arsenal Pact was not the final end of the SDAP's attempts to work with the conservative Austrian authorities, and Julius Deutsch continued to interact with the government as a parliamentary army commissioner into 1932 when he advocated for post office jobs for army veterans. However, the collapse of the Arsenal Pact ended a long-standing, trusting, private relationship among elites from various parties. The few lingering structures that tied socialists to the state like the parliamentary commissioner and regular Nationalrat sessions would be dismantled in 1932 and 1933, which brought the anti-government and anti-Christian Social feelings of the socialist base closer to the party leaders.[54] For Deutsch and the SDAP leadership, the conservative government was no longer a trustworthy partner, even in private. Political rivals who had been willing to co-operate when interests overlapped finally became true enemies. Rivals fight each other in elections; however, enemies go to war against each other. Tragically, that happened in Austria during the civil war of 1934.[55]

Walther Lambach: From Conservative Trade Unionist to Target of a Radicalizing Party

The fictional German parliamentarian Herr Müller-Hinterwalden had uncovered the age-old tension between cross-cutting political interconnections and all-powerful political parties. By the time Julius Deutsch and Carl Vaugoin were wrestling with the needs of their parties versus co-operation with rivals, they had ascended to the top ranks of interwar Austria's politics. There was more wiggle room at these political heights for building interconnections with colleagues. However, the tension between an ideologically regimented political group and an openness to work with partners beyond one's own party could also shape the political careers of ordinary rank-and-file parliamentarians. Herr Müller-Hinterwalden's own creator, Walther Lambach, ultimately fell victim to the wrath of the radicalizing conservative German nationalist DNVP because he had been willing to seek out interconnections with political partners of varying political stripes.

Walther Lambach was a Protestant Rhinelander and white-collar conservative trade union mandarin. Lambach had first trained in business and then worked as a clerk at various companies in and around Düsseldorf as he rose through the ranks of the German National Union of Commercial Employees (Deutschnationaler Handlungsgehilfen-Verband, DHV). The DHV was founded in 1893 as a small trade union that spewed antisemitic propaganda for anti-Marxist Christian workers. Over time, however, it slowly moved in a slightly less rabid direction to become the largest white-collar trade union in interwar Germany. The DHV co-operated with other elements of the non-socialist Christian labour movement and was not tied to one political party. The DHV instead worked across the centre right of the Weimar political spectrum, particularly reaching out to Protestant clerks and tradespeople. Although some DHV leaders were members of the right-liberal German People's Party (Deutsche Volkspartei, DVP), Lambach was one of the most prominent in the more conservative DNVP, and he was elected to the Reichstag for that party in 1920. Although the DNVP was often linked to eastern Junker agricultural interests and Rhenish industrialists, it was also dependent on the votes of the more middle-class white-collar labour movement, which included Lambach's DHV.[56]

Although Lambach and the DHV were on the relative left of the DNVP, there was not a progressive bone in Lambach's body. His early interwar publications embraced the antisemitism, anti-Marxism, and base populism of the Weimar right.[57] However, in 1926, his publications took a turn, first with his fictionalized account of the humdrum and horse-trading of the Weimar-era Reichstag in *Die Herrschaft der Fünfhundert* (The Rule of the 500). This was the book with Müller-Hinterwalden as protagonist, but surprising for a work of fiction, Lambach claimed in the foreword that his avowed aim was to contribute to "making German parliamentary work factual and objective."[58] One might assume that as a DNVP parliamentarian who ostensibly hated the republican system and valued Prussian mores, Lambach would have advanced an anti-democratic line in the book, but he did not. The best evidence for his even-handedness is the book's favourable review by Friedrich Stampfer, a socialist and fellow member of the Reichstag: "This book is pleasantly surprising [...] such an enjoyable and interesting book about German politics has been written so that both a social democrat can read it with delight and a German nationalist can see value in it." Stampfer particularly praised the candid, amateur photographs that another DNVP colleague had taken and that Lambach had reproduced in the book. Müller's fictional life was thus illustrated with real photos that brought the reader behind the closed doors of Reichstag committee rooms, to tables in the parliamentary restaurant, and into private conversations between political rivals. Stampfer sensed an implicit acceptance of parliamentarism in the book's "pithy and biting refutation of reactionary demagoguery." Stampfer reasoned that if Lambach really wanted to eviscerate the republican system, he would not have written a fictionalized account that explored both the positive and negative aspects of parliamentary life.[59]

In 1926, Walther Lambach published in the more traditional genre of political non-fiction with his edited collection *Politische Praxis 1926*.

Figure 7.2. Candid photos of interwar German parliamentarians reproduced in Walther Lambach's *Die Herrschaft der Fünfhundert*, 1926.

Lambach asked specific colleagues in the DNVP to write short essays for a lay audience on their policy area of expertise. These essays covered everything from women as legislators to DNVP support for vintners. The articles tended to be dry, fact-filled, and deeply rooted in contemporary political concerns. Lambach contended that this new publication also should "serve to render factual and objective the political work of the German people."[60] *Politische Praxis 1926* was not the reactionary tract of a man bent on destroying the republican system. The contributors proposed policy solutions within the current governmental framework. Moreover, the contributors Lambach enlisted from within the DNVP in 1926 were a veritable who's who of politicians driven out of the right-wing party as it radicalized later. Of the 25 contributors, 15 left the DNVP and several more were not re-elected in 1930. Lambach was enabling these German nationalist political luminaries to develop a practical conservative rapprochement with their republican colleagues where interconnections could be found on a "factual and objective" basis.[61]

Walther Lambach is known to historians not so much for his white-collar union leadership or his political publications but because of a later scandal that played a key role in the radicalization of Germany's chief conservative party. After the DNVP's electoral defeat in the May 1928 national election, Lambach wrote an article trying to understand why the party had lost votes and strategizing about how to recapture its political support. However, his dispassionate election post-mortem was blown wildly out of proportion by the DNVP's right wing for political gain.[62] In his article, Lambach argued that the DNVP's insistence on its traditional monarchism cost it votes the election, particularly with younger voters. Lambach desired a big-tent DNVP "as the meeting place [...] of conservative forces" with the broad-church motto: "Monarchists and republicans join our ranks!"[63] For an advocate of interconnections with non-monarchist parties, Lambach's political calculation of appealing to the centre right seemed natural. However, this challenge to the core conservative tenet of monarchism was immediately seized on by more radical forces in the party that were coalescing around the industrialist and soon-to-be party leader Alfred Hugenberg.[64]

The 1928 Lambach Affair was a turning point in the DNVP's radicalization. The party's right understood that Lambach's challenge to monarchism was linked to the larger question of whether the DNVP should acquiesce to the republican system. Both Larry Eugene Jones and Daniel Ziblatt have focused on the Lambach Affair and the opportunistic use of the moment to wrest control of the DNVP from its traditional conservative leaders. Hugenberg and his allies first tried to topple the party leader Kuno von Westarp from his leadership of the DNVP parliamentary party using Westarp's inaction on the Lambach issue to allege that Westarp was weak. The DNVP parliamentarians voted to retain Westarp, so Hugenberg and his allies moved to force Westarp out of the separate office of party chair. Ziblatt has argued that even earlier radicalization of local DNVP groups contributed to Hugenberg's ultimate capture of the party. In the end, forcing the pragmatic Westarp out pushed the party in an even more anti-system direction. Despite the scholarly interest in the Lambach Affair as a momentous turning point, at the time, Lambach experienced this scandal as yet another contest between him and other factions in the party.[65]

These long-running interpersonal disputes between Walther Lambach, as well as his allies from the white-collar unions, and DNVP members closer to the employers' associations had sometimes moved into the party's honour court (*Ehrengericht*) system. Party discipline and mediation between members was often carried out through these so-called honour courts. Even through their name, there was a clear link between political discipline, towing the party line, and gentlemanly honour. Before the 1928 Lambach Affair, however, the DNVP honour courts had often been used to make peace between the party's factions. For instance, on one occasion, when the parliamentary party reviewed an honour court decision in Lambach's favour against another parliamentarian, the party set aside that decision in the interests of comity. Lambach and his opponent were instead required to "declare on their word of honour" that they would stop personally insulting each other. Since honour was satisfied through this process, the ultimate goal of this party disciplinary procedure was to restore party unity rather than impose exacting sanctions to enforce ideological purity.[66]

After Lambach's explosive article on monarchism in mid-1928, however, more radical members of the DNVP hounded Lambach through the party honour courts with a different goal in mind. Paul Bang, a fellow DNVP member of the Reichstag and close ally of Alfred Hugenberg, accused Lambach of slander for allegedly saying of Bang in a speech: "If that man believes [Germans should work 14 hours a day], then he is dimwitted; if he is just phrasing it in that way, then he is a silly demagogue."[67] The honour court process first tried to mediate between the two men as it had done before. However, under pressure from the right in the DNVP, Lambach's radicalized local party organization in Potsdam moved to expel him from the entire party. The DNVP parliamentarians helped set aside that expulsion order, but internal party disciplinary processes continued unabated against Lambach. In fact, old cases against Lambach that had been settled by the party honour courts in the past were dredged up, and past allegations were lodged again to restart party judicial processes. Lambach saw this mobilization of party discipline against him as "attacks made in concert with instigators and opponents in the press." Hounded by these cases within the party, Lambach finally resigned from the DNVP for a conservative splinter party in 1929.[68]

Walther Lambach's relative centrism had envisioned a big-tent DNVP, and it had grown out of his DHV union's long-standing belief in cross-party ties that stretched across the bourgeois right of Weimar politics.[69] Lambach's pragmatic political interconnections were in opposition to the more radically right-wing and smaller DNVP "fused together by the iron hammer of Weltanschauung" that Hugenberg supported.[70] The 1928 Lambach Affair marked the turning point when a DNVP that welcomed people like Lambach veered to the far right and purged the centrists as ideologically impure. At its core, the Lambach Affair was not about monarchism but sprung from the deeper tension that Lambach had noticed in his books published back in 1926. *Die Herrschaft der Fünfhundert* fictionally balanced the power of party with the cross-party influence of interconnections. *Politische Praxis* implicitly argued that the DNVP should work with colleagues in parliament to achieve political ends on certain policy goals. When Lambach was attacked in the wake of his monarchism article, he was also directly challenged for his long-standing push for building up these pragmatic, centrist interconnections "right through the parties."[71] Lambach's DHV union newspaper pled in vain for conservatives to see the value in these political interconnections: "A genuine politician, someone who contains just one spark of true political passion, would be grateful that there are interconnections tied to his political group, since these make it possible for him to enter into fruitful relationships with others when the time is ripe." After 1928, however, party purity within the DNVP trumped pragmatic cross-party co-operation. Lambach's fuzzy, co-operative brand of conservativism rooted in right-wing unions was purged in favour of a conservative politics that embraced the radical right.[72]

Siegfried von Kardorff: An Honourable Patrician Leaving Two Conservative Parties

Compared to the nationalist union functionary Walther Lambach, Siegfried von Kardorff cut a very different figure in interwar German conservative politics. Kardorff was an aristocrat who slowly stepped towards the political centre and reached out a hand of friendship beyond his natural social milieu. Kardorff's more middle-of-the-road stances meant that he left or was expelled from two different Weimar-era conservative parties. In turn, Kardorff's willingness to collaborate across party lines bred resentment among more conservative figures, and his opportunities to rise into the interwar German cabinet were spoiled by members of his own political party rather than by his rivals. Although Kardorff ultimately was elected vice president of the Reichstag from 1928 to 1932, he was later and permanently ushered off the political stage for failing to follow party instructions by casting a key vote in accordance with his more pragmatically inclined conscience.

Siegfried von Kardorff was born into an aristocratic East Elbian political family, and his father had served in Otto von Bismarck's Reichstag. The younger Kardorff also went into politics, was elected for the Free Conservative Party (Freikonservative Partei) to the Prussian parliament in 1910, and became a district administrator in part of Prussian Poland.

Surprisingly for the scion of a storied noble family, Kardorff converted to the cause of reform and spearheaded progressive changes to the Prussian voting system in the final years of the First World War. Advocating for these liberalizing reforms earned Kardorff the formal censure of his fellow conservatives in 1918 and prompted the enduring skepticism of his more right-wing colleagues throughout the Weimar years. Despite this widening gulf between him and others on the Wilhelmine right, Kardorff nevertheless followed fellow imperial conservatives into the postwar DNVP. When he served in the newly republican Prussian legislature, he gravitated towards the more pragmatic wing of the party, but he broke definitively with the DNVP in 1920 and decamped to the right-liberal DVP.[73]

This decision to leave the DNVP in 1920 and abandon the natural political home of most Wilhelmine patricians was a defining moment in Kardorff's life. Years later, this choice would still be seen by the interwar public as the key turning point of his career. In marking Kardorff's 60th birthday in early 1933, a society newsletter in Berlin claimed he left the DNVP "because he did not approve of its monarchism and antisemitism." The *Vossische Zeitung* also congratulated Kardorff on this birthday in a brief article that noted the tension between Kardorff being "conservative-bourgeois in tradition and inclination" and his "incorruptible devotion to his convictions." The *Neue Freie Presse* in Vienna placed Kardorff's break with the DNVP in the context of interwar German democracy: "In this party [the DNVP] that clung to the past and tried to turn the clock back, there was no space for a politician who was conservative – no doubt – but looked towards the future and recognized that Germany had to progress on the path of democratic development."[74]

Although Kardorff's break with the DNVP came to be cast in moral terms, his 1919 correspondence when he was still a member of the party pointed to more pragmatism. Kardorff wanted to position the newly formed DNVP on the centre right as a potential party of government. In mid-1919, for example, Kardorff expressed his exasperation with DNVP hotheads who attacked the Catholic Centre Party as no better than the socialists, since this undercut a potential governing coalition partner. Kardorff was also leery of antisemites active in the DNVP: "These activities [of antisemitic provocateurs] are both a public danger and a danger for the party."[75] One might be inclined to praise Kardorff as an enlightened conservative who rejected antisemitism outright, but his centrism was based more in pragmatism. In correspondence about the new DNVP party program, for instance, Kardorff tried to tone down a blanket DNVP antisemitic indictment of "Jewry" with the still antisemitic condemnation of "certain Jewish circles." Perhaps most surprisingly given Lambach's later tussle with the DNVP over monarchism, in 1919, Kardorff advocated minimizing the party's allegiance to monarchy: "In the question of monarchy, objectively – and you will believe me – I agree complete with you, namely I also want the restoration of the imperial and royal rule of the Hohenzollerns. Nevertheless, I doubt whether it is expedient to state this in black-and-white terms in the manifesto." Kardorff wanted to position the DNVP as a centre-right party of government rather than a reactionary party on the far-right fringe.[76]

By early 1920, Kardorff's attempts to create a political party that was centre right in its stated positions made him *persona non grata* for the DNVP's right-wing majority. His opponents within the party criticized his public speeches in the conservative press and ganged up on him in private meetings. Kardorff understood this treatment as part of the larger project of sidelining the DNVP's "left wing" in favour of the "old conservative show horses." In Kardorff's earliest correspondence from 1920 after leaving the party, he began the somewhat revisionist project of framing his departure in more ethical terms, claiming that "the differences that exist between [the party leadership and me] are irreconcilable differences of world view." Moreover, Kardorff began to emphasize his horror with the DNVP's response to the Kapp Putsch of 1920. Kardorff believed that some of his DNVP colleagues were co-conspirators with the putschists and that the party moved to protect them in the wake of the failed coup.[77] Kardorff decried everyone who helped cover up for those involved in plotting the putsch as "fellow travellers in the Kapp affair." Kardorff's rejection of the coup should be seen as an early implicit acceptance of the republican order from a man who sought out middle ground and interconnections with the new status quo.[78]

The interwoven nature of interwar politics and sociability is clear in that Kardorff paid a steep personal and political price for defecting from the DNVP. Weimar's political landscape was not only made up of parties but also defined social milieux. Kardorff's decision to leave the DNVP meant turning his back on his own patrician social world. Kardorff wrote of this within weeks of leaving the DNVP: "When I tell you that I almost exclusively socialize in DNVP circles, that all my student fraternity colleagues vote DNVP, when you understand that my affiliation with the party has brought me into close friendly contact with countless people in the DNVP, then you will believe me when I say that this step was exceptionally difficult for me."[79] Years later, Kardorff took to lecturing on Otto von Bismarck, and he paused at a similar point in the Iron Chancellor's life when Bismarck's friends turned against him: "Prince Bismarck was a conservative statesman, and since he was a conservative statesman, the attacks on him from the Conservative Party deeply wounded him in his heart of hearts. Ultimately, these were men – who were of the same flesh and blood as he was – they were his professional colleagues, his social brethren, and his childhood friends who all agitated and slurred him in this way." Although Kardorff was ostensibly reflecting on Bismarck's life, one cannot help but read Kardorff's own experiences of being shunned in his biography of the Wilhelmine chancellor: "I nevertheless believe that these fights with [Bismarck's] own friends perhaps stirred the most bitter sentiments within him." Kardorff's departure from the DNVP tore apart long-standing friendships and forced him to remake his social world.[80]

As his DNVP social milieu collapsed, Kardorff met his future wife on the night of the 1920 Reichstag election when both were victorious Reichstag candidates for the right-liberal DVP. Katharina von Oheimb was herself a trailblazing woman, and after the two politicians carried on a relationship for some time as colleagues, they married in 1927. Oheimb and Kardorff would come to be known for their Berlin salon, which even Walther Lambach referenced as a social event the fictional Müller-Hinterwalden considered attending. Kardorff and his paramour only served in the Reichstag together for four years, with Oheimb departing in 1924. However, during their joint parliamentary service, the two politicians worked to reconcile the new republican reality with their German nationalist and upper-class social milieu. In parliamentary politics, they both took a centrist course, voting against the more conservative DVP majority on free votes in the Reichstag, to the ire of some of their DVP colleagues who would have preferred far more party unity.[81]

Throughout the 1920s, Siegfried von Kardorff was busy befriending colleagues from across the politician spectrum. When he collected four of his speeches on the life of Otto von Bismarck into a book, Kardorff distributed copies to his friends in the Reichstag. Ludwig Kaas, the leader of the Catholic Centre Party, which had been one of Bismarck's main opponents during the Iron Chancellor's lifetime, took the time to read Kardorff's book and sent comments to the author applauding his depiction of "the dry charm that surrounded this powerful and often such richly contradictory person." Even the socialist President of the Reichstag Paul Löbe responded to Kardorff's gift copy of the book waning nostalgically about the politics of the Wilhelmine past. In the context of the fraught politics of the Weimar Republic, Kardorff believed that the conservative Bismarck could be a unifying centre in German political history who would resonate even with Catholics and socialists. On some level, Kardorff was trying to position Bismarck as the focus of a unifying, cross-party parliamentary interconnection.[82]

In reflecting on her late husband's biography after his death, Katharina von Kardorff-Oheimb characterized the "highlight – I daresay, triumph" of Kardorff's political career as a 1927 speech that marked his most public move into the moderate political middle ground. The Reichstag organized an annual speech marking the republic's Constitution Day, and conservative politicians generally skipped out on this event. However, when an aristocrat of Kardorff's pedigree was the invited guest speaker, even a Junker skeptical of democracy was hard pressed to play hooky.[83] In Kardorff's speech, the DVP politician did his best to chart a middle path invoking both presidents of the German republic, the socialist Friedrich Ebert and conservative Paul von Hindenburg: "This should be a day on which the political conflict between parties ceases, a day on which we remember that which unites us, a day on which we want to speak about the German past, the German present, and the German future, when we want to speak about German suffering, about German hope, and about German faith in a better era." For this celebration of the Weimar constitution, Kardorff distanced himself from the revolutionary character of 1918 and 1919 to instead focus on Germany's unity in an attempt to find common ground across Weimar's political divisions. Kardorff's speech was an attempt to create a new centre in Weimar political discourse where everyone could accept the status quo of the republic while distancing themselves from the left-wing utopian desires of the revolutionaries of 1918.[84]

As Kardorff publicly warmed to the republican status quo over the course of the 1920s, he was not done tangling with his old conservative social milieu. He was still captive to the sense of gentlemanly honour of the Wilhelmine elite. Kardorff's conservative peers' understanding of honour in politics and his own came into conflict. For instance, in May 1921, Kardorff voted in the Reichstag for rapprochement with the Allies, and two of his fellow aristocrats challenged this decision as dishonourable. Thilo von Trotha, a member of Kardorff's old student fraternity Saxo-Borussia zu Heidelberg, referred him to the organization's honour council (Ehrenrat) for a "violation of national honour" for his political stance. Trotha demanded that Kardorff be expelled from the fraternity's alumni group. A commission of five aristocrats on the council rejected the complaint as beyond their purview.[85]

However, Kardorff's same 1921 Reichstag vote prompted a far more dramatic showdown with Diether Prinz zu Ysenburg und Büdingen. The prince wrote an open letter to the *Frankfurter Nachrichten* newspaper that provocatively challenged Kardorff's honour. Ysenburg und Büdingen rhetorically asked Kardorff "how can you square [this vote] with your sense of duty and your honour" and claimed that Kardorff's vote was "a sign of weakness of will, dishonesty, and cowardice."[86] This was the Wilhelmine aristocratic equivalent of throwing down the gauntlet, and Kardorff responded by immediately appointing a second to arrange a duel with the prince. The two seconds negotiated to find a time and location for the fight: "A spot can easily be found in my woodland that would almost completely preclude the arrival of any unwelcome guests. I can make vehicles available for both parties, and I will ensure that a doctor is present."[87] Ultimately, however, scheduling difficulties, problems procuring pistols, and allegations of slow-walking the process meant that satisfaction was sought in a less deadly way. Ysenburg und Büdingen's second forwarded the issue to the honour chamber (Ehrenkammer) of the Hessian officers' association, and Kardorff, in turn, forwarded the matter to his student fraternity's honour council. A duel was ultimately averted when the Hessian officers' association honour chamber stepped in to negotiate a "compromise proposal" that both parties accepted to settle the whole affair.[88]

Kardorff's showdowns ultimately moved from the dueling field to the honour courts that policed patrician Wilhelmine respectability even into the republican years. Within Kardorff's traditional conservative social milieu, his pragmatism and centrist parliamentary votes were not merely understood as political decisions but as questions of honour. Kardorff's continued centrism was so noxious to some in this social world that in 1930, Thilo von Trotha, the embittered student fraternity member from Saxo-Borussia zu Heidelberg who was frustrated that the fraternity's honour council did not expel Kardorff in the early 1920s, sent a pointed letter to Kardorff: "Considering the political stance you have taken for years that in no way reflects the monarchist traditions of Saxo-Borussia, I hereby respectfully inform you that this letter dissolves the outward expressions of any remaining fraternal relationship to you." Political differences and party purges were not merely a matter of high politics, but they trickled into the social world in which a man like Kardorff moved and resonated with the ideas of honour that shaped this milieu.[89]

Turning to 1932, there is a sense of déjà vu when considering Kardorff's political denouement. Once again, Kardorff bucked a political party that was moving in a more conservative direction, although this time it was the DVP rather than the DNVP. After the long-serving DVP leader and foreign minister Gustav Stresemann died, the party took a more conservative and obstructionist turn in a futile attempt to compete with the DNVP and the Nazis for right-wing voters. Kardorff opposed this trend; he had always positioned himself on the more constructive and co-operative wing of the DVP. Right-wing rank-and-file members of the party singled out Kardorff as the embodiment of everything that was wrong with the DVP. For instance, in one overly antisemitic and conspiracy-theory-laden resignation letter, a former party member wrote that Kardorff was a "political Judas," betraying the DVP like German Jewish prisoners of war during the First World War who sided with the French. Kardorff's long-standing rejection of antisemitism earned him the ire of true believers of the stab-in-the-back myth who resented that he stood in the way of the DVP racing quickly to the far right.[90]

Kardorff began to run into trouble with the new right-wing DVP party leadership that objected to his honest conversations with party members in which Kardorff challenged the emerging right-wing orthodoxy. When Kardorff was reprimanded for speaking his mind, he furiously responded to the DVP leader who chastised him: "No one – not even you – has the right to forbid me to speak to my election committee. If a decision in this direction were taken and published, perhaps you would have the right to regret such an action 'out of collegial concern.' However, that did not occur." Kardorff pointed out that the new party leadership was trafficking in rumours and building up a system of political spies to keep tabs on and intimidate politicians like himself. This policing of Kardorff's social world, private conversations, and political connections by the party only produced more resentment on the part of the German patrician.[91]

As with Lambach in the DNVP, Kardorff's problems with the rightward drift of the party ended up in the party's disciplinary honour courts. From 1931, Kardorff and his wife were involved in a legal quandary over a family inheritance. Embarrassing financial investigations and legal inventories of the couple's properties were made, and the attorney opposing the Kardorffs, Ludwig Schultz, happened to be a leader within the DVP and member of one of its more right-wing local party groups. Since the Berlin press did not report in depth on all the lurid steps of the legal process against the couple, Schultz personally dragged Kardorff's name through the mud within the DVP. Kardorff elected to challenge Schultz in the party honour courts rather than through a more public libel lawsuit. Eventually, the inheritance issues were settled, but Kardorff continued to pursue the honour court process. Ultimately in December 1932, the special honour court determined that Kardorff's honour was unaffected by this legal affair and dismissed the case, leaving the Kardorff's reputation intact. This resolution was actually long after the aristocrat had departed elected politics, but it was crucial for Kardorff's personal patrician sense of honour.[92]

When the DVP sponsored a motion of no confidence in Catholic Centre party Chancellor Heinrich Brüning's government in February 1932, the DVP parliamentary party implemented strict disciplinary procedures to automatically expel any member who did not vote in favour. Kardorff purposefully missed the vote in order to avoid voting against a centre-right government he supported. Kardorff knew what to expect for disobeying the party, and he soon received a formal letter from the party chief severing all party-political ties with him. Without another party to join, Kardorff unceremoniously left active politics soon afterwards. This automatic DVP expulsion for a parliamentary vote that the nobleman skipped anti-climatically drove him out of politics, and Kardorff did not run for re-election in the July 1932 elections that the Nazis won by a landslide.[93]

Even after Kardorff was expelled from the parliamentary party and subsequently left the Reichstag, he actually remained a member of the DVP and stayed in close contact with the party leadership. During this time, Kardorff campaigned for uniting political parties of the bourgeois middle, and he did not give up hope on the DVP. In fact, Kardorff was approached to speak at two election rallies in Pomerania on behalf of the party, and he accepted the invitation. The DVP leadership learned about these events and hastily ordered the local party to disinvite Kardorff or face consequences. Afterwards, the DVP's top brass issued instructions banning Kardorff from speaking at any party-political events. Specifically, Kardorff was targetted because of his push for co-operation among moderate parties, particularly against a right-wing alliance that might embrace the Nazis. The leaders of the DVP wanted to keep their options open to partner with the radical right, and Kardorff's presence was a reminder of the party's earlier centrism.[94]

Pragmatism, Sociability, and Besieged Interconnections

Walther Lambach and Siegfried von Kardorff both participated in inter-war Europe's continent of colleagues by advocating for more pragmatism within their German conservative parties. They were opposed by ascendant figures like Alfred Hugenberg who stressed ideological purity over pragmatism. In 1928, Hugenberg had provocatively asked the question whether the DNVP wanted to be a "bloc or mush." This was a creative formulation of a question that vexes political parties to this very day. Should a political party aspire to be an ideologically pure, radical group or a big-tent movement with a more pragmatic centrism? In the late 1920s and early 1930s, the DNVP and DVP both opted to become more defined right-wing parties that embraced reactionary politics. This transition led to the purging of moderates like Lambach and Kardorff. In the end, interwar Germany's conservative parties turned their back on centrist interconnections in an attempt to compete in a radical political space dominated by the Nazi Party. Instead of booking any electoral gains, these German parties dug the grave of the republican middle ground, serving as midwives of the Third Reich.[95]

Carl Vaugoin and Julius Deutsch's relationship brought together lawmakers who simultaneously held roles as elite figures within their own political parties. They combined party-political roles with formal offices as army minister and parliamentary commissioner. Despite the oft-repeated refrain that interwar democracies failed because of a lack of democrats who were ready to make difficult compromises, in fact, elites were often willing to compromise but were held back by rank-and-file party members. Vaugoin and Deutsch's working relationship reflected an elite Austrian consociationalism and its democratic potential; however, this elite co-operation also represented increasing tension between party leadership and an uncompromising political grassroots. Out of public view, Vaugoin and Deutsch's long-standing personal ties enabled pragmatic concessions in order to hide weapons at the Viennese Arsenal. Over time, more tension was injected into this personal and political relationship, and the pitched 1930 Austrian election campaign finally snuffed out this example of consociational co-operation.[96]

In the end, Deutsch, Vaugoin, Kardorff, and Lambach all represented robust, cross-party interconnections among pragmatic politicians who were willing to make concessions to govern and legislate in their countries. As a trade unionist, Lambach understood the value of building coalitions, and he took this experience to the Reichstag. However, the principle of seeking out and cultivating cross-party interconnections broke down under rising political pressure from radicalizing conservative parties. In keeping with Daniel Ziblatt's insight that conservative parties were key for democratization, when both the DNVP and DVP radicalized and turned away from the state, these two parties purged Lambach and Kardorff for representing a more pragmatic past.[97] In the Austrian case, although the Christian Socials were not radicalized during the 1930 election to the extent they would be when building an authoritarian, anti-democratic state several years later, there was growing political polarization from 1927. In the 1930 election, Vaugoin played up his anti-Marxist credentials and his alliance with the paramilitaries. The heightened tension in the Austrian federal election with the Christian Socials embracing the openly anti-democratic right provided the final blow to both the Arsenal Deal and to the behind-the-scenes relationship between Deutsch and Vaugoin.[98]

The ultimate fate of these cross-party connections cannot negate the fact that for years European legislators moved within an interwar continent of colleagues. These private backroom networks, friendships, and social spaces were even bound by unwritten rules of interwar sociability. The violation of private confidence could cause the severing of behind-the-scenes ties, as happened to the working relationship between Carl Vaugoin and Julius Deutsch when Vaugoin pushed the envelope too far in the 1930 election campaign. As was shown in Chapter 6, even among avowed anti-parliamentary parties like the Sudeten German Party in Czechoslovakia or the National Socialist Movement in the Netherlands, while legislators dutifully delivered anti-democratic speeches in public, they were willing to play by more of the social and political rules in private. For parliamentarians between the world wars, this gap between public statements and private actions meant that radical politicians could still be tied into the republican system through behind-the-scenes, cross-cutting interconnections. This system tying political rivals together lasted longer than anyone has imaged. Ultimately, however, when the private became public – when hidden weapons caches become a political cudgel, for instance – these ties frayed, and interwar democracy was in greater danger.

Republics of Friends: Informal Institutions or Damaging Democracy?

In the world of past politics, contemporaries sometimes had insights that would take a historian an entire monograph to reconstruct. The French journalist Robert de Jouvenel wrote a telling guide to the chummy political system of France's Third Republic on the eve of the First World War. In 1914, Jouvenel published *La république des camarades* (The Republic of Friends) with the gritty realities of French politics on full display. Jouvenel took his reader on a tour of the four separate political powers – the legislative, the executive, the judicial, and the press. This was a modernized version of Montesquieu's ideas, with the press as Jouvenel's addition. Jouvenel wrote: "In principle, the powers continue to be separated. But, they are neighbours." This proximity meant that "among the men who are entrusted with any roles in this world of public affairs, an intimacy is established."[1] Jouvenel's book moved both humourously and critically through the realities of republican legislative life before proceeding to chapters on the work of ministers, judges, lawyers, and press barons. Jouvenel's chapter on being elected to the Chamber of Deputies began: "One becomes a parliamentarian however one can. The easiest way is obviously to have a father who is a deputy. Or, many did well enough with a father-in-law." If family ties were not in the cards, Jouvenel suggested milking industry links or climbing the greasy pole from local politics up to a parliamentary seat. Unafraid to spotlight the republic's graft and nepotism, Jouvenel framed his description so his audience would chuckle.[2]

Although *La république des camarades* included a healthy dose of criticism about France's Third Republic, any reading of Jouvenel as antirepublican is off the mark. By the 1930s, the book was praised by French fascists, but this far right-wing interpretation departs from Jouvenel's own reformist left-wing politics. More convincing is the argument that this text was "a critique of the republic made in the name of republican ideals themselves."[3] Jouvenel fundamentally respected how political institutions could turn rivals into colleagues: "There are fewer differences between two parliamentarians, one of whom is a revolutionary and the other who is not, than between two revolutionaries, one of whom is a parliamentarian and the other who is not." On balance, Jouvenel thought that it was a good thing that opponents could mingle "in ministerial antechambers, in newsrooms, out about in the world, and even in the café – there cordial relationships are born." As has been demonstrated, forging friendly, cross-party relationships was not only true of French politicians during the Third Republic. During the 1920s and 1930s, these cordial relationships stretched across an entire continent of political colleagues.[4]

However, the changing reception of *La république des camarades* suggests increasing tension between the backroom world of politics and democratic sensibilities during the interwar decades. In 1914, a glimpse into the Third Republic's political sausage being made was worthy of a cringeworthy laugh. By the 1930s, however, the French far right read Robert de Jouvenel's exposé of politics' dirty secrets as an indictment of the "complicity" of an entire bankrupt political system.[5] After the First World War, new "republics of friends" had cropped up across Europe, and legislators brought their cross-party sociability into their transnational work. However, the public feeling that politics was becoming too enmeshed with backroom dealings came to be reflected by eagle-eyed humourists. For instance, the Austrian satirical magazine *Kikeriki* mocked political sociability in a February 1930 cartoon in which a wealthy Austrian couple was preparing to leave for a festive evening. A fashionably dressed woman was applying lipstick when her monocle-wearing husband cut in: "Make sure to apply lots of red, Ella – We're off to the City of Vienna's Formal Ball." An interwar Austrian would have chuckled, since the "red" socialists-controlled Vienna's city government, yet this annual ball was the embodiment of elite sociability. *Kikeriki* often embraced the far right and ridiculed Austria's left in antisemitic terms. In this case, however, the joke referenced the gulf between the working-class image of left wing politicians and the elite social world in which their public roles placed them.[6]

Politicians in high society were also caricatured by the German satirical periodical *Simiplicissimus* with a more explicit reference to parliamentarians in Berlin's social world. After the Nazi Reichstag election victory of 1930, a *Simiplicissimus* cartoon entitled "Berlin reorganizes: 1. High Society" depicted formally dressed men and women at a classy dinner party with the caption: "At Banker Goldstein's one always meets the season's most prominent guests: Toller, Einstein, Tagore and this year even Dr.

Figure 8.1. Cartoon about Nazis in Berlin high society from *Simiplicissimus*, November 10, 1930. The cartoon reads: "Berlin Reorganizes: 1. High Society / At Banker Goldstein's one always meets the season's most prominent guests: Toller, Einstein, Tagore and this year even Dr. Goebbels!"

Source: *Simiplicissimus* (November 10, 1930).

Goebbels!" The Nazi parliamentarian and propagandist Goebbels was drawn sulking at the head of the table with Berlin's social elite. For the more democratically oriented *Simplicissimus*, the joke was in the tension between Goebbels's radicalism and the social world in which politicians moved. The readers of *Simplicissimus* and *Kikeriki* could laugh at this gulf between the private goings-on of the political elite and the public debate presented to ordinary voters.[7]

This book has demonstrated that even in an era of intense polarization there was a behind-the-scenes world that helped structure the interwar political game. Transnational and backroom sociability was not a fleeting cultural phenomenon that amounted to the "décor" of past politics, but it was an institutionalized aspect of interwar parliamentary life.[8] The political scientists Gretchen Helmke and Steven Levitsky have shown that formal institutions like parliaments can have associated informal institutions, which are the "socially shared rules, usually unwritten, that are created, communicated, and enforced outside officially sanctioned channels." Informal institutions can range from unwritten codes that determine presidential succession to clannish norms that shape political activity. In comparative work on Latin America, Helmke and Levitsky have studied how informal institutions can complement or even substitute for weaker formal institutions.[9]

The interwar era's private world of parliamentary politics helped structure political life between the world wars. There were implicit rules in this backroom ecosystem, and violations of norms were punished. One shared rule was that information obtained in confidence could not be used publicly for political gain against a rival. When German and Dutch national socialist politicians flaunted these rules and leaked information to the press, they were excluded. This informal world of politics could even promote the kind of trust and respect that was required for parties to enter governing coalitions. For instance, although Dutch socialists were publicly tarred as revolutionary outsiders, in fact, they had been integrated into The Hague's private parliamentary culture long before they first entered a governing coalition in 1939. The collegial informal institution surrounding the Dutch parliament promoted constructive governance by bringing rivals together; this ultimately paved the way for socialists to enter government. Among elected politicians, these parliamentary informal institutions did not subvert democracy but could promote more constructive and inclusive political outcomes. This was a boon for interwar republics.[10]

However, a functioning informal institution that worked for the political elite could also breed resentment among ordinary voters. Compromises made over drinks and secret negotiations that walked back public statements could damage faith in democracy. Moreover, democratic processes of legislating and governing could be displaced into those backrooms. This situation was encapsulated in yet another *Simiplicissimus* cartoon from January 29, 1933. The magazine's front cover marked the beginning of the annual carnival season with a cartoon that featured two costumed carnival-goers appearing at a hotel. The hotel staff member says: "I'm sorry, but there are no more private hotel rooms available – they are all full of politicians!" Behind the curtains, there are three men, one wearing a military uniform, who are deep in conversation.

Figure 8.2. The cover of the satirical magazine *Simiplicissimus* from January 29, 1933. The text reads: "The Politics of Private Conversations: I'm sorry there are no more private hotel rooms available; they're all full of politicians!"

The entire cartoon is captioned "The Politics of Private Conservations." The humourous idea was that mustachioed conservative politicians were wheeling and dealing to determine Germany's political future in Berlin's backrooms. This cartoon would seem to be an accurate representation of an informal institution, as defined by political scientists. However, this backroom politicking is also depicted as glaringly undemocratic, since governing had been displaced out of public view. Tragically, this satirical take on German politics could not have been more apt. The very next day, as a result of private, behind-the-scenes conversations, Adolf Hitler was appointed chancellor of Germany. When processes of governing are displaced into backrooms, they can support interwar democratic ideals – as happened with the national right-wing Sudeten German Party reluctantly working with the Czechoslovak state and in First Republic Austria with the close relationship between the socialist Julius Deutsch and the Christian Social Carl Vaugoin. However, behind-the-scenes politicking and horse-trading can also lead to events like Adolf Hitler's appointment as chancellor.[11]

The Postwar Legacy of Interwar Parliamentary Networks

After the Second World War, there was a groundswell of support for European integration. Parliamentarians took their place in this transnational world, as they had done after the First World War. The chief advocate for legislators' involvement was the cosmopolitan Richard von Coudenhove-Kalergi, a Bohemian nobleman with a Japanese mother and Austrian father who had championed European integration from the early interwar years. His 1923 manifesto *Pan-Europa* had called for a "parliamentary campaign" to fuel the project of European integration, and he returned to this parliamentary strategy after 1945. En route to Zurich in 1946, the former British prime minister Winston Churchill met with the Coudenhove-Kalergi to discuss European unity. Referencing Coudenhove-Kalergi directly in his Swiss speech, Churchill famously threw his weight behind the project of European integration and called for the creation of a "United States of Europe."[12]

With Churchill's backing and momentum building, Richard Coudenhove-Kalergi sent a survey to over 4,000 postwar European parliamentarians that contained the sole question: "Are you in favour of a European Federation within the framework of the U.N.O.?" Coudenhove-Kalergi received almost 1,500 replies. 1,450 of the responses were in favour of European integration and only 42 were opposed. The count had gotten so many responses that he could prove there were absolute majorities for a European federation in the Italian and Dutch parliaments. Belgium, France, and Greece also had wildly lopsided survey results in favour of European unification. Coudenhove-Kalergi had always placed his faith in parliaments, having written in 1923, "as soon as the Pan-Europeans achieve majorities in all the parliaments of this part of the world, implementing a federation will be assured." In 1947, the count was on the cusp of parliamentary majorities across Western Europe in favour of his pan-European goals.[13]

Emboldened by this "indirect plebiscite," Richard Coudenhove-Kalergi convened a conference of European legislators in Gstaad, Switzerland. In September 1947, around 120 people gathered for the first meeting of the European Parliamentary Union (EPU). Delegations from Belgium,

Britain, Denmark, the Netherlands, France, Greece, Italy, Sweden, and Switzerland took their seats in the Gstaad Palace Hotel's large festival hall. Almost 50 per cent of the delegates were from Italy and France, but there were also former parliamentarians as observers, as well as anti-Communist representatives from Eastern European countries.[14] Press coverage of the conference was cloyingly positive. An op-ed in *Le Monde* argued that parliamentarians best represented the people and should lead any new European league: "Let us never forget that the League of Nations failed largely because it was a league of governments. It might perhaps have succeeded if it had been a league of peoples."[15] One American newspaper went so far to dub the EPU a "European Parliament" because represented the European body politic and the desire for a "European Union" better than any government.[16]

Many of these early postwar parliamentary cheerleaders for European integration were themselves veterans of international interwar organizations. The leadership of the European Parliamentary Union included a number of participants from the Inter-Parliamentary Union's final conference in Oslo in August 1939. The Belgian chair of the EPU, as well as vice chairs from France and the Netherlands had all been active in the IPU. Leon Maccas, the Greek vice chair of the EPU, had even attended the League of Nations Assembly with the Greek delegation in the 1920s. In subsequent years, even more of the older political faces from the 1920s and 1930s, including Eleftherios Venizelos of Greece, Paul van Zeeland of Belgium, and Édouard Herriot of France re-emerged in this pan-European parliamentary space. In the 1950s, they were joined by German parliamentarians including Paul Löbe, when West Germany was admitted to these European organizations.[17]

In May 1948, many of the new groups pushing for European integration came together at the Congress of Europe in The Hague, and Coudenhove-Kalergi ensured that the EPU and parliamentarians were well represented. The Congress' final resolution even called for a "European Assembly chosen by the Parliaments of the participating nations." This new Assembly was to influence the European public – and parliamentary – opinion to win hearts and minds for the European project. The presence of parliamentarians in this late-1940s drive for European unity earned the continent's elected lawmakers permanent seats at the table. When the first formal organization of European integration, the Council of Europe, came into being in 1949, the first session of the Council's parliamentary Assembly met in the lecture hall of the Strasbourg university. For the national legislators who attended this event, it would have seemed similar to the inter-parliamentary gatherings in the years between the world wars.[18]

Richard Coudenhove-Kalergi's insistence on recruiting parliamentarians for this postwar European project meant that these legislators were there from the beginning. This ultimately laid the groundwork for the myriad of parliamentary assemblies that still exist today. The European Coal and Steel Community created a parliamentary body that, in turn, prompted members of the North Atlantic Treaty Organization to, likewise, campaign for a parliamentary assembly. Today, even the Organization for Security and Co-operation in Europe has its own parliamentary assembly. The most well-known supranational parliamentary body is the European Parliament, a directly elected legislature for the European Union. Ultimately, the networks, sociability, interconnections, and internationalism of interwar parliamentarians collapsed into the anti-democratic morass of late 1930s, but that era's continent of colleagues left an enduring legacy in this postwar European project.[19]

Notes

Introduction: Public Political Outsiders to Behind-the-Scenes Insiders

1 Proceedings of the International Working-men's Congress in Paris (1889),
Marxists Internet Archive, accessed Nov. 27, 2023, https://www.marxists
.org/history/international/social-democracy/1889/marxists-congress
/index.htm; F. Domela Nieuwenhuis, Parlement.com, accessed Nov. 27, 2023,
https://www.parlement.com/id/vg09lkzxa0tl/f_domela_nieuwenhuis.
2 Handwritten Text, likely 1929, N Geck 1440, Adolf Geck, GLK.
3 F. Domela Nieuwenhuis, Speech on Legislation for the Eight Hour Day,
Marxists Internet Archive, accessed Nov. 27, 2023, https://www.marxists
.org/archive/nieuwenhuis/1889/eighthours.htm.
4 Tweede Kamer 2 juli 1918, Kiesraad, accessed Nov. 27, 2023, https://www
.verkiezingsuitslagen.nl/verkiezingen/detail/TK19180702; De invoering van
het vrouwenkiesrecht, Tweede Kamer der Staten-Generaal, accessed Nov.
26, 2023, https://www.tweedekamer.nl/hoe_werkt_het/tweede_kamer
_door_de_eeuwen_heen/1848-1922_strijd_voor_rechten/vernieuwing; Bas
van Dongen, *Revolutie of Integratie: De Sociaal Democratische Arbeiders Partij in
Nederland (SDAP) tijdens de Eerste Wereldoorlog* (Amsterdam: IISG, 1992), 693;
Ernest Hueting, Frits de Jong Edz., and Rob Ney, *Ik moet, het is mijn roeping:
Een politiek biografie van Pieter Jelles Troelstra* (Amsterdam, Bert Bakker, 1981),
134–59.
5 Alexander van Kessel, "Bekritisserd Instituut in een Verzuilde Context: De
Tweede Kamer tussen Pacificatie en Wereldoorlog," in *In Dit Huis: Twee
Eeuwen Tweede Kamer*, eds. Remieg Aerts, et al. (Amsterdam: Boom, 2015),
360–1.
6 Troelstra to Marchant, Feb. 19, 1929, Collectie 151, Inv. nr. 264, H.P.
Marchant, NAH.
7 Albarda to Ruys de Beerenbrouck, Feb. 1, 1933, Inv. 85, Johan Willem
Albarda, and Wibaut to Colijn, Feb. 18, 1932, Wibaut to de Veer, May 17,

1929, and de Veer to Wibaut, May 18, 1929, Inv. 335, Florentinus Marinus Wibaut, all IISG; Jan Willem Stutje, *Ferdinand Domela Nieuwenhuis: Een romantische revolutionair* (Amsterdam: Atlas Contact, 2012), 216–20.

8 Charles Maier, *Recasting Bourgeois Europe* (Princeton: Princeton, 1975), 88–109; Remieg Aerts et al., eds, *Land van kleine gebaren: Een politieke geschiedenis van Nederland, 1780–1990* (Nijmegen: SUN, 1999); Sheri Berman, *The Social Democratic Moment : Ideas and Politics in the Making of Interwar Europe* (Cambridge, MA: Harvard, 1998); Tara Zahra, *Against the World: Anti-Globalism and Mass Politics Between the World Wars* (New York: Norton, 2023); George Papuashvili, "Post-World War I comparative constitutional developments in Central and Eastern Europe," *International Journal of Constitutional Law* 15, no. 1 (Jan. 2017): 137–72.

9 *Address of the President of the United States: Delivered At a Joint Session of the Two Houses of Congress, January 8, 1918* (Washington: Government Printing Office, 1918), 5.

10 Maureen Healy, *Vienna and the Fall of the Habsburg Empire: Total War and Everyday Life in World War I* (New York: Cambridge University Press, 2004), 8–10; Pamela E. Swett, *Neighbors and Enemies: The Culture of Radicalism in Berlin, 1929–1933* (New York: Cambridge University Press, 2004), 7; Belinda J. Davis, *Home Fires Burning: Food, Politics, and Everyday Life in World War I Berlin* (Chapel Hill: University of North Carolina Press, 2000), 93–113.

11 Larry Eugene Jones, ed., *The German Right in the Weimar Republic: Studies in the History of German Conservatism, Nationalism, and Anti-Semitism* (New York: Berghahn, 2014), 3–4.

12 Giovanni Capoccia, *Defending Democracy: Reactions to Extremism in Interwar Europe* (Baltimore: Johns Hopkins University Press, 2005), 15, 242–5.

13 Jan Wintr, *Proměny Parlamentní Kultury* (Prague: Auditorium, 2021), 7–64.

14 Thomas Mergel, "Überlegungen zu einer Kulturgeschichte der Politik," *Geschichte und Gesellschaft* 28 (2002): 573–93; Barbara Stollberg-Rilinger, ed, *Was heißt Kulturgeschichte des Politischen?* (Berlin: Dunker&Humblot, 2005).

15 "Sonderforschungsbereich 584: Das Politische als Kommunikationsraum in der Geschichte," Universität Bielefeld, last modified June 30, 2012, https://www.uni-bielefeld.de/(de)/geschichte/forschung/sfb584/; Association for Political History, accessed Dec. 5, 2023, http://www.associationforpolitical history.org/.

16 Thomas Mergel, *Parlamentarische Kultur in der Weimarer Republik* (Düsseldorf: Droste, 2005), 13–34; Karl Dietrich Bracher, *Die Auflösung der Weimarer Republik* (Düsseldorf: Droste, 1978), 26–57; Michael Koß, *Parliaments in Time: The Evolution of Legislative Democracy in Western Europe, 1866–2015* (Oxford: Oxford University Press, 2018), 1–15; Philipp Austermann, *Der Weimarer Reichstag: Die schleichende Ausschaltung, Entmachtung und Zerstörung eines Parlaments* (Wien: Böhlau Verlag, 2020), 20–37.

17 Thomas Mergel, "Überlegungen zu einer Kulturgeschichte der Politik," *Geschichte und Gesellschaft* 28 (2002): 602.

18 Jouke Turpijn, *Mannen van gezag: De uitvinding van de Tweede Kamer, 1848–1888* (Amsterdam: Wereldbibliotheek, 2008), 17–18.

19 Lewis Namier, *The Structure of Politics at the Accession of George III* (London: Macmillan, 1965); Lawrence Stone, "Prosopography." *Daedalus* 100, no. 1 (1971): 46–79; Henry R. Winkler, "Sir Lewis Namier," *The Journal of Modern History* 35, no. 1 (1963): 2–19.

20 Jens Ivo Engels and Volker Köhler, "Moderne Patronage – Mikropolitik in der Moderne Konturen und Herausforderungen eines neuen Forschungsfeldes," *Historische Zeitschrift* 309, no. 1 (2019): 43; Volker Köhler, *Genossen – Freunde – Junker: Die Mikropolitik personaler Beziehungen im politischen Handeln während der Weimarer Republik* (Göttingen: Wallstein Verlag, 2018); Jens Ivo Engels, "Politische Korruption in der Moderne: Debatten und Praktiken in Großbritannien und Deutschland im 19. Jahrhundert," *Historische Zeitschrift* 282, 2 (Apr. 2006): 324–5.

21 Volker Köhler, *Genossen – Freunde – Junker: Die Mikropolitik personaler Beziehungen im politischen Handeln während der Weimarer Republik* (Göttingen: Wallstein Verlag, 2018), 9–44.

22 Fernand Braudel, *The Mediterranean and the Mediterranean World in the Age of Philip II*, trans. Siân Reynolds (New York: Harper & Row, 1972), 22.

23 This happened in the vast majority of the German Reichstag's records that had not previously been transferred to archives. For more, see the description in Invenio for R 101 Reichstag des Deutschen Reiches, https://invenio.bundesarchiv.de/

24 See folders 64–2 Échanges internationaux–documents parlementaires and 58–1 Parlements étrangers, ACB.

25 See, for example, the edited volumes: Bettina Bab et al., eds., *Mit Macht zur Wahl: 100 Jahre Frauenwahlrecht in Europa* (Bonn: Frauenmuseum, 2006) and Sylvia Paletschek and Bianka Pietrow-Ennker, eds., *Women's Emancipation Movements in the Nineteenth Century: A European Perspective* (Stanford: Stanford University Press, 2004).

26 For two recent innovative works that push German history beyond Central Europe, see H. Glenn Penny, *German History Unbound: From 1750 to the Present* (Cambridge: Cambridge University Press, 2022) and David Blackbourn, *Germany in the World: A Global History, 1500–2000* (New York: Liveright, 2023).

27 Erez Manela, *The Wilsonian Moment: Self-Determination and the International Origins of Anticolonial Nationalism* (Oxford: Oxford University Press, 2007); Susan Pedersen, *The Guardians: The League of Nations and the Crisis of Empire* (Oxford: Oxford University Press, 2015).

28 Carole Fink, *Writing 20th Century International History: Explorations and Examples* (Göttingen: Wallstein Verlag, 2017); Madeleine Lynch Dungy,

Order and Rivalry: Rewriting the Rules of International Trade after the First World War (Cambridge: Cambridge University Press, 2023); Patricia Clavin, *Securing the World Economy: The Reinvention of the League of Nations, 1920–1946* (Oxford: Oxford University Press, 2013); Natasha Wheatley, *The Life and Death of States: Central Europe and the Transformation of Modern Sovereignty* (Princeton: Princeton University Press, 2023).

29 Jamie Martin, *The Meddlers: Sovereignty, Empire, and the Birth of Global Economic Governance* (Cambridge: Harvard University Press, 2022); Quinn Slobodian, *Globalists: The End of Empire and the Birth of Neoliberalism* (Cambridge: Harvard University Press, 2018); Tara Zahra, *Against the World: Anti-Globalism and Mass Politics between the World Wars* (New York: Norton, 2023).

30 The one exception is a Scandinavia-focused article on "parliamentary diplomacy": Norbert Götz, "On the Origins of 'Parliamentary Diplomacy': Scandinavian 'Bloc Politics' and Delegation Policy in the League of Nations," *Cooperation and Conflict* 40, no. 3 (2005): 263–79.

31 Peter Baldwin, *The Politics of Social Solidarity: Class Bases of the European Welfare State, 1875–1975* (Cambridge: Cambridge University Press, 1990); John Connelly, *Captive University: The Sovietization of East German, Czech, and Polish Higher Education, 1945–1956*. Chapel Hill: University of North Carolina Press, 2000); Charles Maier, *Recasting Bourgeois Europe* (Princeton: Princeton University Press, 1975); Jürgen Kocka, "Comparison and Beyond," *History and Theory: Studies in the Philosophy of History* 42, no. 1 (2003): 40. https://doi.org/10.1111/1468-2303.00228.

32 Deborah Cohen and Maura O'Connor, "Introduction: Comparative History, Cross-National History, Transnational History – Definitions," *Comparison and History: Europe in Cross-National Perspective*, eds. Deborah Cohen and Maura O'Connor (New York: Routledge, 2004), xv.

33 Jürgen Kocka, "Comparison and Beyond," *History and Theory: Studies in the Philosophy of History* 42, no. 1 (2003): 40.

34 Jeffrey Herf, *Reactionary Modernism: Technology, Culture, and Politics in Weimar and the Third Reich* (Cambridge: Cambridge University Press, 1984), 20.

35 See, for example, the links between German and Austria explored in Erin R. Hochman, *Imagining a Greater Germany: Republican Nationalism and the Idea of Anschluss* (Ithaca: Cornell University Press, 2016).

36 For references to faculty, degree programs, and current research projects of political historians across the Netherlands, see Research School Political History–Onderzoekschool Politieke Geschiedenis, accessed Aug. 9, 2024, https://onderzoekschoolpolitiekegeschiedenis.nl/homepage/

37 Jürgen Kocka, "Comparison and Beyond," *History and Theory: Studies in the Philosophy of History* 42, no. 1 (2003): 44.

38 Charles Maier, *Recasting Bourgeois Europe* (Princeton: Princeton University Press, 1975, 5.

39 Larry Eugene Jones, *Hitler versus Hindenburg: The 1932 Presidential Elections and the End of the Weimar Republic* (Cambridge: Cambridge, 2016); Larry Eugene Jones, *The German Right, 1918–1930: Political Parties, Organized Interests, and Patriotic Associations in the Struggle against Weimar Democracy* (Cambridge: Cambridge, 2020); William L. Patch, "German Liberalism and the Origins of Presidential Government in the Weimar Republic," *The Journal of Modern History* 92, no. 4 (2020): 774–816.

40 The entire corpus of Reichstag minutes have been made available for this research; see Reichstagsprotokoll-Korpus, accessed Dec. 4, 2023, https://www.deutschestextarchiv.de/reichstag/.

41 See, Folder Sache Ky, R 30606, PAAA.

42 Andreas Rühl/Deutsches Rundfunkarchiv, email attachment sent to the author, May 12, 2021; Otto von Sethe, "Freytagh-Loringhoven, Axel Freiherr von," *Neue Deutsche Biographie* 5 (1961), https://www.deutsche-biographie.de/pnd123561485.html#ndbcontent.

1. Entering the Smoke-Filled Backrooms: German, Austrian, and Dutch Women as Interwar Parliamentary Newcomers

1 P.W. Wilson, "Women Storm House of Lords," *The New York Times Magazine*, June 12, 1925, ProQuest; "Katinka Pulls the Reichstag Strings," *The New York Times Magazine*, June 14, 1925, https://nyti.ms/45T8PAu; "Women and the House of Lords," UK Parliament, accessed July 15, 2024, https://www.parliament.uk/about/living-heritage/transformingsociety/electionsvoting/womenvote/overview/womenthelords/.

2 "Katinka Pulls the Reichstag Strings," *The New York Times Magazine*, June 14, 1925.

3 "Finnish Voting Reforms in 1906, as Reported in Historic Newspapers," Europeana Newspapers, last modified Jan. 28, 2015, http://www.europeana-newspapers.eu/the-story-of-women-and-the-right-to-vote-in-finland/; "Anna Rogstad – første kvinne på Stortinget i 1911," Storting, last modified Feb. 15, 2011, https://www.stortinget.no/annarogstad; Jytte Nielsen, "How Danish women got the vote," KVINFO, accessed Nov. 26, 2016, http://kvinfo.org/history/how-danish-women-got-vote.

4 Rochelle Goldberg Ruthschild, "Russia: The Great War and Women's Political Rights," in *The Palgrave Handbook of Women's Political Rights*, Susan Franceschet, et al. (London: Palgrave Macmillan, 2019), 375–87.

5 "Women's Suffrage: A World Chronology of the Recognition of Women's Rights to Vote and to Stand for Election," IPU, accessed Dec. 5, 2023, http://www.ipu.org/wmn-e/suffrage.htm

6 "Women Suffrage and Beyond: Confronting the Democratic Deficit," accessed May 10, 2025, https://web.archive.org/web/20160313033722

/http://womensuffrage.org/?page_id=97; Parliament (Qualification of Women) Act, 1918, 8 and 9, Geo 5, c. 47.

7 Jouke Turpijn, *Mannen van gezag: De uitvinding van de Tweede Kamer, 1848–1888* (Amsterdam: Wereldbibliotheek, 2008), 161–77; Erie Tanja, *Goede politiek: De parlementaire cultuur van de Tweede Kamer, 1866–1940* (Amsterdam: Boom, 2010), 209–240; Carla Hoetink, *Macht der gewoonte: Regels en rituelen in de Tweede Kamer na 1945* (Nijmegen: Vantilt, 2018), 205–67.

8 Program for the Visit of the Hungarian Prime Minister and Invitation List for "Herrendiner," Nov. 22, 1930, N 1005/64, Hermann Pünder, BAK.

9 Comparative work on topics like women's suffrage is often done in edited volumes. See, for example, Sylvia Paletschek and Bianka Pietrow-Ennker, eds., *Women's Emancipation Movements in the Nineteenth Century: A European Perspective* (Stanford: Stanford University Press, 2004).

10 Raufhon Salahodjaev and Dilyafruz Jarilkapova, "Women in Parliament and Deforestation: Cross-Country Evidence," *Journal for Nature Conservation* 55 (2020); Dinuk S. Jayasuriya and Paul J. Burke, "Female Parliamentarians and Economic Growth: Evidence from a Large Panel," *Applied Economics Letters* 20, no. 3 (2013): 304–7.

11 See Angelique Leszczawski-Schwerk, "Dynamics of Democratization and Nationalization: The Significance of Women's Suffrage and Women's Political Participation in Parliament in the Second Polish Republic," *Nationalities Papers* 46, no. 5 (Sep. 2018): 809–22.

12 Hannelore Mabry, *Unkraut ins Parlament: Die Bedeutung weiblicher parlamentarischer Arbeit für die Emanzipation der Frau* (Munich: Ernst Vögel, 1971), 24–5; Gabriella Hauch, "'Against the Mock Battle of Words': Therese Schlesinger, Neé Eckstein (1863–1940), a Radical Seeker," in *Austrian Lives*, ed. Günter Bischof, et al. (New Orleans: University of New Orleans Press, 2012), 77; Gabriella Hauch, "Im Parlament! Akteurinnen, Themen und Politische Kultur in der Ersten Republik," in *"Sie meinen es politisch!" 100 Jahre Frauenwahlrecht in Österreich: Geschlechterdemokratie als gesellschaftspolitische Herausforderung* (Vienna: Löcker Verlag, 2019), 98.

13 On minimizing women's political role in the foreign policy realm, see J. Ann Tickner, *Gender in International Relations: Feminist Perspectives on Achieving Global Security* (New York: Columbia University Press, 1992), 1.

14 Gabriele Abels and Anne Cress, "Vom Kampf Ums Frauenwahlrecht Zur Parité: Politische Repräsentation von Frauen Gestern Und Heute," *Zeitschrift Für Parlamentsfragen* 50, no. 1 (2019): 167; Thomas Mergel, *Parlamentarische Kultur in der Weimarer Republik* (Düsseldorf: Droste, 2005), 43–4.

15 Jennifer Striewski, "Marie Juchacz (1879–1956), Begründerin der Arbeiterwohlfahrt," Portal Rheinische Geschichte, last modified March 3,

2013, http://www.rheinische-geschichte.lvr.de/persoenlichkeiten/J
/Seiten/MarieJuchacz.aspx

16 Lily Tonger-Erk and Martina Wagner-Egelhaaf, *Einspruch! Reden von Frauen* (Stuttgart: Reclam, 2011), 104–10.

17 Angelika Schaser, *Helene Lange und Getrud Bäumer: Eine politische Lebensgemeinschaft* (Weimar: Böhlau, 2010), 240; Christl Wickert, *Unsere Erwählten: Sozialdemokratische Frauen im Deutschen Reichstag und im Preußischen Landtag, 1919 bis 1933*, vol. 1 (Göttingen: Sovec, 1986), 166–77, 240–51; Antrag Dr. Baum, Oct. 22, 1919, N 1151/169, Marie-Elisabeth Lüders, BAK.

18 Christl Wickert, *Unsere Erwählten: Sozialdemokratische Frauen im Deutschen Reichstag und im Preußischen Landtag, 1919 bis 1933*, vol. 1 (Göttingen: Sovec, 1986), 169–70; Hermann Mosler, ed., *Die Verfassung der Weimarer Republik* (Stuttgart, Reclam, 2009), 39.

19 *Reichstags-Handbuch*, I. Wahlperiode 1920, (Berlin, 1920), 295; Katharina von Kardorff-Oheimb, *Politik und Lebensbeichte* (Tübingen: Hopfer Verlag, 1962), 90–1.

20 Anita Blasberg, "Sie nahm sich, was sie wollte," *Die Zeit*, 23 Jan. 2014, http://www.zeit.de/2014/05/katharina-von-oheimb-abgeordnete; Katharina von Kardorff-Oheimb, *Politik und Lebensbeichte* (Tübingen: Hopfer Verlag, 1962), 93, 209; Raffael Scheck, *Mothers of the Nation: Right-Wing Women in Weimar Germany* (Oxford: Berg, 2004), 34–5; "Katinka Pulls the Reichstag Strings," *The New York Times Magazine*, June 14, 1925; also see the extensive collection of German and foreign newspaper clippings, as well as the score of "Kathinka hat ein Höschen an!," in N 1039/47, 48, and 49, Katharina von Kardorff, BAK.

21 *Verhandlungen des Reichstags*, I. Wahlperiode 1920, Band 348, 2734.

22 Cornelia Baddack, *Katharina von Kardorff-Oheimb (1879–1962) in der Weimarer Republik* (Göttngen: V&R unipress, 2016), 224.

23 Undated and untitled list, N 1039/21a, and Lüders to "Marquise" (Oheimb), Oct. 1, 1924, N 1039/19, Katharina von Kardorff, BAK.

24 Undated and untitled list, N 1039/21a, Katharina von Kardorff, BAK.

25 Cornelia Baddack, *Katharina von Kardorff-Oheimb (1879–1962) in der Weimarer Republik* (Göttingen: V&R unipress, 2016), 229. Baddack never cites N 1039/21a where this list is located.

26 *Verhandlungen des Reichstages*, I. Wahlperiode 1920, Band: 348, 2734.

27 *Verhandlungen des Reichstages*, I. Wahlperiode 1920, Band: 345, 1198.

28 Katharina von Kardorff-Oheimb, *Politik und Lebensbeichte* (Tübingen: Hopfer Verlag, 1962), 136.

29 *Verhandlungen des Reichstages*, I. Wahlperiode 1920, Band: 345, 1198.

30 *Verhandlungen des Reichstages*, I. Wahlperiode 1920, Band: 345, 1198; Katharina von Kardorff-Oheimb, *Politik und Lebensbeichte* (Tübingen: Hopfer Verlag, 1962), 136.

31 For Oheimb's friendship with Mirbach, see her letters to him in N 1039/19a, Katharina von Kardorff, BAK.

32 Thomas Mergel, *Parlamentarische Kultur in der Weimarer Republik* (Düsseldorf: Droste, 2005), 135–7.

33 Lüders to Dessauer, 26 Feb. 1927 and Lüders to Dessauer, Oct 1926, FD 6, Friedrich Dessauer, KFZ.

34 Anita Blasberg, "Sie nahm sich, was sie wollte," *Die Zeit,* Jan. 23, 2014, http://www.zeit.de/2014/05/katharina-von-oheimb-abgeordnete; Oheimb to Kardorff, Feb. 3,1921, N 1040/1, Siegfried von Kardorff, BAK.

35 Cornelia Baddack, *Katharina von Kardorff-Oheimb (1879–1962) in der Weimarer Republik* (Göttingen: V&R unipress, 2016), 131.

36 von Kardorff-Oheimb, *Politik und Lebensbeichte*, 132.

37 Cornelia Baddack, *Katharina von Kardorff-Oheimb (1879–1962) in der Weimarer Republik*, 215; "Katinka Pulls the Reichstag Strings," *The New York Times Magazine,* June 14, 1925.

38 von Kardorff-Oheimb, *Politik und Lebensbeichte*, 137–8.

39 *Verhandlungen des Reichstages*, I. Wahlperiode 1920, Band: 345, 1198.

40 Lüders to "Marquise von O" (Oheimb), Sep. 29, 1924, N 1039/19, Katharina von Kardorff, BAK.

41 Letters between Oheimb and Stresemann in N 1039/21, Katharina von Kardorff, BAK.

42 Oheimb to Charlotte Mühsam, 31 Oct. 1924, N 1039/19a, Katharina von Kardorff, BAK.

43 Cornelia Baddack, *Katharina von Kardorff-Oheimb (1879–1962) in der Weimarer Republik* (Göttingen: V&R unipress, 2016), 233.

44 "Politische Lebenserinnerungen," n.d., N 1019/1, Paul Moldenhauer, BAK.

45 von Kardorff-Oheimb, *Politik und Lebensbeichte*, 95–105.

46 Büro des Reichspräsidenten, June 20, 1922, N 1039/13c and Fritz Mittelmann to Oheimb, 25 Sep. 1924, N 1039/19a, Katharina von Kardorff, BAK.

47 von Kardorff-Oheimb, *Politik und Lebensbeichte*, 103.

48 von Kardorff-Oheimb, *Politik und Lebensbeichte*, 146.

49 Oheimb to Löbe, 20 Dec. 1956, N 1039/61 and Löbe to Oheimb Postcard, March 15, 1929, N 1039/19, Katharina von Kardorff, BAK.

50 Katharina von Kardorff to Müller, July 8, 1928, 1/HMAG00001, Hermann Müller, FES.

51 Kardorff to Müller, Apr. 2, 1930, 1/HMAG00040, Hermann Müller, FES.

52 Sir Philip Dawson to Oheimb, March 25, 1927, N 1039/3, Katharina von Kardorff, BAK.

53 Wilhelm Kube to Oheimb, March 26, 1927, N 1039/3, Katharina von Kardorff, BAK; *Reichstags-Handbuch*, IX. Wahlperiode 1933 (Berlin: Reichsdruckerei, 1934), 240.

54 "Katinka Pulls the Reichstag Strings," *The New York Times Magazine*, June 14, 1925; Walther Lambach, *Die Herrschaft der Fünfhundert: Ein Bild des parlamentarischen Lebens im neuen Deutschland* (Hamburg: Hanseatische Verlagsanstalt, 1926), 86.

55 Katharina von Kardorff-Oheimb, *Politik und Lebensbeichte*, 215.

56 Kurt Tucholsky, *Ausgewählte Werke* (Neu-Isenburg: Melzer, 2006), 875; Riccardo Bavaj, *Von links gegen Weimar: Linkes antiparlamentarisches Denken in den Weimarer Republik* (Bonn: Dietz, 2005), 415–28.

57 *Verhandlungen des Reichstags*, I. Wahlperiode 1920, Band: 348, 2734.

58 Werner Sabitzer, "100 Jahre Frauen im Parlament," *Öffentliche Sicherheit* 1–2 (2019): 81–2.

59 "Gabriele Proft," Republik Österreich Parlament, accessed Nov. 16, 2016, https://www.parlament.gv.at/WWER/PAD_01313/; "Anna Boschek," Republik Österreich Parlament, accessed Nov. 16, 2016, https://www .parlament.gv.at/WWER/PAD_00155/index.shtml; Biographies of Anna Boschek and Gabriele Proft, c. 1928, Karton 110, Mappe 14/1, S.D. Parl. Klub, VGA.

60 Ernst Hanisch, *Österreichische Geschichte, 1890–1990: Der lange Schatten des Staates: Österreichische Gesellschaftsgeschichte im 20. Jahrhundert* (Vienna: Ueberreuter, 1994), 268–70; Helmut Rumpler, "Parlamentarismus und Demokratieverständnis in Österreich, 1918–1933," in *Das Parteiwesen Österreichs und Ungarns in der Zwischenkriegszeit*, eds. Anna M. Drabek, Richard G. Plaschka, and Helmut Rumpler (Vienna: Verlag der Österreichischen Akademie der Wissenschaften, 1990), 8–17.

61 Anton Pelinka, "Parlament," in *Handbuch des politischen Systems Österreichs, Erste Republik, 1918–1933*, eds. Tálos et al. (Vienna: Manzsche Verlags- und Universitätsbuchhandlung, 1995), 61–5.

62 Erin R. Hochman, "The Failed Republic, 1918–1933?," in *Democracy in Austria*, eds. Günter Bischof and David M. Wineroither (New Orleans: University of New Orleans Press, 2019), 59–63.

63 Evan Burr Bukey, *Hitler's Hometown: Linz, Austria, 1908–1945* (Bloomington: Indiana University Press, 1986), 59–66.

64 Helmut Widder, "Die Entstehung und Entwicklung des Parlamentarismus der Republik Österreich," and Helmut Widder, "Der Nationalrat," in *Österreichs Parlamentarismus: Werden und System*, ed. Herbert Schambeck (Berlin: Duncker & Humblot, 1986), 229–50, 281–301.

65 Konstituierende Nationalversammlung für Deutschösterreich, *Stenographische Protokolle* (1919), 342–3, 447–9, 1351–3; Konstituierende Nationalversammlung d. Republik Österreich, *Stenographische Protokolle* (1920), 1817–23 and 3362; Gabriella Hauch, *Vom Frauenstandpunkt Aus: Frauen im Parlament, 1919–1933* (Vienna: Verlag für Gesellschaftskritik, 1995), 248.

66 Konstituierende Nationalversammlung für Deutschösterreich, *Stenographische Protokolle* (1919), 290–1, 683–4; Konstituierende Nationalversammlung d. Republik Österreich, *Stenographische Protokolle* (1920), 1766–7 and 2751–61.

67 Konstituierende Nationalversammlung für Deutschösterreich, *Stenographische Protokolle* (1919), 342–3.

68 Konstituierende Nationalversammlung d. Republik Österreich, *Stenographische Protokolle* (1920), 1824–1829; Gabriella Hauch, "'Against the Mock Battle of Words': Therese Schlesinger, Neé Eckstein (1863–1940), a Radical Seeker," in *Austrian Lives*, ed. Günter Bischof, et al. (New Orleans: University of New Orleans Press, 2012), 81–2.

69 See Tom Bottomore and Patrick Goode, *Austro-Marxism* (Oxford: Clarendon Press, 1978), and Walter Göhring, *Anna Boschek: erste Gewerkschafterin im Parlament: Biografie einer außergewöhnlichen Arbeiterin* (Vienna: Österreichischer Gewerkschaftsbund, 1998).

70 Ludwig Czech to Gabriele Proft, Nov. 23, 1929, Mappe 27, Gabriele Proft, VGA.

71 Hanna to Boschek, Feb. 16, 1925, Mappe 1 – Korrespondenzen von Gertrud Hanna, ZPH 1241, Anna Boschek, WIR.

72 Red Vienna would also be the focus of post-Second World War accounts of women's political activity in the First Republic. See, for example, Gabriele Proft, *Der Weg zu Uns! Die Frauenfrage im neuen Österreich*, Sozialistische Hefte (Vienna: SPÖ, 1945), 6–7; "Politikerinnen in der Ersten Republik," Wien Geschichte Wiki, Nov. 29, 2023, https://www.geschichtewiki.wien.gv.at /Politikerinnen_in_der_Ersten_Republik.

73 Sozialdemokratisches Frauen-Zentralkomitee to Members of the Committee, Nov. 29, 1929, Mappe 9/2, Karton 4, Gabriele Proft, VGA; Walter Göhring, ed, *Anna Boschek: erste Gewerkschafterin im Parlament: Biografie einer außergewöhnlichen Arbeiterin* (Vienna: Österreichischer Gewerkschaftsbund, 1998).

74 "Arbeiterinnenschule vom 6. bis 25. September 1926," Mappe 9/5, Karton 5, Gabriele Proft, VGA.

75 "Nordamerika-Reise: Veranstaltet vom Studienreisekomitee der Bildungszentrale in Wien vom 15. Juli bis 15. August 1930," Mappe 12, Karton 5, Nachlass Gabriele Proft, VGA; Folder Dr. Robert Danneberg, Amerikareise, 1930, Karton 183, AAng BKA-AA NPA Neues Politisches Archiv, Archiv der Republik, ÖSTA.

76 Konstituierende Nationalversammlung für Deutschösterreich, *Stenographische Protokolle* (1919), 342–3; Walter Göhring, *Anna Boschek: Erste Gewerkschafterin im Parlament: Biographie einer aussergewöhnlichen Arbeiterin* (Vienna: Österreichischer Gewerrkschaftsbund, 1998), 146–52; Mundt to Boschek, Feb. 6, 1931, and Wlcek to Boschek, May 16, 1931, Mappe 1, ZPH 1241, Anna Boschek, WIR.

77 Walter Göhring, *Anna Boschek: Erste Gewerkschafterin im Parlament: Biographie einer aussergewöhnlichen Arbeiterin* (Wien: Österreichischer Gewerrkschaftsbund, 1998), 154–65; International Labor Office to Boschek, Mar. 2, 1935, Mappe 1, ZPH 1241, Anna Boschek, WIR; C. Earl Edmondson, *The Heimwehr and Austrian Politics, 1918–1936* (Athens: University of Georgia Press, 1978), 231.

78 For more on elections and blocs during the interwar years, see Martin Kitchen, *Europe Between the Wars* (Harlow, UK: Pearson, 2006).

79 "Hors d'oeuvre-Weekpraatje," *De Maasbode*, July 7, 1918, as quoted in Carla van Baalen, "Suze Groeneweg en Carry Pothuis-Smit: De eerste vrouwen in de Staten-Generaal," Tweede Kamer der Staten-Generaal, Sep. 6, 2019, 29, https://www.tweedekamer.nl/sites/default/files/atoms/files/de_eerste _vrouwelijke_parlementariers_def.pdf; "News in Brief." *Times*, April 2, 1917, 7, The Times Digital Archive; De invoering van het vrouwenkiesrecht, Tweede Kamer der Staten-Generaal, accessed Nov. 26, 2016, https://www .tweedekamer.nl/hoe_werkt_het/tweede_kamer_door_de_eeuwen _heen/1848–1922_strijd_voor_rechten/vernieuwing

80 Paul van der Steen, *De ongehoorde helft: De eerste vrouwen op het politieke pluche* (Nijmegen: Vantilt, 2019), 39–41.

81 "De zitting der Tweede Kamer," *De Telegraaf*, Sep. 18, 1918, as quoted in Carla van Baalen, "Suze Groeneweg en Carry Pothuis-Smit: De eerste vrouwen in de Staten-Generaal," Tweede Kamer der Staten-Generaal, Sep. 6, 2019, 31, https://www.tweedekamer.nl/sites/default/files/atoms/files /de_eerste_vrouwelijke_parlementariers_def.pdf.

82 Carla van Baalen, "Suze Groeneweg en Carry Pothuis-Smit: De eerste vrouwen in de Staten-Generaal," Tweede Kamer der Staten-Generaal, 6 Sep. 2019, 16, https://www.tweedekamer.nl/sites/default/files/atoms/files /de_eerste_vrouwelijke_parlementariers_def.pdf.

83 "Tweede Kameroverzicht," *Haagsche Courant*, Oct. 21, 1918 and "Het vrouwenkiesrecht – En Suze Groeneweg?" *De Telegraaf*, Oct. 28, 1918 as quoted in Carla van Baalen, "Suze Groeneweg en Carry Pothuis-Smit: De eerste vrouwen in de Staten-Generaal," Tweede Kamer der Staten-Generaal, Sep. 6, 2019, 31, https://www.tweedekamer.nl/sites/default/files/atoms /files/de_eerste_vrouwelijke_parlementariers_def.pdf.

84 *Handelingen der Tweede Kamer* (7 Nov 1918), 296–300; *De Telegraaf*, Nov. 8, 1918, as quoted in Carla van Baalen, "Suze Groeneweg en Carry Pothuis-Smit: De eerste vrouwen in de Staten-Generaal," Tweede Kamer der Staten-Generaal, Sep. 6, 2019, 31, https://www.tweedekamer.nl/sites/default /files/atoms/files/de_eerste_vrouwelijke_parlementariers_def.pdf.

85 This information is a product of searching on parlement.com.

86 "Mr. C.F. (Frida) Katz," Parlement & Politiek, accessed Nov. 18, 2016, http://www.parlement.com/id/vg09ll33l2xw/c_f_frida_katz.

87 *Handelingen der Tweede Kamer* (Nov. 22, 1922), 579.

88 *Handelingen der Tweede Kamer* (Nov. 23, 1922), 601.

89 *Handelingen der Tweede Kamer* (March 20, 1923), 1928.

90 J.R. McSpadden III, "Spel, Spelbrekers en Parlementaire Cultuur: Het Informele Leven van de Nederlandse Kamer gedurende het Interbellum" (Master's thesis, Universiteit Leiden, 2010), 28–31.

91 D.J. Wijnkoop to F. Katz, n.d., Inv. 8, 2.21.190, C. Frida Katz Fam., NAH

92 Albarda to Frida Katz, June 30, 1939, Inv. 88, 2.21.190, C. Frida Katz Fam., NAH.

93 J.P. de Valk and A.C.M. Kappelhof, eds., *Dagboeken van P.J.M. Aalberse 1902–1947* (The Hague: Instituut voor Nederlandse Geschiedenis, 2006), 660–1.

94 Ephemera available in Inv. 90, 2.21.190, C. Frida Katz Fam., NAH.

95 Menu, XXIIème Conférence Interparlementaire, Berne et Genève, Aug. 26, 1924, Inv. 90, 2.21.190, C. Frida Katz Fam., NAH; "Spencer, Selden Palmer (1862–1925), *Biographical Dictionary of the United States Congress*, accessed Nov. 26, 2016, http://bioguide.congress.gov/scripts/biodisplay .pl?index=s000730

96 Everything here is found on various pieces of ephemera available in Inv. 80, 2.21.190, C. Frida Katz Fam., NAH; André Niedostadek, "Der letzte Präsident des Reichsgerichts: Der stumme Richer," Legal Tribune Online (July 5, 2014), http://www.lto.de/recht/feuilleton/f/rechtsgeschichte -reichsgericht-praesident-erwin-bumke/; John E. Hansan, "Hastings Hornell Hart (1851–1932): Prison Authority, Children's Advocate and President the National Conference of Charities and Correction in 1893," The Social Welfare History Project, Virginia Commonwealth University, accessed 16 Nov 2016, http://socialwelfare.library.vcu.edu/eras/civil-war -reconstruction/hart-hastings-h/; Shinguma Motoji (1876–1947), Portraits of Modern Japanese Historical Figures, accessed 16 Nov 2016, http://www .ndl.go.jp/portrait/e/datas/397.html?cat=118.

97 Plan of Tables, Inv. 80, 2.21.190, C. Frida Katz Fam., NAH.

98 Photo labelled Union Internationale des Avocats, 28–31 Juli 1932 in het Vredespaleis te den Haag, Inv. 21, 2.21.190, C. Frida Katz Fam., NAH; Jim Robinson, "Introducing the UIA," *Law Institute Journal (Victoria)* 202 (1999), http://www.austlii.edu.au/au/journals/LawIJV/1999/202.html.

99 See, for instance, the lists of delegates to the 1927 World Economic Conference: Société des Nations, Conférence Economique Internationale, Deuxième liste provisoire des membres de la conférence, Apr. 26, 1927, 987, Georges Theunis, AEB.

100 Christelijk-Historische Unie, Hoofdbestuur to Frida Katz, May 29, 1922, Inv. 65, 2.21.190 and Handwritten Notes, Inv. 91, 2.21.190, C. Frida Katz Fam., NAH.

101 "De roeping der vrouw in de Tweede Kamer der Staten-Generaal," 1933, Inv. 91, 2.21.190, C. Frida Katz Fam., NAH.

102 Marja Borkus, et al., *Vrouwenstemmen: 100 jaar Vrouwenbelangen, 75 Jaar Vrouwenkiesrecht* (Zutphen: Walburg Pers, 1994), 81; "De roeping der vrouw in de Tweede Kamer der Staten-Generaal," 1933, Inv. 91, 2.21.190, C. Frida Katz Fam., NAH.

103 "Mr. C.F. (Frida) Katz," Parlement & Politiek, accessed 18 Nov. 2016, http://www.parlement.com/id/vg09ll33l2xw/c_f_frida_katz; Marja Borkus, et al., *Vrouwenstemmen: 100 jaar Vrouwenbelangen, 75 Jaar Vrouwenkiesrecht* (Zutphen: Walburg Pers, 1994), 81.

104 "De roeping der vrouw in de Tweede Kamer der Staten-Generaal," 1933, Inv. 91, 2.21.190, C. Frida Katz Fam., NAH.

105 "Mr. C.F. (Frida) Katz," Parlement & Politiek, accessed Nov. 18, 2016, http://www.parlement.com/id/vg09ll33l2xw/c_f_frida_katz.

106 Johan Schot and Vincent Lagendijk, "Technocratic Internationalism in the Interwar Years: Building Europe on Motorways and Electricity Networks," *Journal of Modern European History/Zeitschrift Für Moderne Europäische Geschichte/Revue d'histoire Européenne Contemporaine* 6, no. 2 (2008): 196–217.

107 Brita Skottsberg, *Der österreichische Parlamentarismus* (Göteborg: Elanders Boktryckeri Aktiebolag, 1940), 3–12; Carl Schmitt, *The Crisis of Parliamentary Democracy*, trans. Ellen Kennedy (Cambridge, MA: MIT Press, 1985), 22; Hans Kelsen, *Das Problem des Parlamentarismus* (Vienna: Wilhelm Braumüller, 1926), 3; Wilhelm Medinger, *Die Internationale Diskussion über Die Krise des Parlamentarismus* (Vienna: Wilhelm Braumüller, 1929), 4–6.

2. From Boozy Receptions to Private Clubs: The Social Landscape of Politics in Weimar Berlin

1 Thomas Wieke, *Vom Etablissement zur Oper: Die Geschichte der Kroll-Oper* (Berlin: Haude & Spener, 1993); Uwe Sauerwein, "Nüscht bei Kroll jewesen, nüscht in Berlin jewesen!" *Berliner Morgenpost*, 18 Apr. 2014, https://www.morgenpost.de/kultur/article127095916/Nuescht-bei -Kroll-jewesen-nuescht-in-Berlin-jewesen.html

2 Kroll Wirtschaftsbetrieb General Letter to Reichstag Members, n.d., FD 9, Friedrich Dessauer, KFZ; Thomas Wieke, *Vom Etablissement zur Oper: Die Geschichte der Kroll-Oper* (Berlin: Haude & Spener, 1993).

3 Kroll-Wirtschaftsbetrieb G.m.b.H. to Dessauer, May 24, 1929, FD 9, Friedrich Dessauer, KFZ.

4 Thomas Mergel, *Parlamentarische Kultur in der Weimarer Republik* (Düsseldorf: Droste, 2005), 81–134

5 Thomas Mergel, *Parlamentarische Kultur in der Weimarer Republik* (Düsseldorf: Droste, 2005), 137.

6 "Ledental Tweede en Eerste Kamer sinds 1815," Parlement.com, accessed
  July 17, 2024, https://www.parlement.com/id/vhnnmt7lfkz5/ledental
  _tweede_en_eerste_kamer_sinds; "Nationalrat," Wien Geschichte Wiki, 3
  Nov. 2023, https://www.geschichtewiki.wien.gv.at/Nationalrat; "Weimarer
  Republik," *Informationen zur politischen Bildung* Nr. 346/2021, 16.

7 Max Kaase, "Sinn oder Unsinn des Konzepts Politische Kultur für die
  Vergleichende Politikforschung, oder auch: Der Versuch, einen Pudding
  an die Wand zu nageln," in *Wahlen und politisches System* (Opladen:
  Westdeutscher Verlag, 1983), 144–72.

8 See for instance, List of Guests with Two Columns "ist eingeladen" and
  "hat eingeladen," n.d., N 1135/58, Wolfgang Jaenicke, BAK; Attachment
  to Letter Schnee to Solf, May 7, 1930, N 1053/131, Wilhelm Solf, BAK;
  Various Files in N 2035/1–4, Franz Bracht, BAB; Social Invitations and
  Lists, N 1130/4, Bernhard Dernburg, BAK; All folders in N 1004/179–194,
  Hermann Dietrich, BAK.

9 Thomas Mergel, *Parlamentarische Kultur in der Weimarer Republik* (Düsseldorf:
  Droste, 2005), 135–6; Andreas Biefang, *Die andere Seite der Macht: Reichstag
  und Öffentlichkeit im »System Bismarck«, 1871–1890* (Düsseldorf: Droste,
  2009), 177–8.

10 Horst Groschopp, *Zwischen Bierabend und Bildungsverein: Zur Kulturarbeit in
   der deutschen Arbeiterbewegung vor 1914* (Berlin: Dietz, 1985), 25–30.

11 The shift between "Herrenabend" and "Bierabend" around 1900 can
   be seen with Google Ngrams' German (2019) corpus, which yields early
   sources including: "Verschiedene Nachrichten: Ein Bierabend in Kiel,"
   Zeitschrift für das gesamte Brauwesen XXII, Nr. 29, 389; *Lübeckische Blätter* 40,
   nr. 19 (May 8, 1898): 221.

12 Erich Matthias and Eberhard Pikart, *Die Reichstagsfraktion der Deutschen
   Sozialdemokratie: 1898 bis 1918*, vol. 1 (Düsseldorf: Droste, 1966), 23, 270.

13 Margaret Lavinia Anderson, "Ein Demokratiedefizit?: Das Deutsche
   Kaiserreich in Vergleichender Perspektive," *Geschichte Und Gesellschaft* 44,
   no. 3 (2018): 377–8; Löbe to Ledebour, 30 Oct. 1948, 1/GLAA000001,
   Ledebour and Müller to Juchacz, Sep. 9, 1929, 1/HMAG00039 and
   Postcard from Louise Schröder and Paul Löbe to Müller, July 6, 1929, 1
   /HMAG00001, Hermann Müller, FES.

14 Zetkin to Geck, n.d., NY 4005/74, Clara Zetkin, SAPMO, BAB; Zetkin to
   Geck, March 15. 1928, N Geck 2686, Adolf Geck, GLK; Ina Hochreuther,
   Frauen im Parlament: Südwestdeutsche Parlamentarierinnen von 1919 bis heute
   (Stuttgart: Landtag von Baden-Württemberg, 2002), 44–5; Anne Junk, "Ein
   Leben für die Sozialdemokratie," *Mittelbadische Presse*, Feb. 23 2012, http://
   www.bo.de/lokales/offenburg/ein-leben-fuer-die-sozialdemokratie.

15 Carl Severing, *Mein Lebensweg*, vol. I (Cologne: Greven Verlag, 1950),
   163–4.

16 Lebenserinnerungen von Georg Gothein, Page 332, N 1006/14, Georg Gothein, BAK.

17 "Verzicht auf Repräsentationen," *Vossische Zeitung*, Feb. 7, 1930; "Empfang bei Reichskanzler," *Vossische Zeitung*, June 17, 1921; and Bierabend bei Hindenburg," *Vossische Zeitung*, Feb. 16, 1927, De Gruyter Vossische Zeitung Online.

18 Paul Löbe, *Der Weg war lang* (Berlin: arani, 1954), 138–9.

19 "300 Millionen für Bodenverbesserung," *Vossische Zeitung*, Mar. 8, 1922, De Gruyter Vossische Zeitung Online; Eberhard Kolb, *The Weimar Republic*, trans. P.S. Falla and R.J. Park (London: Routledge, 2005), 224–5.

20 Guests for Parlamentarischer Bierabend, Nov. 19, 1920, R 43-I/1927, Reichskanzlei ("Neue Reichskanzlei"), BAB.

21 Guest List for Reichskanzler's Bierabend, n.d., R 43-I/1927, Reichskanzlei ("Neue Reichskanzlei"), BAB.

22 Bierabend Guest List, May 30, 1925, R 43-I/1927, Reichskanzlei ("Neue Reichskanzlei"), BAB.

23 Paul Löbe, *Der Weg war lang* (Berlin: arani, 1954), 139.

24 Walther Lambach, *Die Herrschaft der Fünfhundert: Ein Bild des parlamentarischen Lebens im neuen Deutschland* (Hamburg: Hanseatische Verlagsanstalt, 1926), 15–16.

25 Paul Löbe, *Der Weg war lang* (Berlin: arani, 1954), 140–1.

26 This can be reconstructed from the number of saved invitations from collections like N 1004/179–194, Hermann Dietrich, BAK.

27 Invitation to the Zehnjährige Verfassungsfeier, Aug. 11, 1929, N 42/4, Kurt von Schleicher, BAF.

28 Wirtschaftshilfe der Deutschen Studentenschaft Invitation, Oct. 25, 1928, FD 8, Friedrich Dessauer, KFZ; Reichsverkehrsminister Invitation to Müller, June 20, 1928, N 2200/1, Hermann Müller, BAB.

29 Invitation to Exhibition Opening "Die künstlerische Formgebung des Reichs," Oct. 29, 1926 and Invitation from Reichminister des Innern to visit the Moltke-Gedächtniszimmer, Oct. 31, 1926, N 1069/19, Walther Lambach, BAK.

30 Martin Sabrow, *Der Rathenaumord und die deutsche Gegenrevolution* (Göttingen: Wallstein, 2022), 98–116; *Verhandlungen des Reichstags*, I. Wahlperiode 1920, Band 355, 8033–8039; Walther Rathenau Gedächtnisfeier, July 6, 1923, N 1039/37, Katharina von Kardorff, BAK.

31 See the Invitations and Programs from March 1925, N 1039/52, Katharina von Kardorff, BAK.

32 *Reichstags-Handbuch*, III. Wahlperiode 1924 (Berlin: Reichsdruckerei, 1925), 237.

33 Löbe to Frau Rosset, Apr. 29, 1926, N Fehrenbach 120, Constantin Fehrenbach, GLK.

34 Invitation to "Aussprache-Abend" des Westfälischen Bauernbundes, Mar. 22, 1932, FD 12, Friedrich Dessauer, KFZ; Invitation to the Deutsche Bühnen-Klub, May 12, 1924, N 2178/97, Paul Löbe, BAB; Invitation to the Stadt- und Kurverwaltung des Radium-Solbades Kreuznach, Feb. 13, 1929, N 42/4, Kurt von Schleicher, BAF.

35 Invitation to Deutscher Reiter- und Pferdzüchter-Tag, Oct. 20, 1928, and Invitation Kolonialgesellschaft und Frauenverein, Nov. 9, 1929, N 42/4, Kurt von Schleicher, BAF; Reichs-Landbund Invitation, Nov. 3, 1926, N 1069/19, Walther Lambach, BAK.

36 "Ausstellungseröffnung: Was die Märkische Scholle bringt," n.d., and Zentralinstitut für Erziehung und Unterricht Invitation, Nov. 6, 1926, N 1069/19, Walther Lambach, BAK.

37 Flakverein e.V. Invitation, Dec. 5, 1929, N 42/4, Kurt von Schleicher, BAF; Einladung des außenpolitischen Komitees, Nov. 11, 1926, N 1069/19, Walther Lambach, BAK; Verlag der Vossischen Zeitung, Dec. 11, 1923 N 2178/97, Paul Löbe, BAB.

38 Rudolf Pechel's 50th Birthday, n.d., N 2035/3, Franz Bracht, BAB.

39 Ehrenkarten 3. Preußischen Landgemeindetag, Nov. 13, 1926, and Bierabend Invitation from Gereke to Lambach, Nov. 19, 1926, N 1069/19, Walther Lambach, BAK.

40 Arbeitsausschuss Deutscher Verbände to Dessauer, n.d., FD 10, Friedrich Dessauer, KFZ.

41 Verband für Europäische Verständigung Event, 2 Nov 1926, N 1069/19, Walther Lambach, BAK.

42 Giovanni Sartori, *The Theory of Democracy Revisited* (Chatham, NJ: Chatham House Publishers, 1987), 228–30; Sven T. Siefken and Hilmar Rommetvedt, eds., *Parliamentary Committees in the Policy Process* (New York: Routledge, 2022).

43 Behm to Frau Höner, 8 Nov. 1923 and Lange-Hegermann to Frau Höner, Nov. 11, 1923, Mappe 1, Mathias Höner, FES.

44 "Mein Lebenslauf," n.d., 1/KBAB1, Karl Becker, FES.

45 *Verhandlungen des Reichstags*, V. Wahlperiode 1930, Band 451, Anlage Nr. 1080.

46 "Rückblick und Ausblick (1871–1956)," N 1670/1, August Weber, BAK.

47 See, table seatings and invitation lists, N 1005/166, Hermann Pünder, BAK.

48 Heuss to Stolper, June 16, 1930, N 1221/487, Theodor Heuss, BAK.

49 Invitation Reichskuratorium für Jugendertüchtigung, Oct. 27, 1932, N 2035/3, Franz Bracht, BAB; Pünder to Schleicher, Jan. 6, 1931, N 42/4, Kurt von Schleicher, BAF.

50 Memo "Betrifft: Rheinischer Abend am 9. 1926," N 1005/506, Hermann Pünder, BAK.

51 Schacht an Seeckt, 14 June 1928, N 247/182, Hans von Seeckt, BAF.

52 Invitation Riesser to Müller, N 2200/1, Hermann Müller, BAB.

53 Deutschnationale Reichstagsfraktion Invitation for Dinner to Müller, March 24. 1927 and Müller to Vorstand der Deutschnationalen Reichstagsfraktion, March 19, 1927, N 2200/1, Hermann Müller, BAB.

54 See folder on the Walter Rathenau Gesellschaft, N 1005/150, Hermann Pünder, BAK; Members of German IPU Group, April 1, 1921, N 1051-F/96, Walther Schücking, BAK.

55 Protokoll der Sitzung des Präsidiums der Deutschen Liga für Völkerbund, Feb. 16, 1927, N 1051-F/93, Walther Schücking, BAK.

56 Report on International on Parliamentarism, n.d., R58/3436, Reichssicherheitshauptamt, BAB; Memo from Deutsches Comitte für Europäische Cooperation, n.d., N 1051-F/100, Walther Schücking, BAK.

57 Joseph Walk, "Das 'Deutsche Komitee Pro Palästina' 1926–1933," *Leo Baeck Institute Bulletin* 50 (1976): 163–70.

58 Letter from Deutsches Komitee Pro Palästina signed Dr. M. Rosenblüth, May 4, 1932, N 1040/9, Siegfried von Kardorff, BAK.

59 Kurt Blumenfeld, *Erlebte Judenfrage: Ein Vierteljahrhundert deutscher Zionismus* (Stuttgart: Deutsche Verlags-Anstalt, 1962), 177.

60 Flyer for Jubiläums-Meeting, May 15, 1927, R 8071/1, Wissenschaftlich-humanitäres Komitee, BAB.

61 See, for instance, the response from Max Liebermann, April 24, 1927, R 8071/1, Wissenschaftlich-humanitäres Komitee, BAB.

62 Löbe to WhK, April 29, 1927, R 8071/1, Wissenschaftlich-humanitäres Komitee, BAB.

63 Dernburg to WhK, R 8071/1, Wissenschaftlich-humanitäres Komitee, BAB.

64 Mitteilungen des Wissenschaftlich-humanitäres Komitees e.V., Nr. 7, May–June 1927, R 8071/1, Wissenschaftlich-humanitäres Komitee, BAB.

65 See, for example, Soviet Ambassador Invitation to Dessauer, Nov. 7, 1929, FD 9, Friedrich Dessauer, KFZ.

66 See invitations from diplomats in N 42/4, Kurt von Schleicher, BAF; Polish Consul to Hermann Müller, N 2200/3, Hermann Müller, BAB.

67 Hausmusik Invitation List, Nov. 18, 1931, N 2020/72, Georg Bernhard, BAB.

68 List of People Invited to Social Events, n.d., N 1130/4, Bernhard Dernburg, BAK.

69 Invitation to Event with King and Queen of Afghanistan, Feb. 23, 1928, N 2200/2, Hermann Müller, BAB.

70 Program for the Visit of the Hungarian Prime Minister and Invitation List for "Herrendiner," Nov. 22, 1930, N 1005/64, Hermann Pünder, BAK.

71 Japanese Ambassador to Dessauer, FD 9, Friedrich Dessauer, KFZ.

72 Industrie und Handelskammer zu Berlin to Dessauer, Sep. 24, 1929, FD 9, Friedrich Dessauer, KFZ.

73 Coudenhove-Kalergi to Külz, Oct. 7, 1929, N 1042/155, Wilhelm Külz, BAK.

74 Invitation for Dinner at the Hotel Adlon Max Blokzijl, Dec. 3, 1932, N 2035/3, Franz Bracht, BAB.

75 Alvarez del Vayo to Löbe, Jan. 31, 1924, N/2178/97, Paul Löbe, BAB.

76 Photo and Caption from Keystone View Co, Nov. 9, 1931, E I: 1 – Fotos, Hausarchiv, VAP.

77 Banquet Table Settings for the Verein, 1926–1933, F III: 1, VAP.

78 Abschrift, n.d., N 2178/99, Paul Löbe, BAB.

79 Paul Löbe, *Der Weg war lang* (Berlin: arani, 1954), 140–1.

80 André François-Poncet to Siegfried von Kardorff, Oct. 23, 1938, N 1040/12, Siegfried von Kardorff, BAK;

81 Invitation for Ressource zur Unterhaltung Christmas "Politischer Abend," Walther Lambach, N 1069/19, BAK; Uta Motschmann, "Ressource zur Unterhaltung" in *Handbuch der Berliner Vereine und Gesellschaften, 1786–1815*, ed. Uta Motschmann (Berlin: Walter de Gruyter, 2015), 713–17; "Geschichte des Clubs," Club von Berlin, accessed May 10, 2025, https://web.archive .org/web/20230223124355/http://www.clubvonberlin.de/index.php/ueber /geschichte.

82 Calendars with Daily Appointments, N 1009/426 and 427, Hans Luther, BAK; Memo, 1 June 1931, N 1231/38, Alfred Hugenberg, BAK; Harbou to Schleicher, Sep. 16, 1932, N 42/7, Kurt von Schleicher, BAF.

83 Invitation to Lawn-Tennis-Tunier-Club's Weihnachtsball, Dec. 7, 1929, Kurt von Schleicher, N 42/4, BAF.

84 Walther F. Kleffel, "Eine geschlossene Gesellschaft von Gentlemen," *Die Zeit*, Aug. 25, 1967, http://www.zeit.de/1967/34/eine-geschlossene-gesellschaft -von-gentleman.

85 See the Union-Klub letterhead used by Franz von Papen in N 1005/637, Hermann Pünder, and in N 1040/13, Siegfried von Kardorff, both BAK.

86 Invitation to Festessen im Unionklub, Oct. 21, 1928, N 42/4, Kurt von Schleicher, BAF.

87 Damenclub Event with Maria von Bunsen "Aus der Bülow Zeit," Oct. 13, 1931, and Invitation from the Vorstand des Damenclubs 1930 to Schleicher to Event with Lancken-Wakenitz, 5Mar. 5, 1931, N 42/4, Kurt von Schleicher, BAF.

88 Reichsklub der deutschen Volkspartei Invitation, 7 Oct. 1931, N 42/4, Kurt von Schleicher, BAF; Deutsche Volkspartei/Reichsklub, *Mitgliederverzeichnis /Reichsklub Der Deutschen Volkspartei e.V.* 1923 https://doi.org/10.17192 /eb2014.0094.

89 Kardorff to Stresemann, 1 May 1925, N 1040/13, Siegfried von Kardorff, BAK.

90 Demokratischer Klub to Schücking, Dec. 15, 1926, N 1051-F/96, Walther Schücking, BAK.

91 Mittwochs-Gesellschaft, Verzeichnis der in den Sitzungen 638 bis 900 gehaltenen Vorträge, R 106/25, Mittwochs-Gesellschaft, BAB; Stresemann to Westarp, 20 Sep. 20, 1919 and Westarp to Stresemann, Sep 22, 1919, N 2329/40, Kuno von Westarp, BAB.

92 Invitations for SeSiSo events are signed "v. Seekt Simons Solf," and can be found in either N 2035/3, Franz Bracht, BAB and N 42/4, Kurt von Schleicher, BAF; Eberhard von Vietsch, *Wilhelm Solf: Botschafter Zwischen den Zeiten* (Tübingen: Rainer Wunderlich Verlag, 1961), 306.

93 Eberhard von Vietsch, *Wilhelm Solf: Botschafter Zwischen den Zeiten* (Tübingen: Rainer Wunderlich Verlag, 1961), 306.

94 Small Book on the Deutscher Herrenklub, N 42/7, Kurt von Schleicher, BAF.

95 Freiherr von Gleichen-Russwurm to Schleicher, Nov. 23, 1927, N 42/7, Kurt von Schleicher, BAF.

96 Deutscher Herrenklub Vorstandsmitglied to Schleicher, Oct. 16, 1929, N 42/7, Kurt von Schleicher, BAF.

97 Manfred Schoeps, "Der Deutsche Herrenklub: Ein Beitrag zur Geschichte des Jungkonservatismus in der Weimarer Republik," (PhD Dissertation, Friedrich-Alexander-Universität Erlangen-Nürnberg, 1974), 1–7, 48, 149–51; Larry Eugene Jones, *The German Right, 1918–1930: Political Parties, Organized Interests, and Patriotic Associations in the Struggle against Weimar Democracy* (New York: Cambridge University Press, 2020), 296–8.

98 "Hitler entlarvt!" *Vorwärts,* July 1, 1932, and "Fort mit Mauerei und Herrenklub!" *Reichswart,* June 11, 1933, in R 1501/126017, Reichsministerium des Innern, BAB.

99 Manfred Schoeps, "Der Deutsche Herrenklub: Ein Beitrag zur Geschichte des Jungkonservatismus in der Weimarer Republik," (PhD Dissertation, Friedrich-Alexander-Universität Erlangen-Nürnberg, 1974), 56.

100 Deutscher Herrenklub Vorstandsmitglied to Schleicher, Oct. 16, 1929, and Various Unsigned Invitations to DHK Events, N 42/7, Kurt von Schleicher, BAF; Statistische Abteilung der Reichsbank Memo, Dec. 5, 1928, R 2501/6572, Deutsche Reichsbank, BAB.

101 Gerhard Feldbauer, "Nationalklub, 1919–1943," *Die Bürgerlichen Partien in Deutschland: Handbuch der Geschichte der bürgerlichen Parteien und anderer bürgerlicher Interessenorganization vom Vormärz bis zum Jahre 1945*, ed. Dieter Fricke (Leipzig: Bibliographisches Institut, 1968), 341.

102 Nationaler Klub to Frau von Oheimb, March 12, 1921, N 1039/13, Katharina von Kardorff, BAK.

103 Kreth to Kardorff, Oct. 8, 1930, N 1040/11, Siegfried von Kardorff, BAK.

104 Gerhard Feldbauer, "Nationalklub, 1919–1943," *Die Bürgerlichen Partien in Deutschland: Handbuch der Geschichte der bürgerlichen Parteien und anderer bürgerlicher Interessenorganization vom Vormärz bis zum Jahre 1945*, ed. Dieter Fricke (Leipzig: Bibliographisches Institut, 1968), 341–2.

105 Bertold Petzinna, *Beziehung zum Deutschen Lebensstil: Ursprung und Entwicklung des jungkonservativen "Ring"-Kreises, 1918–1933* (Berlin: Akademie Verlag, 2000), 226.

106 See invitations for Civil-Casino Events in N 2035/3, Franz Bracht, BAB and N 42/4, Kurt von Schleicher, BAF. Also, see Calendars with Daily Appointments, N 1009/426 and 427, Hans Luther, BAK.

107 Hermann Brügelmann, *Politische Ökonomie in Kritische Jahren: Die Friedrich List Gesellschaft e.V. von 1925–1935* (Tübingen: J.C.B. Mohr, 1956), 9–11 and 68–69.

108 Friedrich List Gesellschaft, Teilnehmerverzeichnis für die Aussprache in Berlin am 15. und 16. November 1928 and Teilnehmerverzeichnis für die Aussprache in Pyrmont am 5. und 6. Juni 1928, N 1009/452, Hans Luther, BAK.

109 Hermann Brügelmann, *Politische Ökonomie in Kritische Jahren: Die Friedrich List Gesellschaft e.V. von 1925–1935* (Tübingen: J.C.B. Mohr, 1956), 137.

110 Sebastian Panwitz, "Gesellschaft der Freunde [GdF]" and "Ressource der Gesellschaft der Freunde [RGdF]," in *Handbuch der Berliner Vereine und Gesellschaften, 1786–1815*, ed. Uta Motschmann (Berlin: Walter de Gruyter, 2015), 837–843 and 851–852; Preußischen Landgemeindetag Ehrenkarten, 13 Nov. 1926, N 1069/19, Walther Lambach, BAK.

111 Eberhard von Vietsch, *Wilhelm Solf: Botschafter Zwischen den Zeiten* (Tübingen: Rainer Wunderlich Verlag, 1961), 143.

112 "The Kaiser Speaks from the Balcony of the Royal Palace (August 1, 1914)," trans. Jeffrey Verhey, accessed July 11, 2018, http://germanhistorydocs.ghi -dc.org/sub_document.cfm?document_id=815&language=english

113 Eberhard von Vietsch, *Wilhelm Solf: Botschafter Zwischen den Zeiten* (Tübingen: Rainer Wunderlich Verlag, 1961), 143–4.

114 Jäckh to Fehrenbach, 17 Feb 1920, N Fehrenbach 18, Constantin Fehrenbach, GLK.

115 Rausch to "Verehrter Genosse," 28 June 1923, N 2178/108, Paul Löbe, BAB.

116 Deutsche Gesellschaft 1914 Invitation, 14 Juni 1932, N 1135/59, Wolfgang Jaenicke, BAK.

117 Walther-Rathenau-Gesellschaft Invitation, Dec. 7, 1932, N 2035/3, Franz Bracht, BAB.

118 Deutsche Gesellschaft 1914 e.V. List of Lectures, 31 Jan. 1933, N 2035/1, Franz Bracht, BAB; Invitation Vortrag von Herrn André Maurois, N 42/4, Kurt von Schleicher, BAF; Deutsche Gesellschaft 1914 e.V. Memo, 13 Dec. 1924, R 57/3149, Deutsches Ausland-Institut, BAB.

119 See the lists of presentations in R 57/3149, Deutsches Ausland-Institut, BAB.

120 Seth Alexander Thévoz, *Club Government: How the Early Victorian World was Ruled from London Clubs* (London: I.B. Tauris, 2018), 2–20.

121 SPD-Plakat von 1932 in Michael Sauer, "Historische Plakate,"
Bundeszentrale für politische Bildung, last modified Feb. 2, 2007, https://
www.bpb.de/themen/medien-journalismus/bilder-in-geschichte-und
-politik/73211/historische-plakate/; NSDAP Election Poster "Bonzen und
Herrenklub mit dem Juden," Wahlplakate in der Weimarer Republik,
accessed Oct. 17, 2023, http://www.wahlplakate-archiv.de/wahlen
/reichstagswahl-1933-maerz/.

122 Amy Milne-Smith, *London Clubland: A Cultural History of Gender and Class in
Late Victorian Britain* (New York: Palgrave Macmillan, 2011), 1–10.

123 J.R. van Stuwe, "Clubleven in Engeland: Clubbability," *Club Kroniek*, 1,
no. 4 (September 1926): 49; J.R. van Stuwe, "Clubleven in Engeland: De
Nationaal Liberal Club I," *Club Kroniek*, 2, no. 2 (July 1927): 27–8; J.R.
van Stuwe, "Clubleven in Engeland: Vrouwenclubs," *Club Kroniek*, 3, no. 9
(February 1929): 219; "Het Biljartspel" and "Het Schaakspel," *Club Kroniek*,
3, no. 1 (June 1928): 20–1.

124 Mathieu Arnouts and Boudien de Vries, "Een 'heerlijk' onderonsje: De
Nieuwe of Littéraire Societeit De Witte, 1880–1914," *De Negentiende Eeuw*,
23 (1999): 4–5, 203.

125 Amy Milne-Smith, *London Clubland: A Cultural History of Gender and Class in
Late Victorian Britain* (New York: Palgrave Macmillan, 2011), 206.

126 Pfeiffer to Dingeldey, 1 July 1933, Reichsklub vom 30. Januar Satzung,
Reichsklub vom 30. Januar Anmeldung zur Mitgliedschaft, and Blank
Zahlkarte, N 1002/97, Eduard Dingeldey, BAK.

127 Thomas Mergel, *Parlamentarische Kultur in der Weimarer Republik*
(Düsseldorf: Droste, 2005), 135.

128 Program for the Visit of the Hungarian Prime Minister and Invitation
List for "Herrendiner," Nov. 22, 1930, N 1005/64, Hermann Pünder,
BAK.

129 Joseph Goebbels, *Tagebücher 1924–1945*, vol. 1, ed. Ralf Georg Reuth,
(Munich: Piper, 2003), 332.

130 "Reichstag und Bierabend," *Pariser Tageszeitung*, Feb. 18, 1938, https://
portal.dnb.de/bookviewer/view/1026584388#page/2/mode/1up; *Das
deutsche Führerlexikon 1934/1935* (Berlin: Otto Stollberg, 1934), 194, 257,
and 494.

3. From the League of Nations to Electioneering Abroad: Transnational Parliamentary Connections Between the World Wars

1 Folder "Mezinárodní parlamentní obcohní delgace," inv. č. 701 and
Nishiōji Yoshimitsu Speech, May 24, 1923, inv. č. 701/B, D 2016/32,
Archivní fond KPR, 1919–1947, AKPR. Thanks to Michael Thornton for
the translation of this document from Japanese.

2 Memo, Nov. 17, 1920, inv. č. 104, D 3/2020/20, Folder "Ivan Makarenko, poslanec kubáňského parlamentu," inv. č. 104, D 3/1896/20, D 3 inv. č. 104, Folder "Paul Kalning," inv. č. 312, and Folder "Francouzský ministr Paul Painlevé," inv. č. 753, D 7909/33, all Archivní fond KPR, 1919–1947, AKPR; Folder "Norský ministr Eyde," inv. č. 139, A 960/21, Folder "Slingenberg, holandský ministr sociální péče," inv. č. 683, A 1483/36, Folder "Pierre Vienot, poslanec francouzské socialistické strany," inv. č. 698, and Folder "Poslanci Labour party – zájezd do ČSR," inv. č. 483, all Archivní fond KPR – protokol A (audience), AKPR.

3 For more on the various politicians who stopped by Prague en route to spa towns like Karlsbad/Karlovy Vary, see, Diary Entries from 1928, DO-41, MM-29, Ferdinand Marek, IZV.

4 Folder "Suzuki, viceprezident socialistické lidové strany japonské," inv. č. 545 and Folder "Subhas Chandra Bose, indický politik," inv. č. 788, Archivní fond KPR – protokol A (audience), AKPR.

5 Giovanni Capoccia, *Defending Democracy: Reactions to Extremism in Interwar Europe* (Baltimore: Johns Hopkins University Press, 2005), 103–7.

6 The detailed AKPR finding aids for the First Republic makes this clear. See KPR, 1919–1947 and KPR – protokol A (audience), https://www .prazskyhradarchiv.cz/cs/archivkpr/archivni-fondy-a-sbirky/archivni-fondy -a-sbirky. The French visitors can be cross listed with the information at "Base de données des députés français depuis 1789," Assemblé nationale, http://www2.assemblee-nationale.fr/sycomore/recherche, to find their party affiliation, and the British visitors can be cross listed with the History of Parliament's database, http://www.historyofparliamentonline.org /research/members. Specific folders include:

   Folder "Skupina francouzských poslanců (Grouppe Alliance Democratique)," inv. č. 853, A 754/38, and "Sir Thomas Moore, anglický poslanec," inv. č. 910, Archivní fond KPR – protokol A (audience), AKPR.

7 United Kingdom, *Hansard Parliamentary Debates*, HL Deb, October 3, 1938, vol 110, 1309–1315; George Frost Kennan, *From Prague After Munich* (Princeton: Princeton University Press, 2015), xiii–xxiv.

8 Antero Holmila and Pasi Ihalainen, "Debating Internationalisms: Contexts, Concepts and Historiography," in *Nationalism and Internationalism Intertwined: A European History of Concepts beyond the Nation State*, eds. Pasi Ihalainen and Antero Holmila (New York: Berghahn, 2022), 5–7; Akira Iriye, *Global Community: The Role of International Organizations in the Making of the Contemporary World* (Berkeley: University of California Press, 2002), 9–16; Glenda Sluga and Patricia Clavin, "Rethinking the History of Internationalism" in *Internationalisms: A Twentieth-Century History*, eds. Glenda Sluga and Patricia Clavin (Cambridge: Cambridge University Press, 2017), 4–5; Martin Kristoffer Hamre, "'Nationalists of All Countries,

Unite!': Hans Keller and Nazi Internationalism in the 1930s," *Contemporary European History* 33, no. 2 (2024): 477–8; David Motadel, "Nationalist Internationalism in the Modern Age," *Contemporary European History* 28, no. 1 (2019): 77; Tara Zahra, *Against the World: Anti-Globalism and Mass Politics between the World Wars* (New York: Norton, 2023), xiv–xxv.

 9 Johan Schot and Vincent Lagendijk, "Technocratic Internationalism in the Interwar Years: Building Europe on Motorways and Electricity Networks," *Journal of Modern European History/Zeitschrift Für Moderne Europäische Geschichte /Revue d'histoire Européenne Contemporaine* 6, no. 2 (2008): 196–217; Christoph Cornelißen and Dirk van Laak, "Einleitung: Die (Ent-)Provinzialisierung Weimars," in *Weimar und die Welt: Globale Verflechtungen der ersten deutschen Republik*, eds. Christoph Cornelißen and Dirk van Laak (Göttingen: Vandenhoeck&Ruprecht, 2020), 14–15; Heidi J.S. Tworek, *News from Germany: The Competition to Control World Communications, 1900–1945* (Cambridge, MA: Harvard University Press, 2019); Stephen G. Gross, *Export Empire: German Soft Power in Southeastern Europe, 1890–1945* (Cambridge: Cambridge University Press, 2015); Sean Andrew Wempe, *Revenants of the German Empire: Colonial Germans, Imperialism, and the League of Nations* (Oxford: Oxford University Press, 2019).

10 Peter Weber, "Ernst Jäckh and the National Internationalism of Interwar Germany," *Central European History* 52, no. 3 (2019): 402–23.

11 "Aus meinen Erlebnissen beim Völkerbund," n.d., N 1626/3, Nachlass Thusnelda Lang-Brumann, Bundesarchiv-Koblenz.

12 Viscount Norwich, quoted in Andrew Webster, "The Transnational Dream: Politicians, Diplomats and Soldiers in the League of Nations' Pursuit of International Disarmament, 1920–1938," *Contemporary European History* 14, 4 (2005): 509, doi:10.1017/S0960777305002730.

13 Susan Pedersen, *The Guardians: The League of Nations and the Crisis of Empire* (Oxford: Oxford University Press, 2015), 6.

14 Frederick Pollock, *The League of Nations* (London: Steven and Sons, 1920), 190.

15 Woodrow Wilson, "Address at the San Francisco Civic Auditorium in San Francisco, California," Sep. 17, 1919, The American Presidency Project, accessed Nov. 8, 2023, http://www.presidency.ucsb.edu/ws/index .php?pid=117386

16 Erez Manela, *The Wilsonian Moment: Self-Determination and the International Origins of Anticolonial Nationalism* (Oxford: Oxford University Press, 2007), 3–34.

17 Mai'a K. Davis Cross, *The European Diplomatic Corps: Diplomats and International Cooperation from Westphalia to Maastricht* (New York: Palgrave Macmillan, 2007), 106.

18 Sean Andrew Wempe, *Revenants of the German Empire: Colonial Germans, Imperialism, and the League of Nations* (Oxford: Oxford University Press, 2019), 16–17.

19 Lord Hankey, *Diplomacy by Conference: Studies in Public Affairs, 1920–1946* (London: Ernest Benn, 1946), 11–39.

20 Susan Pedersen, *The Guardians: The League of Nations and the Crisis of Empire* (Oxford: Oxford University Press, 2015), 5–24; "List of Assembly Delegates and Substitutes," League of Nations Photo Archive, last modified October 2002, http://www.indiana.edu/~league/; Norbert Götz, "On the Origins of 'Parliamentary Diplomacy': Scandinavian 'Bloc Politics' and Delegation Policy in the League of Nations," *Cooperation and Conflict* 40, no. 3 (2005): 263–79.

21 World Peace Foundation, "The First Assembly of the League of Nations," *A League of Nations* IV, no. 1 (Feb. 1921), 197–9.

22 Susan Pedersen, *The Guardians: The League of Nations and the Crisis of Empire,* 5–7; World Peace Foundation, "The First Assembly of the League of Nations," *A League of Nations* IV, no. 1 (Feb. 1921), 197–9.

23 World Peace Foundation, "The First Assembly," 197–9.

24 World Peace Foundation, "The First Assembly," 197–9.

25 Margaret E. Burton, *The Assembly of the League of Nations* (Chicago: University of Chicago Press, 1941), 98; World Peace Foundation, "The First Assembly," 197–9; Cosme de la Torriente, *La Liga de las Naciones: Trabajos de la Segunda Asamblea* (Havana: Impr. y papeleria de Rambla, Bouza y ca, 1922), 10; "Fourth Assembly, Geneva, September 3–September 29, 1923," League of Nations Photo Archive, last modified October 2002, https://web.archive.org/web/20160827145631/http://www.indiana.edu/~league/4thassemb.htm; Booklet "List of Delegates and Members of Delegations (revised)", Geneva 1925, M3609/1, NAA.

26 Roger Fourès, "Des développements apportés par la Société des Nations à la notion de Représentation Étatique" (Doctoral thesis, Université de Paris, 1938), 42–3; Abschrift: Müller to Breitscheid, Aug. 3, 1927, N 2200/2, Hermann Müller, BAB; on Dutch socialists, international travel, and governing coalitions, see Wibaut to Griffier der Eerste Kamer, 13 October 1927, Inv. 331, Florentinus Marinus Wibaut, IISG.

27 "First Assembly, Geneva, November 15–December 18, 1920," League of Nations Photo Archive, last modified October 2002, https://web.archive.org/web/20160827145559/http://www.indiana.edu/~league/1thordinaryassemb.htm; Decypher of cable sent to Joseph Cook, London, 29 March 1924 and Decypher of cablegram, London, December 17, 1925, A3934/SC32/6, NAA.

28 Office Notice (E. 15640/ 21/25): Payments to Members of Parliament, 4 June 1925, and Hubert Montgomery to Sir Russell Scott Memo, 16 July 1926, FO 366/840, NAK; "Thirteenth Ordinary Session of the Assembly, Geneva, September 26–October 17, 1932," League of Nations Photo Archive, last modified October 2002, https://web.archive.org/web/20160412004902/http://www.indiana.edu/~league

/13thordinaryassemb.htm; List of Delegates and Members of Delegations (Provisional), Thirteenth Ordinary Session of the Assembly of the League of Nations, 1932, N 1310/163, Konstantin Freiherr von Neurath, BAK.

29 Roger Fourès, "Des développements apportés par la Société des Nations à la notion de Représentation Étatique" (Doctoral thesis, Université de Paris, 1938), 110–26.

30 Congressional Research Service, "United Nations Issues: Congressional Representatives to the U.N. General Assembly," Sep. 16, 2022, https://sgp.fas.org/crs/row/IF10464.pdf

31 John Tilley, British Embassy, Tokyo to Austen Chamberlain, 9 Oct. 1926, A11804/1927/71, NAA; Report "Lundi, 16 juillet 1932 – visite par: (Japon), 58 Parlements étrangers, ACB; 67 Congressional Record S3062 (1921).

32 O. Clough to M. Pawels, 4 Sep. 1923, 58–1 Parlements étrangers, as well as Raoul Brandon to A.M. Poncelet, 19 July 1935, and Kennisgeving, 12 July 1935, and Program Amitié Franco-Belge & Luxembourgeoise, 16 July 1937, 58 Parlements étrangers, ACB.

33 Robert James Maddox, *William E. Borah and American Foreign Policy* (Baton Rouge: LSU Press, 1969), 215; Borah to Henry Haye, 23 Nov. 1931, and Henry Haye to Borah, 10 Nov. 1931, Folder: Foreign Affairs, Box 313, William Edgar Borah papers, 1905–1940, LOC.

34 Robert James Maddox, *William E. Borah and American Foreign Policy* (Baton Rouge: LSU Press, 1969), 248.

35 See both John Chalmers Vinson, *William E. Borah and the Outlawry of War* (Athens, GA: UGA Press, 1957) and "Es war einmal … Erinnerungen an die Zeit von 1870 bis 1932," N 1771/1, Wilhelm Friedrich Kalle, BAK.

36 Empire Parliamentary Association (United Kingdom Branch), Some Urgent African Problems Address by Mr. G. Heaton Nicholls, M.P. (Union of South Africa), 16 November 1938; Clipping "A Parliamentary Picnic: Jaunt to South Africa," 21 July 1923, *The Age*, A3934 SC32/6, Clipping "Parliamentary Tourists: Arrival at Durban," 19 Aug. 1924, *The Argus*, A461 E4/1/9, Memo: TC/BE Visting of Members of the Commonwealth Parliament to South Africa, 1924, A461 E4/1/9, all in NAA; Empire Parliamentary Association (Dominion of Canada Branch), Conferences of the Empire Parliamentary Association held in the Senate Chamber, Ottawa, and the Legislative Assembly Chambers of the Canadian Provinces, August, September, October 1928.

37 Stefan Berger, "Internationalismus als Lippenbekenntnis? Die transnationale Kooperation sozialdemokratischer Parteien in der Zwischenkriegszeit," in *Politische Parteien und europäische Integration Entwicklung und Perspektiven transnationale Parteienkooperation in Europa,* ed. Jürgen Mittag (Essen, Klartext, 2006), 198; see also: Carl E. Schorske, *German social democracy, 1905–1917: the development of the great schism*

(Cambridge: Harvard UP, 1983), William Lee Blackwood, "Socialism, Nationalism, and 'the German Question' from World War I to Locarno and Beyond" (PhD diss, Yale University, 1995), and Talbot C. Imlay, *The Practice of Socialist Internationalism: European Socialists and International Politics, 1914–1960* (Oxford: Oxford University Press, 2018).

38 Freie Vereinigung sozialistischer Akademiker der deutschen Hochschulen in Prag to Levi, 2 Oct 1922, NY 4126/15, Paul Levi, SAPMO, BAB; Renner to Austerlitz, 26 Oct. 1926, M85, Partei-Archiv vor 1934 and Det norske Arbeiderparti to Deutsch, 22 May 1930, M45, Partei Archiv vor 1934, VGA; Löbe to Müller, 28 Dec. 1928, 1/HMAG00001, Hermann Müller, FES.

39 Sender illegible to Parteivorstand SDAP, 16 Sep. 1926, M 130, Czech to SDAP, 3 Dec. 1924, M 129, and Parteisekretariat Kreisvertretung Troppau to Unnamed [SDAP], Troppau, 20 June 1922, M 129, Taub to Danneberg, 6 Oct. 1930, M 130, all Partei-Archiv vor 1934, VGA.

40 SDAP/Organisation Wien to SPD Parteivorstand, Mar. 3, 1927, and SDAP /Organisation Wien to Müller, n.d.; Deutsch to Müller, N 2200/1, Hermann Müller, BAB; "Das Osterfest des Arbeitersports," *Arbeiter-Zeitung*, Apr. 19, 1927, ANNO; Glöckel to Deutsch, Mar. 30, 1925, M 128, Partei-Archiv vor 1934, VGA.

41 SDP, Bezirksverband Schleswig-Holstein to Deutsch, Dec. 15, 1930, M44, Partei Archiv vor 1934, VGA.

42 Deutsch to Renner, Aug. 8, 1930, and April 20, 1928, AVA Nachlässe NN Renner 83, Allgemeines Verwaltungsarchiv, ÖSTA.

43 Taub to Danneberg, Oct. 27, 1925, M 129, SDAP Parteileitung to Kreis-Organisation (Tratenau), Oct. 6, 1926, M 130, and Deutsch to Reese, Sep. 11, 1929, M45, all Partei-Archiv vor 1934, VGA.

44 Telegrams Hilferding (June 27, 1932), Breitscheid (June 28, 1932), and Voigt (June 30, 1932) to Wilkinson, and "TO OUR COMRADES OF THE GERMAN SOCIAL DEMOCRATIC PARTY," July 1, 1932, LP/ID/GER/7, Labour Party Archives, PHM; David Clay Large, *Between Two Fires: Europe's Path in the 1930s* (New York: Norton, 1991), 201–9.

45 Albarda to Müller, Sep. 27, 1928, 1/HMAG00034, Lenz to Müller, Aug. 20, 1928, 1/HMAG00042, and Albarda to Müller, Sep. 27, 1928, 1/ HMAG00034, all Hermann Müller, FES; Heinrich August Winkler, *Weimar, 1918–1933: die Geschichte der ersten deutschen Demokratie* (Munich: Beck, 1993), 332–3.

46 Johannes Großman, *Die Internationale der Konservativen: Transnationale Elitenzirkel und private Außenpolitik in Westeuropa seit 1945* (Munich: Oldenbourg, 2014), 1–2 and 555; Vockel to Dessauer, May 21, 1928, and Dessauer to Brüning, May 3, 1933, FD 8, Friedrich Dessauer, KFZ.

47 Entente internationale des partis radicaux et des partis démocratiques similaires, *Compte-Rendu du Congrès de Londres*, Fascicule IV (Paris, 1928);

Provisional Program, May 1928, N 1132/51, Wilhelm Heile, BAK; Heuss to Foreign Office, n.d., N 1221/1, Theodor Heuss, BAK.

48 Verhandlungsschrift der konstituierenden Sitzung, 19 and 20 Nov. 1921, and Mitgliederverzeichnis „Arbeitsgemeinschaft deutscher Parlamentarier," n.d., Karton 10, and Verhandlungsschrift-Innsbruck, 5 June 1926, and Verhandlungsschrift-Salzburg, 18 and 19 Mar. 1922, Karton 11, all AdR BKA BKA-I Parteiarchiv GDVP allgemein Schriftgut der Partei, Archiv der Republik, ÖSTA.

49 Georg Wilhelm Schiele to Unnamed, May 17, 1919, GDVP to DNVP (Görlitz), Oct. 25, 1922, and GDVP to Kollbach (DVP), 4 Jul 1925, Karton 40, AdR BKA BKA-I Parteiarchiv GDVP allgemein Schriftgut der Partei, Archiv der Republik, ÖSTA; David Motadel, "Nationalist Internationalism in the Modern Age," *Contemporary European History* 28: 1 (2019), 77.

50 For examples of politicians meeting in spa towns, see Diary Entries from 1928, DO-41, MM-29, Ferdinand Marek, IZV.

51 Christoph Cornelißen and Dirk van Laak, "Einleitung: Die (Ent-) Provinzialisierung Weimars," in *Weimar und die Welt: Globale Verflechtungen der ersten deutschen Republik*, eds. Christoph Cornelißen and Dirk van Laak (Göttingen: Vandenhoeck&Ruprecht, 2020), 14–15.

52 Schücking to Herriot, n.d., N 1051-F/96, Walther Schücking, BAK; Georges-Henri Soutou, "Édouard Herriot et l'Allemagne: la continuité dans la méfiance," in *Édouard Herriot en quatre portraits*, ed. Bruno Benoit (Villeneuve d'Ascq: Presses universitaires du Septentrion, 2020), 252–5; for a similar example of a letter of introduction, see Business Card of Charles Trevelyan, 1 Feb 1920, N/2200/1, Hermann Müller, BAB.

53 Isabella Löhr, "Deutschland im Völkerbund," in *Weimar und die Welt: Globale Verflechtungen der ersten deutschen Republik*, eds. Christoph Cornelißen and Dirk van Laak (Göttingen: Vandenhoeck&Ruprecht, 2020), 288–302; Nomination Archive: Walther Adrian Schücking, accessed July 23, 2024, https://www.nobelprize.org/nomination/archive/show_people .php?id=8298; see the Table of Contents and Articles in *Die Friedens-Warte*, Vol. 35, No. 5 (1935), https://www.jstor.org/stable/i23794594.

54 Ellenbogen to Müller, July 22, 1927, N 2200/2, Hermann Müller, BAB.

55 Müller to Ellenbogen, July 7, 1927 and Müller to Siemens, July 7, 1927, N 2200/2, Hermann Müller, BAB.

56 Ellenbogen to Müller, July 22, 1927, N/2200/2, Hermann Müller, BAB.

57 Erinnerungsalbum, Mappe 17, Karton 5, Gabriele Proft, VGA,

58 Breitscheid to Hoegner, May 25, 1934, ED 120/2, Wilhelm Hoegner, IZM; "Frau Seger Released," *Times*, May 24, 1934 and "Concentration Camp Prisoners," *Times*, May 16, 1934, The Times Digital Archive.

59 Brookhart to Renner, Mar. 31, 1934, Taub to Renner, Apr. 20, 1934, and Jeanne Vandervelde to Renner, Apr. 18, 1935, Mappe 2, Karl Renner, VGA.

60 Czech to Danneberg, Dec. 29, 1931, Jan. 12, 1932, and Jan. 21, 1932, and Danneberg to Czech, Jan. 13, 1932, M130, Partei-Archiv vor 1934, VGA.

61 Vandervelde to Hansson, Engberg, and Sandler, Feb. 28, 1926, EV/IV/532 and Vandervelde to Hansson, Jan. 8, 1935, EV/III/67 Archives d'Émile Vandervelde, IÉV.

62 Curtius to Müller, Mar. 14, 1930, 1/HMAG0000 and Müller to Curtius, Mar. 18, 1930, 1/HMAG00036, Hermann Müller, FES.

63 Vandervelde to Blum, Aug. 28, 1935, EV/IV/64, Archives d'Émile Vandervelde, IÉV; P. Aspeslagh, F. Verleden, N. Matheve, C. Heyneman, E. Gerard, *Belelite: Databank van de Belgische regeringen sinds 1831*, accessed Aug. 15, 2023, www.koninklijkecommissiegeschiedenis.be/belelite.

64 Advertisement for GRANDE DEMONSTRATION INTERNATIONAL, *Le Drapeau Rouge*, Sep. 7, 1935, 1, BelgicaPress.

65 Vandervelde to Blum, Aug. 28, 1935, EV/IV/64, Archives d'Émile Vandervelde, IÉV; Julian Jackson, *The Popular Front in France defending democracy, 1934–38* (Cambridge: Cambridge, 1988), 42–61.

66 "Basècles Tombola," *Le Drapeau Rouge*, Oct. 12, 1935, 2, BelgicaPress.

67 Günther Guggenberger, "Austria," in *Authoritarianism, History and Democratic Dispositions in Austria, Poland, Hungary and the Czech Republic*, eds. Oliver Rathkolb and Günther Ogris (Innsbruck: Studien Verlag, 2010), 44–5; C. Earl Edmondson, *The Heimwehr and Austrian Politics, 1918–1936* (Athens: University of Georgia Press, 1978), 178–208.

68 *Handelingen der Tweede Kamer* (Nov. 10, 1933), 274–82.

69 For an overview of the press coverage, see "Eine Rede Albardas über Oesterreich," *Arbeiter-Zeitung*, Nov. 28, 1933, 3. ANNO.

70 "Hochverratsaffäre der Austromarxisten," *Neues Wiener Journal*, Nov. 28, 1933, 4, ANNO.

71 Albarda to Austrian Diplomat as an attachment to Ruijs de Beerenbrouck, Nov. 29, 1933, 2.21.244, Inv. 39, Ruijs de Beerenbrouck, NAH.

72 Searching ANNO did not include references to subsequent stories on the issue.

73 Michael Habersack, *Friedrich Dessauer (1881–1963): Eine politische Biographie des Frankfurter Biophysikers und Reichstagsabgeordneten* (Paderborn: Ferdinand Schöningh, 2011), 84–97, 177–265; Dessauer to Brüning, 11 Jan. 1932, FD 12, Friedrich Dessauer, KFZ.

74 Dessauer sent several key letters on April 12, 1932, after the second round of the German presidential election and before both the Prussian election and French national election. On the elections, see Larry Eugene Jones, *Hitler versus Hindenburg: The 1932 Presidential Elections and the End of the Weimar Republic* (Cambridge: Cambridge University Press, 2016), 314–15; Vincent Adoumié, *De la république à l'État français, 1918–1944* (Paris:

Hachette, 2005), 64–6; Serge Berstein, *La France des Années 30* (Paris: Armand Colin, 2011), 67–8.

75 Dessauer to Fetzer, Apr. 12, 1932, FD 12, Friedrich Dessauer, KFZ.

76 Dessauer to Brüning Apr. 12, 1932, FD 12, Friedrich Dessauer, KFZ.

77 "Édouard Herriot et l'Allemagne: la continuité dans la méfiance," in *Édouard Herriot en quatre portraits*, ed. Bruno Benoit (Villeneuve d'Ascq: Presses universitaires du Septentrion, 2020), 254–5.

78 Patricia Clavin, *Securing the World Economy: The Reinvention of the League of Nations, 1920–1946*, (Oxford: Oxford, 2013), 82.

79 See, David Marquand, *Ramsay MacDonald* (London: Jonathan Cape, 1977), especially 1–10 and 792–5.

80 "Pariser Arbeiterforderungen," May 30, 1919, "Nach Georgien," Aug. 29, 1920, and "Genosse Ramsay MacDonald," Feb. 1, 1922, all *Vorwärts*, available at Historische Presse der deutschen Sozialdemokratie online; "To our Guests from abroad," n.d., PRO 30/69/1402, NAK.

81 "Labour-Party and China-Politik," *Vorwärts*, Jan. 28, 1927, HPDS; MacDonald to Vandervelde, 14 Jan 1927, and Vandervelde to MacDonald, 18 Jan. 1927, EV/IV/357, Archives d'Émile Vandervelde, IÉV.

82 "MacDonald besucht Berlin," *Vorwärts*, Oct. 8, 1925, HPDS; Calendar, Oct. 14 and 25, 1928, RMD/2/25, Ramsay MacDonald Papers, JRL.

83 "MacDonald in Paris," *Vorwärts*, Dec. 24, 1925, HPDS.

84 Voize to MacDonald, Nov. 24, 1928, and MacDonald's staff to Léon Blum, Nov. 8, 1928, PRO 30/69/1487, NAK.

85 Bernd Braun and Joachim Eichler, eds., *Arbeiterführer, Parlamentarier, Parteiveteran: Die Tagebücher des Sozialdemokraten Hermann Molkenbuhr, 1905 bis 1927* (Munich: Oldenbourg, 2000), 137; "Labour Party und Einigkeit," July 22, 1921, and "Minister Simons im Kreuzfeuer," July 28, 1920, in *Vorwärts*, HPDS.

86 "Die Zukunft der 2. Internationale," *Vorwärts*, July 27, 1920, HPDS.

87 Calendar, May 24, 1922, N 1027/17, Eduard David, BAK; Card of Charles Trevelyan, 1 Feb 1920, N/2200/1, Hermann Müller, BAB; Müller to MacDonald, Sep. 26, 1928, 1/HMAG00043, Hermann Müller, FES.

88 MacDonald to Müller, June 13, 1929, 1/HMAG00001, Hermann Müller, FES.

89 Wels to MacDonald, 4 Oct. 4, 1933, and Note to Prime Minister in Neville Butler's hand, n.d., PRO 30/69/282, as well as Agenda and Conclusions of the Meeting of October 9, 1933, "Conclusions of Meetings of Cabinet," p. 77–89, CAB 23/77, all NAK.

90 Norbert Götz, "On the Origins of 'Parliamentary Diplomacy': Scandinavian 'Bloc Politics' and Delegation Policy in the League of Nations," *Cooperation and Conflict* 40, no. 3 (2005): 263–79.

91 MacDonald to Müller, 13 June 1929, 1/HMAG00001, Hermann Müller, FES.

4. The Inter-Parliamentary Union, International Parliamentary Commercial Conference, and Interwar Parliamentary Democracy

1 Excerpt "Antikomintern" herausgegebenen "NACHRICHTENDIENST" 2. Jahrgang Nr. 20 v. 15.12.1935, R 58/3436, Reichssicherheitshauptamt, BAB.

2 See, for example, Andrew Webster, "The League of Nations, Disarmament and Internationalism," in *Internationalisms: A Twentieth-Century History*, eds. Glenda Sluga and Patricia Clavin (Cambridge: Cambridge University Press, 2017): 139–69.

3 For publication sponsored by the Swedish national group, see Frederik Sterzel, *The Inter-Parliamentary Union* (Stockholm: Norstedt & Söner, 1968); Yefime Zarjevski, *The People Have the Floor: A History of the Inter-Parliamentary Union*, trans. Nicholas Albrecht (Aldershot: Dartmouth, 1989), 64–90.

4 Ralph Uhlig, *Die interparlamentarische Union, 1889–1914* (Stuttgart: Franz Steiner, 1988); Claudia Kissling, *Die Interparlementarische Union im Wandel: Rechtspolitische Ansätze einer repräsentativ-parlamentarischen Gestaltung der Weltpolitik* (Frankfurt: Peter Lang, 2005); Leonida Tedoldi, "Understanding Globalization. The Inter-Parliamentary Union From the Late Nineteenth to Early Twentieth Century," *History Research*, no. 1 (2014): 21–30.

5 Martin Albers, "Between the Crisis of Democracy and World Parliament: The Development of the Inter-Parliamentary Union in the 1920s." *Journal of Global History* 7, no. 2 (2012): 208–9.

6 Martin Albers, "Between the Crisis of Democracy and World Parliament," 193–208.

7 O.B., "Bücherschau: Parlamentarismus," *Der Kampf: Sozialdemokratische Monatsschrift*, 1 Feb. 1914, 237–9, ANNO; Carl Schmitt, *The Crisis of Parliamentary Democracy*, trans. Ellen Kennedy (Cambridge, MA: MIT Press, 1985).

8 See the expert reports in Box 392, Inter-Parliamentary Union Archive-Geneva as well as the summaries of these materials, in addition to published reports in Wilhelm Medinger, *Die Internationale Diskussion über Die Krise des Parlamentarismus* (Vienna: Wilhelm Braumüller, 1929), 12–51.

9 Liste der prominenten außerdeutschen Teilnehmer, R 53712, PAAA.

10 Inter-Parliamentary Bureau, *The Inter-Parliamentary Union: Its Work and Its Organization* (Geneva: Inter-Parliamentary Bureau, 1930), 1; J.R.M., "Sir William Randal Cremer," in *Dictionary of National Biography, Second Supplement*, Vol 1, (New York: The MacMillan Company, 1912), 441–2.

11 *L'Union interparlementaire de 1889 à 1939: Ouvrage publié par les soins du Bureau interparlementaire à l'occasion du cinquantenaire de l'Union* (Lausanne: Payot & c, 1939), 375–81; James Douglas, *A Century of Parliamentary Diplomacy: A Short History of the British Group of the Inter-Parliamentary Union, 1889–1989* (Cambridge, England: Pentlands Publications, 1989), 6–7; Weardale, et al., Memo, Dec. 3, 1917, Folder Groupes 1917, Box 282, IPU.

12 Inter-Parliamentary Bureau, *The Inter-Parliamentary Union: Its Work and Its Organization* (Geneva: Inter-Parliamentary Bureau, 1930), 2.

13 Aufzeichnung, 9 Sep. 1928, R 53712, PAAA; Union interparlementaire, *Compte rendu de la XXVme conférence tenue à Berlin du 23 au 28 août 1928* (Lausanne, Librairie Payot & Cie, 1928), 27; Invitation for Berlin IPU Conference, Inv. 90, 2.21.190, C. Frida Katz Fam., NAH; Invitations for IPU-related Events, N 1004/183, Hermann Dietrich, BAK; Aufzeichnung, 9 Sep 1928, R 53712, PAAA.

14 Heym, Betrifft: Tagung der Interparlamentarischen Union, 20 Nov. 1927, R 43-I/563, Reichskanzlei, BAB.

15 Hindenburg to Reichskanzler, July 16, 1928 and Interparlamentarische Union, XXV. Konferenz, Berlin 1928 to Reichskanzler, Aug. 8, 1928, R 43-I/563, Reichskanzlei, BAB.

16 Aufzeichnung, 9 Sep 1928, R 53712, PAAA. Other versions of this list can be found at PAAA in R 70085 and R 83524. There is also a copy at R 43-I/563, BAB.

17 Stampfer to Schücking, Aug. 21, 1928, Folder Com. exc., Berlin, Aug 1928, Box 259, IPU; Letter to the President and Members of of the XXV. Inter-Parliamentary Conference from Filippo Amedeo, et al., Aug. 18, 1928, Folder Com. exc., Berlin, août 1928, Box 259, IPU.

18 Macek and Krnjevic to Löbe, Aug. 20, 1928, and Stellvertretender Präsident des Interparlamentarischen Rates to Mazek, Aug. 24, 1928, Folder Com. exc., Berlin, Aug. 1928, Box 259, IPU; Elinor M. Despalatović, "The Roots of the War in Croatia," *Neighbors at War: Anthropological Perspectives on Yugoslav Ethnicity, Culture, and History*, eds. Joel M. Halpern and David A. Kideckel (University Park, PA: Pennsylvania State University Press, 2000), 86–7; Mark Biondich, *Stjepan Radić, the Croat Peasant Party, and the Politics of Mass Mobilization, 1904–1928* (Toronto: University of Toronto Press, 2000), 242.

19 "Egypt. Parliament Dissolved. No Meeting for Three Years," *The Advertiser* (Adelaide) (July 21, 1928); Telegram, Martius to Diplogerma, Alexandrien Nr. 54, Aug. 30, 1928, Telegram, Pilger to AA, Aug. 27, 1928, and Untitled Memo (VM 4258), Aug. 27, 1928, R 53712, PAAA.

20 Telegram, Pilger to AA, Oct. 20, 1928, Letter from Deutsche Gesandtschaft, San Stefano to AA, Telegram, Pilger to AA, 27 Aug. 27, 1928, Telegram, AA to Diplogerma Alexandrien Nr. 54, Aug. 30, 1928, and IPU, Tagesordnung: Sitzung des Interparlamentarischen Rates, Dienstag, den 28. 1928, R 53712, PAAA.

21 Martin Albers, "Between the Crisis of Democracy and World Parliament: The Development of the Inter-Parliamentary Union in the 1920s." *Journal of Global History* 7, no. 2 (2012): 194.

22 Inter-Parliamentary Bureau, *The Inter-Parliamentary Union: Its Work and Its Organization* (Geneva: Inter-Parliamentary Bureau, 1930), 6–7; Speech

for Luncheon H[ouse] of C[ommons], July 17, 1919, Folder Groupes 1919, Box 282, IPU; James Douglas, *A Century of Parliamentary Diplomacy: A Short History of the British Group of the Inter-Parliamentary Union, 1889–1989* (Cambridge, England: Pentlands Publications, 1989), 11; Diarmid Coffey to Léopold Boissier, June 4, 1936, Folder Groupes 1936, Box 289, IPU.

23 La Liste de Groupe Japonais d'Union Interparlementaire, n.d., Folder Groupes 1924, Box 282, and Sender illegible to Generalsekretär, June 17, 1936, and Liste des membres du group du Volksraad des Indes Néerlandaises, Jan. 1936, Folder Groupes 1936, Box 289, IPU.

24 Slaydon to Undefined, Nov. 1917, Groupes 1917, Box 282, IPU.

25 Memo from Plenary Session of the Czechoslovak Group, June 17, 1925, Folder Groupes 1924, Box 282, IPU.

26 Mitglieder der deutschen Gruppe der Interparlamentarischen Union, Apr. 1, 1921, N 1051-F/96, Walther Schücking, BAK; for information on party affiliation of members of the Reichstag, see "Verhandlungen des Deutschen Reichstags," accessed Oct. 22, 2016, http://www.reichstagsprotokolle.de/index.html.

27 Selby to Boissier, Feb. 19, 1936, Folder Groupes 1936, Box 289 and F.W. Pethick Lawrence to Lange, Nov. 13, 1931, Folder Groupes 1931 Box 287, IPU.

28 See, for example, Union interparlementaire, *Compte rendu de la XXVme Conference Interparlementaire* (Lausanne, Librairie Payot & Cie, 1928), for a list of members of the 1928 delegations to get a sense of numbers.

29 Boissier and Lykke, Circular to the Groups, Inter-Parliamentary Union, Aug. 19, 1939, A981/CONF167/PART 2, NAA.

30 Boyé to Lange, Mar. 24, 1928, Folder Groupes 1928 I, Box 282, IPU.

31 Löbe to Bülow, Apr. 4, 1933, R 98279, PAAA; Convention for limiting the Manufacture and regulating the Distribution of Narcotic Drugs, accessed Oct. 20, 2023, https://treaties.un.org/pages/ViewDetails.aspx?src=TREATY&mtdsg_no=VI-8-a&chapter=6&clang=_en

32 Invitation from Deutsche Gruppe der IPU, Dr. Braun (Franken), June 30, 1925, FD 3 and Invitation from the Deutsche Gruppe der IPU, Schücking, Feb. 12, 1926, FD 5, Friedrich Dessauer, KFZ.

33 Maddison to Lange, Feb. 9, 1920, Folder Groupes 1920, Box 283, IPU.

34 Invitation from the Nederlandsche Groep der Interparlementaire Unie, Feb. 12, 1929, Inv. 332, Florentinus Marinus Wibaut, IISG.

35 Union interparlementaire group du Volksraad to Léopold Boissier, 17 Mar. 1936, Folder Groupes 1936, Box 289, IPU.

36 Coffey to Boissier, June 4, 1936, Folder Groupes 1936, Box 289, IPU.

37 Boyé to Schücking, June 29, 1930, N 1051-F/96, Walther Schücking, BAK; Löbe to Lange, 4 Mar. 1932, Box 480, IPU.

38 Coffey to Boissier, May 20, 1935 and Boissier to Coffey, May 22, 1935, Folder Löbe, Box 289, IPU.

39 Union interparlementaire, Reunion des groups français et Suisse tenue à Lausanne, Sep. 11, 1930, Lange to Merlin, Dec. 5, 1931, Lange to Löbe, Nov. 21, 1931, and Löbe to Boissier, 6 Jun 1932, Box 480, IPU.

40 Attachment to Letter from President of the Belgian Group to British Group, Feb. 20, 1919, Folder Groupe belge etc. 1919, Box 282, IPU.

41 Lange to Vandervelde, July 24, 1922, and "De Internationale Vereeniging der Parlementairen," *De Standaard,* July 13, 1922, Box 283, IPU; "De Interparlementaire Unie te Bern," 13 July 13, 1922, "In de Interparlementaire Unie: Oneenigheid onder de Belgische leden," Aug. 15–16, 1927, "Om het Parlement: Interparlementaire Unie," May 21, 1930, "De Interparlementarie Conferentie te Berlijn," Aug. 23, 1928, all in *De Standaard,* BelgicaPress.

42 Drexel to Deutsche Gruppe der IPU, July 19, 1928; R 43-I/563, Reichskanzlei, BAB; Speech for Luncheon, July 17, 1919, Folder Groupes 1919, Box 282, IPU; James Douglas, *A Century of Parliamentary Diplomacy: A Short History of the British Group of the Inter-Parliamentary Union, 1889–1989* (Cambridge, England: Pentlands Publications, 1989), 11.

43 Papers of Heinrich Brüning, Uncatalogued Accession, Photo of Delegation to Inter-parliamentary Conference (1927) among Photos, Acs. 13632, Box 5, HUA; Oscar Meyer, *Von Bismarck zu Hitler: Erinnerungen und Betrachtungen,* (Offenbach a.M.: Bollwerk-Verlag Karl Drott, 1948), 139.

44 Oscar Meyer, *Von Bismarck zu Hitler,* 139; Pistor, Deutsche Gesandtschaft Rio de Janeiro to AA, Sep. 17, 1927, R 401/1047, Vorläufiger Reichswirtschaftsrat, BAB.

45 "Parlamentarische Handelskonferenz von Rio de Janeiro-Sept. 1927," Folder Comité exécutif, 2 et 3 décembre 1927 (Genève), Box 259, IPU; Pistor, Deutsche Gesandtschaft Rio de Janeiro to AA, 17 Sep. 1927, R 401/1047, Vorläufiger Reichswirtschaftsrat, BAB.

46 Stresemann to Lejeune-Jung, Nov. 10, 1927, Bd. 61, Gustav Stresemann, PAAA; "Parlamentarische Handelskonferenz von Rio de Janeiro-Sept. 1927," Folder Comité exécutif, 2 et 3 décembre 1927 (Genève), Box 259, IPU.

47 Brüning, General Correspondence, Letter, Brüning to Hans von Raumer (Apr. 13, 1946) in folder Hans von Raumer, Stephanie von Raumer, HUG FP 93.10, Box 26, HUA.

48 Oscar Meyer, *Von Bismarck zu Hitler: Erinnerungen und Betrachtungen* (Offenbach a.M.: Bollwerk-Verlag Karl Drott, 1948), 139–41.

49 Jointly signed postcard to Elisabeth Thesing, 1/RHAB000010, Rose Hilferding, FES; Postcard to Hermann Meyer, Aug. 25, 1927, AR 7243, Oscar Meyer Collection, LBI.

50 Conférence parlementaire international du commerce, *Cinquième assemblée plénière: notices relatifs aux questions inscrites à son programme* (Brussels: Bureau permanent de Bruxelles, 1919), 3–4.

51 Conférence parlementaire international du commerce, *Douzième assemblée plénière: Historique, Assemblées plénières, Horaire, Programme des travaux, liste de delegations*, May 1926, p. 14, in Cl. No. 10, Doc. No. 49706, Dossier No. 44049, LON.

52 Conférence parlementaire international du commerce, *Dix-huitième assemblée plénière. assemblée plénière: rapports et notices relatifs aux questions inscrites à son programme* (Brussels: Bureau permanent de Bruxelles, 1933), 7–8.

53 Conférence parlementaire international du commerce, *Douzième assemblée plénière: Historique, Assemblées plénière, Horaire, Programme des travaux, liste de delegations*, May 1926, p. 16, in Cl. No. 10, Doc. No. 49706, Dossier No. 44049, LON; Baie to Theunis, Apr. 25, 1926, 983, Georges Theunis, AEB; Official Secretary, Australia House, to The Secretary, Prime Minister's Department, Melbourne, Dec. 12, 1921, A457/K107/5, NAA; Richard Weiskirchner to Bundesminister für Ausseres, July 29, 1922, Karton 53, AdR AAng BKA-AA HP Handelspolitik, Abteilung 14, Archiv der Republik, ÖSTA; Richard Linton to S.M. Bruce, 5 Nov. 1928, A 981/CONF167/PART 1, NAA.

54 Pistor, Deutsche Gesandtschaft Rio de Janeiro to AA, Sep. 17, 1927, R 401/1047, Vorläufiger Reichswirtschaftsrat, BAB; "Parlamentarische Handelskonferenz von Rio de Janeiro-Sept. 1927," Folder Comité exécutif, 2 et 3 décembre 1927 (Genève), Box 259, IPU.

55 See "Union interparlementaire," *Compte rendu de la XXVme conférence tenue à Berlin du 23 au 28 août 1928* (Lausanne, Librairie Payot & Cie, 1928), as well as the other annual *comptes rendus* of the conferences; Memo, Conférence Parlementaire Internationale du Commerce, Douzième assemblée plénière, March 1926, I 494, 983, Georges Theunis, AEB.

56 Un. iprl. Conférence parlementaire du Commerce, Congrès de Prague, n.d., Box 721, IPU; Inter-parliamentary Commercial Conference, Versailles, June 19 to 22, 1928," A 981/CONF/167/PART 1, NAA.

57 Un. iprl. Conférence parlementaire du Commerce, Congrès de Prague, n.d., Box 721, IPU.

58 Martin Albers, "Between the Crisis of Democracy and World Parliament: The Development of the Inter-Parliamentary Union in the 1920s." *Journal of Global History* 7, no. 2 (2012): 198–203; Nitobe to Lange, Feb. 19, 1920 and Lange to Nitobe, Mar. 18, 1920, Section No. 13, Document No. 3132, Dossier No. 1666, LON.

59 Dr. H. Parodi, Memorandum adressé au secrétaire-général, Oct. 6, 1920, and Untitled Memo, Oct. 13, 1920, Cl. No. 11, Doc. 7362, Dossier 7362, LON.

60 Slayden to Lange, Sep. 25, 1918, Folder Groupes 1918, Box 282, Otero to Presidente de la Unión Interpalamentaría, Dec. 13, 1930 and República

Chile Senado, Unnamed "Acta," 21 Nov 1930, Folder Groupes 1931, Box 287, IPU.

61 *L'Union interparlementaire de 1889 à 1939: Ouvrage publié par les soins du Bureau interparlementaire à l'occasion du cinquantenaire de l'Union* (Lausanne: Payot & c, 1939), 380–1.

62 Conférence parlementaire international du commerce, *Cinquième assemblée plénière: notices relatifs aux questions inscrites à son programme* (Brussels: Bureau permanent de Bruxelles, 1919), 3–4; Ministère des Affaires étrangères to Hymans, Poullet, Sep. 20, 1921, 10.740, folder 1, ADB.

63 Un. iprl. Conférence parlementaire du Commerce, Congrès de Prague, n.d., Box 721, IPU.

64 Inter-Parliamentary Union, Circular to the Groups No. 6 (1928): Multiplicity of Inter-Parliamentary Organizations, Apr. 12, 1928, Box 721, IPU.

65 Un. iprl. Conférence parlementaire du Commerce, Congrès de Prague, n.d., L.A. Kesper to Christian Lange, 17 Feb. 17, 1930, and Albert François to Christian Lange, May 5, 1931, Box 721, IPU.

66 Sitzung der Deutschen Gruppe der Interparlamentarischen Union, June 27, 1929, N 1132/110, Wilhelm Heile, BAK; Memo, German Embassy Tokyo, June 11, 1928, R 83524, PAAA.

67 The photo at Papers of Heinrich Brüning, Uncatalogued Accession, Photo of Delegation to Inter-parliamentary Conference (1927) among Photos, Acs. 13632, Box 5, HUA, has been mislabeled as from an IPU conference, when it was really a CPIC conference.

68 Martin Albers, "Between the Crisis of Democracy and World Parliament" 206–7.

69 Union interparlementaire, Procès-verbaux du Conseil interparlementaire XXIV bis Partie confidentielle, Aug. 25, 1927, Box 8, IPU.

70 Boissier to Allen, Jan. 30, 1935, and Boissier to Call, Feb. 2, 1935, Folder Löbe, Box 289, IPU.

71 Action en faveur de M. Loebe and Souscription au fonds Loebe, Box 289, n.d., IPU. As an example of requesting to be confidential, see Davies to Boissier, Mar. 12, 1935, Box 289, IPU.

72 Boissier to Schücking, Apr. 3, 1935, Box 289, IPU.

73 Abschrift: 83 Teilnehmer der Konferenz der Interparlamentarischen Union fordern Gnade für Robert Stamm, n.d., R58/6282, Reichssicherheitshauptamt, BAB.

74 Inter-Parliamentary Union, Circular to the Groups No. 6 (1928): Multiplicity of Inter-Parliamentary Organizations, Apr. 12, 1928, Box 721, IPU; "French 'Insult' Moves Fascists To Quit Parley" *New York Herald Tribune* (July 23, 1932).

75 AA, Ref.D. 3176 to Reichstagspräsident Göring, July 31, 1933, R 98279, PAAA.

76 Bülow to Göring, Jan. 24, 1935, R 99205, PAAA.

77 *Verhandlungen des Reichstags*, VII. Wahlperiode 1933, Band 457, 40–1, http://www.reichstagsprotokolle.de; Michael Habersack, *Friedrich Dessauer (1881–1963): Eine politische Biographie des Frankfurter Biophysikers und Reichstagsabgeordneten* (Paderborn: Ferdinand Schöningh, 2011), 259–65.

5. "Wolves Among Lambs": Nazis in the German Reichstag

1 See generally, Heinrich Himmler, *Der Reichstag 1930: Das sterbende System und der Nationalsozialismus* (Munich: F. Eher, 1931).

2 Heinrich Himmler, *Der Reichstag 1930: Das sterbende System und der Nationalsozialismus* (Munich: F. Eher, 1931), 41–61; Peter Longerich, *Heinrich Himmler*, trans. Jeremy Noakes and Lesley Sharpe (Oxford: Oxford University Press, 2012), 116.

3 *Die Verlagserscheinungen des Zentralverlages der NSDAP* (Leipzig: Bibliographischen Abteilung des Börsenvereins der Deutschen Buchhändler, 1941), 12–21; Wilhelm Frick, *Die Nationalsozialisten im Reichstag, 1924–1931* (Munich: Franz Eher, 1932).

4 Nationalsozialistischer Parlamentsdienst, Feb. 22, 1932, NS 46/53, Nationalsozialistische Reichstagsfraktion, BAB.

5 Nationalsozialistischer Parlamentsdienst, Feb. 6, 1932, Feb. 13, 1932, and Feb. 22, 1932, NS 46/53, Nationalsozialistische Reichstagsfraktion, BAB.

6 Volker Ullrich, *Hitler: Ascent, 1889–1939*, trans. Jefferson Chase (New York: Alfred A. Knopf, 2016), 243.

7 Ian Kershaw, *Hitler, 1889–1936: Hubris* (New York: Norton, 1999), 229; Benjamin Carter Hett, *The Death of Democracy: Hitler's Rise to Power and the Downfall of the Weimar Republic* (New York: St. Martin's Griffin, 2018), 66–8.

8 Benjamin Carter Hett, *The Death of Democracy: Hitler's Rise to Power and the Downfall of the Weimar Republic* (New York: St. Martin's Griffin, 2018), 128.

9 Richard J. Evans, *The Coming of the Third Reich* (New York: Penguin, 2003), 275.

10 Martin Döring, *"Parlamentarischer Arm der Bewegung:" Die Nationalsozialisten im Reichstag der Weimarer Republik* (Düsseldorf: Droste, 2001), 15.

11 See, for example, Eberhard Kolb, *The Weimar Republic*, trans. P.S. Falla and R.J. Park (London: Routledge, 2005), 116–35.

12 Martin Döring, *"Parlamentarischer Arm der Bewegung:" Die Nationalsozialisten im Reichstag der Weimarer Republik* (Düsseldorf: Droste, 2001), 20–1.

13 Martin Döring, *"Parlamentarischer Arm der Bewegung,"* 462.

14 Martin Döring, *"Parlamentarischer Arm der Bewegung,"* 425–9.

15 Paul Löbe, *Der Weg war lang* (Berlin: arani, 1954), 138–143.

16 *Der Großdeutsche Reichstag 1938*, IV. Wahlperiode (nach dem 30. Januar 1933) (Berlin: R.v. Decker's Verlag, 1938), 200; "Fabricius, Hans (Eugen

Stephan)," "Akten der Reichskanzlei. Weimarer Republik"
online, accessed Nov. 12, 2023, https://www.bundesarchiv.de
/aktenreichskanzlei/1919-1933/0011/adr/adrag/kap1_6/para2_2.html.

17 Hans Fabricius, *Geschichte der nationalsozialistischen Bewegung* (Berlin:
Industrieverlag Spaeth & Linde, 1937), 5.

18 Fabricius' contemporaries generally glossed over the Nazis' early
parliamentary career, see Wilhelm Fanderl, *Von 7 Mann zum Volk: Illustrierte
Geschichte der NSDAP und der SA* (Oldenburg: Verlag Gerhard Stalling,
1933), and SS-Hauptamt/IV, Lehrplan für Sechsmonatige Schulung
(Berlin: SS-Hauptamt/IV, n.d.). The work of NSDAP parliamentarians
was also minimized by contemporary opponents. See, Konrad Heiden,
Geschichte des Nationalsozialismus (Berlin: Rowohlt, 1932).

19 Richard Suchenwirth, *Deutsche Geschichte: von der gemanischen Vorzeit bis
zur Gegenwart* (Leipzig: Georg Dollheimer, 1941), 601; Friedrich Stieve,
Geschichte des deutschen Volkes (Munich: Oldenbourg, 1943), 456–8.

20 Joachim Lilla, ed., *Statisten in Uniform: Die Mitglieder des Reichstags, 1933–
1945: Ein biographisches Handbuch* (Düsseldorf, Droste, 2004), 131; Martin
Döring, *"Parlamentarischer Arm der Bewegung:" Die Nationalsozialisten im
Reichstag der Weimarer Republik* (Düsseldorf: Droste, 2001), 15–16.

21 Hans Fabricius, *Geschichte der nationalsozialistischen Bewegung* (Berlin:
Industrieverlag Spaeth & Linde, 1937), 33.

22 Diary Entry for May 14, 1928, N 1101/97, Franz Ritter von Epp, BAK;
Hans Fabricius, *Geschichte der nationalsozialistischen Bewegung* (Berlin:
Industrieverlag Spaeth & Linde, 1937), 34; Joseph Goebbels, *Der Angriff:
Aufsätze aus der Kampfzeit* (Munich: Franz Eher, 1935), 73. Hitler's exact
phrase was "Hechte im Karpfenteich," literally "pike in the carp pond,"
but wolves among the lambs captures the metaphor more effectively
in English. This was the phrase mostly commonly recited by NSDAP
parliamentarians, but Goebbels wrote instead of being like wolves among a
herd of sheep.

23 Hans Fabricius, *Geschichte der nationalsozialistischen Bewegung* (Berlin:
Industrieverlag Spaeth & Linde, 1937), 33.

24 Joseph Goebbels, *Tagebücher 1924–1945*, Band 1, ed. Ralf Georg Reuth,
(Munich: Piper, 2003), 332.

25 Hans Fabricius, *Geschichte der nationalsozialistischen Bewegung* (Berlin:
Industrieverlag Spaeth & Linde, 1937), 33–4.

26 Fabricius, *Geschichte der nationalsozialistischen Bewegung*, 33.

27 Joseph Goebbels, *Der Angriff: Aufsätze aus der Kampfzeit* (Munich: Franz Eher,
1935), 61–82; Peter Longerich, *Goebbels: A Biography*, trans. Alan Bance,
Jeremy Noakes, and Lesley Sharpe (New York: Random House, 2015), 100.

28 Thomas Mergel, *Parlamentarische Kultur in der Weimarer Republik*
(Düsseldorf: Droste, 2005), 118–19; Hans Fabricius, *Geschichte der*

nationalsozialistischen Bewegung (Berlin: Industrieverlag Spaeth & Linde, 1937), 33.

29 Wissenschaftliche Dienste des Deutschen Bundestages, "Das Diätenrecht des Reichstages (1871–1918) und der Weimarer Nationalversammlung" (Nov. 27, 2008), https://www.bundestag.de/blob/413332/3ab719bf37 bfe3d44488c84bfe6bdb56/wd-1-254-08-pdf-data.pdf; Hermann Mosler, ed., *Die Verfassung der Weimarer Republik* (Stuttgart, Reclam, 2009), 17; Hans Fabricius, *Geschichte der nationalsozialistischen Bewegung* (Berlin: Industrieverlag Spaeth & Linde, 1937), 33.

30 Unpublished Memiors, originally "Auferstehung oder Untergang," retitled "Auf dem Wege", p. 18, N 1676/4, Maria Reese, BAK.

31 Hermann Mosler, ed., *Die Verfassung der Weimarer Republik* (Stuttgart, Reclam, 2009), 15–16.

32 Hans Stetter, "Aus dem Leben eines Proletariers," p. 22, 1/JSAG000002, Johannes Stetter, FES; Hans Stetter, *Der kommunitische Sumpf: Mein Ausschluss aus der K.P.D.* (Stuttgart: Schwäbische Tagwacht, 1927).

33 Peter Longerich, *Goebbels: A Biography*, trans. Alan Bance, Jeremy Noakes, and Lesley Sharpe (New York: Random House, 2015), 100–47.

34 Hans Fabricius, *Geschichte der nationalsozialistischen Bewegung*, 33.

35 Richard J. Evans, *The Coming of the Third Reich* (New York: Penguin, 2003), 275; Volker Ullrich, *Hitler: Ascent, 1889–1939*, trans. Jefferson Chase (New York: Alfred A. Knopf, 2016), 243.

36 Henk te Velde, "Parliamentary Obstruction and the 'Crisis' of European Parliamentary Politics Around 1900," *Redescriptions* 16, no. 1 (01, 2013): 125–42.

37 Peter D. Stachura, *Gregor Strasser and the Rise of Nazism* (London: George Allen & Unwin, 1983), 92.

38 Margaret Lavinia Anderson, *Practicing Democracy: Elections and Political Culture in Imperial Germany* (Princeton: Princeton University Press, 2000), 295–305; Typewritten Manuscript "Wie alles kam. Das Hitlerreich und sein Zusammenbruch von Heinrich Schnee," p. 14, Nr. 13, VI. HA Nl. Schnee, Heinrich Schnee, GSPK.

39 Volker Ullrich, *Hitler: Ascent, 1889–1939*, trans. Jefferson Chase (New York: Alfred A. Knopf, 2016), 242–3; Martin Döring, *"Parlamentarischer Arm der Bewegung:" Die Nationalsozialisten im Reichstag der Weimarer Republik* (Düsseldorf: Droste, 2001), 270–85; "Rückblick und Ausblick (1871–1956)" von Dr. August Weber, p. 156, N 1670/1, August Weber, BAK; Thomas Mergel, *Parlamentarische Kultur in der Weimarer Republik* (Düsseldorf: Droste, 2005), 436–49.

40 Günter Neliba, *Wilhelm Frick: Der Legalist des Unrechtstaates: Eine politische Biografie* (Paderborn: Ferdinand Schöningh, 1992), 48.

41 Martin Döring, *"Parlamentarischer Arm der Bewegung:" Die Nationalsozialisten im Reichstag der Weimarer Republik* (Düsseldorf: Droste, 2001), 273–6.

42 Gregor Strasser to Löbe, n.d., R 2/4462, Reichsfinanzministerium, BAB.

43 "Rückblick und Ausblick (1871–1956)" von Dr. August Weber, p. 156, N 1670/1, August Weber, BAK.

44 Reminiscences of Gerhart Heinrich Seger: 1950, 32–3, NXCP87-A1495, Columbia Center for Oral History, CUA.

45 Reminiscences of Gerhart Heinrich Seger: 1950, 32–3; Brüning's response to Alfred Rosenberg is found in an original Reichstag audio recording available through Südwestrundfunk: 19:15 at Maximilian Schönherr, "Brüning stellt sich gegen Hitler," SWR, 1 Mar 2018, https://www.swr.de /swr2/wissen/broadcastcontrib-swr-22930.html

46 Hindenburg to Ludendorff, Aug. 25, 1925, and July 29, 1925, N 77/16, Erich Ludendorff, BAF.

47 See, *Hitlers Auseinandersetzung mit Brüning* (Munich: Eher Verlag, 1932).

48 Hugenberg to Hitler, Mar. 20, 1932, N 1231/37, Alfred Hugenberg, BAK.

49 Vorstand der SPD, "Die Reichsregierungen und Reichstagswahlergebnisse von 1918–1933," Box 127, German Subject Collection, HLA; Das deutsche Reich: Reichstagswahl 1930," last accessed July 9, 2018, http://www .gonschior.de/weimar/Deutschland/RT5.html; Das deutsche Reich: Reichstagswahl Juli 1932," accessed July 9, 2018, http://www.gonschior.de /weimar/Deutschland/RT6.html.

50 Martin Döring, *"Parlamentarischer Arm der Bewegung:" Die Nationalsozialisten im Reichstag der Weimarer Republik* (Düsseldorf: Droste, 2001), 333–6.

51 Dingeldey to Göring, Feb. 18, 1933, N 1002/56, Eduard Dingeldey, BAK.

52 Heinrich August Winkler, *Weimar, 1918–1933: die Geschichte der ersten deutschen Demokratie* (Munich: Beck, 1993), 522–4.

53 Guido Knopp, *Göring: Eine Karriere* (Munich: C. Bertelsmann, 2006), 52–3; *Verhandlungen des Reichstags*, VI. Wahlperiode 1932, Band 454, 15.

54 Guido Knopp, *Göring: Eine Karriere* (Munich: C. Bertelsmann, 2006), 53; Martin Döring, *"Parlamentarischer Arm der Bewegung:" Die Nationalsozialisten im Reichstag der Weimarer Republik* (Düsseldorf: Droste, 2001), 337–44; *Verhandlungen des Reichstags*, VI. Wahlperiode 1932, Band 454, 15.

55 Martin Döring, *"Parlamentarischer Arm der Bewegung:" Die Nationalsozialisten im Reichstag der Weimarer Republik* (Düsseldorf: Droste, 2001), 341; Guido Knopp, *Göring: Eine Karriere* (Munich: C. Bertelsmann, 2006), 53.

56 Volker Ullrich, *Hitler: Ascent, 1889–1939*, trans. Jefferson Chase (New York: Alfred A. Knopf, 2016), 241; Henk te Velde, "Parliamentary Obstruction and the 'Crisis' of European Parliamentary Politics Around 1900," *Redescriptions* 16, no. 1 (01, 2013): 142–4.

57 For a Nazi-era biography of Franz Ritter von Epp, see Joseph H. Krumbach, *Franz Ritter von Epp: Ein Leben für Deutschland* (Munich: Franz Eher Verlag, 1940); Winfried Becker, "The Nazi Seizure of Power in Bavaria and the Demise of the Bavarian People's Party," in *From Weimar to*

Hitler: Studies in the Dissolution of the Weimar Republic and the Establishment of the Third Reich, 1932–1934, eds. Hermann Beck and Larry Eugene Jones (New York: Berghahn, 2018), 120; A.D. Harvey, "An Early Hitler Speech," *The Historical Journal,* Sep., 1996, Vol. 39, No. 3 (Sep. 1996): 767.

58 Martin Döring, *"Parlamentarischer Arm der Bewegung:" Die Nationalsozialisten im Reichstag der Weimarer Republik* (Düsseldorf: Droste, 2001), 218–19.

59 Günter Neliba, *Wilhelm Frick: Der Legalist des Unrechtstaates: Eine politische Biografie* (Paderborn: Ferdinand Schöningh, 1992), 44.

60 Kube to Frick, Mar. 11, 1936, Box 1, Collection Carl A. Baehr, HLA.

61 Martin Döring, *"Parlamentarischer Arm der Bewegung:" Die Nationalsozialisten im Reichstag der Weimarer Republik* (Düsseldorf: Droste, 2001), 213.

62 ·Martin Döring, *"Parlamentarischer Arm der Bewegung:" Die Nationalsozialisten im Reichstag der Weimarer Republik* (Düsseldorf: Droste, 2001), 212–17; Markus Müller, *Die Christlich-Nationale Bauern- und Landvolkpartei, 1928–1933* (Düsseldorf: Droste, 2001), 358.

63 Heinrich August Winkler, *Der Weg in die Katastrophe: Arbeiter und Arbeiterbewegung in der Weimarer Republik 1930 bis 1933* (Berlin: J.H.W. Dietz Nachf, 1987), 432; Karl Dietrich Bracher, *Die Auflösung der Weimarer Republik* (Düsseldorf: Droste, 1978), 362; Telegram Frick to "Parteivorstand Deutsche Volkspartei," Oct. 10, 1931, N 1002/37 and Seeckt to Dingeldey, 7 Okt 1931, N 1002/89, Eduard Dingeldey, BAK.

64 Joseph Goebbels, *Der Angriff: Aufsätze aus der Kampfzeit* (Munich: Franz Eher, 1935), 72.

65 Report, n.d., Nr. 25, VI. HA Nl. Schnee, Heinrich Schnee, GSPK.

66 Dingeldey to Göring, Oct. 21, 1931, N 1002/98, Eduard Dingeldey, BAK.

67 Erinnerungen von Josef Felder, 1972, p. 26, ED 312/2, Josef Felder, IZM.

68 Copies of Signed Statements, n.d., NS 46/29, Nationalsozialistische Reichstagsfraktion, BAB; Merkblatt I für die Mitglieder der Reichstagsfraktion der NSDAP, Aug. 30, 1932, N 1410/19, Friedrich Wilhelm Krüger, BAK; Martin Döring, *"Parlamentarischer Arm der Bewegung:" Die Nationalsozialisten im Reichstag der Weimarer Republik* (Düsseldorf: Droste, 2001), 449.

69 Hermann Mosler, ed., *Die Verfassung der Weimarer Republik* (Stuttgart, Reclam, 2009), 11; Martin Döring, *"Parlamentarischer Arm der Bewegung,"* 449.

70 Among others, see Eberhard Kolb, The Weimar Republic, trans. P.S. Falla and R.J. Park (London: Routledge, 2005), 113–15.

71 Martin Döring, *"Parlamentarischer Arm der Bewegung,"* 267; Merkblatt I für die Mitglieder der Reichstagsfraktion der NSDAP, Aug. 30, 1932, N 1410/19, Friedrich Wilhelm Krüger, BAK.

72 Frick to Mitglieder der Reichstagsfraktion der NSDAP, Aug. 22, 1932 and NSDAP Fraktionseinladung, n.d., N 1410/19, Friedrich Wilhelm Krüger, BAK.

73 Merkblatt I für die Mitglieder der Reichstagsfraktion der NSDAP, Aug. 30, 1932, N 1410/19, Friedrich Wilhelm Krüger, BAK.

74 *Reichstags-Handbuch,* IV Wahlperiode (Berlin, Reichsdruckerei, 1932), 129; Knickmann to Frick, Nov. 9, 1932, NS 46/56, Nationalsozialistische Reichstagsfraktion, BAB; "Verzeichnis der Mitglieder des Reichstags nach Wahlkreisen in der Reihenfolge der Kreis- und Reichswahlvorschläge geordnet," *Verhandlungen des Reichstags,* VII. Wahlperiode 1932, Band 455, 7; "Änderungen im Alphabetischen Verzeichnis der Mitglieder des Reichstags," *Verhandlungen des Reichstags,* VII. Wahlperiode 1932, Band 456, Nr. 353; Martin Döring, *"Parlamentarischer Arm der Bewegung:" Die Nationalsozialisten im Reichstag der Weimarer Republik* (Düsseldorf: Droste, 2001), 345.

75 Ian Kershaw, *Hitler: 1889–1936: Hubris* (New York: Norton, 1998), 238; Martin Döring, *"Parlamentarischer Arm der Bewegung:" Die Nationalsozialisten im Reichstag der Weimarer Republik* (Düsseldorf: Droste, 2001), 268; Frick to Mitglieder der Reichstagsfraktion der NSDAP, Aug. 22, 1932, N 1410/19, Friedrich Wilhelm Krüger, BAK; Diary Entry, May 24, 1924, ED 874/5, Gottfried Feder, IZM; Guido Knopp, *Göring: Eine Karriere* (Munich: C. Bertelsmann, 2006), 47; Heft 34, p. 2007, ED 60/8, Otto Wagener, IZM.

76 Frühjahr 1932 Gespräch mit Adolf Hitler, "Memoiren: Besondere Erlebnisse," Gustav Hülser, FES.

77 Fabricius Memo, Nov. 17, 1932, NS 46/4, Nationalsozialistische Reichstagsfraktion, BAB.

78 Diary Entry for June 12, 1928, N 1101/97, Franz Ritter von Epp, BAK.

79 Martin Döring, *"Parlamentarischer Arm der Bewegung,"* 218–19.

80 Peter D. Stachura, *Gregor Strasser and the Rise of Nazism* (London: George Allen & Unwin, 1983), 101–120; Udo Kissenkoetter, *Gregor Strasser und die NSDAP* (Stuttgart: Deutsche Verlags-Anstalt, 1978), 63.

81 Peter D. Stachura, *Gregor Strasser and the Rise of Nazism* (London: George Allen & Unwin, 1983), 110–12.

82 Strasser to Rosenberg, Jan. 15, 1930, Box 1, Rolf Stutz Collection, YMA.

83 Hermann Mosler, ed., *Die Verfassung der Weimarer Republik* (Stuttgart, Reclam, 2009), 11.

6. Gentlemanly National Socialists and Co-operating German Nationalists in the Dutch and Czechoslovak Parliaments of the 1930s

1 Dijxhoorn to Schaik, Mar. 12, 1940, Inv. Nr. 3381, 2.02.22, Tweede Kamer der Staten-Generaal, 1815–1945, NAH; United States Holocaust Memorial Museum, "World War II Dates and Timeline," Holocaust Encyclopedia, Nov. 15, 2021, https://encyclopedia.ushmm.org/content/en/article/world-war-ii-key-dates.

2 See the photos of the military visit in Inv. Nr. 3381, and the folder of invitations, Inv. Nr. 3381, 2.02.22, Tweede Kamer der Staten-Generaal, 1815–1945, NAH

3 Correspondence and List related to Bezoek verdedigingswerken, March 1940, Inv. Nr. 3381 and Commandant van het Veldleger to Griffier including Photos, April 5, 1940, Inv. Nr. 3395, 2.02.22, Tweede Kamer der Staten-Generaal, 1815–1945, NAH; E. Fraenkel-Verkade, "Inleiding," in *Correspondentie van Mr. M.M. Rost van Tonningen, Deel I: 1921–Mei 1942* (The Hague: Martinus Nijhoff, 1967), 73.

4 Materials for Dinner for Parliamentarians, Feb. 15, 1928, Inv. Nr. 39, 2.21.244, Ruijs de Beerenbrouck, NAH.

5 Folder of Invitations and Attendence Lists, Inv. Nr. 3381, 2.02.22, Tweede Kamer der Staten-Generaal, 1815–1945, NAH.

6 Griffier to Van Steijn, Dec. 11, 1936, Inv. Nr. 3381, 2.02.22, Tweede Kamer der Staten-Generaal, 1815–1945, NAH; L.L.H. (Lou) de Visser, Parlement. com, last accessed Nov. 13, 2023, https://www.parlement.com/id /vg09llc23fqf/l_l_h_lou_de_visser.

7 Stanley G. Payne, *A History of Fascism, 1914–1945* (Madison: University of Wisconsin Press, 1995), 290–397; Robert O. Paxton, *The Anatomy of Fascism* (New York: Vintage, 2005), 73–5; Robert O. Paxton, "The Five Stages of Fascism," *The Journal of Modern History* 70, no. 1 (1998): 1–23; Carl Levy, "Fascism, National Socialism and Conservatives in Europe, 1914–1945: Issues for Comparativists," *Contemporary European History* 8, no. 1 (1999): 97–126.

8 Giovanni Capoccia, *Defending Democracy: Reactions to Extremism in Interwar Europe* (Baltimore: Johns Hopkins University Press, 2005), 79–81; Johann Wolfgang Brügel, *Tschechen und Deutsche, 1918–1938* (Munich: Nymphenburger Verlagshandlung, 1967), 237.

9 This information is from the detailed biographies found using the search function on parlement.com for Max graaf de Marchant et d'Ansembourg, Meinoud Marinus Rost van Tonningen, Jan Woudenberg, and Gerhardus Dieters.

10 C. van Geelkerken, *Voor Volk en Vaderland: Tien Jaren Strijd van de Nationaal-Socialistische Beweging der Nederlanden, 1931–14 December 1941* (Utrecht: Nenasu, 1943), 317; E. Fraenkel-Verkade, "Inleiding," in *Correspondentie van Mr. M.M. Rost van Tonningen, Deel I: 1921-Mei 1942* (The Hague: Martinus Nijhoff, 1967), 47.

11 Hans Fabricius, *Geschichte der nationalsozialistischen* Bewegung (Berlin: Industrieverlag Spaeth & Linde, 1937), 33.

12 Peter Bootsma and Carla Hoetink, *Over lijken: Ontoelaatbare taalgebruik in de Tweede Kamer* (Amsterdam: Boom, 2006), 92.

13 Fabricius, *Geschichte der nationalsozialistischen* Bewegung, 34.

14 Memoirs "… of Moskou," Doc. I 1096 a 12, Archief 248, M.V.E.H.J.M. Marchant et d'Ansembourg, NIOD.

15 E. Fraenkel-Verkade, "Inleiding," in *Correspondentie van Mr. M.M. Rost van Tonningen, Deel I: 1921-Mei 1942* (The Hague: Martinus Nijhoff, 1967), 46.

16 Peter Bootsma and Carla Hoetink, *Over lijken: Ontoelaatbare taalgebruik in de Tweede Kamer* (Amsterdam: Boom, 2006), 23–4; Koen Vossen, *Vrij vissen in het Vondelpark: Kleine politieke partijen in Nederland, 1918–1940* (Amsterdam: Wereldbibliotheek, 2003), 173.

17 Koen Vossen, *Vrij vissen in het Vondelpark: Kleine politieke partijen in Nederland, 1918–1940* (Amsterdam: Wereldbibliotheek, 2003), 174–85.

18 Instructie voor de N.S.B. Statenleden signed by Mussert, June 12, 1935, Inv. Nr. 1359, Archief 123, NSB, NIOD.

19 E. Fraenkel-Verkade, "Inleiding," in *Correspondentie van Mr. M.M. Rost van Tonningen, Deel I: 1921-Mei 1942* (The Hague: Martinus Nijhoff, 1967), 46; Memoires, Eerste Deel, Doc. I 1922, Map F, Arch. Nr. 248, H.J. Woudenberg, NIOD.

20 Memoires, Eerste Deel, Doc. I 1922, Map F, Arch. Nr. 248, H.J. Woudenberg, NIOD; Jakob Tj.J. Sinnema, "Dwaarskijkers en Spelbedervers: De visie van de Nationaal-Socialistische Beweging op de Nederlandse Parlementaire Democratie en een Analyse van het Optreden van de NSB-Tweede Kamerfractie aan de hand van concrete voorbeelden," (Doctoraalscriptie Geschiedenis, Universiteit van Amersterdam, 1989), 107, available at NIOD Scr 312, NIOD.

21 M.P. Bruinsma, "M.V.E.H.J.M. graaf de Marchant et d'Ansembourg" (Doctoraalscriptie Geschiedenis, Vrije Universiteit Amsterdam, 1997), 48, available at NIOD Scr 444, NIOD.

22 Memoires, Eerste Deel, Doc. I 1922, Map F, Arch. Nr. 248, H.J. Woudenberg, NIOD.

23 Merkblatt I für die Mitglieder der Reichstagsfraktion der NSDAP, 30 Aug. 1932, N 1410/19, Friedrich Wilhelm Krüger, BAK; J.P. de Valk en A.C.M. Kappelhof, *Dagboeken van P.J.M. Aalberse, 1902–1947* (The Hague: Instituut voor Nederlandse Geschiedenis, 2006), 711.

24 Bob Moore, "Louis de Jong: Writing the History of Occupied Europe," *Contemporary European History* 13 no. 14 (Aug 2005): 417; Bram Mertens, "'An Explosion of Vitality and Creativity'? Memory and Historiography of the Second World War in Belgium and the Netherlands," *Dutch Crossing* 37, no. 1 (2013): 43; E. Fraenkel-Verkade, "Inleiding," in *Correspondentie van Mr. M.M. Rost van Tonningen, Deel I: 1921-Mei 1942* (The Hague: Martinus Nijhoff, 1967), 97–118; "Mr. M.M. Rost van Tonningen," Parlement & Politiek, accessed 10 Jul 2018, https://www.parlement.com/id/vg091l69w5zh /m_m_rost_van_tonningen; F.S. Rost van Tonningen-Heubel, *Op zoek naar mijn huwelijksring* (Erembodegem, Belgium: De Krijger, n.d.).

25 E. Fraenkel-Verkade, "Inleiding," in *Correspondentie van Mr. M.M. Rost van Tonningen, Deel I: 1921-Mei 1942* (The Hague: Martinus Nijhoff, 1967), 17–45.

26 Peter Bootsma and Carla Hoetink, *Over lijken: Ontoelaatbare taalgebruik in de Tweede Kamer* (Amsterdam: Boom, 2006), 46 and 96–8.

27 D. Barnouw, *Rost van Tonningen: fout tot het bittere eind* (Zutphen: Walburg Pers, 1994), 38–9.

28 Memoires, Eerste Deel, Doc. I 1922, Map F, Arch. Nr. 248, H.J. Woudenberg, NIOD.

29 E. Fraenkel-Verkade, "Inleiding," in *Correspondentie van Mr. M.M. Rost van Tonningen, Deel I: 1921-Mei 1942* (The Hague: Martinus Nijhoff, 1967), 48; Peter Bootsma and Carla Hoetink, *Over lijken: Ontoelaatbare taalgebruik in de Tweede Kamer* (Amsterdam: Boom, 2006), 100; "Handgemeen in de Tweede Kamer," *Het Vaderland* (2 Mar 1939) and "Handgemeen in de Tweede Kamer," *De Telegraaf* (March 1, 1939) reproduced in N. Cramer, *Wandelingen door de Handelingen* (The Hague: Staatsuitgeverij, 1974), 199–200.

30 Memoires, Eerste Deel, Doc. I 1922, Map F, Arch. Nr. 248, H.J. Woudenberg, NIOD; G. Puchinger, *Tilanus vertelde mij zijn leven* (Kampen: Kok, 1966), 165.

31 Memoirs "… of Moskou," p. 26, Doc. I 1096 a 12, Archief 248, M.V.E.H.J.M. Marchant et d'Ansembourg, NIOD.

32 Memoires, Eerste Deel, Doc. I 1922, Map F, Arch. Nr. 248, H.J. Woudenberg, NIOD.

33 M.P. Bruinsma, "M.V.E.H.J.M. graaf de Marchant et d'Ansembourg" (Doctoraalscriptie Geschiedenis, Vrije Universiteit Amsterdam, 1997), p. 5–7, available at NIOD Scr 444, and Memoirs "… of Moskou," p. 11–34, Doc. I 1096 a 12, Archief 248, M.V.E.H.J.M. Marchant et d'Ansembourg, both NIOD; "M.V.E.H.J.M. (Max) graaf de Marchant et d'Ansembourg," Parlement & Politiek, accessed July 10, 2018, https://www.parlement.com /id/vg09ll35q2y8/m_v_e_h_j_m_max_graaf_de_marchant_et_d.

34 Theo Gerritse, *Collaboreren voor een betere wereld: de memoires van vier Nederlandse nationaal-socialisten* (Soesterberg: Aspekt, 2007), 24; Memoirs "… of Moskou," 33–4, Doc. I 1096 a 12, Archief 248, M.V.E.H.J.M. Marchant et d'Ansembourg and Organisatieboek, Openluchtbijeenkomst Amstenrade, Aug. 14, 1939, Inv. Nr. 1714, Archief 123, Nationaal-Socialistische Beweging, NIOD.

35 Memoirs "… of Moskou," p. 35, Doc. I 1096 a 12, Archief 248, M.V.E.H.J.M. Marchant et d'Ansembourg, and D'Ansembourg to M.J.H. Cobbenhagen, 25 Jan. 1937 and Prof. Dr. M.J.H. Cobbenhagen to d'Ansembourg, Jan. 26, 1937, Inv. nr. 1694, Archief 123, Nationaal-Socialistische Beweging, both NIOD.

36 M.P. Bruinsma, "M.V.E.H.J.M. graaf de Marchant et d'Ansembourg" (Doctoraalscriptie Geschiedenis, Vrije Universiteit Amsterdam, 1997), 42, available at NIOD Scr 444, NIOD; M.V.E.H.J.M. (Max) graaf de Marchant et d'Ansembourg, Parlement.com, accessed 28 Jul 2024, https://www

.parlement.com/id/vg09ll35q2y8/m_v_e_h_j_m_max_graaf_de_marchant
_et_d; Eerste Kamerfractie Nationaal-Socialistische Beweging (NSB),
Parlement.com, accessed July 28, 2024, https://www.parlement.com/id
/vjs6lzhff8px/eerste_kamerfractie_nationaal; "Verkiezingen Eerste
Kamer," *De Tijd: godsdienstig-staatkundig dagblad* (26 Jul 1935), Delpher.

37 "De N.S.B. in Indië," *Deli Courant* (Sep. 3, 1938), Delpher.

38 Memoires, Eerste Deel, p. 37, Doc. I 1922, Map F, Arch. Nr. 248, H.J.
Woudenberg, NIOD.

39 M.P. Bruinsma, "M.V.E.H.J.M. graaf de Marchant et d'Ansembourg"
(Doctoraalscriptie Geschiedenis, Vrije Universiteit Amsterdam, 1997), 49,
available at NIOD Scr 444, NIOD.

40 Memoires, Eerste Deel, Doc. I 1922, Map F, Arch. Nr. 248, H.J.
Woudenberg, NIOD.

41 Memoires, Eerste Deel, p. 35, Doc. I 1922, Map F, Arch. Nr. 248, H.J.
Woudenberg, NIOD.

42 Memoirs "… of Moskou," p. 46, Doc. I 1096 a 12, Archief 248,
M.V.E.H.J.M. Marchant et d'Ansembourg, NIOD.

43 Bloch to d'Ansembourg, Feb. 4, 1937, and Feb. 12, 1937, inv. nr. 1694,
Archief 123, Nationaal-Socialistische Beweging, NIOD.

44 Memoirs "… of Moskou," 3, 33–42.

45 Edwin Klijn and Robin te Slaa, *De NSB: Deel 2 Twee werelden botsen, 1936–
1940* (Amsterdam: Boom, 2021), 399–400.

46 Memoires, Eerste Deel, p. 10, 41, Doc. I 1922, Map F, Arch. Nr. 248, H.J.
Woudenberg, NIOD.

47 Piet de Rooy, "Een zoekende tijd: De ongemakkelijke democratie, 1913–
1949" in *Land van kleine gebaren: Een politieke geschiedenis van Nederland, 1780–
1990*, eds. Remieg Aerts et al. (Nijmegen: Uitgeverij SUN, 1999), 196–201;
Piet de Rooy, *Republiek van rivaliteiten: Nederland sinds 1813* (Amsterdam:
Mets&Schilt, 2002), 175–80.

48 Peter van Dam, *Staat van verzuiling: Over een Nederlandse mythe* (Amsterdam:
Wereldbibliotheek, 2011), 14–35.

49 Alexander van Kessel, "Bekritisserd Instituut in een Verzuilde Context:
De Tweede Kamer tussen Pacificatie en Wereldoorlog," in *In Dit Huis:
Twee Eeuwen Tweede Kamer*, eds. Remieg Aerts, et al. (Amsterdam: Boom,
2015), 362–9; Henk te Velde, "Van Grondwet tot Grondwet: Oefenen
met Parlement, Partij en Schaalvergrooting," in *Land van kleine gebaren:
Een politieke geschiedenis van Nederland, 1780–1990*, eds. Remieg Aerts
et al., (Nijmegen: SUN, 1999), 175; Rob Hartmans, *Vijandige broeders?
De Nederlandse social-democratie en het national-socialisme, 1922–1940*
(Amsterdam: Ambo, 2012), 239.

50 Peter van Dam, *Staat van verzuiling: Over een Nederlandse mythe* (Amsterdam:
Wereldbibliotheek, 2011), 59.

51 Peter van Dam, *Staat van verzuiling: Over een Nederlandse mythe* (Amsterdam: Wereldbibliotheek, 2011), 18; Benjamin Carter Hett, *The Death of Democracy: Hitler's Rise to Power and the Downfall of the Weimar Republic* (New York: St. Martin's Griffin, 2018), 67–8.

52 Harry Klepetar, *Seit 1918 … Eine Geschichte der Tschechoslowakischen Republik* (Ostrava: Verlag Julius Kittls Nachfolger, 1937), 16–18; Alice Garrigue Masaryk, *Alice Garrigue Masaryk, 1879–1966: Her life as recorded in her own words and by her friends* (Pittsburgh: University of Pittsburgh University Center for International Studies, 1980), 104; Andrea Orzoff, *Battle for the Castle: The Myth of Czechoslovakia in Europe, 1914–1948* (Oxford: Oxford Univerity Press, 2009), 62; Antonín Boháč, "Die Nationalitäten in der Tschechoslovakischen Republik: Statistik und gegenwärtigen Stand," *Die Tschechoslovakische Republik: Ihre Staatsidee in der Vergangenheit und Gegenwart*, Vol. 2 (Prague: Veritas Verlag, 1937), 71–9; Václav L. Beneš, "Czechoslovak Democracy and Its Problems," in *A History of the Czechoslovak Republic, 1918–1948*, eds. Victor S. Mamatey and Radomír Luža (Princeton: Princeton University Press, 1973), 39–40.

53 Jiří Kopica, *Boj o pohraničí: Demonstrace 4. března 1919 v Československu* (Kadaň: Karolinum, 2012), 20–40; Harry Klepetar, *Seit 1918 … Eine Geschichte der Tschechoslowakischen Republik* (Ostrava: Verlag Julius Kittls Nachfolger, 1937), 95–102.

54 J. Chemelař, "Die nationale Frage seit dem Weltkrieg," *Die Tschechoslovakische Republik: Ihre Staatsidee in der Vergangenheit und Gegenwart*, Vol. 2 (Prague: Veritas Verlag, 1937), 57–58; Hans Krebs, *Kampf in Böhmen* (Berlin: Volk und Reich Verlag, 1938), 124, 173–4; Veronika Arndt, *Die Fahne von Saaz: Konrad Henlein in seiner Zeit* (Magdeburg: Helmuth-Block-Verlag, 1998), 68; F. Spurný, "Spina, Franz" in *Österreichisches Biographisches Lexikon 1815–1950*, Band 13 (Vienna: Verlag der Österreichischen Akademie der Wissenschaften, 2010), 29–30; Martin K. Bachstein, *Wenzel Jaksch und die Sudetendeutsche Sozialdemokratie* (Munich: Oldenbourg, 1974).

55 Franz Jesser, *Volkstumkampf und Ausgleich im Herzen Europas: Erinnerungen eines sudetendeutschen Politikers* (Nuremberg: Helmut Preußler Verlag, 1983), 98–9; Giovanni Capoccia, *Defending Democracy: Reactions to Extremism in Interwar Europe* (Baltimore: Johns Hopkins University Press, 2005), 92–5.

56 Johann Wolfgang Brügel, *Tschechen und Deutsche, 1918–1938* (Munich: Nymphenburger Verlagshandlung, 1967), 237–50; Michael Walsh Campbell, "A Crisis of Democracy: Czechoslovakia and the Rise of Sudeten German Nationalism, 1918–1938," (PhD Diss., University of Washington, 2003), 91–3; František Kolář, et al., eds., *Politická elita meziválečného Československa, 1918–1938: Kdo byl kdo* (Prague: Pražská edice, 1998), 83–6.

57 Tara Zahra, *Kidnapped Souls: National Indifference and the Battle for Children in the Bohemian Lands* (Ithaca: Cornell University Press, 2008), 135, 143; Věra

Olivová, *Dějiny první republiky* (Prague: Karolinum, 2000), 191–2; Antonín Klimek, *Boj o hrad: 2. Kdo po Masarykovi? Vnitropolitický vývoj Československa 1926–1935 na půdorysu zápasu o prezidentské nástupnictví* (Prague: Panevropa, 1998), 399; Jaroslav Kučera, "Hitler u moci a čeští Němci" in *Republika československá, 1918–1939*, eds. Dagmar Hájková and Pavel Horák (Prague: Nakladatelství Lidové noviny, 2018), 811.

58 Jaroslav Kučera, "Hitler u moci a čeští Němci" in *Republika československá, 1918–1939*, eds. Dagmar Hájková and Pavel Horák (Prague: Nakladatelství Lidové noviny, 2018), 808–9.

59 Cartoon "Der Hampelmann und wer ihn an der Strippe hat" in *Nordböhmischer Volksbote*, May 25, 1935, 825/503, inv. číslo 31, číslo kartónu 20, Sudetoněmecká strana (SdP), 1933–1938 – Dodatky, NAP.

60 Reminiscences of Jan Papanek: 1951, p. 81, NXCP87-A621, Columbia Center for Oral History, CUA.

61 Edvard Beneš, *Paměti: Od Mnichova k nové válce a k novému vítězství* (Prague: Naše vojsko, 2004), 467.

62 Mark Cornwall, "Heinrich Rutha and the Unraveling of a Homosexual Scandal in 1930s Czechoslovakia," *GLQ: A Journal of Lesbian and Gay Studies* 8, no. 3 (2002): 323; Giovanni Capoccia, *Defending Democracy: Reactions to Extremism in Interwar Europe* (Baltimore: Johns Hopkins University Press, 2005), 71–8.

63 Věra Olivová, *The Doomed Democracy: Czechoslovakia in a Disrupted Europe, 1914–38*, trans. George Theiner (London: Sidgwick & Jackson, 1972), 191; J.W. Bruegel, "The Germans in Pre-war Czechoslovakia," in *A History of the Czechoslovak Republic, 1918–1948*, eds. Victor S. Mametey and Radomír Luža (Princeton: Princeton University Press, 1973), 182; "Brügel, Johann Wolfgang," ENCYKLOPEDIE ČSSD, accessed 4 July 2018, http://www.historiecssd.cz/b/brugel-johann-wolfgang/; "prof. JUDr. Johann Wolfgang Brügel," Internetová encyklopedie dějin Brna, last modified June 29, 2018, https://encyklopedie.brna.cz/home-mmb/?acc=profil _osobnosti&load=8710; Johann Wolfgang Brügel, *Tschechen und Deutsche, 1918–1938* (Munich: Nymphenburger Verlagshandlung, 1967), 237; Radomír Luža, *The Transfer of the Sudeten Germans: A Study of Czech-German Relations, 1933–1962* (New York: New York University Press, 1964), 60; Věra Olivová, *Dějiny první republiky* (Prague: Karolinum, 2000), 209.

64 Giovanni Capoccia, *Defending Democracy: Reactions to Extremism in Interwar Europe* (Baltimore: Johns Hopkins University Press, 2005), 71–8; Michael Walsh Campbell, "A Crisis of Democracy: Czechoslovakia and the Rise of Sudeten German Nationalism, 1918–1938," (PhD Diss., University of Washington, 2003), 6.

65 Radomír Luža, *The Transfer of the Sudeten Germans: A Study of Czech-German Relations, 1933–1962* (New York: New York University Press, 1964), 60.

66 *Documents on German Foreign Policy, 1918–1945*, Series D, Volume II (Washington: Government Printing Office, 1949), 50–61.

67 Mark Cornwall, *The Devil's Wall: The Nationalist Youth Mission of Heinz Rutha* (Cambridge: Harvard University Press, 2012), 212, 234–54.

68 Věra Olivová, *Dějiny první republiky* (Prague: Karolinum, 2000), 191–6.

69 Mark Cornwall, "'A Leap into Ice-Cold Water': The Manoeuvres of the Henlein Movement in Czechoslovakia, 1933–1938," in *Czechoslovakia in a Nationalist and Fascist Europe, 1918–1948*, eds. Mark Cornwall and R.J.W. Evans (Oxford: Oxford University Press, 2007), 129–42.

70 Milan Sládek, *Němci v Čechách: Německá menšina v českých zemích a československsku, 1848–1946* (Prague: pragma, 2002), 63.

71 Jeremy King, *Budweisers into Czechs and Germans: A Local History of Bohemian Politics, 1848–1948* (Princeton: Princeton University Press, 2002), 169–72.

72 Caitlin E. Murdock, *Changing Places: Society, Culture, and Territory in the Saxon-Bohemian Borderlands, 1870–1946* (Ann Arbor: University of Michigan Press, 2010), 189–95.

73 Ludwig Weichselbaumer, *Walter Brand (1907–1980): Ein sudetendeutscher Politiker um Spannungsfeld zwischen Autonomie und Anschluss* (Munich: Sudetendeutsches Archiv, 2008), 308.

74 Nine Point Memo beginning "SS-Grenzüberwachungsstellen Waldsassen," n.d., 296/435, inv. číslo 28 (složka 1), číslo kartónu 51, and Two Unsigned Letters to Reichsministerium für Volksaufklärung und Propaganda, Abt. Auslandstheater, Dec. 11, 1936, 296/435, inv. číslo 1 (složka 7), číslo kartónu 4, Sudetoněmecká strana (SdP), 1933–1938, NAP.

75 Antonín Klimek, *Boj o hrad: 2. Kdo po Masarykovi? Vnitropolitický vývoj Československa 1926–1935 na půdorysu zápasu o prezidentské nástupnictví* (Prague: Panevropa, 1998), 400; Jaroslav Kučera, "Hitler u moci a čeští Němci" in *Republika československá, 1918–1939*, eds. Dagmar Hájková and Pavel Horák (Prague: Nakladatelství Lidové noviny, 2018), 815; Věra Olivová, *Dějiny první republiky* (Prague: Karolinum, 2000), 196; Milan Sládek, *Němci v Čechách: Německá menšina v českých zemích a československsku, 1848–1946* (Prague: pragma, 2002), 63; Jeremy King, *Budweisers into Czechs and Germans: A Local History of Bohemian Politics, 1848–1948* (Princeton: Princeton University Press, 2002), 171–7; Caitlin E. Murdock, *Changing Places : Society, Culture, and Territory in the Saxon-Bohemian Borderlands, 1870–1946* (Ann Arbor: University of Michigan Press, 2010), 190.

76 Taub to Danneberg, Oct. 27, 1925, M129, Partei-Archiv vor 1934, VGA; Dessauer to Brüning Apr. 12, 1932, FD 12, Friedrich Dessauer, KFZ.

77 Jaroslav Kučera, "Hitler u moci a čeští Němci" in *Republika československá, 1918–1939*, eds. Dagmar Hájková and Pavel Horák (Prague: Nakladatelství Lidové noviny, 2018), photo and caption on 809.

78 Folder "Für den Fall der Auflösung der Partei," Jan 1935, 296/435, inv. číslo 1 (složka 1), číslo kartónu 1, Sudetoněmecká strana (SdP), 1933–1938, NAP.

79 Radomír Luža, *The Transfer of the Sudeten Germans: A Study of Czech-German Relations, 1933–1962* (New York: New York University Press, 1964), 60.

80 Folder "Für den Fall der Auflösung der Partei," Jan 1935, 296/435, inv. číslo 1 (složka 1), číslo kartónu 1, Sudetoněmecká strana (SdP), 1933–1938, NAP.

81 Český statistický úřad, "Volby do Národního shromáždění 1920 až 1935," 31 Mar. 2006, https://www.czso.cz/csu/czso/volby-do-narodniho-shromazdeni-1920-az-1935-n-2hwwxuf57q; "Rundschreiben" of the "Gemeinsamer Parlamentarischer Klub der SdP," n.d., in 296/435, inv. číslo 28 (složka 1), číslo kartónu 51, Sudetoněmecká strana (SdP), 1933–1938, NAP.

82 Alfred von Klement, *Geschichte des Deutschen Hauses in Prag* (Prague: J.G. Calve'sche Universitäts-Buchhandlung, 1938) 26–7; Oskar Ullrich, *Sie kamen aus aller Herren Ländern: Aus dem Tagebuch des SdP-Dolmetschers* (Karlsbad: Adam Kraft Verlag, 1940), 66–70.

83 Gemeinsamer Parlamentarischer Klub der SdP, Rundschreiben Nr. 27, n.d., 296/435, inv. číslo 28 (složka 1), číslo kartónu 51, Sudetoněmecká strana (SdP), 1933–1938, NAP.

84 Konstantin Höß, *Die SdP im Parlament: Ein Jahresbericht 1935/36* (Karlsbad: Verlag Karl H. Frank, 1937), 12; Oskar Ullrich, *Sie kamen aus aller Herren Ländern: Aus dem Tagebuch des SdP-Dolmetschers* (Karlsbad: Adam Kraft Verlag, 1940), 68; Gemeinsamer Parlamentarischer Klub der SdP, Rundschreiben Nr. 17, n.d., 296/435, inv. číslo 28 (složka 1), číslo kartónu 51, Sudetoněmecká strana (SdP), 1933–1938, NAP; R.L. Bytwerk, "Fritz Reinhardt and the Rednerschule der NSDAP," *The Quarterly Journal of Speech* 67, no. 3 (1981): 298–309. https://doi.org/10.1080/00335638109383574.

85 Gemeinsamer Parlamentarischer Klub der SdP, Rundschreiben Nr. 27, n.d., 296/435, inv. číslo 28 (složka 1), číslo kartónu 51, Sudetoněmecká strana (SdP), 1933–1938, NAP.

86 Gemeinsamer Parlamentarischer Klub der SdP, Rundschreiben Nr. 2–4, n.d., 296/435, inv. číslo 28 (složka 1), číslo kartónu 51, Sudetoněmecká strana (SdP), 1933–1938, NAP.

87 Oskar Ullrich, *Sie kamen aus aller Herren Ländern: Aus dem Tagebuch des SdP-Dolmetschers* (Karlsbad: Adam Kraft Verlag, 1940), 57–61; Letters to Labour Party Officials, n.d., 24, Wenzel Jaksch, Sudetendeutsches Archiv, BHSA; *Documents on German Foreign Policy, 1918–1945*, Series D, Volume II (Washington: Government Printing Office, 1949), 124–5; Związek Polaków w Czechosłowacji to Gemeinsamer Parlamentarischer Klub der SdP, 7 Jun

1938, 296/435, inv. číslo 28 (složka 1), číslo kartónu 51, Sudetoněmecká strana (SdP), 1933–1938, NAP.

88 Antonín Klimek, *Boj o hrad: 2. Kdo po Masarykovi? Vnitropolitický vývoj Československa 1926–1935 na půdorysu zápasu o prezidentské nástupnictví* (Prague: Panevropa, 1998), 403.

89 Joseph Goebbels, *Der Angriff: Aufsätze aus der Kampfzeit* (Munich: Franz Eher, 1935), 72.

90 René Küpper, *Karl Hermann Frank (1898–1946): Politische Biographie eines sudetendeutschen Nationalsozialisten* (Munich: R. Oldenbourg Verlag, 2010), 70–2.

91 Manuscript "Die SdP im Parlament," n.d., 296/435, inv. číslo 1 (složka 8), číslo kartónu 4, Sudetoněmecká strana (SdP), 1933–1938, NAP.

92 Küpper, *Karl Hermann Frank (1898–1946,* 70–2; Gemeinsamer Parlamentarischer Klub der SdP, Rundschreiben Nr. 21, n.d., 296/435, inv. číslo 28 (složka 1), číslo kartónu 51, Sudetoněmecká strana (SdP), 1933–1938, NAP.

93 Opis k číslo 23656 pres. min. vnitra, 16 Oct. 1935, inv. č. 1054, D 13444/38/E and Interior Ministry to Kancelář prezidenta republiky, Dec. 27, 1935, inv. č. 1054, D 13444/38/E, Archivní fond KPR, 1919–1947, AKPR

94 Denkschrift from Wollner to Ministers, Jan. 15, 1937, 296/435, inv. číslo 28 (složka 6), číslo kartónu 52, Sudetoněmecká strana (SdP), 1933–1938, NAP.

95 *The Constitution of the Czechoslovak Republic* (Prague: Édition de la société l'effort de la Tchécoslovaquie, 1920), 25.

96 Konstantin Höß, *Die SdP im Parlament: Ein Jahresbericht 1935/36* (Karlsbad: Verlag Karl H. Frank, 1937), 25.

97 Höß, *Die SdP im Parlament,* 27–9.

98 Tara Zahra, *Kidnapped Souls: National Indifference and the Battle for Children in the Bohemian Lands* (Ithaca: Cornell University Press, 2008), 161–2.

99 SdP Unsigned Letter to Rudolf Bechyně, Feb. 17, 1938, Richter to Horn, Feb. 17, 1938, SdP Unsigned Letter to Dostal, Feb. 11, 1938, R to Martha Horn, June, 23, 1938, 296/435, inv. číslo 28 (složka 1), číslo kartónu 51, Sudetoněmecká strana (SdP), 1933–1938, NAP.

100 Ludwig Weichselbaumer, "Walter Brand (1907–1980): Weg und Wirken eines sudetendeutschen Politikers" (PhD diss, Ludwig-Maximilians-Universität zu München, 2004), 249.

101 Ludwig Weichselbaumer, *Walter Brand (1907–1980): Ein sudetendeutscher Politiker um Spannungsfeld zwischen Autonomie und Anschluss* (Munich: Sudetendeutsches Archiv, 2008), 324; Veronika Arndt, *Die Fahne von Saaz: Konrad Henlein in seiner Zeit* (Magdeburg: Helmuth-Block-Verlag, 1998), 7; Walter Brand, *Auf verlorenem Posten: Ein sudetendeutscher Politiker zwischen Autonomie und Anschluß* (Munich: Verlagshaus Sudetenland GmbH, 1985), 64.

102 Walter Brand, *Auf verlorenem Posten: Ein sudetendeutscher Politiker zwischen Autonomie und Anschluß* (Munich: Verlagshaus Sudetenland GmbH, 1985), 93–5.

103 Heidrun Dolezel and Stephan Dolezel, eds., *Deutsche Gesandtschaftsberichte aus Prag*, Vol. IV (Munich: R. Oldenbourg Verlag, 1983), 164.

104 Circular Letter from the Gruppe der Aufrechten in der SHF, Oct. 18, 1934, 296/435, inv. číslo 1 (složka 8), číslo kartónu 4, Sudetoněmecká strana (SdP), 1933–1938, NAP.

105 Konrad Henlein to President Masaryk, Mar. 5, 1935, 296/435, inv. číslo 1 (složka 8), číslo kartónu 4, Sudetoněmecká strana (SdP), 1933–1938, NAP.

106 Beneš to Henlein, Jan. 28, 1936 and June 2, 1936, 296/435, inv. číslo 1 (složka 8), číslo kartónu 4 and Tajemník ministra národní obrany and Henlein, Jan. 18, 1935, Osobní tajemník ministra vnitra to Henlein, 18 Jan. 1935, and Hodža to Henlein, Jan. 19, 1935, 296/435, inv. číslo 1 (složka 8), číslo kartónu 4, Sudetoněmecká strana (SdP), 1933–1938, NAP.

107 Walter Brand, *Auf verlorenem Posten: Ein sudetendeutscher Politiker zwischen Autonomie und Anschluß* (Munich: Verlagshaus Sudetenland GmbH, 1985), 112.

108 Heidrun Dolezel and Stephan Dolezel, eds., *Deutsche Gesandtschaftsberichte aus Prag*, Vol. IV (Munich: R. Oldenbourg Verlag, 1983), 151–4.

109 Ludwig Weichselbaumer, "Walter Brand (1907–1980): Weg und Wirken eines sudetendeutschen Politikers," (PhD diss, Ludwig-Maximilians-Universität zu München, 2004), 248–9; Minutes of Meeting between Sandner and Interior Minister, Oct. 22, 1935, 296/435, inv. číslo 28 (složka 6), číslo kartónu 52, Konrád Henlein Cesty do zahraničí, 1936–1937, 296/435, inv. číslo 1 (složka 5), číslo kartónu 3, Henlein to Prime Minister, Feb. 5, 1936, and Note about Phone Call with Bartoš, Feb. 7, 1936, 296/435, inv. číslo 1 (složka 8), číslo kartónu 4, all Sudetoněmecká strana (SdP), 1933–1938, NAP.

110 Andrea Orzoff, *Battle for the Castle: The Myth of Czechoslovakia in Europe, 1914–1948* (Oxford: Oxford University Press, 2009), 175; Věra Olivová, *Dějiny první republiky* (Prague: Karolinum, 2000), 211–12; Milan Sládek, *Němci v Čechách: Německá menšina v českých zemích a československu, 1848–1946* (Prague: pragma, 2002), 64–5; Mark Cornwall, "'A Leap into Ice-Cold Water': The Manoeuvres of the Henlein Movement in Czechoslovakia, 1933–1938," in *Czechoslovakia in a Nationalist and Fascist Europe, 1918–1948*, eds. Mark Cornwall and R.J.W. Evans (Oxford: Oxford University Press, 2007), 137–9.

111 Konrad Henlein, "The German Minority in Czechoslovakia," *International Affairs (Royal Institute of International Affairs 1931–1939)* 15, no. 4 (1936): 561–72.

112 Aussprache Konrad Henleins mit Herrn Ministerpräsidenten Dr. Hodža, Sep. 16, 1937, 296/435, inv. číslo 28 (složka 6), číslo kartónu 52 and Mitteilung für alle Haup- und Kreisleiter, sowie die Abgeordenten und Senatoren, Sep. 16, 1937, 296/435, inv. číslo 28 (složka 6), číslo kartónu 52, Sudetoněmecká strana (SdP), 1933–1938, NAP.

113 Aussprache Konrad Henleins mit Herrn Ministerpräsidenten Dr.
    Hodža, Sep. 16, 1937, 296/435, inv. číslo 28 (složka 6), číslo kartónu 52,
    Sudetoněmecká strana (SdP), 1933–1938, NAP; Milan Hodža, *Schicksal
    Donauraum: Erinnerungen,* trans. Valerie Neumann (Vienna: Amalthea,
    1995), 229; Arnold Suppan, "Vzájomné zahranično-politické activity Hodžu
    a Schuschnigga v rokoch 1936 a 1937," in *Milan Hodža: Štátnik a Politik,*
    eds. Miroslav Pekník et al. (Bratislava: Veda vydavateľstvo, 2002), 267.
114 Giovanni Capoccia, *Defending Democracy: Reactions to Extremism in Interwar
    Europe* (Baltimore: Johns Hopkins University Press, 2005), 93; Milan
    Hodža, *Schicksal Donauraum: Erinnerungen,* Trans. Valerie Neumann
    (Vienna: Amalthea, 1995), 229.
115 *Documents on German Foreign Policy, 1918–1945,* Series D, Volume II
    (Washington: Government Printing Office, 1949), 25–9.
116 *Documents on German Foreign Policy, 1918–1945,* Series D, Volume II, 234–5.
117 Edvard Beneš, *Mnichovské dny: Paměti* (Prague: Svoboda, 1968), 28–9.
118 *Documents on German Foreign Policy, 1918–1945,* Series D, Volume II
    (Washington: Government Printing Office, 1949), 173–4.
119 *Documents on German Foreign Policy, 1918–1945,* Series D, Volume II, 197–8.
120 *Documents on German Foreign Policy, 1918–1945,* Series D, Volume II, 276.
121 Notes on Conversation between Henlein, Frank, and Hodža, May 23,
    1938, 296/435, inv. číslo 28 (složka 8), číslo kartónu 53 and Minutes of
    Conversation with Beneš, Kundt, Sebekovsky, Aug. 25, 1938, 296/435,
    inv. číslo 28 (složka 6), číslo kartónu 52, Sudetoněmecká strana (SdP),
    1933–1938, NAP.
122 Martin Döring, *"Parlamentarischer Arm der Bewegung:" Die Nationalsozialisten
    im Reichstag der Weimarer Republik* (Düsseldorf: Droste, 2001), 341; Guido
    Knopp, *Göring: Eine Karriere* (Munich: C. Bertelsmann, 2006), 53.
123 C. van Geelkerken, *Voor Volk en Vaderland: Tien Jaren Strijd van de Nationaal-
    Socialistische Beweging der Nederlanden, 1931–14 December 1941* (Utrecht:
    Nenasu, 1943), 317–25.
124 Kundt to Henlein, July 15, 1938, 296/435, inv. číslo 2 (složka 2), číslo
    kartónu 6, Sudetoněmecká strana (SdP), 1933–1938, NAP; Martin Döring,
    *"Parlamentarischer Arm der Bewegung:" Die Nationalsozialisten im Reichstag der
    Weimarer Republik* (Düsseldorf: Droste, 2001), 15–16.
125 Vorstand der SPD, "Die Reichsregierungen und Reichstagswahlergebnisse
    von 1918–1933," Box 127, German Subject Collection, HLA.

7. From Cross-Cutting Interconnections to the Primacy of Parties in Interwar Austria and Weimar Germany

  1 Walther Lambach, *Die Herrschaft der Fünfhundert: Ein Bild des parlamentarischen
    Lebens im neuen Deutschland* (Hamburg: Hanseatische Verlagsanstalt, 1926), 5–7.

2 Walther Lambach, *Die Herrschaft der Fünfhundert*, 11–52

3 Lambach, *Die Herrschaft der Fünfhundert*, 12.

4 Lambach, *Die Herrschaft der Fünfhundert*, 32.

5 Lambach, *Die Herrschaft der Fünfhundert*, 75–7.

6 Lambach, *Die Herrschaft der Fünfhundert*, 72–86.

7 Lambach, *Die Herrschaft der Fünfhundert*, 149–50; *Reichstags-Handbuch*, V. Wahlperiode (1930) (Berlin: Reichsdrückerei, 1930), 374–5.

8 Hans Fabricius, *Geschichte der nationalsozialistischen Bewegung* (Berlin: Industrieverlag Spaeth & Linde, 1937), 33–4; G. Puchinger, *Tilanus vertelde mij zijn leven* (Kampen: Kok, 1966), 165.

9 Copies of Signed Statements, n.d., NS 46/29, Nationalsozialistische Reichstagsfraktion, BAB.

10 Daniel Ziblatt, *Conservative Parties and the Birth of Democracy* (Cambridge: Cambridge University Press, 2017), 297–306, 363–8.

11 C. Earl Edmondson, "Heimwehren und andere Wehrverbände," in *Handbuch des politischen Systems Österreichs, Erste Republik, 1918–1933*, eds. Tálos et al. (Vienna: Manzsche Verlags- und Universitätsbuchhandlung, 1995), 61–5, 270–2; Wolfgang Maderthaner, "12 February 1934: Social Democracy and Civil War," in *Austria in the Twentieth Century*, eds. Rolf Steiniger, Günter Bischof, and Michael Gehler (New Brunswick, NJ: Transaction Publishers, 2002), 50–3.

12 Anton Pelinka, *Die gescheiterte Republik: Kultur und Politik in Österreich, 1918–1938* (Vienna: Böhlau, 2017), 5–9, 281–90; Dieter A. Binder, "Fresko in Schwarz? Das christlichsoziale Lager," and Kurt Bauer, "'Heil Deutschösterreich!' Das deutschnationale Lager zu Beginn der Ersten Republik," in *Das Werden der Ersten Republik … der Rest ist Österreich*, eds. Helmut Konrad and Wolfgang Maderthaner (Vienna: Carl Gerold's Sohn, 2008).

13 Evan Burr Bukey, *Hitler's Hometown: Linz, Austria, 1908–1945* (Bloomington: Indiana University Press, 1986), 39–57; Janek Wasserman, *Black Vienna: The Radical Right in the Red City, 1918–1938* (Ithaca: Cornell University Press, 2014), 8–10.

14 Erin R. Hochman, "The Failed Republic, 1918–1933?," in *Democracy in Austria*, eds. Günter Bischof and David M. Wineroither (New Orleans: University of New Orleans Press, 2019), 45–63.

15 Evan Burr Bukey, *Hitler's Hometown: Linz, Austria, 1908–1945* (Bloomington: Indiana University Press, 1986), 39–60.

16 Erin R. Hochman, "The Failed Republic, 1918–1933?," in *Democracy in Austria*, eds. Günter Bischof and David M. Wineroither (New Orleans: University of New Orleans Press, 2019), 61.

17 Visiting Card Seipel to Danneberg, June 3, 1922, and Seipel to Danneberg, Oct. 1, 1930, Inv. 10, Robert Danneberg, IISG; Janek Wasserman, *Black*

Vienna: The Radical Right in the Red City, 1918–1938 (Ithaca: Cornell University Press, 2014), 1–2; Roland Pacher, *Robert Danneberg. Eine politische Biografie* (Peter Lang, Frankfurt am Main 2014); Klemens von Klemperer, *Ignaz Seipel: Christian Statesman in a Time of Crisis* (Princeton: Princeton University Press, 1973).

18 Julius Deutsch, *Ein weiter Weg: Lebenserinnerungen* (Zurich: Amalthea-Verlag, 1960), 160.

19 Martin Kitchen, *The Coming of Austrian Fascism* (London: Croom Helm, 1980), 119–20; Julius Deutsch, *Ein weiter Weg: Lebenserinnerungen* (Zurich: Amalthea-Verlag, 1960), 154–5; Treaty of Peace between the Allied and Associated Powers and Austria, St. Germain-en-Laye, September 10, 1919, Australian Treaty Series, accessed July 4, 2018, http://www.austlii.edu .au/au/other/dfat/treaties/1920/3.html; "Die Waffenfunde im Arsenal," *Illustrierte Kronen-Zeitung* (Mar. 4, 1927), ANNO; for examples of the work of the Inter-Allied Commission finding and destroying weapons, see Folder "Beschlagnahme von Handgranaten in Wr. Arsenale, 1922," Karton 271, AAng BKA-AA NPA Neues Politisches Archiv, Archiv der Republik, ÖSTA.

20 "Carl Vaugoin," Parlament Republik Österreich, accessed July 4, 2018, https://www.parlament.gv.at/WWER/PAD_01344/index.shtml#tab-Ueberblick; A. Staudinger, "Vaugoin, Carl (1873–1949), Politiker," in *Österreichisches Biographisches Lexikon, 1815–1950*, Bd. 15 (Austrian Centre for Digital Humanities and Cultural Heritage, 2017), 195–6, https://www .biographien.ac.at/oebl/oebl_V/Vaugoin_Carl_1873_1949.xml.

21 "Dr. Julius Deutsch," Parlament Österreich, accessed 18 Nov. 2023, https://www.parlament.gv.at/person/208; Österreichisches Staatsarchiv, "Julius Deutsch," 1914–2014: 100 Jahre Erster Weltkrieg, accessed Nov. 18, 2023, https://wk1.staatsarchiv.at/militarisierung-der-politik/julius -deutsch/index.html; Julius Deutsch spricht über sein Leben Audio File, 1 Mar. 1967, Österreichische Mediathek, https://www.mediathek.at /atom/0178295D-2E8-00781-00000BEC-01772EE2.

22 Carl Vaugoin, "Austria as a Republic," *World Affairs* 98, no. 1 (1935): 27–8; C. Earl Edmondson, *The Heimwehr and Austrian Politics, 1918–1936* (Athens: University of Georgia Press, 1978), 19–20.

23 Raymond Earle Bell, Jr., "The Effectiveness of the Austrian Army and the Organization of Military Unions, 1920–1934" (PhD diss., New York University, 1983), 16, 185, 212; Anton Staudinger, "Bemühungen Carl Vaugoins um Suprematie der Christlichsozialen Partei in Österreich (1930–33)," *Mitteilungen des Österreichischen Staatsarchivs,* Vol 23 (1970): 301–18; "General Theodor Körners Abschied," *Arbeiter-Zeitung* (1 Feb. 1924), 4, ANNO.

24 Militärverband der Republik Österreich in Tirol to SDAP Commissioner, Sep. 24, 1922, Deutsch to Army Minister, 20 Nov. 1922, and Deutsch to Rosenwirt, n.d., M116, Parteiarchiv vor 1934, VGA.

25 Report on the Meetings between Deutsch and Vaugoin, Mar. 26 and
    28, 1924, and Correspondence and Letters from Parlamentskommissär
    on "Assentierung für das österreichische Bundesheer," n.d., M116,
    Parteiarchiv vor 1934, VGA.
26 Anton Staudinger, "Bemühungen Carl Vaugoins um Suprematie der
    Christlichsozialen Partei in Österreich (1930–33)," *Mitteilungen des
    Österreichischen Staatsarchivs*, vol. 23 (1970): 339–41.
27 Julius Deutsch, *Ein weiter Weg: Lebenserinnerungen* (Zurich: Amalthea-Verlag,
    1960), 144; Oliver Rathkolb, "Austrian Historiography and Perspectives on
    World War I: The Long Shadow of the 'Just War,' 1914–2018," in *Writing
    the Great War: The Historiography of World War I from 1918 to the Present*, eds.
    Christoph Cornelissen and Arndt Weinrich (New York: Berghahn Books,
    2021), 192–3; Ivan T. Berend, "A Fascistoid Austrian Demagogue: Ernst
    Rüdiger Starhemberg," in *A Century of Populist Demagogues: Eighteen European
    Portraits, 1918–2018* (Budapest: Central European University Press, 2020), 99.
28 Josef Gerdenitsch, "Das Wiener Arsenal in der Ersten Republik: Die
    politische, wirtschaftliche und militärische Bedeutung in den Jahren 1918–
    1927" (PhD diss.: Universität Wien, 1967), 1–7, 46–69; Ilona Duczynska,
    Der demokratische Bolschewik: Zur Theorie und Praxis der Gewalt (Munich: List
    Verlag, 1975), 78–9; "Arsenalpakt 1922" reproduced in Ilona Duczynska,
    Der demokratische Bolschewik: Zur Theorie und Praxis der Gewalt (Munich: List
    Verlag, 1975), 313–14.
29 Matthew James Frank, *Making Minorities History: Population Transfer in
    Twentieth-Century Europe* (Oxford: Oxford University Press, 2017), 95–9;
    "Die Wahrheit über die Innsbrucker Waffen," *Arbeiter-Zeitung* (Nov. 9,
    1930), 2, ANNO; "Speech in the Chamber, February 6, 1926," accessed
    July 10, 2018, http://bibliotecafascista.blogspot.com/2012/03/speech
    -delivered-in-chamber-february-6.html
30 Martin Kitchen, *The Coming of Austrian Fascism* (London: Croom Helm,
    1980), 117–18; "Wieder Waffen ausgeliefert," *Die Rote Fahne*, 9 Nov
    1930, ANNO; "Vaugoin in Verlegenheit," *Arbeiter-Zeitung*, Nov. 9, 1930,
    ANNO; Anton Staudinger, "Bemühungen Carl Vaugoins um Suprematie
    der Christlichsozialen Partei in Österreich (1930–33)," *Mitteilungen des
    Österreichischen Staatsarchivs*, vol. 23 (1970): 362; "Die Waffensuche: Eine
    Antwort des Nationalrates Dr. Deutsch an den Bundeskanzler Vaugoin,"
    Tagblatt, 9 Nov 1930, ANNO.
31 Handwritten Memo from Körner, Nov. 6, 1925, M122, Parteiarchiv vor
    1934, VGA.
32 "Die Waffenfunde im Arsenal," *Illustrierte Kronen-Zeitung* (Mar. 4, 1927),
    ANNO; Martin Kitchen, *The Coming of Austrian Fascism* (London: Croom
    Helm, 1980), 120–121; "Hinter den Mauern des Arsenals," *Christlichsoziale
    Arbeiter-Zeitung* (Mar. 12, 1927), ANNO.

33 Conversation between Vaugoin, Deutsch, and Hecht about Soldatenversorgungsgesetz, Mar. 28, 1927, M 43, Partei-Archiv vor 1934, VGA.

34 Instruktion für den Herrn Walter Dürr, Mjr. a.D., vom Mai 1927, reproduced in Ilona Duczynska, *Der demokratische Bolschewik: Zur Theorie und Praxis der Gewalt* (Munich: List Verlag, 1975), 318; Deutsch to Vaugoin, May 16, 1927, M43 and Gedächtnisprotokolle: Gespräch mit Dr. Presser, May 18, 1927, and Memo S.B. 4667/27 to Staatsanwaltschaft I., June 13, 1927, M122, all Partei-Archiv vor 1934, VGA.

35 As an example of this earlier historiography, see Peter Huemer, *Sektionschef Robert Hecht und die Zerstörung der Demokratie in Österreich: Eine historisch-politische Studie* (Munich: Oldenbourg, 1975), and Ludwig Jedlicka, *Ein Heer im Schatten der Parteien: Die militärpolitische Lage Österreichs 1918–1938* (Vienna: Böhlau, 1955).

36 Erin R. Hochman, "The Failed Republic, 1918–1933?" in *Democracy in Austria*, eds. Günter Bischof and David M. Wineroither (New Orleans: University of New Orleans Press, 2019), 61; Anton Pelinka, "Parlament," in *Handbuch des politischen Systems Österreichs, Erste Republik, 1918–1933*, eds. Tálos et al. (Vienna: Manzsche Verlags- und Universitätsbuchhandlung, 1995), 61–3.

37 Ernst Hanisch, *Österreichische Geschichte, 1890–1990: Der lange Schatten des Staates: Österreichische Gesellschaftsgeschichte im 20. Jahrhundert* (Vienna: Ueberreuter, 1994), 269–87; Agreement between the Government and Political Parties, 7 June 1929, Karton 20, Mappe 107, SD Parteistellen, VGA.

38 Anton Staudinger, "Bemühungen Carl Vaugoins um Suprematie der Christlichsozialen Partei in Österreich (1930–33)," *Mitteilungen des Österreichischen Staatsarchivs*, Vol. 23 (1970): 362; Julius Deutsch, *Ein weiter Weg: Lebenserinnerungen* (Zurich: Amalthea-Verlag, 1960), 200.

39 Gerhard Botz, "Der '15. Juli 1927': Ablauf, Ursachen und Folgen," in *1927 als die Republik brannte: Von Schattendorf bis Wien*, eds. Norbert Leser and Paul Salier-Wlasits (Vienna-Klosterneuburg: Edition Va Bene, 2002), 33–51; Hugo Portisch, *Österreich: Die unterschätzte Republik* (Vienna: Kremayr & Scheriau, 1989), 298–323.

40 Ergebnis der Besprechung mit dem Minister, 30 Dec. 1927, M122, Parteiarchiv vor 1934, VGA.

41 Vaugoin to Deutsch, Apr. 12, 1928, M122, Parteiarchiv vor 1934, VGA.

42 Deutsch to Vaugoin, Oct. 30, 1928, reproduced in Ilona Duczynska, *Der demokratische Bolschewik: Zur Theorie und Praxis der Gewalt* (Munich: List Verlag, 1975), 319; "Waffenfabrik," WienGeschichteWien, last modified 6 June 6, 2017, https://www.wien.gv.at/wiki/index.php/Waffenfabrik.

43 "Die Waffenbestände des Arsenals an die Regierung ausgeliefert," *Die Rote Fahne*, May 20, 1927, ANNO; Deutsche Gesandtschaft Wien Memo "Waffenbestände in Österreich," May 20, 1927, RZ 206 242495, PAAA;

"Legende und Geschichte der Arsenalwaffen," *Arbeiter-Zeitung*, Dec. 3, 1929, ANNO.

44 Anton Staudinger, "Bemühungen Carl Vaugoins um Suprematie der Christlichsozialen Partei in Österreich (1930–33)," *Mitteilungen des Österreichischen Staatsarchivs*, vol. 23 (1970): 302–22; "Carl Vaugoin," Parlament Österreich, accessed Nov. 18, 2023, https://www.parlament.gv.at/WWER/PAD_01344/index.shtml#tab-Ueberblick.

45 Anton Staudinger, "Bemühungen Carl Vaugoins um Suprematie der Christlichsozialen Partei in Österreich (1930–33)," *Mitteilungen des Österreichischen Staatsarchivs*, vol. 23 (1970): 319–20.

46 "Die Waffensuche in Wien," *Freiheit*, Nov. 6, 1930, ANNO; "Ein Racheversuch für die Waffenbeschlagnahme," *Reichspost*, Nov. 7, 1930, ANNO.

47 "Die Wahrheit über die Innsbrucker Waffen," *Arbeiter-Zeitung*, Nov. 9, 1930, ANNO.

48 "Vaugoin in Verlegenheit," *Arbeiter-Zeitung*, Nov. 9, 1930, ANNO.

49 Protokoll vom 8. November 1930, gezeichnet Th. Schubauer, reproduced in Ilona Duczynska, *Der demokratische Bolschewik: Zur Theorie und Praxis der Gewalt* (Munich: List Verlag, 1975), 320.

50 "Bundeskanzler Vaugoin über den austromarxistischen Hochverrat," *Reichspost*, Nov. 8, 1930, ANNO.

51 Vaugoin to Deutsch, Nov. 8, 1930, M 43, Partei-Archiv vor 1934, VGA.

52 Walter Wiltschegg, *Die Heimwehr: Eine unwiderstehliche Volksbewegung?* (Munich: R. Oldenbourg Verlag, 1985), 58–60; Deutsch to Vaugoin, Nov. 10, 1930, M 43, Partei-Archiv vor 1934, VGA.

53 Anton Staudinger, "Bemühungen Carl Vaugoins um Suprematie der Christlichsozialen Partei in Österreich (1930–33)," *Mitteilungen des Österreichischen Staatsarchivs*, vol. 23 (1970): 323–7; Hans Mommsen, "Von der k.u.k. Sozialdemokratie," *Forum: Österreichische Monatsblätter für kulturelle Freiheit* 121 (1964): 22–5.

54 For later co-operation between Deutsch and the government, see Minutes of a meeting with Security Minister Bachinger, Deutsch, and Heinz, March 1, 1932, M 43, Partei-Archiv vor 1934, VGA; Dollfuß to Deutsch, 27 Oct. 1932, Karton 20, Mappe 105, SD Parteistellen, VGA; Anton Pelinka, "Parlament," in *Handbuch des politischen Systems Österreichs, Erste Republik, 1918–1933*, eds. Tálos et al. (Vienna: Manzsche Verlags- und Universitätsbuchhandlung, 1995), 65–7.

55 Ilona Duczynska, *Workers in Arms: The Austrian Schutzbund and the Civil War of 1934* (New York: Monthly Review Press, 1978), 158–245.

56 Franz Menges, "Lambach, Walter" in *Neue Deutsche Biographie* 13 (1982), 425–6, https://www.deutsche-biographie.de/pnd116652179.html#ndbcontent; Larry Eugene Jones, "Between the Fronts: The German National Union of Commercial Employees from 1928 to 1933," *The*

Journal of Modern History 48, no. 3 (1976), 462–6; *Reichstags-Handbuch*, V. Wahlperiode (1930) (Berlin: Reichsdrückerei, 1930), 402; Larry Eugene Jones, *The German Right, 1918–1930: Political Parties, Organized Interests, and Patriotic Associations in the Struggle against Weimar Democracy* (New York: Cambridge University Press, 2020), 89–90.

57   Walther Lambach, *Diktator Rathenau* (Hamburg: Deutschnationale Verlagsanstalt, 1918), 64.

58   Walther Lambach, *Die Herrschaft der Fünfhundert: Ein Bild des parlamentarischen Lebens im neuen Deutschland* (Hamburg: Hanseatische Verlagsanstalt, 1926), 3.

59   Review in *Die Bücherwarte: Zeitschrift für sozialistische Buchkritik*, n.d., N 1069/18, Walther Lambach, BAK; The photos in *Die Herrschaft der Fünfhundert* are on the glossy pages. See the pages between pages 96 and 97 for Friedrich Stampfer's own candid photograph reproduced in the book.

60   Walther Lambach, ed., *Politische Praxis 1926* (Hamburg: Hanseatische Verlagsanstalt, 1926), 5; Lambach, *Die Herrschaft der Fünfhundert*, 3.

61   Lambach, ed., *Politische Praxis 1926*, 7–8. This analysis of political careers is possible when comparing the list of contributors in the book with http://www.reichstagsprotokolle.de/index.html and confirming that with https://www.deutsche-biographie.de/home.

62   Larry Eugene Jones, "German Conservatism at the Crossroads: Count Kuno von Westarp and the Struggle for Control of the DNVP, 1928–30," *Contemporary European History* 18, no. 2 (2009): 152–3.

63   Lambach's Article in "Politische Wochenschrift" as quoted in *Der Fall Lambach (System Hugenberg gegen D.H.V.)* (Berlin: Jungdeutschen Orden), 3.

64   Hans Mommsen, *Die verspielte Freiheit: Der Weg der Republik von Weimar in den Untergang, 1918 bis 1933* (Frankfurt: Propyläen, 1990), 264–5; Larry Eugene Jones, "German Conservatism at the Crossroads: Count Kuno von Westarp and the Struggle for Control of the DNVP, 1928–30," *Contemporary European History* 18, no. 2 (2009): 152–3.

65   Hermann Weiß and Paul Hoser, eds., *Die Deutschnationalen und die Zerstörung der Weimarer Republik: Aus dem Tagebuch von Reinhold Quaatz, 1928–1933* (Munich: R. Oldenbourg, 1989), 44; Lambach, *Die Herrschaft der Fünfhundert*, 96; Larry Eugene Jones, *The German Right, 1918–1930: Political Parties, Organized Interests, and Patriotic Associations in the Struggle against Weimar Democracy* (New York: Cambridge University Press, 2020), 416–20; Daniel Ziblatt, *Conservative Parties and the Birth of Democracy* (Cambridge: Cambridge University Press, 2017), 301–24.

66   Lambach to Graf von Westarp, May 5, 1927, and Schlange to Thomsen, n.d., N 1069/9, Walther Lambach, BAK.

67   Bang to Lambach, June 16, 1928, N 1069/10, Walther Lambach, BAK.

68 John A. Leopold, *Alfred Hugenberg: The Radical Nationalist Campaign against the Weimar Republic* (New Haven: Yale University Press, 1977), 47–79; Lambach to Albert Zimmerman, July 20, 1931, N 1069/9, Walther Lambach, BAK; Frank Lambach, *Mein Grossvater Walther Lambach Politiker der Weimarer Zeit* (Berlin: epubli, 2012), 37.

69 Larry Eugene Jones, *The German Right, 1918–1930: Political Parties, Organized Interests, and Patriotic Associations in the Struggle against Weimar Democracy* (New York: Cambridge University Press, 2020), 417.

70 Larry Eugene Jones, "Between the Fronts: The German National Union of Commercial Employees from 1928 to 1933," *The Journal of Modern History* 48, no. 3 (1976), 466.

71 Oberfinanzrat Dr. Bang, M.d.R. as quoted in *Der Fall Lambach (System Hugenberg gegen D.H.V.)* (Berlin: Jungdeutschen Orden), 6.

72 *Deutsche Handels-Wacht* article of July 25, 1928 as quoted in *Der Fall Lambach (System Hugenberg gegen D.H.V.)* (Berlin: Jungdeutschen Orden), 15.

73 *Reichstags-Handbuch*, V. Wahlperiode (1930) (Berlin: Reichsdrückerei, 1930), 385; Konrad Reiser, "Kardorff, Siegfried von" in: *Neue Deutsche Biographie* 11 (1977), 149–50, https://www.deutsche-biographie .de/pnd101265956.html#ndbcontent; Deutscher Zentral-Verein der Vereinigten Konservativen der Provinz Posen to Kardorff, June 24, 1918, N 1040/9 and Speech by Moldenhauer, Feb. 7, 1943, N 1040/5, Siegfried von Kardorff, BAK.

74 Excerpt of *Korrespondenz der Gesellschaft*, January 25, 1933: "Civilcourage," *Vossiche Zeitung*, Berlin Clipping, 4 Feb. 1933, and *Neue freie Presse*, Wien Clipping, Feb. 11, 1933, all N 1040/4, Siegfried von Kardorff, BAK.

75 Kardorff to Hergt, August 21, 1919, N 1040/10, Siegfried von Kardorff, BAK.

76 Kardorff to Westarp, December 21, 1919, N 1040/14, Siegfried von Kardorff, BAK.

77 Kardorff to Neuhaus, Apr. 19, 1920, N 1040/16, Siegfried von Kardorff, BAK.

78 Kardorff to Lindeiner, Jan. 30, 1921, N 1040/11, Siegfried von Kardorff, BAK.

79 Kardorff to Neuhaus, Apr. 19, 1920, N 1040/16, Siegfried von Kardorff, BAK.

80 Siegfried von Kardorff, *Bismarck: Vier Vorträge Ein Beitrag zur Deutschen Parteigeschichte* (Berlin: Ernst Rowohlt Verlag, 1929), 34.

81 Katharina von Kardorff-Oheimb, *Politik und Lebensbeichte* (Tübingen: Hopfer Verlag, 1962), 94; Lambach, *Die Herrschaft der Fünfhundert*, 86; Excerpt of *Korrespondenz der Gesellschaft*, Jan. 25, 1933: "Civilcourage," N 1040/4, Siegfried von Kardorff, BAK; Cornelia Baddack, *Katharina von Kardorff-Oheimb (1979–1962) in der Weimarer Republik* (Göttingen: V & R unipress, 2016), 195–200; "Politische Lebenserinnerungen," n.d., N 1019/1, Paul Moldenhauer, BAK.

82 Siegfried von Kardorff, *Bismarck: Vier Vorträge, Ein Beitrag zur Deutschen Parteigeschichte* (Berlin: Ernst Rowohlt Verlag, 1929); Kaas to Kardorff, June 19, 1929, N 1040/11 and Löbe to Kardorff, n.d., N 1040/5, both Siegfried von Kardorff, BAK.

83 Katharina von Kardorff-Oheimb, *Politik und Lebensbeichte* (Tübingen: Hopfer Verlag, 1962), 166.

84 Rede des Herrn Reichstagsabgeordneten Siegfried von Kardorff anlässlich des Verfassungstages im Reichstagsgebäude am 11. August 1927, (Berlin: Verlag von Georg Stilke, 1927), 1, https://portal.dnb.de/bookviewer /view/1131560752#page/7/mode/1up.

85 Decision and Attachments from Der Ehrenrat des Alten-Herrenvereins des Corps der Saxo-Borussia zu Heidelberg, Nov. 14, 1922, N 1040/5a, Siegfried von Kardorff, BAK.

86 Diether Prinz zu Ysenburg und Büdingen to Kardorff, May 12, 1921, N 1040/5a, Siegfried von Kardorff, BAK.

87 Kardorff to Reischach, May 16, 1921, Diether Prinz zu Ysenburg und Büdingen to Reischach, May 22, 1921, Reischach to Carl Fürst zu Ysenburg, 30 June 1930? [*sic*], and Carl Fürst zu Ysenburg und Büdingen to Reischach, May 22, 1921, all N 1040/5a, Siegfried von Kardorff, BAK.

88 Carl Fürst zu Ysenburg und Büdingen to Reischach, May 30, 1921 and Reischach to Carl Fürst zu Ysenburg und Büdingen, June 1, 1921, and Der Ehrenrat II des Vereins der Offiziere des Hessischen Leibgarde-Infanterie-Regiments to Kardorff, June 30, 1921, all N 1040/5a, Siegfried von Kardorff, BAK.

89 Thilo von Trotha to Siegfried von Kardorff, February 14, 1930, Siegfried von Kardorff, N 1040/5a, BAK.

90 Hans Mommsen, *Die verspielte Freiheit: Der Weg der Republik von Weimar in den Untergang, 1918 bis 1933* (Frankfurt: Propyläen, 1990), 292–3, 460–1; E. Schmidt to Dingeldey, March 16, 1931, N 1002/61, Eduard Dingeldey, BAK.

91 Kardorff to Dingeldey, 27 February 1931, N 1002/61, Eduard Dingeldey, BAK.

92 Cornelia Baddack, *Katharina von Kardorff-Oheim (1979–1962) in der Weimarer Republik* (Göttingen: V & R unipress, 2016), 538–40; Dingeldey to Kardorff, 3 Aug 1931, Schultz to Dingeldey Aug. 24, 1931, Schutz to Dingeldey, 7 Mar. 1932, Kardorff to Dingeldey, Apr. 27, 1932, and Haack, Stendel, Kriege to Dingeldey, Dec. 10, 1932, Siegfried von Kardorff, N 1040/16, BAK.

93 *Verhandlungen des Reichstags*, V. Wahlperiode 1930, Band 446, 2454–65; Dingeldey to Kardorff, Feb. 27, 1932, N 1040/16 and Excerpt of *Korrespondenz der Gesellschaft*, Jan. 25, 1933: "Civilcourage," N 1040/4, both Siegfried von Kardorff, BAK.

94 Dingeldey to Kardorff, Oct. 28, 1932, Dingeldey to Kardorff, Nov. 2, 1932, and Nov. 9, 1932, Kardorff to Dingeldey, Nov. 7, 1932, N 1040/61, Siegfried von Kardorff, BAK.

95 Larry Eugene Jones, "Between the Fronts: The German National Union of Commercial Employees from 1928 to 1933," *The Journal of Modern History* 48, no. 3 (1976), 466.

96 Thomas Raithel, "Die Haltung von Eliten, Verbänden und Parteien: Überlegungen zur Stabilität und Instabilität parlamentarischer Demokratien zwischen den Weltkriegen," in *Demokratie in der Krise: Europa in der Zwischenkriegszeit*, ed. Christoph Gusy (Baden-Baden: Nomos, 2008), 119; Erin R. Hochman, "The Failed Republic, 1918–1933?," in *Democracy in Austria*, eds. Günter Bischof and David M. Wineroither (New Orleans: University of New Orleans Press, 2019), 45–63.

97 Daniel Ziblatt, *Conservative Parties and the Birth of Democracy* (Cambridge: Cambridge University Press, 2017), 325–31.

98 Anton Pelinka, "Parlament," in *Handbuch des politischen Systems Österreichs, Erste Republik, 1918–1933*, eds. Tálos et al. (Vienna: Manzsche Verlags- und Universitätsbuchhandlung, 1995), 65–7.

Conclusion: Republics of Friends

1 Robert de Jouvenel, *La république des camarades* (Paris: B. Grasset, 1914), 1–2; Guy Thuillier, "La République Des Camarades: Comment Robert de Jouvenel Voyait l'administration En 1914," *La Revue Administrative* 44, no. 259 (1991): 16–24.

2 Robert de Jouvenel, *La république des camarades* (Paris: B. Grasset, 1914), 10–19.

3 Jacques de SaintVictor and Nicolas Branthôme, preface to *La république des camarades* (Paris: Équateurs, 2014), 7–8.

4 de Jouvenel, *La république des camarades*, 2–17; Paul Morand, preface to *La république des camarades* (Paris: B. Grasset, 1934), 9–30.

5 Éric Desmons, Review of *La République des camarades* by Robert de Jouvenel, *Revue Française d'Histoire des Idées Politiques* (2015): 259–64; Paul Morand, preface to *La république des camarades* (Paris: B. Grasset, 1934), 9–30.

6 Cartoon "Vor dem Balle," *Kikeriki*, 2 Feb 1930, ANNO; Matthias Marschik, "Depicting Hakoah: Images of a Zionist Sports Club in Interwar Vienna," *Historical Social Research/Historische Sozialforschung* 43, no. 2 (164) (2018): 131.

7 Cartoon "Berlin stellt sich um," *Simplicissimus*, Nov. 10, 1930, 395, http://www.simplicissimus.info

8 Thomas Mergel, "Überlegungen zu einer Kulturgeschichte der Politik," *Geschichte und Gesellschaft* 28 (2002): 586.

9 Gretchen Helmke and Steven Levitsky, "Introduction," *Informal Institutions and Democracy: Lessons from Latin America*, Eds. Gretchen Helmke and Steven Levitsky (Baltimore: Johns Hopkins University Press, 2006), 5.

10 Gretchen Helmke and Steven Levitsky, "Informal Institutions and Comparative Politics: A Research Agenda." *Perspectives on Politics* 2, no. 4 (2004): 725–40; G. Puchinger, *Tilanus vertelde mij zijn leven* (Kampen: Kok, 1966), 165; Kabinet-De Geer II (1939–1940), Parlement.com, accessed Dec. 5, 2023, https://www.parlement.com/id/vh8lnhrp8ws1/kabinet_de _geer_ii_1939_1940.

11 Cartoon "Politik der Privatgespräche," *Simplicissimus,* Jan. 29, 1933, front page, http://www.simplicissimus.info; Henry Ashby Turner, Jr., *Hitler's Thirty Days to Power: January 1933* (Reading, MA: Addison-Wesley, 1996), 109–61.

12 Richard N. Coudenhove-Kalergi, *Pan-Europa* (Vienna: Pan-Europa, 1923), 162; Richard Coudenhove-Kalergi, *Ein Leben für Europa: Meine Lebenserinnerungen* (Cologne: Kiepenheuer & Witsch, 1966), 284–8; "Mr Winston Churchill speaking in Zurich, 19th September 1946," The Churchill Society, accessed Feb. 23, 2018, http://www.churchill-society -london.org.uk/astonish.html

13 Questionnaire Response, 10 Aug. 1947, IPU 477, IPU; Richard Coudenhove-Kalergi, *Ein Leben für Europa: Meine Lebenserinnerungen* (Cologne: Kiepenheuer & Witsch, 1966), 290; Richard N. Coudenhove-Kalergi, *Pan-Europa* (Vienna: Pan-Europa, 1923), 162–7; Richard Coudenhove-Kalergi, *Kampf um Europa* (1949), CVCE.eu.

14 Richard Coudenhove-Kalergi, *Kampf um Europa* (1949), CVCE.eu; Report on M. Robinet de Clery's Attendance at the Gstaad Meetings, Sep. 1947, IPU 477, IPU.

15 "Will we have a European Parliament?," from *Le Monde* (14 September 1947), CVCE.eu.

16 "European Union," *The Washington Post*, Sep. 15, 1947, ProQuest Historical Newspapers.

17 The Members of the Provisional Council of the EPU (Gstaad, September 10, 1947), Cvce.edu; 35th Inter-Parliamentary Conference, Oslo 1939, Provisional List of Delegates, Inv. 463, W. Drees, NAH; Sixth Assembly of the League of Nations, *List of Delegates and Members of Delegations* (Geneva, 1925), 32; Report on M. Robinet de Clery's Attendance at the Gstaad Meetings, Sep 1947, IPU 477, IPU; Mitgliederliste der Deutschen Parlamentarischen Sektion der Europäischen Bewegung, Mar. 1, 1950, N 1005/442, Herman Pünder, BAK.

18 Political Resolution of the Hague Congress (May 7–10, 1948), CVCE.eu; Forerunner of Council of Europe Parliamentary Assembly first met 75 years ago, Council of Europe, Aug. 9, 2024, https://www.coe.int/en

/web/portal/-/forerunner-of-council-of-europe-parliamentary-assembly
-first-met-75-years-ago; Frederick F Ritsch, "ORIGINS OF THE COUNCIL
OF EUROPE: Part One: The Post-War Unity Movements to the Hague
Congress," Il Politico 35, no. 1 (1970): 76–92.

19 "Six Nations Form Europe Assembly in Coal-Steel Pool," *The New York
Times*, Sep. 11, 1952, ProQuest Historical Newspapers; Joseph Harned
and Gerhard Molly, *Atlantic Assembly: Proposals and Prospects* (London: The
Hansard Society, 1965); Stelios Stavridis and Davor Jančić, "Introduction:
The Rise of Parliamentary Diplomacy in International Politics," in
Parliamentary Diplomacy in European and Global Governance, eds. Stelios
Stavridis and Davor Jančić (Leiden: Brill, 2017), 1–15.

Bibliography

Abbreviations of Archives

ACB	Les archives de la Chambre/Archief van de Kamer, Brussels
ADB	Archives diplomatiques/Diplomatiek Archief, Brussels
AEB	Archives de l'État en Belgique/Rijksarchief in België, Brussels
AKPR	Archiv Kanceláře prezidenta republiky, Prague
BAB	Bundesarchiv, Berlin-Lichterfelde
BAF	Bundesarchiv, Freiburg
BAK	Bundesarchiv, Koblenz
BHSA	Bayerisches Hauptstaatsarchiv, Munich
CUA	Columbia University Archives, New York City
FES	Archiv der sozialen Demokratie der Friedrich-Ebert-Stiftung, Bonn
GLK	Generallandesarchiv, Karlsruhe
GSPK	Geheimes Staatsarchiv Preußischer Kulturbesitz, Berlin
HLA	Hoover Institution Library and Archives, Stanford
HUA	Harvard University Archives, Cambridge
IÉV	Institut Émile Vandervelde, Brussels
IZM	Institut für Zeitgeschichte, Munich
IZV	Institut für Zeitgeschichte, Vienna
IISG	Internationaal Instituut voor Sociale Geschiedenis, Amsterdam
IPU	Inter-Parliamentary Union Archive, Geneva
JRL	John Rylands Library, University of Manchester, Manchester
KFZ	Kommission für Zeitgeschichte, Bonn
LBI	Leo Baeck Institute-Center for Jewish History, New York
LOC	Library of Congress Manuscripts Division, Washington, DC
LON	League of Nations Archives, Geneva
NAA	National Archives of Australia, Canberra
NAH	Nationaal Archief, The Hague

NAK   National Archives, Kew
NAP   Národní archiv, Prague-Chodovec
NIOD   NIOD Instituut voor Oorlogs-, Holocaust- en Genocidestudies,
       Amsterdam.
ÖSTA   Österreichisches Staatsarchiv, Vienna
PAAA   Politisches Archiv des Auswärtigen Amts, Berlin
PHM   People's History Museum, Manchester
VAP   Archiv des Vereins der Ausländischen Presse e.V., Berlin
VGA   Verein für Geschichte der ArbeiterInnenbewegung, Vienna
WIR   Wienbibliothek im Rathaus, Vienna
YMA   Manuscripts and Archives, Yale University Library

Archival Sources

AUSTRIA

Institut für Zeitgeschichte, Vienna (IZV)

MM-29 Ferdinand Marek

Österreichisches Staatsarchiv, Vienna (ÖSTA)

AdR AAng BKA-AA HP Handelspolitik, Abteilung 14
AdR AAng BKA-AA Neues Politisches Archiv
AdR BKA BKA-I Parteiarchive GDVP allgemein Schriftgut der Partei
Allgemeines Verwaltungsarchiv
Archiv der Republik, Bundeskanzleramt/Auswärtige Angelegenheiten
Archiv der Republik, Großdeutsche Volkspartei
AVA Nachlässe NN Renner

Verein für Geschichte der ArbeiterInnenbewegung, Vienna (VGA)

Altes Parteiarchiv / Partei-Archiv vor 1934
Sozialdemokratische Parteistellen
Sozialdemokratischer Parlamentsklub
(Teil)Nachlass Gabriele Proft
(Teil)Nachlass Karl Renner

Wienbibliothek im Rathaus, Vienna (WIR)

Teilnachlass Anna Boschek (LQH0025005)

AUSTRALIA

National Archives of Australia, Canberra (NAA)

A457 Prime Minister's Department / Department of External Affairs [II], Central Office, Correspondence files, multiple number series, first system
A461 Prime Minister's Department/Department of External Affairs [II], Central Office, Correspondence files, multiple number series (third system)
A981 Department of External Affairs [II], Correspondence files, alphabetical series
A3934 Prime Minister's Department, Correspondence files, SC secret and confidential series, (old files)
A11804 General Correspondence of Governor-General (excluding War files)
M3609 Documents and photographs accumulated as Australia's representative to the Imperial War Conference and Cabinet, the Versailles Peace Conference and the League of Nations

BELGIUM

Les archives de la Chambre/Archief van de Kamer, Brussels (ACB)

58 and 58–1   Parlements étrangers
64–2   Échanges internationaux – documents parlementaires

Archives de l'État en Belgique/Rijksarchief in België, Brussels (AEB)

Archives Georges Theunis

Archives diplomatiques/Diplomatiek Archief, Brussels (ADB)

10.740   League of Nations, Second Assembly

Institut Émile Vandervelde, Brussels (IÉV)

Archives d'Émile Vandervelde (EV/III and EV/IV)

CZECH REPUBLIC

Archiv Kanceláře prezidenta republiky, Prague (AKPR)

Archivní fond KPR – protokol A (audience)
Archivní fond KPR, 1919–1947

Národní archiv, Prague-Chodovec (NAP)

Sudetoněmecká strana (SdP), 1933–1938
Sudetoněmecká strana (SdP), 1933–1938 – Dodatky

GERMANY

Archiv der sozialen Demokratie der Friedrich-Ebert-Stiftung, Bonn (FES)

Nachlass Gustav Hülser
Nachlass Hermann Müller
Nachlass Johannes Stetter
Nachlass Karl Becker
Nachlass Mathias Höner
Nachlass Paul Löbe
Nachlass Rose Hilferding

Bundesarchiv, Berlin-Lichterfelde (BAB)

N 2020   Nachlass Georg Bernhard
N 2035   Nachlass Franz Bracht
N 2178   Nachlass Paul Löbe
N 2200   Nachlass Hermann Müller
N 2329   Nachlass Kuno von Westarp
NS 46   Nationalsozialistische Reichstagsfraktion
R 2   Reichsfinanzministerium
R 43-I   Reichskanzlei ("Neue Reichskanzlei")
R 57   Deutsches Ausland-Institut
R 58   Reichssicherheitshauptamt
R 106   Mittwochs-Gesellschaft
R 401   Vorläufiger Reichswirtschaftsrat
R 1501   Reichsministerium des Innern
R 2501   Deutsche Reichsbank
R 8071   Wissenschaftlich-humanitäres Komitee

Bundesarchiv, Freiburg (BAF)

N 42   Nachlass Kurt von Schleicher
N 77   Nachlass Erich Ludendorff
N 247   Nachlass Hans von Seeckt

Bundesarchiv, Koblenz (BAK)

N 1002   Nachlass Eduard Dingeldey
N 1004   Nachlass Hermann Dietrich
N 1005   Nachlass Hermann Pünder
N 1006   Nachlass Georg Gothein
N 1009   Nachlass Hans Luther
N 1019   Nachlass Paul Moldenhauer
N 1027   Nachlass Eduard David
N 1039   Nachlass Katharina von Kardorff
N 1040   Nachlass Siegfried von Kardorff
N 1042   Nachlass Wilhelm Külz
N 1051-F   Nachlass Walther Schücking
N 1053   Nachlass Wilhelm Solf
N 1069   Nachlass Walther Lambach
N 1101   Nachlass Franz Ritter von Epp
N 1130   Nachlass Bernhard Dernburg
N 1132   Nachlass Wilhelm Heile
N 1135   Nachlass Wolfgang Jaenicke
N 1151   Nachlass Marie-Elisabeth Lüders
N 1221   Nachlass Theodor Heuss
N 1231   Nachlass Alfred Hugenberg
N 1310   Nachlass Konstantin Freiherr von Neurath
N 1410   Nachlass Friedrich Wilhelm Krüger
N 1626   Nachlass Thusnelda Lang-Brumann
N 1670   Nachlass August Weber
N 1676   Nachlass Maria Reese
N 1771   Nachlass Wilhelm Friedrich Kalle

Deutsches Rundfunkarchiv, Frankfurt am Main

Email correspondence and audio files sent by Andreas Rühl in 2021.

Geheimes Staatsarchiv Preußischer Kulturbesitz, Berlin (GSPK)

VI. HA Nl C.H. Becker   Nachlass C.H. Becker
VI. HA Nl. Schnee   Nachlass Heinrich Schnee

Generallandesarchiv, Karlsruhe (GLK)

N Fehrenbach   Nachlass Constantin Fehrenbach
N Geck Nachlass Adolf Geck

Institut für Zeitgeschichte, Munich (IZM)

ED 60   Otto Wagener
ED 120   Wilhelm Hoegner
ED 312   Josef Felder
ED 874   Gottfried Feder

Kommission für Zeitgeschichte, Bonn (KFZ)

Nachlass Friedrich Dessauer

Politisches Archiv des Auswärtigen Amts, Berlin (PAAA)

NL Stresemann Nachlass Gustav Stresemann
R 30606   Verständigungsbestrebungen des britischen
                           Parlamentsabgeordneten Cmdr. Joseph Montague
                           Kenworthy, 1921–22
R 53712   Völkerrechtsakten der Rechtsabteilung, über IPU
R 70085, R 83524   Akten der Länderabteilungen II, III und IV: IPU
R 98279, R 99205   Akten des Sonderreferats Deutschland: IPU
RZ 206 242495   Österreich – Waffen (1922–1936)

Stiftung Archiv der Parteien und Massenorganisationen der DDR im Bundesarchiv, Berlin-Licherfelde (BAB)

NY 4005   Nachlass Clara Zetkin
NY 4126   Nachlass Paul Levi

Sudetendeutsches Archiv im Bayerischen Hauptstaatsarchiv, Munich (BHSA)

Nachlass Wenzel Jaksch

Archiv des Vereins der Ausländischen Presse e.V., Berlin (VAP)

Hausarchiv (This collection was in the early 2000s returned to the association
    in Berlin from Sweden.)

THE NETHERLANDS

Internationaal Instituut voor Sociale Geschiedenis, Amsterdam (IISG)

Collectie Florentinus Marinus Wibaut
Collectie Johan Willem Albarda
Collectie Robert Danneberg

Nationaal Archief, The Hague (NAH)

2.02.22   Collectie Tweede Kamer der Staten-Generaal, 1815–1945
2.21.117   Collectie Mr. H.P. Marchant
2.21.190   Collectie C. Frida Katz Fam.
2.21.244   Collectie C. Ruijs de Beerenbrouck
2.21.286   Collectie W. Drees

NIOD Instituut voor Oorlogs-, Holocaust- en Genocidestudies, Amsterdam (NIOD)

Collectie H.J. Woudenberg
Collectie M.V.E.H.J.M. Marchant et d'Ansembourg
Collectie NSB
Unpublished Thesis Collection (NIOD Scr 312 and NIOD Scr 444)

SWITZERLAND

Inter-Parliamentary Union Archive, Geneva (IPU)

Archival boxes from this private organizational archive from before 1945 were
consulted.

League of Nations Archives, Geneva (LON)

Classement No. 10   Economic & Financial
Classement No. 11   Political
Classement No. 13   Internationale Bureaux

UNITED KINGDOM

John Rylands Library, University of Manchester (JRL)

Ramsay MacDonald Papers (RMD)

National Archives, Kew (NAK)

CAB 23   War Cabinet and Cabinet: Minutes
FO 366   Foreign Office
PRO 30/69   James Ramsay MacDonald and predecessors and successors:
Papers

People's History Museum, Manchester (PHM)

LP/ID Labour Party Archives, International Department

UNITED STATES

Columbia Center for Oral History, Columbia University Archives, New York City, New York (CUA)

NXCP87-A621   Reminiscences of Jan Papanek: 1951
NXCP87-A1495   Reminiscences of Gerhart Heinrich Seger: 1950

Harvard University Archives, Cambridge, Massachusetts (HUA)

Papers of Heinrich Brüning

Hoover Institution Library and Archives, Stanford, California (HLA)

93072   Collection Carl A. Baehr
XX741   German Subject Collection

Leo Baeck Institute, New York City, New York (LBI)

AR 7243   Oscar Meyer Collection

Library of Congress, Manuscripts Division, Washington, DC (LOC)

William Edgar Borah papers, 1905–1940

Manuscripts and Archives, Yale University Library, New Haven, Connecticut (YMA)

Rolf Stutz Collection

Periodicals

AUSTRIA

Arbeiter-Zeitung
Christlichsoziale Arbeiter-Zeitung
Die Rote Fahne
Freiheit
Illustrierte Kronen-Zeitung
Kikeriki
Neue Freie Presse
Neues Wiener Journal
Protokolle des Ministerrates der Ersten Republik
Reichspost

Stenographische Protokolle (Konstituierende Nationalversammlung für
    Deutschösterreich and Konstituierende Nationalversammlung d. Republik
    Österreich)
Tagblatt

AUSTRALIA

The Advertiser (Adelaide)

BELGIUM

De Standaard
Le Drapeau Rouge

FRANCE

Le Monde
Pariser Tageszeitung

GERMANY

Berliner Morgenpost
Die Friedens-Warte
Die Zeit
Mittelbadische Presse
Reichstags-Handbuch
Simplicissimus
Verhandlungen des Reichstags
Vorwärts
Vossische Zeitung

THE NETHERLANDS AND DUTCH EAST INDIES

Club Kroniek
Deli Courant
De Telegraaf
De Tijd: godsdienstig-staatkundig dagblad
Handelingen Tweede Kamer (Staten-Generaal Digitaal)
Het Vaderland

UNITED KINGDOM

Hansard Parliamentary Debates
Times

UNITED STATES

Congressional Record
New York Herald Tribune
New York Times
New York Times Magazine
The Washington Post

Published Primary Sources

Address of the President of the United States: Delivered at a Joint Session of the Two Houses of Congress, January 8, 1918. Washington: Government Printing Office, 1918.

Beneš, Edvard. *Mnichovské dny:* Paměti. Prague: Svoboda, 1968.

– *Paměti: Od Mnichova k nové válce a k novému vítězství.* Prague: Naše vojsko, 2004.

Brand, Walter. *Auf verlorenem Posten: Ein sudetendeutscher Politiker zwischen Autonomie und Anschluß.* Munich: Verlagshaus Sudetenland GmbH, 1985.

Braun, Bernd and Joachim Eichler, eds. *Arbeiterführer, Parlamentarier, Parteiveteran: Die Tagebücher des Sozialdemokraten Hermann Molkenbuhr, 1905 bis 1927.* Munich: Oldenbourg, 2000.

Conférence parlementaire international du commerce. *Cinquième assemblée plénière: notices relatifs aux questions inscrites à son programme.* Brussels: Bureau permanent de Bruxelles, 1919.

– *Dix-huitième assemblée plénière. assemblée plénière: rapports et notices relatifs aux questions inscrites à son programme.* Brussels: Bureau permanent de Bruxelles, 1933.

The Constitution of the Czechoslovak Republic. Prague: Édition de la société l'effort de la Tchécoslovaquie, 1920.

Coudenhove-Kalergi, Richard N. *Pan-Europa.* Vienna: Pan-Europa, 1923.

– *Ein Leben für Europa: Meine Lebenserinnerungen.* Cologne: Kiepenheuer & Witsch, 1966.

de Jouvenel, Robert. *La république des camarades.* Paris: B. Grasset, 1914.

– *La république des camarades.* Paris: B. Grasset, 1934.

– *La république des camarades.* Paris: Équateurs, 2014.

de la Torriente, Cosme. *La Liga de las Naciones: Trabajos de la Segunda Asamblea.* Havana: Impr. y papeleria de Rambla, Bouza y ca, 1922.

de Valk, J.P., and A.C.M. Kappelhof, eds. *Dagboeken van P.J.M. A e 1902–1947.* The Hague: Instituut voor Nederlandse Geschiedenis, 2006.

Der Fall Lambach (System Hugenberg gegen D.H.V.). Berlin: Jungdeutschen Orden, n.d.

Deutsch, Julius. *Ein weiter Weg: Lebenserinnerungen.* Zurich: Amalthea-Verlag, 1960.

Deutsche Volkspartei/Reichsklub. *Mitgliederverzeichnis / Reichsklub Der Deutschen Volkspartei E.V.* (1923).

Die Verlagserscheinungen des Zentralverlages der NSDAP. Franz Eher Nachf. G.m.b.H. München, Berlin, Wien, 1921–1941. Leipzig: Bibliographischen Abteilung des Börsenvereins der Deutschen Buchhändler, 1941.

Documents on German Foreign Policy, 1918–1945. Series D. Volume II. Washington: Government Printing Office, 1949.

Dolezel, Heidrun, and Stephan Dolezel, eds. *Deutsche Gesandtschaftsberichte aus Prag. Vol. IV.* Munich: R. Oldenbourg Verlag, 1983.

Empire Parliamentary Association (Dominion of Canada Branch). Conferences of the Empire Parliamentary Association held in the Senate Chamber, Ottawa, and the Legislative Assembly Chambers of the Canadian Provinces. August, September, October 1928.

Entente internationale des partis radicaux et des partis démocratiques similaires. *Compte-Rendu du Congrès de Londres.* Paris, 1928.

Fabricius, Hans. *Geschichte der nationalsozialistischen Bewegung.* Berlin: Industrieverlag Spaeth & Linde, 1937.

Fanderl, Wilhelm. *Von 7 Mann zum Volk: Illustrierte Geschichte der NSDAP und der SA.* Oldenburg: Verlag Gerhard Stalling, 1933.

Fourès, Roger. "Des développements apportés par la Société des Nations à la notion de Représentation Étatique." Doctoral thesis, Université de Paris, 1938.

Fraenkel-Verkade, E., ed. *Correspondentie van Mr. M.M. Rost van Tonningen.* Deel I: 1921-Mei 1942. The Hague: Martinus Nijhoff, 1967.

Frick, Wilhelm. *Die Nationalsozialisten im Reichstag, 1924–1931.* Munich: Franz Eher, 1932.

Goebbels, Joseph. *Der Angriff: Aufsätze aus der Kampfzeit.* Munich: Franz Eher, 1935.

– *Tagebücher 1924–1945.* Edited by Ralf Georg Reuth. Munich: Piper, 2003.

Hankey, Lord. *Diplomacy by Conference: Studies in Public Affairs, 1920–1946.* London: Ernest Benn, 1946.

Heiden, Konrad. *Geschichte des Nationalsozialismus.* Berlin: Rowohlt, 1932.

Himmler, Heinrich. *Der Reichstag 1930: Das sterbende System und der Nationalsozialismus.* Munich: F. Eher, 1931.

Hitlers Auseinandersetzung mit Brüning. Munich: Eher Verlag, 1932.

Höß, Konstantin. *Die SdP im Parlament: Ein Jahresbericht 1935/36.* Karlsbad: Verlag Karl H. Frank, 1937.

Hodža, Milan. *Schicksal Donauraum: Erinnerungen.* Translated by Valerie Neumann. Vienna: Amalthea, 1995.

Inter-Parliamentary Bureau. *The Inter-Parliamentary Union: Its Work and Its Organization.* Geneva: Inter-Parliamentary Bureau, 1930.

Jesser, Franz. *Volkstumkampf und Ausgleich im Herzen Europas: Erinnerungen eines sudetendeutschen Politikers.* Nuremberg: Helmut Preußler Verlag, 1983.

Kelsen, Hans. *Das Problem des Parlamentarismus.* Vienna: Wilhelm Braumüller, 1926.

Krebs, Hans. *Kampf in Böhmen.* Berlin: Volk und Reich Verlag, 1938.

L'Union interparlementaire de 1889 à 1939: Ouvrage publié par les soins du Bureau interparlementaire à l'occasion du cinquantenaire de l'Union. Lausanne: Payot & c, 1939.

Lambach, Walther. *Diktator Rathenau.* Hamburg: Deutschnationale Verlagsanstalt, 1918.

– *Die Herrschaft der Fünfhundert: Ein Bild des parlamentarischen Lebens im neuen Deutschland.* Hamburg: Hanseatische Verlagsanstalt, 1926.

– ed. *Politische Praxis 1926.* Hamburg: Hanseatische Verlagsanstalt, 1926.

Löbe, Paul. *Der Weg war lang.* Berlin: arani, 1954.

Masaryk, Alice Garrigue. *Alice Garrigue Masaryk, 1879–1966: Her life as recorded in her own words and by her friends.* Compiled by Ruth Crawford Mitchell. (Pittsburgh: University of Pittsburgh University Center for International Studies, 1980.

Matthias, Erich and Eberhard Pikart. *Die Reichstagsfraktion der Deutschen Sozialdemokratie: 1898 bis 1918.* Düsseldorf: Droste, 1966.

Medinger, Wilhelm, *Die Internationale Diskussion über Die Krise des Parlamentarismus.* Vienna: Wilhelm Braumüller, 1929.

Meyer, Oscar. *Von Bismarck zu Hitler: Erinnerungen und Betrachtungen.* Offenbach a.M.: Bollwerk-Verlag Karl Drott, 1948.

Mosler, Hermann, ed. *Die Verfassung der Weimarer Republik.* Stuttgart, Reclam, 2009.

Proft, Gabriele. *Der Weg zu Uns! Die Frauenfrage im neuen Österreich.* Sozialistische Hefte. Vienna: SPÖ, 1945.

Puchinger, G. *Tilanus vertelde mij zijn leven.* Kampen: Kok, 1966.

Rede des Herrn Reichstagsabgeordneten Siegfried von Kardorff anlässlich des Verfassungstages im Reichstagsgebäude am 11. August 1927. Berlin: Verlag von Georg Stilke, 1927.

Rost van Tonningen-Heubel, F.S. *Op zoek naar mijn huwelijksring.* Erembodegem, Belgium: De Krijger, n.d.

Schmitt, Carl. *The Crisis of Parliamentary Democracy.* Translated by Ellen Kennedy. Cambridge, MA: MIT Press, 1985.

Severing, Carl. *Mein Lebensweg.* Cologne: Greven Verlag, 1950.

Sixth Assembly of the League of Nations. *List of Delegates and Members of Delegations.* Geneva, 1925.

Skottsberg, Brita. *Der österreichische Parlamentarismus.* Göteborg: Elanders Boktryckeri Aktiebolag, 1940.

SS-Hauptamt/IV. Lehrplan für Sechsmonatige Schulung. Berlin: SS-Hauptamt/IV, n.d.

Stetter, Hans. *Der kommunitische Sumpf: Mein Ausschluss aus der K.P.D.* Stuttgart: Schwäbische Tagwacht, 1927.

Stieve, Friedrich. *Geschichte des deutschen Volkes.* Munich: Oldenbourg, 1943.

Suchenwirth, Richard. *Deutsche Geschichte: von der gemanischen Vorzeit bis zur Gegenwart.* Leipzig: Georg Dollheimer, 1941.

Tonger-Erk, Lily, and Martina Wagner-Egelhaaf. *Einspruch! Reden von Frauen.* Stuttgart: Reclam, 2011.

Tucholsky, Kurt. *Ausgewählte Werke.* Neu-Isenburg: Melzer, 2006.

Ullrich, Oskar. *Sie kamen aus aller Herren Ländern: Aus dem Tagebuch des SdP-Dolmetschers.* Karlsbad: Adam Kraft Verlag, 1940.

Union interparlementaire. *Compte rendu de la XXVme conférence tenue à Berlin du 23 au 28 août 1928.* Lausanne, Librairie Payot & Cie, 1928.

United Kingdom Parliament. Parliament (Qualification of Women) Act, 1918.

van Geelkerken, C. *Voor Volk en Vaderland: Tien Jaren Strijd van de Nationaal-Socialistische Beweging der Nederlanden, 1931–14 December 1941.* Utrecht: Nenasu, 1943.

Vaugoin, Carl. "Austria as a Republic." *World Affairs* (Washington) 98, no. 1 (1935): 27–30.

von Kardorff, Siegfried. *Bismarck: Vier Vorträge Ein Beitrag zur Deutschen Parteigeschichte.* Berlin: Ernst Rowohlt Verlag, 1929.

von Kardorff-Oheimb, Katharina. *Politik und Lebensbeichte.* Tübingen: Hopfer Verlag, 1962.

Weiß, Hermann and Paul Hoser, eds. *Die Deutschnationalen und die Zerstörung der Weimarer Republik: Aus dem Tagebuch von Reinhold Quaatz, 1928–1933.* Munich: R. Oldenbourg, 1989.

World Peace Foundation. "The First Assembly of the League of Nations." *A League of Nations* IV, no. 1 (Feb 1921).

Secondary Sources

Abels, Gabriele, and Anne Cress. "Vom Kampf Ums Frauenwahlrecht Zur Parité: Politische Repräsentation von Frauen Gestern Und Heute." *Zeitschrift Für Parlamentsfragen* 50, no. 1 (2019): 167–86.

Adoumié, Vincent. *De la république à l'État français, 1918–1944.* Paris: Hachette, 2005.

Aerts, Remieg, Carla van Baalen, Joris Oddens, Diederik Smit, and Henk te Velde, eds. *In Dit Huis: Twee Eeuwen Tweede Kamer.* Amsterdam: Boom, 2015.

Aerts, Remieg, Herman de Liagre Böhl, Piet de Rooy, and Henk te Velde, eds. *Land van kleine gebaren: Een politieke geschiedenis van Nederland, 1780–1990.* Nijmegen: Uitgeverij SUN, 1999.

Albers, Martin. "Between the Crisis of Democracy and World Parliament: The Development of the Inter-Parliamentary Union in the 1920s." *Journal of Global History* 7, no. 2 (2012): 189–209.

Anderson, Margaret Lavinia. *Practicing Democracy: Elections and Political Culture in Imperial Germany.* Princeton: Princeton University Press, 2000.

– "Ein Demokratiedefizit?: Das Deutsche Kaiserreich in Vergleichender Perspektive." *Geschichte Und Gesellschaft* 44, no. 3 (2018): 367–98.

Arndt, Veronika. *Die Fahne von Saaz: Konrad Henlein in seiner Zeit.* Magdeburg: Helmuth- Block-Verlag, 1998.

Arnouts, Mathieu, and Boudien de Vries, "Een 'heerlijk' onderonsje: De Nieuwe of Littéraire Societeit De Witte, 1880–1914," *De Negentiende Eeuw* 23 (1999): 203–17.

Austermann, Philipp. *Der Weimarer Reichstag: Die schleichende Ausschaltung, Entmachtung und Zerstörung eines* Parlaments. Vienna: Böhlau Verlag, 2020.

Bab, Bettina et al., eds. *Mit Macht zur Wahl: 100 Jahre Frauenwahlrecht in Europa.* Bonn: Frauenmuseum, 2006.

Bachstein, Martin K. *Wenzel Jaksch und die Sudetendeutsche Sozialdemokratie.* Munich: Oldenbourg, 1974.

Baddack, Cornelia. *Katharina von Kardorff-Oheimb (1879–1962) in der Weimarer Republik.* Göttingen: V&R unipress, 2016.

Baldwin, Peter. *The Politics of Social Solidarity: Class Bases of the European Welfare State, 1875–1975.* Cambridge: Cambridge University Press, 1990.

Barnouw, D. *Rost van Tonningen: fout tot het bittere eind.* Zutphen: Walburg Pers, 1994.

Bavaj, Riccardo. *Von links gegen Weimar: Linkes antiparlamentarisches Denken in den Weimarer Republik.* Bonn: Dietz, 2005.

Beck, Hermann, and Larry Eugene Jones, eds. *From Weimar to Hitler: Studies in the Dissolution of the Weimar Republic and the Establishment of the Third Reich, 1932–1934.* New York: Berghahn, 2018.

Bell, Jr., Raymond Earle. "The Effectiveness of the Austrian Army and the Organization of Military Unions, 1920–1934." Ph.D. diss., New York University, 1983.

Belliard, Corinne M. "An Echo in France of the British Women's Suffrage Campaign." *Women's History Review* 29, no. 6 (2020): 1075–83.

Benoit, Bruno, ed. *Édouard Herriot en quatre portraits.* Villeneuve d'Ascq: Presses universitaires du Septentrion, 2020.

Berend, Ivan T. *A Century of Populist Demagogues: Eighteen European Portraits, 1918–2018.* Budapest: Central European University Press, 2020.

Berman, Sheri. *The Social Democratic Moment : Ideas and Politics in the Making of Interwar Europe.* Cambridge, MA: Harvard, 1998.

Berstein, Serge. *La France des Années* 30. Paris: Armand Colin, 2011.

Biefang, Andreas. *Die andere Seite der Macht: Reichstag und Öffentlichkeit im »System Bismarck«, 1871–1890.* Düsseldorf: Droste, 2009.

Biondich, Mark. *Stjepan Radić, the Croat Peasant Party, and the Politics of Mass Mobilization, 1904–1928.* Toronto: University of Toronto Press, 2000.

Bischof, Günter, et al. *Austrian Lives*. New Orleans: University of New Orleans Press, 2012.

– eds., and David M. Wineroither. *Democracy in Austria*. New Orleans: University of New Orleans Press, 2019.

Blackbourn, David. *Germany in the World: A Global History, 1500–2000*. New York: Liveright, 2023.

Blackwood, William Lee. "Socialism, Nationalism, and 'the German Question' from World War I to Locarno and Beyond." PhD diss., Yale University, 1995.

Blaustrumpf, ed. *"Sie meinen es politisch!" 100 Jahre Frauenwahlrecht in Österreich: Geschlechterdemokratie als gesellschaftspolitische Herausforderung*. Vienna: Löcker Verlag, 2019.

Blumenfeld, Kurt. *Erlebte Judenfrage: Ein Vierteljahrhundert deutscher Zionismus*. Stuttgart: Deutsche Verlags-Anstalt, 1962.

Bootsma, Peter, and Carla Hoetink. *Over lijken: Ontoelaatbare taalgebruik in de Tweede Kamer*. Amsterdam: Boom, 2006.

Borkus, M., T. den Hartog, and H. Lakmaker, eds. *Vrouwenstemmen: 100 jaar Vrouwenbelangen, 75 Jaar Vrouwenkiesrecht*. Zutphen: Walburg Pers, 1994.

Bottomore, Tom, and Patrick Goode. *Austro-Marxism*. Oxford: Clarendon Press, 1978.

Bracher, Karl Dietrich. *Die Auflösung der Weimarer Republik*. Düsseldorf: Droste, 1978.

Braudel, Fernand. *The Mediterranean and the Mediterranean World in the Age of Philip* II. Translated by Siân Reynolds. New York: Harper & Row, 1972.

Brügel, Johann Wolfgang. *Tschechen und Deutsche, 1918–1938*. Munich: Nymphenburger Verlagshandlung, 1967.

Brügelmann, Hermann. *Politische Ökonomie in Kritische Jahren: Die Friedrich List Gesellschaft e.V. von 1925–1935*. Tübingen: J.C.B. Mohr (Paul Siebeck), 1956.

Bukey, Evan Burr. *Hitler's Hometown: Linz, Austria, 1908–1945*. Bloomington: Indiana University Press, 1986.

Burton, Margaret E. *The Assembly of the League of Nations*. Chicago: University of Chicago Press, 1941.

Bytwerk, R.L. "Fritz Reinhardt and the Rednerschule der NSDAP." *The Quarterly Journal of Speech* 67, no. 3 (1981): 298–309.

Campbell, Michael Walsh. "A Crisis of Democracy: Czechoslovakia and the Rise of Sudeten German Nationalism, 1918–1938." PhD diss., University of Washington, 2003.

Canning, Kathleen. "The Politics of Symbols, Semantics, and Sentiments in the Weimar Republic." *Central European History* 43, no. 4 (2010): 567–80.

Capoccia, Giovanni. *Defending Democracy: Reactions to Extremism in Interwar Europe*. Baltimore: Johns Hopkins University Press, 2005.

Clavin, Patricia. *Securing the World Economy: The Reinvention of the League of Nations, 1920–1946*. Oxford: Oxford University Press, 2013.

Cohen, Deborah, and Maura O'Connor, eds. *Comparison and History: Europe in Cross-National Perspective.* New York: Routledge, 2004.

Connelly, John. *Captive University: The Sovietization of East German, Czech, and Polish Higher Education, 1945–1956.* Chapel Hill: University of North Carolina Press, 2000.

Cornelißen, Christoph, and Dirk van Laak, eds. *Weimar und die Welt: Globale Verflechtungen der ersten deutschen Republik.* Göttingen: Vandenhoeck & Ruprecht, 2020.

Cornelissen, Christoph, and Arndt Weinrich, eds. *Writing the Great War: The Historiography of World War I from 1918 to the Present.* New York: Berghahn Books, 2021.

Cornwall, Mark. "Heinrich Rutha and the Unraveling of a Homosexual Scandal in 1930s Czechoslovakia." *GLQ: A Journal of Lesbian and Gay Studies* 8, no. 3 (2002): 319–47.

– *The Devil's Wall: The Nationalist Youth Mission of Heinz Rutha.* Cambridge: Harvard University Press, 2012.

Cornwall, Mark, and R.J.W. Evans, eds. *Czechoslovakia in a Nationalist and Fascist Europe, 1918–1948.* Oxford: Oxford University Press, 2007.

Cramer, N. *Wandelingen door de Handelingen.* The Hague: Staatsuitgeverij, 1974.

Cross, Mai'a K. Davis. *The European Diplomatic Corps: Diplomats and International Cooperation from Westphalia to Maastricht.* New York: Palgrave Macmillan, 2007.

Das deutsche Führerlexikon 1934/1935. Berlin: Otto Stollberg G.m.b.H, 1934.

Davis, Belinda J. *Home Fires Burning: Food, Politics, and Everyday Life in World War I Berlin.* Chapel Hill: University of North Carolina Press, 2000.

de Rooy, Piet. *Republiek van rivaliteiten: Nederland sinds 1813.* Amsterdam: Mets&Schilt, 2002.

Desmons, Éric. Review of *La République des camarades* by Robert de Jouvenel, Jacques de Saint Victor and Nicolas Branthôme. *Revue Française d'Histoire des Idées Politiques* (2015): 259–64.

Die Tschechoslovakische Republik: Ihre Staatsidee in der Vergangenheit und Gegenwart. Prague: Veritas Verlag, 1937.

Döring, Martin. *"Parlamentarischer Arm der Bewegung:" Die Nationalsozialisten im Reichstag der Weimarer Republik.* Düsseldorf: Droste, 2001.

Douglas, James. *A Century of Parliamentary Diplomacy: A Short History of the British Group of the Inter-Parliamentary Union, 1889–1989.* Cambridge: Pentlands Publications, 1989.

Drabek, Anna M., Richard G. Plaschka, and Helmut Rumpler, eds. *Das Parteiwesen Österreichs und Ungarns in der Zwischenkriegszeit.* Vienna: Verlag der Österreichischen Akademie der Wissenschaften, 1990.

Duczynska, Ilona. *Der demokratische Bolschewik: Zur Theorie und Praxis der Gewalt.* Munich: List Verlag, 1975.

– *Workers in Arms: The Austrian Schutzbund and the Civil War of 1934.* New York: Monthly Review Press, 1978.

Dungy, Madeleine Lynch. *Order and Rivalry: Rewriting the Rules of International Trade after the First World War.* Cambridge: Cambridge University Press, 2023.

Edmondson, C. Earl. *The Heimwehr and Austrian Politics, 1918–1936.* Athens: University of Georgia Press, 1978.

Engels, Jens Ivo. "Politische Korruption in der Moderne: Debatten und Praktiken in Großbritannien und Deutschland im 19. Jahrhundert." *Historische Zeitschrift* 282, 2 (Apr 2006): 313–50.

Engels, Jens Ivo, and Volker Köhler. "Moderne Patronage – Mikropolitik in der Moderne Konturen und Herausforderungen eines neuen Forschungsfeldes." *Historische Zeitschrift* 309, no. 1 (2019): 36–69.

Evans, Richard J. *The Coming of the Third Reich.* New York: Penguin, 2003.

Fink, Carole. *Writing 20th Century International History: Explorations and Examples.* Göttingen: Wallstein Verlag, 2017.

Franceschet, Susan, et al., eds. *The Palgrave Handbook of Women's Political Rights.* London: Palgrave Macmillan, 2019.

Frank, Matthew James. *Making Minorities History: Population Transfer in Twentieth-Century Europe.* Oxford: Oxford University Press, 2017.

Fricke, Dieter, ed. *Die Bürgerlichen Partien in Deutschland: Handbuch der Geschichte der bürgerlichen Parteien und anderer bürgerlicher Interessenorganization vom Vormärz bis zum Jahre 1945.* Leipzig: Bibliographisches Institut, 1968.

Gerdenitsch, Josef. "Das Wiener Arsenal in der Ersten Republik: Die politische, wirtschaftliche und militärische Bedeutung in den Jahren 1918–1927." PhD diss.: Universität Wien, 1967.

Gerritse, Theo. *Collaboreren voor een betere wereld: de memoires van vier Nederlandse nationaal-socialisten.* Soesterberg: Aspekt, 2007.

Göhring, Walter, ed. *Anna Boschek: erste Gewerkschafterin im Parlament: Biografie einer außergewöhnlichen Arbeiterin.* Vienna: Österreichischer Gewerkschaftsbund, 1998.

Götz, Norbert. "On the Origins of 'Parliamentary Diplomacy': Scandinavian 'Bloc Politics' and Delegation Policy in the League of Nations." *Cooperation and Conflict* 40, no. 3 (2005): 263–79.

Großman, Johannes. *Die Internationale der Konservativen: Transnationale Elitenzirkel und private Außenpolitik in Westeuropa seit 1945.* Munich: Oldenbourg, 2014.

Groschopp, Horst. *Zwischen Bierabend und Bildungsverein: Zur Kulturarbeit in der deutschen Arbeiterbewegung vor 1914.* Berlin: Dietz, 1985.

Gross, Stephen G. *Export Empire: German Soft Power in Southeastern Europe, 1890–1945.* Cambridge: Cambridge University Press, 2015.

Gusy, Christoph, ed. *Demokratie in der Krise: Europa in der Zwischenkriegszeit.* Baden-Baden: Nomos, 2008.

Habersack, Michael. *Friedrich Dessauer (1881–1963): Eine politische Biographie des Frankfurter Biophysikers und Reichstagsabgeordneten.* Paderborn: Ferdinand Schöningh, 2011.

Hájková, Dagmar, and Pavel Horák, eds. *Republika československá, 1918–1939.* Prague: Nakladatelství Lidové noviny, 2018.

Halpern, Joel M., and David A. Kideckel, eds. *Neighbors at War: Anthropological Perspectives on Yugoslav Ethnicity, Culture, and History.* University Park, PA: Pennsylvania State University Press, 2000.

Hamre, Martin Kristoffer. "'Nationalists of All Countries, Unite!': Hans Keller and Nazi Internationalism in the 1930s," *Contemporary European History* 33, no. 2 (2024): 477–96.

Hanisch, Ernst. *Österreichische Geschichte, 1890–1990: Der lange Schatten des Staates: Österreichische Gesellschaftsgeschichte im 20. Jahrhundert.* Vienna: Ueberreuter, 1994.

Harned, Joseph, and Gerhard Molly. *Atlantic Assembly: Proposals and Prospects.* London: The Hansard Society, 1965.

Hartmans, Rob. *Vijandige broeders? De Nederlandse social-democratie en het national-socialisme, 1922–1940.* Amsterdam: Ambo, 2012.

Harvey, A.D. "An Early Hitler Speech." *The Historical Journal* Vol. 39, No. 3 (Sep 1996): 767–9.

Hauch, Gabriella. *Vom Frauenstandpunkt Aus: Frauen im Parlament, 1919–1933.* Vienna: Verlag für Gesellschaftskritik, 1995.

Healy, Maureen. *Vienna and the Fall of the Habsburg Empire: Total War and Everyday Life in World War I.* Cambridge: Cambridge University Press, 2004.

Helmke, Gretchen and Steven Levitsky. "Informal Institutions and Comparative Politics: A Research Agenda." *Perspectives on Politics* 2, no. 4 (2004): 725–40.

– eds. *Informal Institutions and Democracy: Lessons from Latin America.* Baltimore: Johns Hopkins University Press, 2006.

Herf, Jeffrey. *Reactionary Modernism: Technology, Culture, and Politics in Weimar and the Third Reich.* Cambridge: Cambridge University Press, 1984.

Hett, Benjamin Carter. *The Death of Democracy: Hitler's Rise to Power and the Downfall of the Weimar Republic.* New York: St. Martin's Griffin, 2018.

Hochman Erin R. *Imagining a Greater Germany: Republican Nationalism and the Idea of Anschluss.* Ithaca: Cornell University Press, 2016.

Hochreuther, Ina. *Frauen im Parlament: Südwestdeutsche Parlamentarierinnen von 1919 bis heute.* Stuttgart: Landtag von Baden-Württemberg, 2002.

Hoetink, Carla. *Macht der gewoonte: Regels en rituelen in de Tweede Kamer na 1945.* Nijmegen: Vantilt, 2018.

Howard-Ellis, C. *The Origin and Structure & Working of the League of Nations.* Boston: Houghton Mifflin, 1928.

Huemer, Peter. *Sektionschef Robert Hecht und die Zerstörung der Demokratie in Österreich: Eine historisch-politische Studie.* Munich: Oldenbourg, 1975.

Hueting, Ernest, Frits de Jong Edz., and Rob Ney. *Ik moet, het is mijn roeping: Een politiek biografie van Pieter Jelles Troelstra.* Amsterdam, Bert Bakker, 1981.

Ihalainen, Pasi, and Antero Holmila, eds. *Nationalism and Internationalism Intertwined: A European History of Concepts beyond the Nation State.* New York: Berghahn, 2022.

Imlay, Talbot C. *The Practice of Socialist Internationalism: European Socialists and International Politics, 1914–1960.* Oxford: Oxford University Press, 2018.

Iriye, Akira. *Global Community: The Role of International Organizations in the Making of the Contemporary World.* Berkeley: University of California Press, 2002.

Jackson, Julian. *The Popular Front in France Defending Democracy, 1934–38.* Cambridge: Cambridge, 1988.

Jayasuriya, Dinuk S., and Paul J. Burke. "Female Parliamentarians and Economic Growth: Evidence from a Large Panel." *Applied Economics Letters* 20, no. 3 (2013): 304–7.

Jedlicka, Ludwig. *Ein Heer im Schatten der Parteien: Die militärpolitische Lage Österreichs 1918–1938.* Vienna: Böhlau, 1955.

Jones, Larry Eugene. "Between the Fronts: The German National Union of Commercial Employees from 1928 to 1933." *The Journal of Modern History* 48, no. 3 (1976): 462–482.

– "German Conservatism at the Crossroads: Count Kuno von Westarp and the Struggle for Control of the DNVP, 1928–30." *Contemporary European History* 18, no. 2 (2009): 147–77.

– ed. *The German Right in the Weimar Republic: Studies in the History of German Conservatism, Nationalism, and Anti-Semitism.* New York: Berghahn, 2014.

– *Hitler versus Hindenburg: The 1932 Presidential Elections and the End of the Weimar Republic.* Cambridge: Cambridge University Press, 2016.

– *The German Right, 1918–1930: Political Parties, Organized Interests, and Patriotic Associations in the Struggle against Weimar Democracy.* New York: Cambridge University Press, 2020.

Kaase, Max, and Hans-Dieter Klingemann, eds. *Wahlen und politisches System.* Opladen: Westdeutscher Verlag, 1983.

Kędzia, Zdzisław, and Agata Hauser. "The impact of political party control over the exercise of the parliamentary mandate." Inter-Parliamentary Union. Geneva: Inter-Parliamentary Union, 2011.

Kennan, George Frost. *From Prague After Munich.* Princeton: Princeton University Press, 2015.

Kershaw, Ian. *Hitler: 1889–1936: Hubris.* New York: Norton, 1998.

King, Jeremy. *Budweisers into Czechs and Germans: A Local History of Bohemian Politics, 1848–1948.* Princeton: Princeton University Press, 2002.

Kissenkoetter, Udo. *Gregor Strasser und die NSDAP.* Stuttgart: Deutsche Verlags-Anstalt, 1978.

Kissling, Claudia. *Die Interparlementarische Union im Wandel: Rechtspolitische Ansätze einer repräsentativ-parlamentarischen Gestaltung der Weltpolitik*. Frankfurt: Peter Lang, 2005.

Kitchen, Martin. *The Coming of Austrian Fascism*. London: Croom Helm, 1980.

– *Europe Between the Wars*. Harlow, UK: Pearson, 2006.

Klepetar, Harry. *Seit 1918 … Eine Geschichte der Tschechoslowakischen Republik*. Mährisch-Ostrau: Verlas Julius Kittls Nachfolger, 1937.

Klijn, Edwin, and Robin te Slaa. *De NSB: Deel 2 Twee werelden botsen, 1936–1940*. Amsterdam: Boom, 2021.

Klimek Antonín. *Boj o hrad: 2. Kdo po Masarykovi? Vnitropolitický vývoj Československa 1926–1935 na půdorysu zápasu o prezidentské nástupnictví*. Prague: Panevropa, 1998.

Knopp, Guido. *Göring: Eine Karriere*. Munich: C. Bertelsmann, 2006.

Koß, Michael. *Parliaments in Time: The Evolution of Legislative Democracy in Western Europe, 1866–2015*. Oxford: Oxford University Press, 2018.

Kocka, Jürgen. "Comparison and Beyond," *History and Theory: Studies in the Philosophy of History* 42, no. 1 (2003): 39–44.

Köhler, Volker. *Genossen – Freunde – Junker: Die Mikropolitik personaler Beziehungen im politischen Handeln während der Weimarer Republik*. Göttingen: Wallstein Verlag, 2018.

Kolář, František, et al., eds. *Politická elita meziválečného Československa, 1918–1938: Kdo byl kdo*. Prague: Pražská edice, 1998.

Kolb, Eberhard. *The Weimar Republic*. Translated by P.S. Falla and R.J. Park. London: Routledge, 2005.

Konrad, Helmut, and Wolfgang Maderthaner, eds. *Das Werden der Ersten Republik … der Rest ist Österreich*. Vienna: Carl Gerold's Sohn, 2008.

Kopica, Jiří. *Boj o pohraničí: Demonstrace 4. března 1919 v Československu*. Kadaň: Karolinum, 2012.

Krumbach, Joseph H. *Franz Ritter von Epp: Ein Leben für* Deutschland. Munich: Franz Eher Verlag, 1940.

Küpper, René. *Karl Hermann Frank (1898–1946): Politische Biographie eines sudetendeutschen Nationalsozialisten*. Munich: R. Oldenbourg Verlag, 2010.

Lambach, Frank. *Mein Grossvater Walther Lambach Politiker der Weimarer Zeit*. Berlin: epubli, 2012.

Large, David Clay. *Between Two Fires: Europe's Path in the 1930s*. New York: Norton, 1991.

Lee, Sidney, ed. *Dictionary of National Biography, Second Supplement*. New York: MacMillan, 1912.

Leopold, John A. *Alfred Hugenberg: The Radical Nationalist Campaign against the Weimar Republic*. New Haven: Yale University Press, 1977.

Leser, Norbert, and Paul Salier-Wlasits, eds. *1927 als die Republik brannte: Von Schattendorf bis Wien*. Vienna-Klosterneuburg: Edition Va Bene, 2002.

Leszczawski-Schwerk, Angelique. "Dynamics of Democratization and Nationalization: The Significance of Women's Suffrage and Women's Political Participation in Parliament in the Second Polish Republic." *Nationalities Papers* 46, no. 5 (Sep 2018): 809–22.

Levy, Carl. "Fascism, National Socialism and Conservatives in Europe, 1914–1945: Issues for Comparativists." *Contemporary European History* 8, no. 1 (1999): 97–126.

Lilla, Joachim, ed. *Statisten in Uniform: Die Mitglieder des Reichstags, 1933–1945: Ein biographisches Handbuch.* Düsseldorf, Droste, 2004.

Longerich, Peter. *Goebbels: A Biography.* Translated by Alan Bance, Jeremy Noakes, and Lesley Sharpe. New York: Random House, 2015.

Luža, Radomír. *The Transfer of the Sudeten Germans: A Study of Czech-German Relations, 1933–1962.* New York: New York University Press, 1964.

Mabry, Hannelore. *Unkraut ins Parlament: Die Bedeutung weiblicher parlamentarischer Arbeit für die Emanzipation der Frau.* Munich: Ernst Vögel, 1971.

Maddox, Robert James. *William E. Borah and American Foreign Policy.* Baton Rouge: Louisiana State University Press, 1969.

Maier, Charles. *Recasting Bourgeois Europe.* Princeton: Princeton University Press, 1975.

Mamatey, Victor S., and Radomír Luža, eds. *A History of the Czechoslovak Republic, 1918–1948.* Princeton: Princeton University Press, 1973.

Manela, Erez. *The Wilsonian Moment: Self-Determination and the International Origins of Anticolonial Nationalism.* Oxford: Oxford University Press, 2007.

Marquand, David. *Ramsay MacDonald.* London: Richard Cohen, 1997.

Marschik, Matthias. "Depicting Hakoah: Images of a Zionist Sports Club in Interwar Vienna," *Historical Social Research / Historische Sozialforschung* 43, no. 2 (164) (2018): 129–47.

Martin, Jamie. *The Meddlers: Sovereignty, Empire, and the Birth of Global Economic Governance.* Cambridge: Harvard University Press, 2022.

McSpadden III, J.R. "Spel, Spelbrekers en Parlementaire Cultuur: Het Informele Leven van de Nederlandse Kamer gedurende het Interbellum." Master's thesis, Universiteit Leiden, 2010.

Mergel, Thomas. "Überlegungen zu einer Kulturgeschichte der Politik." *Geschichte und Gesellschaft* 28 (2002): 573–606.

– *Parlamentarische Kultur in der Weimarer Republik.* Düsseldorf: Droste, 2005.

Mertens, Bram. "'An Explosion of Vitality and Creativity'? Memory and Historiography of the Second World War in Belgium and the Netherlands." *Dutch Crossing* 37, no. 1 (2013): 41–56.

Milne-Smith, Amy. *London Clubland: A Cultural History of Gender and Class in Late Victorian Britain.* New York: Palgrave Macmillan, 2011.

Mittag, Jürgen, ed. *Politische Parteien und europäische Integration Entwicklung und Perspektiven transnationale Parteienkooperation in Europa.* Essen: Klartext, 2006.

Mommsen, Hans. "Von der k.u.k. Sozialdemokratie," *Forum: Österreichische Monatsblätter für kulturelle Freiheit* 121 (1964): 22–5.

–. *Die Verspielte Freiheit: Der Weg der Republik von Weimar in den Untergang, 1918 bis 1933.* Frankfurt: Propyläen, 1990.

Moore, Bob. "Louis de Jong: Writing the History of Occupied Europe." *Contemporary European History* 13 no. 14 (August 2005): 415–17.

Motadel, David. "Nationalist Internationalism in the Modern Age." *Contemporary European History* 28, no. 1 (2019): 77–81.

Motschmann, Uta, ed. *Handbuch der Berliner Vereine und Gesellschaften, 1786–1815.* Berlin: Walter de Gruyter, 2015.

Müller, Markus. *Die Christlich-Nationale Bauern- und Landvolkpartei, 1928–1933.* Düsseldorf: Droste, 2001.

Murdock, Caitlin E. *Changing Places : Society, Culture, and Territory in the Saxon-Bohemian Borderlands, 1870–1946.* Ann Arbor: University of Michigan Press, 2010.

Namier, Lewis. *The Structure of Politics at the Accession of George III.* London: Macmillan, 1965.

Neliba, Günter. *Wilhelm Frick: Der Legalist des Unrechtstaates: Eine politische Biografie.* Paderborn: Ferdinand Schöningh, 1992.

Olivová, Věra. *The Doomed Democracy: Czechoslovakia in a Disrupted Europe, 1914–38.* Translated by George Theiner. London: Sidgwick & Jackson, 1972.

–. *Dějiny první republiky.* Prague: Karolinum, 2000

Orzoff, Andrea. *Battle for the Castle: The Myth of Czechoslovakia in Europe, 1914–1948.* Oxford: Oxford Univerity Press, 2009.

Österreichisches Biographisches Lexikon 1815–1950. Vienna: Verlag der Österreichischen Akademie der Wissenschaften, 2010.

Pacher, Roland. *Robert Danneberg. Eine politische Biografie.* Peter Lang, Frankfurt am Main 2014.

Paletschek, Sylvia, and Bianka Pietrow-Ennker, eds. *Women's Emancipation Movements in the Nineteenth Century: A European Perspective.* Stanford: Stanford University Press, 2004.

Papuashvili, George. "Post-World War I Comparative Constitutional Developments in Central and Eastern Europe." *International Journal of Constitutional Law* 15, no 1 (Jan 2017): 137–72.

Patch, William L. "German Liberalism and the Origins of Presidential Government in the Weimar Republic." *The Journal of Modern History* 92, no. 4 (2020): 774–816.

Patel, Kiran Klaus. "Provincialising European Union: Co-Operation and Integration in Europe in a Historical Perspective." *Contemporary European History* 22, no. 4 (2013): 649–73.

Paxton, Robert O. "The Five Stages of Fascism." *The Journal of Modern History* 70, no. 1 (1998): 1–23.

–. *The Anatomy of Fascism.* New York: Vintage, 2005.

Payne, Stanley G. *A History of Fascism, 1914–1945.* Madison: University of Wisconsin Press, 1995.

Pedersen, Susan. *The Guardians: The League of Nations and the Crisis of Empire.* Oxford: Oxford University Press, 2015.

Pekník, Miroslav, et al., eds. *Milan Hodža: Štátnik a Politik.* Bratislava: Veda vydavateľstvo, 2002.

Pelinka, Anton. *Die gescheiterte Republik: Kultur und Politik in Österreich, 1918–1938.* Vienna: Böhlau, 2017.

Penny, Glenn. *German History Unbound: From 1750 to the Present.* Cambridge: Cambridge University Press, 2022.

Petzinna, Bertold. *Beziehung zum Deutschen Lebensstil: Ursprung und Entwicklung des jungkonservativen "Ring"-Kreises, 1918–1933.* Berlin: Akademie Verlag, 2000), 226.

Pollock, Frederick. *The League of Nations.* London: Steven and Sons, 1920.

Portisch, Hugo. *Österreich: Die unterschätzte Republik.* Vienna: Kremayr & Scheriau, 1989.

Rathkolb, Oliver, and Günther Ogris, eds. *Authoritarianism, History and Democratic Dispositions in Austria, Poland, Hungary and the Czech Republic.* Innsbruck: Studien Verlag, 2010.

Ritsch, Frederick F. "ORIGINS OF THE COUNCIL OF EUROPE: Part One: The Post-War Unity Movements to the Hague Congress." *Il Politico* 35, no. 1 (1970): 76–92.

Robinson, Jim. "Introducing the UIA." *Law Institute Journal* (Victoria) 202 (1999): 39–41.

Rossmann, Eva. *Unter Männern: Frauen im österreichischen Parlament.* Vienna: Folio Verlag, 1995.

Sabitzer, Werner. "100 Jahre Frauen im Parlament." *Öffentliche Sicherheit* 1–2 (2019): 81–2.

Sabrow, Martin. *Der Rathenaumord und die deutsche Gegenrevolution.* Göttingen: Wallstein, 2022.

Salahodjaev, Raufhon, and Dilyafruz Jarilkapova. "Women in Parliament and Deforestation: Cross-Country Evidence." *Journal for Nature Conservation* 55 (2020).

Sartori, Giovanni. *The Theory of Democracy Revisited.* Chatham, NJ: Chatham House Publishers, 1987.

Schambeck, Herbert, ed. *Österreichs Parlamentarismus: Werden und System.* Berlin: Duncker & Humblot, 1986.

Schaser, Angelika. *Helene Lange und Getrud Bäumer: Eine politische Lebensgemeinschaft.* Weimar: Böhlau, 2010.

Scheck, Raffael. *Mothers of the Nation: Right-Wing Women in Weimar Germany.* Oxford: Berg, 2004.

Schoeps, Manfred. "Der Deutsche Herrenklub: Ein Beitrag zur Geschichte des Jungkonservatismus in der Weimarer Republik." PhD diss., Friedrich-Alexander-Universität Erlangen-Nürnberg, 1974.

Schorske, Carl E. *German Social Democracy, 1905–1917: The Development of the Great Schism.* Cambridge: Harvard University Press, 1983.

Schot, Johan, and Vincent Lagendijk. "Technocratic Internationalism in the Interwar Years: Building Europe on Motorways and Electricity Networks." *Journal of Modern European History / Zeitschrift Für Moderne Europäische Geschichte / Revue d'histoire Européenne Contemporaine* 6, no. 2 (2008): 196–217.

Siefken, Sven T., and Hilmar Rommetvedt, eds. *Parliamentary Committees in the Policy Process.* New York: Routledge, 2022.

Sládek, Milan. *Němci v Čechách: Německá menšina v českých zemích a československsku, 1848–1946.* Prague: pragma, 2002.

Slobodian, Quinn. *Globalists: The End of Empire and the Birth of Neoliberalism.* Cambridge: Harvard University Press, 2018.

Sluga, Glenda, and Patricia Clavin, eds. *Internationalisms: A Twentieth-Century History.* Cambridge: Cambridge University Press, 2017.

Stachura, Peter D. *Gregor Strasser and the Rise of Nazism.* London: George Allen & Unwin, 1983.

Staudinger, Anton. "Bemühungen Carl Vaugoins um Suprematie der Christlichsozialen Partei in Österreich (1930–33)." *Mitteilungen des Österreichischen Staatsarchivs,* vol 23 (1970): 301–318.

Stavridis, Stelios, and Davor Jančić, eds. *Parliamentary Diplomacy in European and Global Governance.* Leiden: Brill, 2017.

Steiniger, Rolf, Günter Bischof, and Michael Gehler, eds. *Austria in the Twentieth Century.* New Brunswick, NJ: Transaction Publishers, 2002.

Sterzel, Frederik. *The Inter-Parliamentary Union.* Stockholm: Norstedt & Söner, 1968.

Stollberg-Rilinger, Barbara, ed. *Was heißt Kulturgeschichte des Politischen?* Berlin: Dunker&Humblot, 2005.

Stone, Lawrence. "Prosopography." *Daedalus* 100, no. 1 (1971): 46–79.

Stutje, Jan Willem. *Ferdinand Domela Nieuwenhuis: Een romantische revolutionair.* \ Amsterdam: Atlas Contact, 2012.

Swett, Pamela E. *Neighbors and Enemies: The Culture of Radicalism in Berlin, 1929–1933.* New York: Cambridge University Press, 2004.

Tálos et al., eds. *Handbuch des politischen Systems Österreichs, Erste Republik, 1918–1933.* Vienna: Manzsche Verlags- und Universitätsbuchhandlung, 1995.

Tanja, Erie. *Goede politiek: De parlementaire cultuur van de Tweede Kamer, 1866–1940.* Amsterdam: Boom, 2010.

Te Velde, Henk. "Parliamentary Obstruction and the 'Crisis' of European Parliamentary Politics Around 1900." *Redescriptions* 16, no. 1 (01, 2013): 125–47.

Tedoldi, Leonida. "Understanding Globalization: The Inter-Parliamentary Union From the Late Nineteenth to Early Twentieth Century." *History Research* no. 1 (2014): 21–30.

Thévoz, Seth Alexander. *Club Government: How the Early Victorian World was Ruled from London Clubs.* London: I.B. Tauris, 2018.

Thuillier, Guy. "La République des Camarades: Comment Robert de Jouvenel Voyait l'administration en 1914." *La Revue Administrative* 44, no. 259 (1991): 16–24.

Tickner, J. Ann. *Gender in International Relations: Feminist Perspectives on Achieving Global Security.* New York: Columbia University Press, 1992.

Turner, Jr., Henry Ashby. *Hitler's Thirty Days to Power: January 1933.* Reading, MA: Addison-Wesley, 1996.

Turpijn, Jouke. *Mannen van gezag: De uitvinding van de Tweede Kamer, 1848–1888.* Amsterdam: Wereldbibliotheek, 2008.

Tworek, Heidi J.S. *News from Germany: The Competition to Control World Communications, 1900–1945.* Cambridge, MA: Harvard University Press, 2019.

Uhlig, Ralph. *Die interparlamentarische Union, 1889–1914.* Stuttgart: Franz Steiner, 1988.

Ullrich, Volker. *Hitler: Ascent, 1889–1939.* Translated by Jefferson Chase. New York: Alfred A. Knopf, 2016.

Van der Steen, Paul. *De ongehoorde helft: De eerste vrouwen op het politieke pluche.* Nijmegen: Vantilt, 2019.

van Dongen, Bas. *Revolutie of Integratie: De Sociaal Democratische Arbeiders Partij in Nederland (SDAP) tijdens de Eerste Wereldoorlog.* Amsterdam: IISG, 1992.

Vinson, John Chalmers. *William E. Borah and the Outlawry of War.* Athens, GA: University of Georgia Press, 1957.

von Klement, Alfred. *Geschichte des Deutschen Hauses in Prag.* Prague: J.G. Calve'sche Universitäts-Buchhandlung, 1938.

von Klemperer, Klemens. *Ignaz Seipel: Christian Statesman in a Time of Crisis.* Princeton: Princeton University Press, 1972.

von Vietsch, Eberhard. *Wilhelm Solf: Botschafter Zwischen den Zeiten.* Tübingen: Rainer Wunderlich Verlag Hermann Leins, 1961.

Vossen, Koen. *Vrij vissen in het Vondelpark: Kleine politieke partijen in Nederland, 1918–1940.* Amsterdam: Wereldbibliotheek, 2003.

Walk, Joseph. "Das 'Deutsche Komitee Pro Palästina' 1926–1933." *Leo Baeck Institute Bulletin* 50 (1976): 162–93.

Wasserman, Janek. *Black Vienna: The Radical Right in the Red City, 1918–1938.* Ithaca: Cornell University Press, 2014.

Weber, Peter. "Ernst Jäckh and the National Internationalism of Interwar Germany." *Central European History* 52, no. 3 (2019): 402–23.

Webster, Andrew. "The Transnational Dream: Politicians, Diplomats and Soldiers in the League of Nations' Pursuit of International Disarmament, 1920–1938." *Contemporary European History* 14, 4 (2005): 493–518.

Weichselbaumer, Ludwig. "Walter Brand (1907–1980): Weg und Wirken eines sudetendeutschen Politikers." PhD diss., Ludwig-Maximilians-Universität zu München, 2004.

–. *Walter Brand (1907–1980): Ein sudetendeutscher Politiker um Spannungsfeld zwischen Autonomie und Anschluss.* Munich: Sudetendeutsches Archiv, 2008.

"Weimarer Republik" Issue, *Informationen zur politischen Bildung* Nr. 346/2021.

Wempe, Sean Andrew. *Revenants of the German Empire: Colonial Germans, Imperialism, and the League of Nations.* Oxford: Oxford University Press, 2019.

Wheatley, Natasha. *The Life and Death of States: Central Europe and the Transformation of Modern Sovereignty.* Princeton: Princeton University Press, 2023.

Wickert, Christl. *Unsere Erwählten: Sozialdemokratische Frauen im Deutschen Reichstag und im Preußischen Landtag, 1919 bis 1933.* Göttingen: Sovec, 1986.

Wieke, Thomas. *Vom Etablissement zur Oper: Die Geschichte der Kroll-Oper.* Berlin: Haude & Spener, 1993.

Wiltschegg, Walter. *Die Heimwehr: Eine unwiderstehliche Volksbewegung?* Munich: R. Oldenbourg Verlag, 1985.

Winkler, Heinrich August. *Der Weg in die Katastrophe: Arbeiter und Arbeiterbewegung in der Weimarer Republik 1930 bis 1933.* Berlin: J.H.W. Dietz Nachf, 1987.

–. *Weimar, 1918–1933: Die Geschichte der ersten deutschen Demokratie.* Munich: Beck, 1993.

Winkler, Henry R. "Sir Lewis Namier." *The Journal of Modern History* 35, no. 1 (1963): 2–19.

Wintr, Jan. *Proměny Parlamentní Kultury.* Prague: Auditorium, 2021.

Zahra, Tara. *Kidnapped Souls: National Indifference and the Battle for Children in the Bohemian Lands.* Ithaca: Cornell University Press, 2008.

–. *Against the World: Anti-Globalism and Mass Politics between the World Wars.* New York: Norton, 2023.

Zarjevski, Yefime. *The People Have the Floor: A History of the Inter-Parliamentary Union.* Translated by Nicholas Albrecht. Aldershot: Dartmouth, 1989.

Ziblatt, Daniel. *Conservative Parties and the Birth of Democracy.* Cambridge: Cambridge University Press, 2017.

Electronic Sources

Akten der Reichskanzlei. Weimarer Republik online. https://www.bundesarchiv.de/aktenreichskanzlei/1919-1933/0011/index.html.

Archiv Kanceláře prezidenta republiky. http://www.prazskyhradarchiv.cz
    /archivKPR/cz/.

Aspeslagh, P., F. Verleden, N. Matheve, C. Heyneman, and E. Gerard,
    eds. *Belelite: Databank van de Belgische regeringen sinds 1831.* www
    .koninklijkecommissiegeschiedenis.be/belelite.

Assemblée Nationale. http://www2.assemblee-nationale.fr/.

Association for Political History. "APH: Association for Political History."
    http://www.associationforpoliticalhistory.org/.

Baalen, Carla van. "Suze Groeneweg en Carry Pothuis-Smit: De eerste vrouwen
    in de Staten-Generaal." Tweede Kamer der Staten-Generaal. September 6,
    2019. https://www.tweedekamer.nl/sites/default/files/atoms/files/de
    _eerste_vrouwelijke_parlementariers_def.pdf.

Bayerische Akademie der Wissenschaften. *Neue Deutsche Biographie.* http://www
    .ndb.badw-muenchen.de/.

Bayerische Staatsbibliothek. *Verhandlungen des Deutschen Reichstags.* http://www
    .reichstagsprotokolle.de/index.html.

Biblioteca Fascista. http://bibliotecafascista.blogspot.com/

Biographical Dictionary of the United States Congress, 1774-present. https://bioguide
    .congress.gov/.

bpk Bildagentur. www.bpk-bildagentur.de.

Bundesarchiv, Invenio, https://invenio.bundesarchiv.de/.

Centre virtuel de la connaissance sur l'Europe (CVCE). https://www.cvce.eu/.

Český statistický úřad. "Volby do Národního shromáždění 1920 až 1935." March
    31, 2006. https://www.czso.cz/csu/czso/volby-do-narodniho-shromazdeni
    -1920-az-1935-n-2hwwxuf57q.

Club von Berlin. "Geschichte des Clubs." https://web.archive.org/web
    /20160312085738/http://www.clubvonberlin.de/index.php/ueber
    /geschichte.

Commonwealth of Australia and Department of Foreign Affairs and Trade.
    Australian Treaty Series. http://www.austlii.edu.au/au/other/dfat/treaties/.

Congressional Research Service. "United Nations Issues: Congressional
    Representatives to the U.N. General Assembly." September 16, 2022. https://
    sgp.fas.org/crs/row/IF10464.pdf.

Domela Nieuwenhuis, F. Speech on Legislation for the Eight Hour Day.
    Marxists Internet Archive. https://www.marxists.org/archive/nieuwenhuis
    /1889/eighthours.htm.

ENCYKLOPEDIE ČSSD. 2013. http://www.historiecssd.cz/b/brugel-johann
    -wolfgang/.

German Historical Institute. "German History in Documents and Images."
    http://germanhistorydocs.ghi-dc.org/index.cfm.

Gonschior, Andreas. Wahlen in der Weimarer Republik, 2001–2005, http://
    www.gonschior.de/weimar/index.htm.

Google Books Ngram Viewer. https://books.google.com/ngrams/.

Institute of Historical Research. "The History of Parliament: British Political, Social & Local History." http://www.historyofparliamentonline.org/.

Inter-Parliamentary Union. "Women's Suffrage: A World Chronology of the Recognition of Women's Rights to Vote and to Stand for Election." http:// www.ipu.org/wmn-e/suffrage.htm.

Internetová encyklopedie dějin Brna. Last modified 29 June 2018. https:// encyklopedie.brna.cz/.

IPU Parline: Global Data on National Parliaments. https://data.ipu.org/.

Kiesraad. Databank Verkiezingsuitslagen. https://www.verkiezingsuitslagen.nl/.

League of Nations Archives and Center for the Study of Global Change. League of Nations Photo Archive. Last modified October 2002. https://web.archive .org/web/20160827145559/http://www.indiana.edu/~league /1thordinaryassemb.htm.

LVR-Institut für Landeskunde und Regionalgeschichte and Landschaftsverband Rheinland. Portal Rheinische Geschichte. http://www.rheinische-geschichte .lvr.de.

Mergel, Thomas. "Kulturgeschichte der Politik." *Docupedia-Zeitgeschichte.* October 22, 2012. http://docupedia.de/zg/Kulturgeschichte_der_Politik _Version_2.0_Thomas_Mergel.

Ministry of Foreign Affairs of the Republic of Serbia. "List of the Ministers for Foreign Affairs Since the Forming of the First Government in 1811." http:// www.mfa.gov.rs/en/diplomatic-tradition/ministers-through-history.

National Diet Library, Japan. *Portraits of Modern Japanese Historical Figures.* 2013. http://www.ndl.go.jp/portrait/e/.

Niedostadek, André. "Der stumme Richter." *Legal Tribune Online.* July 5, 2014. http://www.lto.de/recht/feuilleton/f/rechtsgeschichte-reichsgericht -praesident-erwin-bumke/.

Nielsen, Jytte. "How Danish women got the vote." KVINFO. http://kvinfo.org /history/how-danish-women-got-vote.

The Nobel Prize. https://www.nobelprize.org/.

Österreichische Mediathek, Julius Deutsch spricht über sein Leben Audio File, March 1, 1967. https://www.mediathek.at/atom/0178295D-2E8-00781 -00000BEC-01772EE2.

Österreichisches Staatsarchiv. "Julius Deutsch," 1914–2014: 100 Jahre Erster Weltkrieg." https://wk1.staatsarchiv.at/militarisierung-der-politik/julius -deutsch/index.html.

Oxford University Press. *Oxford Dictionary of National Biography.* 2018. http:// www.oxforddnb.com/.

Parlement & Politiek. https://www.parlement.com/.

Peters, Gerhard, and John T. Woolley. The American Presidency Project. 1999–2018. http://www.presidency.ucsb.edu/index.php

Proceedings of the International Working-men's Congress in Paris (1889). Marxists Internet Archive. Accessed Nov. 27, 2023. https://www.marxists.org /history/international/social-democracy/1889/marxists-congress/index.htm.

Reichstagsprotokoll-Korpus. https://www.deutschestextarchiv.de/reichstag/.

Republik Österreich Parlament. https://www.parlament.gv.at/.

Research School Political History – Onderzoekschool Politieke Geschiedenis,, https://onderzoekschoolpolitiekegeschiedenis.nl/homepage/.

Sauer, Michael, ed. "Historische Plakate." Bundeszentrale für politische Bildung. https://www.bpb.de/themen/medien-journalismus/bilder-in -geschichte-und-politik/73211/historische-plakate/.

Schönherr, Maximilian. "Brüning stellt sich gegen Hitler." SWR. March 1, 2018. https://www.swr.de/swr2/wissen/broadcastcontrib-swr-22930.html.

Staatsbibliothek zu Berlin-Preußischer Kulturbesitz. "Europeana Newspapers." http://www.europeana-newspapers.eu/.

Stadt Wien. "WienGeschichteWien." https://www.geschichtewiki.wien.gv.at/.

Storting. "Anna Rogstad – første kvinne på Stortinget i 1911." Last modified February 15, 2011. https://www.stortinget.no/annarogstad.

Tweede Kamer der Staten-Generaal. https://www.tweedekamer.nl/.

UK Parliament. https://www.parliament.uk/.

United Nations. United Nations Treaty Collection. https://treaties.un.org/.

United States Holocaust Memorial Museum. Holocaust Encyclopedia. https://encyclopedia.ushmm.org/.

Universität Bielefeld. "Sonderforschungsbereich 584: Das Politische als Kommunikationsraum in der Geschichte." Last modified 30 June 2012. https://www.uni-bielefeld.de/(de)/geschichte/forschung/sfb584/.

Virginia Commonwealth University. VCU Libraries: Social Welfare History Project. Last modified October 14, 2017. http://socialwelfare.library.vcu .edu/.

Wahlplakate in der Weimarer Republik. http://www.wahlplakate-archiv.de/.

"Winston Churchill speaking in Zurich, 19th September 1946." The Churchill Society. Accessed February 23, 2018. http://www.churchill-society-london .org.uk/astonish.html.

Wissenschaftliche Dienste des Deutschen Bundestages. "Das Diätenrecht des Reichstages (1871–1918) und der Weimarer Nationalversammlung." November 27, 2008. https://www.bundestag.de/blob/413332/3ab719bf37bf e3d44488c84bfe6bdb56/wd-1-254-08-pdf-data.pdf.

Index

GERMAN AND EUROPEAN STUDIES

General Editor: James Retallack